Women's Writing

IN STUART ENGLAND

The Mothers' Legacies of Dorothy Leigh,
Elizabeth Joscelin, and Elizabeth Richardson

EDITED BY
SYLVIA BROWN

SUTTON PUBLISHING

First published in 1999 by
Sutton Publishing Limited · Phoenix Mill
Thrupp · Stroud · Gloucestershire · GL5 2BU

Cover illustration: *Anne Hale, Mrs Hoskins*, 1629, by Marcus Gheeraerts the Younger (Private Collection/Bridgeman Art Library, London)

British Library Cataloguing in Publication Data
A catalogue record for this book is available from the British Library

ISBN 0 7509 1854 3 (hb)
      0 7509 1855 1 (pb)

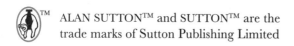
Typeset in 10/12 pt Baskerville MT.
Typesetting and origination by
Sutton Publishing Limited.
Printed in Great Britain by
Biddles Limited, Guilford, Surrey.

CONTENTS

ILLUSTRATIONS

ACKNOWLEDGEMENTS

My interest in mothers' legacies and in women's manuscripts began when I 'discovered' Elizabeth Joscelin's autograph legacy in the British Library in the course of my doctoral research. So my thanks must extend back, first of all, to Donald and Mary Hyde, who funded my first trip to England through their generous endowment of a Princeton English Department bursary for research abroad.

As my interest in mothers' legacies has developed, I have benefited from the feedback and help of Cedric Brown, Danielle Clarke, Elizabeth Clarke, Lorna Hutson, Victoria Kahn, Peter Lake, Lynne Magnusson, Jeremy Maule, Diane Purkiss, Nigel Smith, the members of the Renaissance and Early Modern Colloquium at Princeton, the Renaissance English Text Society, and the fellows and junior members of Keble College. By far the greatest excitement was provided by Victoria Burke, who generously shared with me her own discoveries of Elizabeth Ashburnham's (Richardson's) early manuscripts, and by Sophie Blacksell, who fulfilled every instructor's dream by going off to the Bodleian Library to write an essay on mothers' legacies and coming back to tell me about a copy of Richardson's *A Ladies Legacie* annotated in her own hand – and to give me a brilliant essay as well.

This edition of mothers' legacies could never have been completed without the material aid of the Social Sciences and Humanities Research Council of Canada, which gave me a postdoctoral fellowship; Keble College, Oxford, which made me Douglas Price Junior Research Fellow; and the University of Alberta, which supported the final research. I am also grateful to the staff of the Bruce Peel Special Collections Library at the University of Alberta (particularly to John Charles and Jeannine Green), the East Sussex Record Office, the Folger Library (particularly Laetitia Yeandle and Georgianna Ziegler), the Bodleian Library, and the British Library Manuscripts Students' Room. I thank Kim Feyen, Rachel Fitz and Krissy Lundberg for their help with the preparation of text. A useful conversation with Elaine Hobby helped me to clarify my thoughts about editorial practice at a crucial stage. Paul Considine kindly shared his knowledge of Leicestershire with me. Finally, I am indebted to Christopher Feeney and Helen Gray at Sutton Publishing for seeing it through to the end. This edition could never have been begun, however, without Malcolm Parkes and Roger Thorp, and I thank them for their original interest in the project.

Of all the generous and learned people who have helped me along the way, none has been more free with his help and his learning than John Considine, to whom this edition is dedicated.

THE MOTHER'S LEGACY

T he mother's legacy is a genre which seems at once alien and familiar to us. Parents still, and probably will always, give advice to their children, but the particular form in which some seventeenth-century women chose to give maternal advice is strange and arresting. Drawing on the language of the deathbed – and sometimes literally writing from the deathbed – these women decided to leave their advice in the form of a written 'legacy' or 'blessing' which would speak for them after they were gone. As a result, some mothers' legacies, like the one written by Elizabeth Joscelin out of a seemingly prophetic sense of her imminent death in childbirth, can produce an uncanny effect of immediacy and intimacy: as of a mother's voice speaking to her child from the grave.

More often, however, the mothers' legacies of Dorothy Leigh, Elizabeth Joscelin, and Elizabeth Richardson reproduced in this collection remind us how far from immediate these texts are, how embedded in their own particular time and place. Their authors rely heavily on the rhetorical effect of producing what seems to be a present, speaking voice. But whether advising, supplicating, admonishing, or preaching, how strange these voices are: Dorothy Leigh, for instance, affecting to address Satan directly, arguing with him to produce an edifying spectacle of godliness triumphing over temptation; or Elizabeth Richardson, praying, as she puts it, 'while I have breath to call upon thee, before I am laid into the darke dungeon of the earth, when the wormes shall eat my corrupt flesh'. What is strange to us in these mothers' legacies is precisely what connects them to their origins in early modern English culture. They reflect, and indeed contributed to, the pervasive fashion for meditating on death in Stuart England, drawing on the extraordinary authority that deathbed pronouncements or blessings were acknowledged to have. They are also deeply engaged with the question of how to live and propagate the true Christian religion. They build on the sixteenth-century Protestant reformers' promotion of household godliness, and in particular the godly mother's duty to instruct her children when they are young and impressionable – taking that instruction one step further into writing.[1]

But while the mothers' legacies reflect their originary culture, they also reflect and reproduce that culture's paradoxes and contradictions. One of the principal paradoxes of the mothers' legacy books is their evident popularity at a time when silence was an ideal female virtue, and writing (let alone publishing) women were anomalous. Until about 1640, very few women wrote; even fewer had their works printed.[2] Those who did aspire to write had to contend with models of authorship where men were seen as the active engenderers of texts, while women provided the symbolic material: as muses, or as subjects for praise, satire, or regulation.[3] General proscriptions on female speech also encouraged silence: a man could be eloquent, but a woman interested in words was merely garrulous.

Yet Dorothy Leigh, Elizabeth Joscelin, and Elizabeth Richardson all wrote and were published during this unpropitious time. The posthumous texts of Leigh and Joscelin, moreover, became what could be called 'bestsellers': the printed version of Joscelin's text, *The Mothers Legacie to her Vnborne Childe*, saw eight editions between 1624 and 1684, while Leigh's *The Mothers Blessing*, with twenty-three editions between 1616 and 1674, was the most reprinted woman's text of the seventeenth century. Together, Leigh and Joscelin produced what amounted to a fashion. An anonymous text of 1627, *A Mothers Teares ouer Hir Seduced Son*, refers to both as if they were well known. Although Leigh and Joscelin are invoked as models, *A Mothers Teares* does not actually follow their format but is written as an epistolary dialogue between a pious Protestant mother and her apostate son at Douai, a popular place of exile for English Catholics.[4] Yet the reference to Joscelin and Leigh is significant. It not only invokes their authority as exemplary maternal guardians of Protestant orthodoxy; it shows also that certain women, notably *mothers*, so far overcame cultural obstacles to women's authorship that they themselves became originators of influential textual models.

Later books of maternal advice were probably influenced by the example of Leigh or Joscelin or both.[5] When Elizabeth Richardson emended the title of presentation copies of *A Ladies Legacie* to read *A Mothers Legacie*, she may have had the title of Joscelin's published legacy in mind. Dorothy Leigh's affirmation of a godly mother's care for her child – 'will shee not blesse it euery time it suckes on her brests, when shee feeleth the bloud come from her heart to nourish it?' – found an answering voice in Elizabeth Clinton's *The Countesse of Lincolnes Nurserie* (1622), a tract advising godly women to breastfeed their children instead of sending them out to wetnurses. Later in the century, Margaret Blagge, like Elizabeth Joscelin, composed a mother's legacy because she predicted (correctly) that she would die in childbirth. Anne, Lady Halkett, wrote her 'Mothers Will to her vnborne child' for similar reasons in 1656, but she survived to write instructions 'To My Son Robert Halkett' in 1670. Halkett's and others' mothers' legacies remain in manuscript. Katherine Austen's 'Discours to my children', for instance, was written into her commonplace book. Anne Bradstreet left a collection of prose meditations, poems, and aphorisms as a manuscript legacy to her family. Finally, Anne Wentworth's husband stole papers of hers which included 'A mother's legacy to her daughter', dated 22 September 1677.[6]

Mothers' legacies continued to be written and published into the eighteenth century; their popularity did not in fact wane until the nineteenth. Mr Wentworth was an exception (in fact, he disapproved not of Anne's mother's legacy in particular but of her writing generally). Mothers' legacies were not only a favoured genre with women, but had a wide readership as well.[7] The general approbation that the genre enjoyed from the beginning suggests it did as much to confirm normative gender ideology as it did to disrupt it by giving women an authoritative voice and enabling them to write and publish. This is one of the troubling paradoxes of the genre: women speak authoritatively in the mother's legacy, but only as mothers, and often as mothers on the point of dissolution. The authors of these texts are themselves caught between the contradictory self-assertion which the genre allows, and the self-negation it demands. Elizabeth Joscelin, for instance, wrests a justification for her writing out of sanctioned 'motherly zeale' and the need to be religiously prepared to die. Yet the same ideological framework which allows mothers to express their zeal by writing a spiritual inheritance for their children also marks that particular kind of expression as exceptional. The assumptions about women's general unfitness for authorship remain intact – hence Joscelin's worries, evident especially in the self-corrections of her manuscript, about her qualifications for eloquence, or even 'skil to write'.[8]

On the other hand, we can also consider what productive use writers of mothers' legacies made of the contradictions of the genre. Elizabeth Richardson, for example, takes advantage of the feminization of private devotion to transform a conventional apology for her writing into an assertion of her expertise. Like Leigh and Joscelin, Richardson feels the need to justify her maternal legacy before she begins to write it: 'I thus excuse, the matter is but devotions or prayers, which surely concernes and belongs to women.' Richardson's characterization of devotion as 'female' is both a concession and a challenge to the limits placed on seventeenth-century women. On the one hand, it seems to accept that women's proper sphere is not the public sphere, but rather the 'private' one of devotion. Moreover, the abjection which prayer demands – the humble obeisance of a subject to a divine monarch, the obedience of a child to a heavenly father – surely comes more 'naturally' to the sex which is born into subjection. On the other hand, Richardson is also appropriating *for* women the privileges of prayer and devotion, modes which command unimpeachable respect and even deference by their association with the sacred. Richardson's movement from humble apology to self-authorization is completed when she finishes her sentence by stating that prayer belongs not only to women, but also to 'the best learned men'. At their best, men are like women!

Writers of mothers' legacies, then, evidently *did* find the materials for female authorship in their patriarchal culture – although the materials necessarily remained complicated by that culture – creating a genre which was at once distinctively female, but also acceptable and even authoritative. The mothers' legacies are therefore, in a sense, groundbreaking texts in the history of female authorship. But they remain unresolvedly paradoxical. Their authors are able to step outside the bounds imposed by feminine silence and domesticity because they anchor themselves firmly within the limits of the household and the maternal role. Their voices are achieved, but at the cost of loss, absence, and death.[9]

Still, as Margaret Ezell has cautioned in *Writing Women's Literary History*, we ourselves risk silencing early women writers when we impose our own anachronistic expectations of what does or does not constitute successful (or even what we might call in this case 'healthy') authorship. Ezell argues that our model for female authorship has been largely a nineteenth- and twentieth-century one, which has seen women's literary history moving progressively towards the emancipated woman writer: professional, published, secular, and angry. Judged against this model, earlier women who wrote primarily for manuscript circulation, or whose mode was devotion rather than explicit protest, have tended to be overlooked.[10] But when early women writers are recontextualized, we are able to see them not as less, but different; not as failed novelists, but as resourceful shapers of the cultural materials available to them.

We are able to understand not only their strategies of accommodation, but also their culturally specific strategies for self-assertion, and even dissent. We can recognize, for instance, that religious politics as well as sexual politics informed their writing. Through a shared wish that their sons might become ministers, Elizabeth Joscelin and Dorothy Leigh used their maternal advice to assert the value of a preaching ministry and more generally to criticize a society in need of reformation. Their maternal zeal carried them into the Puritan pulpit. Elizabeth Richardson, on the other hand, by placing her prayers into public circulation at the precise moment *The Book of Common Prayer* was withdrawn, was making a critical statement from the other end of the spectrum of English Protestantism. The writings of all three were intensely engaged with the religious life of the nation as it touched (as it always did in this period) their private lives of prayers and devotion and of household piety. This collection of the writings of three Stuart women to their children thus not only gives us a sense of being let into an intimate family conversation, it also allows us to hear some of the first voices to emerge from the silence imposed on early modern women and to reconstruct the particular authority that those voices carried.

Notes

1. On the importance of domestic godliness for reformed religion, see Margo Todd, 'The Spiritualized Household', in *Christian Humanism and the Puritan Social Order* (Cambridge, 1987). For women's part in domestic religious instruction, see Patricia Crawford, *Women and Religion in England 1500–1720* (London, Routledge, 1993), p. 87.

2. For a graphic representation of the number of books published by women in the seventeenth century, see Patricia Crawford, 'Women's Published Writings 1600–1700', in *Women in English Society 1500–1800*, ed. Mary Prior (London, Routledge, 1991), p. 212. Crawford notes that in the half-decade in which Dorothy Leigh's mother's legacy appeared, only eight new works by women were published.

3. For a discussion of the gendering of authorship in the early modern period, see Wendy Wall, *The Imprint of Gender: Authorship and Publication in the English Renaissance* (Ithaca, Cornell University Press, 1993); Stephanie H. Jed, *Chaste Thinking: The Rape of Lucretia and the Birth of Humanism* (Bloomington, Indiana University Press, 1989); and Lorna Hutson, 'The Housewife and the Humanists', in *The Usurer's Daughter: Male Friendship and Fictions of Women in Sixteenth-Century England* (London, Routledge, 1994), pp. 17–51.

4. *A Mothers Teares ouer Hir Seduced Son* ([London], 1627), sig. A2r. This work has been attributed to Joscelin, but she of course had no son, dying in 1622 after the birth of her only daughter. *A Mothers Teares* is in fact an expanded version (adding the introduction mentioning Leigh and Joscelin) of Ez. W., *The Answere of a Mother vnto Hir Seduced Sonnes Letter* printed in Amsterdam in 1627. 'Ez.' suggests 'Elizabeth'.

5. Although the texts of Leigh and Joscelin were probably the most influential exemplars, a number of mother's legacy texts predate them. Lady Frances Abergavenny's prayers, a deathbed gift to her daughter, were printed in Thomas Bentley's *Monument of Matrones* (1582). The Catholic Elizabeth Grymeston's *Miscelanea. Meditations. Memoratiues*, addressed to her son Bernye, were first printed in 1604. Elizabeth Richardson anticipates both Leigh and Joscelin with a manuscript book of 'Instructions for my children, or any other Christian', dated 1606. (See Richardson, 'Introduction' and Appendix 1.)

One of the earliest printed examples is actually by a male author: Nicholas Breton wrote *The Mothers Blessing* (1602) in the person of the mother of the addressee. Breton's text is further evidence of the recognized cultural authority of the maternal voice. See Kristen Poole, ' "The fittest closet for all goodness": Authorial Strategies of Jacobean Mothers' Manuals', *SEL*, 35.1 (winter 1995), 69–70.

6. Halkett's 'Mothers Will' and instructions 'To My Son' are in the National Library of Scotland (MSS 6489, 6492). Katherine Austen's commonplace book is in the British Library (Add. MS 4454). I am grateful to Victoria Burke and Elizabeth Clarke, respectively, for drawing my attention to these manuscripts. For Bradstreet's legacy, see *The Works of Anne Bradstreet*, ed. Jeannine Hensley (Cambridge, Massachusetts, Belknap Press, 1967), pp. 240–95. Information on the legacies of Margaret Godolphin (née Blagge) and Anne Wentworth may be found in *A Biographical Dictionary of English Women Writers 1580–1720*, ed. Maureen Bell *et al.* (New York, Harvester Wheatsheaf, 1990).

Printed mothers' legacies of the seventeenth century also include *The Mothers Counsell, Or, Live Within Compasse* by 'M.R.' (entered in the Stationer's Register 1624 but possibly printed 1630), and Susanna Bell, *The Legacy of a Dying Mother to her Mourning Children* (1673).

7. For nineteenth-century appreciation of Joscelin's mother's legacy, including the Reverend C.H.G. Craufurd's collection of editions of Joscelin, see Sylvia Brown, 'The Approbation of Elizabeth Jocelin', *English Manuscript Studies 1100–1700*, 10 (2000). Joscelin's text even enjoyed an early international reputation, translated into Dutch as *Uyterste Wille van een Moeder aan haar Toekomende Kint* (a second edition was published at Amsterdam in 1699).

8. See Joscelin, 'Introduction'.

9. The dependence of mothers' legacy texts on self-negation is explored by Wendy Wall, 'Dancing in a Net: The Problems of Female Authorship', in *The Imprint of Gender*, and by Teresa Feroli in '"Infelix Simulacrum": The Rewriting of Loss in Elizabeth Jocelin's *The Mothers Legacie*', *English Literary History* 61 (spring 1994), 89–102.

10. See 'A Tradition of Our Own: Writing Women's Literary History in the Twentieth Century', in Margaret Ezell, *Writing Women's Literary History* (Baltimore, Johns Hopkins Press, 1993).

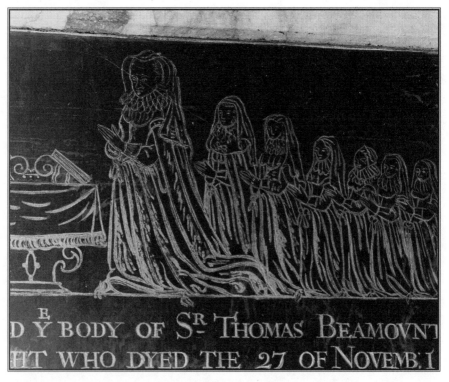

Detail from a monument erected by Elizabeth Richardson in memory of her parents, St Mary's Church, Stoughton, Leicestershire (1631). (*Photograph by S. Brown*)

EDITORIAL PRACTICE: APPROACHES AND CONVENTIONS

APPROACHES

This edition is intended for a dual audience. For the specialist reader I have provided a detailed picture of the textual histories of the mothers' legacies through the critical apparatus and the appendices of excerpts from Richardson's manuscripts. For Joscelin's and Richardson's texts I have documented substantive revisions – in Joscelin's case, both self-revisions and the often ideological revisions of the first male editor of her text in 1624 – which tell fascinating stories not only about editorial appropriation, but also about the choices, conflicts, and allegiances out of which these texts were produced.

I hope, though, that textual variants (sometimes admittedly a dry subject) will engage non-specialist readers as well. They should: after all, these variants *do* tell stories about the practice of individual writers, and about their relationships to the culture in which they lived and wrote. The changes which Thomas Goad made to Joscelin's text, for instance, give us a very precise glimpse of how gender roles were defined in Stuart England. What specific things did Goad find unacceptable to his view of how a godly mother should write and represent herself? Moreover, we can look at the changes Joscelin made to her own text and read not just what she said, but what she tried to say, or nearly said, or could not say. What did Joscelin herself find unsayable as she tried to write and represent herself?

Introductory discussions of each of the three women whose legacies are reproduced here integrate their changing writing practices with their personal histories, and also place them and their texts in a wider cultural and historical context. Distinct from the critical apparatus at the foot of the page, endnotes give further contextual and glossarial information. And as each of the three authors makes continuous, allusive use of scripture, endnotes also give and sometimes expand biblical references in order to reconstruct something of the intertextual reading experience available to a godly seventeenth-century reader, thoroughly immersed in the Bible. Further readings, with the undergraduate user in mind, are suggested at the end of the collection.

EDITORIAL CONVENTIONS

Original spelling, including the use of i/j and u/v, has been retained. Abbreviations have also been retained; in some cases, for the sake of clarity, they have been expanded by interpolating letters enclosed in square brackets as in, for example, 'p[ro]tection'. Generally, interpolated material appears in square brackets [ ], material appearing in the margin is enclosed in curly brackets { }, and manuscript revisions inserted over the line are enclosed in half-square brackets ⌈ ⌉.

In Joscelin's manuscript and the appendices from Richardson's manuscripts, line breaks are indicated by a gap of four spaces. In all texts, original paragraphing is maintained by indentation. But where the original has very long blocks of text, I have broken them up for the sake of readability – using whenever I can the rhetorical indications of the original texts to find 'natural' places for breaks, but signalling my editorial intervention by *not* indenting and by interposing a blank line instead.

When I have been working from a printed copytext (for Leigh and Richardson), I have not maintained the sometimes seemingly arbitrary distinction between large and small capital letters, and I have silently emended obvious typographical errors.

BIBLIOGRAPHIC CONVENTIONS

In their biblical quotations, all three authors are closest to the Geneva version. (This is not surprising, as the annotated Geneva Bible was the generally preferred Bible for personal study.) My own biblical quotations therefore, except where explicitly indicated to the contrary, are all taken from this version: I have used an edition with the Tomson/Junius annotations, printed by Robert Barker in London in 1610.

I have also made frequent use of the following works, and have indicated them by abbreviation in my notes.

BCP   *The Book of Common Prayer* (1559 or 'Elizabethan' version with the revisions of 1604).

DNB   *The Dictionary of National Biography*, eds. Leslie Stephen and Sidney Lee (Oxford, Oxford University Press, 1971).

OED   *The Oxford English Dictionary*.

Tilley   M.P. Tilley, *A Dictionary of the Proverbs in England in the Sixteenth and Seventeenth Centuries* (Ann Arbor, University of Michigan Press, 1950).

Where no place of publication is stated in bibliographical references, it should be assumed to be London. Finally, in giving dates, I assume that the New Year begins 1 January (not 25 March).

Part I

DOROTHY LEIGH

1

INTRODUCTION TO DOROTHY LEIGH

The Mothers Blessing (1616)

D orothy Leigh's mother's legacy was overwhelmingly popular with its first readers, running to twenty-three editions between 1616 and 1674: seven in the first five years alone. *The Mothers Blessing* has therefore been described, with some justification, as the bestselling book by a woman in the seventeenth century.[1] It is also one of the earliest examples of the genre, although Elizabeth Grymeston's miscellaneous collections for her son Bernye (titled *Miscelanea. Meditations. Memoratives*) was published in 1604, and Elizabeth Richardson began a mother's legacy book in manuscript at least as early as 1606 (see Richardson, Appendix I). Still, if we are looking for the 'mother' of the genre, Dorothy Leigh is a good candidate. *The Mothers Blessing* was likely an example for and an influence on Richardson's subsequent collections of prayers, and on her decision to have them printed in 1645 as *A Ladies Legacie* – which Richardson manually corrected to 'A Mothers Legacie'. An early edition of Leigh was almost certainly in Joscelin's library, given the frequent parallels between their two treatises.

What might account for the popularity of *The Mothers Blessing* then, both as a bestselling book and as a model for other women writers? If the only acceptable face of the Stuart woman-in-print was pious, meek, and self-effacing, then Dorothy Leigh ought not to have been the oft-reprinted author that she was. She is, in fact, the most outspoken of the writers of mothers' legacies. She is scathing, for instance, on worldly ministers who spend more time on lawsuits than on preaching. In her final chapter on '*The right vse of goods*', she writes with vehement emphasis on the subject:

> wheras *they should draw many vnto Christ* by their liberalitie and true preaching, they driue many from Christ by loue of their owne (as they say) & by their idlenes & negligence in preaching (as I say) & I say, this loue of their own, as they call it, is a thousand times worse in them, & doth a multitude more of hurt, then in other ordinarie men.

The lack of good preachers was a characteristic concern of Puritans in the period, who gave it as a reason for the evident incompleteness of godly reformation in England. One remedy, which circumvented the established Church's seeming unwillingness to do something about the problem, was the endowment of Puritan lectureships, the godly members of a parish paying a lecturer of their choice for extra preaching. But while a remedy for the idleness, negligence, or simple non-residence of an incumbent, lectureships effectively created an alternative church within the Church. (For that reason, the arch-proponent of conformity, Archbishop William Laud, would work hard to suppress them in the 1630s.) Leigh seems not only to endorse this alternative, but to recommend general activism in the interest of furthering godly reformation: 'Moue the people to prouide themselues a Preacher, tell them of their wants, speake to the Magistrates, mourne to see the Alehouses full, and the Church of God emptie.'

Here Leigh herself speaks like a preacher, exhorting her readers to work for godly reformation: not just in the private, but in the public sphere. Even where she writes about prayer – which, as Elizabeth Richardson writes, 'surely concernes and belongs to women' – Leigh adopts, not the voice of the private suppliant, but that of an authoritative teacher on the subject. 'Me thinks if I were a man and a preacher of Gods word,' she writes, '. . . I surely perswade my selfe, that through Gods grace I should bring many to pray rightly, which now pray vnaduisedly or not at all.'

On the other hand, Leigh is very much aware that she is not a man and that, as a woman, it is not her place to be (as she says of preachers) one of 'the Captaines of the Church'. In fact, she says that she writes to encourage women 'to giue men the first and chiefe place' (Chapter 5). Yet this very encouragement to women to embrace their traditionally subordinate role is couched in another call for activism: for women to labour to cast out sin from themselves and their posterity, even if that means showing their 'infirmities' in published writing. Perhaps it was just this combination of boldness and compliance which appealed to Leigh's seventeenth-century readers. Leigh managed to endorse ideas which held in place female domestic subservience – such as the notion that woman's cold nature fitted her to be subject to her husband's desire – while at the same time stepping boldly outside the private domestic realm by publication, and by warmly exhorting her readers to further godly reformation.

Leigh's intended readership is itself simultaneously private and public. She addresses the work to her three sons, George, John, and William; but she chooses to do so in print. Like Joscelin (although not so urgently), she sees herself 'going out of the world' and her sons 'but comming in'. And therefore, as Joscelin also would do, Leigh decides to take the unusual step of writing to make certain that her sons will receive the religious instruction which it is the special duty of parents to provide. Leigh characterizes her writing not only as maternal, but as wifely duty. Her husband, predeceasing her, urged her in his will to see his children 'well instructed and brought up in knowledge', and in the prefatory epistle to her sons, Leigh construes the writing of her own legacy as the execution of that paternal will and husbandly command. Here, like Joscelin in her own preface to her husband, Leigh seems hesitant to own her text as an author. She seems much more interested in casting her writing as an extension of her sanctioned familial roles of mother and wife.

Yet, once she has characterized the writing of her legacy as a family duty, Leigh characteristically expands and even undermines her own orthodox position, overleaping the bounds of the family. She goes on in her prefatory epistle to justify her decision not just to write but to publish, to send her embodied maternal advice 'abroad': 'for should it be left with the eldest, it is likely the youngest should haue but little part in it'. If that were her worry, could she not have had three manuscript copies made? By publishing, and moreover by publishing for this explicit reason, she rejects not only a kind of primogeniture, but also the rigid, closed domestic economy which is created by the 'rules' of primogeniture and female subservience and enclosure. In the closed domestic economy, maternal advice is only for private circulation. But as the title page to the *The Mothers Blessing* states, Leigh's published text inevitably finds a wider audience, and is declared to be 'profitable for all Parents, to leave as a Legacy to their Children'.

Throughout her legacy – but especially from her concentration on the subject of prayer from Chapter 16 on – Leigh seems to be conscious of a readership beyond her three school-age sons.[2] In the context of ruminating on the conventionally female subject of prayer, she takes up questions which, in the early decades of the seventeenth century, were part of a wider public discussion among the godly of how to further reformation of manners, morals, and especially, religion. Some are also picked up by Joscelin: the relative merits of set and extemporaneous prayer, sabbath observance, proper and improper uses of worldly wealth, the importance of restricting one's business dealings and marital alliances to the godly, and towards the end of the book, the faults of worldly and negligent preachers. Throughout, however, Leigh maintains the connection between the more general social criticism she offers, and the ostensible origin of her writing in maternal cares and fears. More than once, she expresses her wish (a wish she shares with Joscelin) that her sons will become preachers. This anxiously expressed maternal wish allows her to write normatively about what sort of preachers they should become, as well as the current examples they should scorn to imitate. It also, perhaps, gives her the vicarious pleasure of imagining, through her sons, what *she* would do if she were 'a man and a preacher of Gods word, as (I hope),' she continues, 'some of you shall be'.

In her epistle to her 'Beloued sonnes', Dorothy Leigh positions herself and her writing in relation to the male members of her family: her husband authorizing her with a dying wish, her sons justifying her by their need for instruction. But Leigh also invokes a powerful female protector from outside her family. Even before the epistle to her sons, she dedicates her work to Elizabeth, daughter of James I of England and wife to the Elector Palatine: a powerful Protestant princess, and like Dorothy Leigh, a mother. By her marriage in February 1613 to the Calvinist Frederick, who was First Elector of the Holy Roman Empire, Elizabeth had cemented an alliance between England and one of the most influential Protestant princes on the continent. Their child Frederick Henry, born

January 1614, was King James's first grandchild and secured the Protestant successsion.

In her dedication to Elizabeth, Leigh's conceit is to give this kindly princess her 'scroule' for safekeeping: her children being 'too young to receiue it, my selfe too old to keepe it, men too wise to direct it to'. Yet Princess Elizabeth is not merely a female friend for Leigh's legacy and for Leigh herself. In her political connections, and in Leigh's vision of her as one of the princely elect, she is a star of international Protestantism. The 'numerous posterity' Leigh wishes her will be occupied with the 'continuall defence and propagation' of 'true Religion' against the forces of the Counter-Reformation in Europe. By seeking her patronage, Leigh aligns herself with Princess Elizabeth and thereby sets her own writerly effort to propagate true religion among her posterity not merely on a public, but on an international stage.

LIFE

Dorothy Leigh was born Dorothy Kempe, into a gentry family that could trace its pedigree back to the reign of Edward I. Her great-aunt was Jane Colt, the unformed girl whom Sir Thomas More chose to marry and educate: Dorothy was thus first cousin once removed to perhaps the most celebrated of the learned ladies of the sixteenth century, Margaret More Roper.[3]

Dorothy was one of four children of Robert Kempe and Elizabeth Higham or Heigham. On her mother's side, as on her father's, her connections were impressive. Elizabeth was the daughter of Sir Clement Heigham, Privy Councillor and Speaker of the House of Commons under Queen Mary, and Lord Chief Baron of the exchequer from 1558 until 1559. She was the widow of her first husband (named Edon) when she married Robert Kempe and came to live at Spains Hall, the seat of the Kempes near Finchingfield in Essex. Spains Hall still stands: the present building is a large Elizabethan house of red brick a mile north-west of the village, built in the time of Dorothy's parents.[4]

As well as evidently prosperous, the family in which Dorothy grew up was decidedly godly. In her legacy, a love of sermons marks out the heavenly-minded child of God. Dorothy's own uncle, John Kempe of London, left money in his will for 300 sermons: 100 to be preached at St Antholin's in London, 100 at Finchingfield, and the remaining 100 at the discretion of Dorothy's father Robert and her other uncle George. Dorothy's brother William (who died in 1623) left money for monthly catechizing by the minister at Finchingfield and for bread to be distributed to the catechumens.[5] The Kempes also had the rectory of Finchingfield in their gift, which they bestowed on a series of godly preachers, including Thomas Pickering, the editor of the works of the influential Puritan divine William Perkins, and Stephen Marshall, who with fellow Essex ministers was castigated by Laud for nonconformity.[6] The sustained interest of *The Mothers Blessing* in the qualities of the true preacher of God's Word – often defined against his worldly, self-serving opposite – is perhaps attributable as much to an ongoing family commitment to godly patronage as to Dorothy's personal wishes for her sons' callings.

Both the gentility and the godliness of Dorothy's pedigree are well documented. This contrasts sharply with the lack of verifiable information about her marriage to Ralph Leigh. They presumably lived in Sussex, for the pedigree for the Kempe family in the 1621 Visitation of Essex puts him down as 'Raphe Lee of Sussex ar'. In a manuscript pedigree, he is stated to be 'of A family of Leigh in Cheshire' and to have been 'a soldier under Robert E[arl] of Essex when he tooke Cadiz in Spaine'.[7] The lack of more specific information about his origins is surprising. There were a number of well-documented families of Leigh in Cheshire, each entitled to a coat of arms, and each associated with a particular place-name. However, no Ralph Leigh, married, with male offspring, and of the appropriate generation, shows up in any of the pedigrees or heraldic visitations for Chester. This is particularly surprising as any alliance with the impeccably connected Dorothy Kempe would have been worth the heralds' recording as confirmation of gentry status.[8] The trail is equally cold in Sussex. There were Lees in Fittleworth, Sussex, until 1634, but again, no 'Raphe Lee'.[9]

The lack of evidence, however, is itself suggestive. The Kempes are well documented in visitations and pedigrees because they are undeniably of gentry status. As the title page to her legacy states, Dorothy was a 'Gentle-woman'. Could it be that in forming an alliance with Ralph Leigh, she was was marrying beneath her station? Listed as 'ar.' in the 1621 Essex Visitation, as an armiger entitled to heraldic arms, Ralph Leigh should be traceable, but is not. His participation in the Cadiz expedition of 1587 (as one of 10,000 soldiers rather than as one of the 60 knights who were controversially created on the spot) further suggests a man who had to make his own way in the world.[10] It is possible, then, that Dorothy or her family chose him, not because he was rich in the gifts of the world, but rather because he was believed to be rich in the gifts of the Spirit.

From Dorothy's legacy we know that Ralph shared his wife's concern that their children be brought up 'godlily': he left specific instructions in his will to that effect. Dorothy also is certain that her deceased husband is in heaven, 'my selfe being a witnesse of his Faith in Christ'. Whether or not Leigh did in fact choose godliness over wealth and station, she advises her sons to do just that. The twelfth chapter of her legacy, on 'Choyse of Wiues', assures them that 'a little with a godly woman is better then great riches with the wicked'. She is particularly concerned that they should avoid alliances with those who superstitiously pray to Saints, pray in Latin, or believe in purgatory (Catholics, but also sufficiently unreformed Protestants), writing, 'Let no riches or mony bring your posterity to this kinde of tradition'. Throughout *The Mothers Blessing*, Leigh returns again and again to the superiority of spiritual riches over worldly wealth, which she denounces as 'trash' destined to be 'consumed with fire & brimstone'. One of the main reasons she writes her legacy, she tells her children in Chapter 6, is to persuade them never to fear poverty: 'alwaies know, it is the state of the children of GOD to bee poore in the world'.

The antagonism between the children of God and the world characterizes much Puritan writing and characteristically informs the Puritan sense of self; but the very persistence of economic themes and metaphors in Leigh's legacy, as well as the sustained vehemence with which Leigh denounces covetousness, worldly pride, and earthly weath, suggest a personal, serious, and perhaps costly commitment to the struggle. On the other hand, Leigh's injunction, 'Loue not the vngodly', is followed by the advice, 'marry with none, except you loue her, and be not changeable in your loue'. Perhaps Leigh simply married for love.

A PURITAN LEGACY

'Nature telleth me, that I cannot long bee here to speake vnto you, and this my mind will continue long after mee in writing.' As with Joscelin, Leigh's words carry the weight and authority of a parental deathbed blessing. Her legacy was probably composed, and certainly dedicated to Princess Elizabeth, around 1614 or 1615, at which time she seems to have recognized herself, correctly, to be near death: the first edition of *The Mothers Blessing* in 1616 describes her as 'not long since deceased'. Her dedication too helps to narrow the possibilities. Princess Elizabeth is addressed, first of all, as wife to the Count Palatine of the Rhine, whom she married in 1613. Leigh's 'vision' of the Princess, moreover, with 'the sweet slips of her vertue' growing upward suggests a date after the birth of Elizabeth's first child on 2 January 1614. (A 'slip' is a small shoot or cutting from a plant; around 1600 the word was often used figuratively to denote offspring.) At the other end, the will of her brother Robert, buried 28 July 1615, mentions relatives comprehensively but does not mention her – presumably because she was already dead.[11]

Like Joscelin, Leigh saw her text as a kind of surrogate mother which would complete the unfinished job of maternal instruction after her death. And, as with Joscelin, the yet unformed child's *need* for instruction is emphasized as a justification for writing. At the time she composed her legacy, Leigh saw her sons George, John, and William as 'too young to receiue it', being not yet 'of iudgement'. From the internal evidence of the legacy, it seems that they were at grammar school, learning the seven liberal arts and the languages which would help them to a true understanding of God's Word.[12] At least one of her sons did go on to use this education in the way that his mother's legacy instructed him to do. William became a preacher, and, moreover, just the sort of preacher Dorothy Leigh might have liked to be herself: scorning both worldly ambition and the remnants of popish religion in the Church.

In 1625 William Leigh was actually one of the candidates for the living at Finchingfield (although the job went to Stephen Marshall). In that year, he was curate at Denston in Suffolk, and in 1626, became rector of Groton in the same county.[13] Like Finchingfield, the living at Groton was in the hands of a godly patron: in this case, John Winthrop, who would emigrate to Massachusetts in 1630 and be elected its governor a year later. Winthrop and future emigrants sought to escape increasing pressure to conform to what they saw as 'Antichristian innovations'. Leigh, who remained behind, at first resisted, but at last was forced into an uneasy accommodation in order to maintain his calling to preach. In 1635, the conformist Bishop of Norwich, Matthew Wren, collected evidence against Leigh – evidence which marked him as a troublesome Puritan. He had, for instance, misused the enforced observance of Holy Days (which Puritans saw as a reversion to papistry) as an excuse for more preaching, and he had failed to read the 'Book of Sports', which authorized secular recreations on the Sabbath. Leigh was finally excommunicated on 5 April, although he soon submitted to the authorities for his 'ministries sake'.[14] It is not hard to imagine that he was influenced by his mother's condemnations of 'dumb dog' ministers who neglect preaching, and of 'such sports and recreations, which haue no warrant in the Word of God'.[15] It is harder to imagine what Dorothy Leigh would have thought of her son's submission.

Writing nearly two decades before the Laudian persecutions, Dorothy Leigh advocates neither separation (Winthrop's solution), nor resistance to evident ecclesiastical corruptions. Her activist injunction to her readers to 'speake to the Magistrates' is founded in an earlier strain of Puritanism, still hopeful that it can reform the state Church from within. The enemy, for her, is still Catholicism, and she more than once denounces Catholic 'superstitions' like praying the rosary or believing in purgatory. She declares herself thankful that England is Protestant. Her characteristic themes – the call for a preaching ministry, the importance of private prayer and Bible study, the necessity for the children of God to separate themselves from the world – are also those of reformist Protestantism in general, yet the energy and focus which she brings to these themes mark her out as one of the 'hotter' sort of Protestant. On the subject of literacy, for instance, she is unusually specific in her instructions that both male and female children should learn to read, beginning at the age of four or earlier. They are to acquire this skill exclusively for the purpose of reading the English Bible, which Leigh sees as nearly a patriotic duty: 'beginning at foure yeeres old or before . . . let them learne till ten, in which time they are not able to do any good in the Commonwealth, but to learne how to serue God, their King & Country by reading'. Furthermore, she advises anyone asked to be 'Witness' at a Baptism (she prefers this distinctively Puritan term to the more usual 'Godfather' or 'Godmother') to refuse unless the parents promise to teach the child to read as soon as it can, and to continue until it can read the Bible. Illiterate servants are to be taught to read at least the Ten Commandments, and persuaded to use all their spare time practising, 'so they may come the better to know the will of God written in his Word'. Universal literacy, so that all would have immediate access to the saving grace of the Word, was a Protestant ideal. But if this ideal was to guarantee social order by promoting an obedient knowledge of 'the will of God', it would also (especially in the 1640s and 1650s) have the opposite effect by democratizing interpretation: what *was* the will of God, according to a servant or a woman? The dismantling of social hierarchies is already present even in Leigh's socially conservative Puritan manual, in her levelling concern for literacy across gender and class.

Can we even see here a foremother of the radical female preachers of the 1640s and 1650s? In addition to promoting preaching, Leigh's text is itself a model of Puritan plain-style preaching. At its best, her prose is clear, balanced, pithy, and conversational. It is sometimes acerbic. Her homely analogies and parables have an engaging immediacy which set them apart from the relentlessly didactic parts of her legacy. As, for example, her extended analogy of the devil to a 'cunning fisher' in Chapter 38:

> when the diuell maketh all his poysonous baits, wherewith hee draweth an innumerable company of soules to hell, hee couereth them all with some worldly thing or other, that they may not see the hooke; some hee couereth with gold, some with siluer, some with earth, some with clay, some with honour, some with beautie, some with one thing, and some with another.

The analogy is so elaborated (it goes on for some pages), so vivid, so full of the practical arts of the fisher (the devil uses 'alteration of baits'), that one suspects Leigh must have fished herself. Equally effective, although less exuberant, is Leigh's simile for a soul which lacks the Holy Spirit in Chapter 30:

> . . . without [the Holy Spirit] we are like a house which is built faire on the outside: but there are no windowes to shew any light at all into it, and then the house is good for nothing, because there remaines nothing but darknes in it: euen so darke is the earth of *Adam*, which we are made of. . . .

Her most scathing prose, however, is reserved for the misuse of the things of the world. On this subject, she even creates her own parable, taking her images not from the Bible, but from seventeenth-century land management and patronage relations.[16] Her sustained attack on worldly interests culminates in the last chapters of her book, where she tells her sons to become preachers and to scorn advancement as the world measures it.

THE TEXT

The text of *The Mothers Blessing* which follows is that of the first edition of 1616, printed at London for John Budge, for sale 'at the great South-dore of Paules, and at Britaines Burse'. The first edition had no table of contents, although later

editions did, and I have included the table from the 1618 edition (with the
appropriate adjustments to page numbering) for convenience of reference. As with
Joscelin's and Richardson's legacies, I have used the convention of a blank line to
break up long blocks of text, using the rhetorical indications of the text (e.g.
marginal headnotes) to decide where breaks should occur, and also taking cues
from the 1618 edition, which introduces some new paragraph breaks. I distinguish
between the paragraph breaks of the 1616 edition, where I have indented the first
line of the new paragraph, and my own additional breaks, where I have not.

Leigh's scriptural quotations are on the whole closer to the Geneva Bible than
to any other version; thus, for my notes, I use the text and marginal commentary
of a Tomson/Junius Geneva Bible, printed by Robert Barker in London in 1610.
Leigh's reading and use of the Bible as an intertext for her legacy is even freer
and more creative than Joscelin's. Leigh seems happy not just to rewrite
scriptural passages, but to add to them as well. Leigh has no trouble at all, for
instance, putting words into the mouth of Christ: 'He that will be my Disciple',
she writes, freely paraphrasing the first half of Matthew 16:24, 'must forsake
himselfe, take vp his crosse and follow mee, and assuredly I will saue him.' The
final assurance of salvation is her own addition.[17] Her paraphrases and additions
often contribute to the homely directness of her style, as when she gives the
serpent tempting Eve the unscriptural, but somehow all-too-familiar line, 'It is
but an apple.'[18] This freedom with scripture, and her frequent miscitation of
chapter and verse suggests, even more than for Joscelin, that Leigh is mostly
using the Bible from memory. If so, she must have internalized an impressive
collection of specific verses.

She must have gathered her internal collection, moreover, from a variety of
sources and settings. Leigh is certainly most intimately acquainted with the Geneva
version; it was the Bible most frequently used for private study. Her quotations are
not only closest to the Geneva; in some cases they reproduce it word for word, and
in one instance she is clearly relying on its marginal commentary.[19] But she also
evidently cites from the King James Bible, published in 1611.[20] Moreover, 'Come
vnto mee, all yee that labour, and are ladẽ, & I wil ease you,' could only have been
taken from Tyndale's translation or the 'Great Bible'.[21] It is entirely possible that
Leigh had access to multiple versions of the Bible. She may also have heard and
remembered this particular verse from church: Elizabeth I had ordered a copy of
the 'Great Bible' to be placed in every church, and it was also the translation used
for *The Book of Common Prayer*. Leigh's unique formulation of Matthew 11:28, 'Come
vnto me, all yee that labour, and be heauy laden, and I will ease you,' may well
have been a composite of what she read at home and what she heard in church: the
first clause is King James, but the second is Great Bible or possibly Geneva.[22]
Finally, like Shakespeare in *Richard II*, Leigh follows *none* of the available
translations when she writes (twice) that it is 'as hard for a rich man to enter into
heauen, as for a Camell to goe thorow the eye of a needle'.[23] Here, Leigh (and

Shakespeare) may be quoting a proverb: a verse of scripture passed into common currency in a slightly altered form.

Leigh's internal Bible is thus distinctly and uniquely her own: made up not only of a composite of versions of scripture – heard publicly in church, studied privately at home, and perhaps even picked up conversationally – but transformed also by rewriting, by her own particular emphases and amplifications. This sort of 'personalization' of the Bible must have been common, among women as well as men, and by no means restricted to evidently subversive interpreters of the Bible. Dorothy Leigh's example cautions us against accepting too rigidly hegemonic a model of the Bible or any of its particular versions: its textual authority, and indeed its textual stability, was not absolutely fixed once a reader began to make it his or her own. Paradoxically, the Bible's textual authority and stability may actually have been the less absolute within what we would consider the 'fundamentalist' culture of scripturally based Puritanism. The intense reading and internalization of scripture that Leigh herself practised, and that she recommended to her sons with images of nourishment and consumption, was the means to living in obedience to the Word. But these same Puritan modes of reading necessitated appropriation, and thus the transformation of scripture. In her obedience to the Word, Dorothy Leigh also makes it entirely her own.

Notes

1. In addition to the frequent reprints of Leigh's book, its general availability may be measured by the cheap format (duodecimo) in which it was printed. A price of 10*d* is marked on the title page of a 1633 edition [Bodleian shelfmark 1 g. 104], placing it among the least expensive books one could have bought in that decade. Compare, for instance, the prices marked in Robert Burton's books bought in the 1630s in Nicholas K. Kiessling, *The Library of Robert Burton* (Oxford, Oxford Bibliographical Society, 1988), Appendix VIII.

2. An exemplary conflation of audience occurs at the beginning of Chapter 39 (p. 62): note the use both of the second person singular 'thy' and the second person plural 'you'.

3. Philip Morant, *The History and Antiquities of the County of Essex*, II (London, 1768), 363–4. For Margaret More Roper and her reputation, see Beilin, *Redeeming Eve*, Chapter 1.

4. Morant, II, 364. *The Visitation of Essex, 1612*, The Harleian Society, XIII (London, 1878), 231. 'Sir Clement Heigham', *DNB*. A photograph and plan of Spains Hall may be found in *Royal Commission on Historical Monuments (England.) An Inventory of the Historical Monuments in Essex*, I (London, His Majesty's Stationery Office, 1916), 90–1. See also Nikolaus Pevsner, *The Buildings of England: Essex* (London, Penguin, 1954), p. 330.

5. Frederick Hitchin-Kemp, *A General History of the Kemp and Kempe Families of Great Britain and her Colonies* (London, Leadenhall Press [1902]), Section III, 5, 10. Dorothy's brother William is reported to have taken a voluntary seven-year vow of silence out of remorse for 'an unjustifiable reflection upon his wife'. The vow is mentioned in his epitaph. See Frederick Chancellor, *The Ancient Sepulchral Monuments of Essex* (London, printed for the Author, 1890), p. 227, and Hitchin-Kemp, III, 8.

6. Marshall was suspected of nonconformity in the 1630s: Tom Webster, *Godly Clergy in Early Stuart England: The Caroline Puritan Movement, c. 1620–1643* (Cambridge University Press, 1997), pp. 194, 240. Marshall is best known, however, as one-fifth of the anti-episcopal publishing collective known as 'Smectymnuus' in the early 1640s, and especially for *Meroz Cursed*, an inflammatory sermon preached before the House of Commons a few months before the outbreak of civil war. Christopher Hill, *The English Bible and the Seventeenth-Century Revolution* (Harmondsworth, Penguin, 1994), pp. 88–9.

7. *Visitation of Essex*, 231. British Library Harleian MS 6071, fol. 203v.

8. Kristen Poole suggests that Dorothy Leigh's husband was the fourth son of Thomas Leigh of Adlington (83–4). The 1613 Visitation of Chester, however, records no marriage for 'Randall' or 'Ralph' Leigh of Adlington, and lists him as 's.p.', without progeny, whereas we know from the legacy that Dorothy Leigh's husband had three surviving sons at that date. *Pedigrees Made at the Visitation of Cheshire, 1613*. Record Society for the Publication of Original Documents Relating to Lancashire and Cheshire, LVIII (1909), 144. A manuscript pedigree similarly lists 'Randalphus', son of Thomas Leigh of Adlington, as unmarried, s.p. British Library Harleian MS 2187, fol. 74v.

One needs to ask why the visitation records for Kempe should be silent on Ralph Lee's parentage if it was as respectable as that of the Leighs of Adlington; or conversely, why those of Leigh of Adlington should be silent on an alliance with Kempes.

9. The Lees of Fittleworth moved to Hertfordshire in 1634. J. Dallaway and E. Cartwright, *Parochial Topography: Rape of Arundel* (1832), p. 343. But no Ralph Lee appears in their pedigree. See manuscript addition to the *1574 Visitation of Hertfordshire*, Harleian Society, XXII, 149.

10. Penry Williams, *The Later Tudors: England 1547–1603* (Oxford, Clarendon Press, 1995) pp. 351–3.

11. Hitchin-Kemp, III, 7.

12. See note 27. It is possible that at least William was already at university, given that he was a serious contender for a good living in 1625 (see below). To justify her legacy, Leigh might have had an interest in exaggerating her sons' youth.

13. Webster, p. 38 and n. 6.

14. Webster, pp. 208–9, 247. Leigh made this excuse in a letter to his former patron, John Winthrop, who had been critical of his 'apostasy'.

15. The names of William Leigh's children may also reflect his mother's advice that biblical names are most suitable (see Leigh, Chapter 9, and note 41): they were John, Mary, Dorothy, Hannah, Philip, Joseph, and Elizabeth. (John also became a minister and Mary, a schoolmistress in Bury.) British Library Harleian MS 6071, fol. 203v.

16. See note 211.

17. Compare the Geneva version of Matthew 16:24: 'Iesus then said to his disciples, If any man will follow mee, let him forsake him selfe, and take vp his crosse, and follow me.' The promise of salvation is referred to obliquely in the next verse. See p. 60.

18. See note 143.

19. Leigh's quotation of Matthew 6:34, for instance, 'Care not for to morrow; let to morrow care for it selfe, the day hath enough with his owne griefe' is distinctly Geneva; only the Geneva Bible, and none of the other versions available to Leigh, has the last clause. For evidence of her use of the Geneva commentary, see note 187.

20. See notes 102 and 203.

21. See *The New Testament Octapla: English Versions of the New Testament*, (ed.) Luther A. Weigle (New York, Thomas Nelson, [1962]), Matthew 11:28 and note 112.

22. See note 80.

23. All versions rather make it 'easier for the camel'. See note 30.

THE

MOTHERS

BLESSING.

OR

The godly counsaile of a Gentle-woman not long since deceased, left behind her for her CHILDREN:

Containing many good exhortations, and godly admonitions, profitable for all Parents to leaue as a Le-
gacy to their Children, but especially
for those, who by reason of their
young yeeres stand most in
need of Instruction.[1]

By M^ris. DOROTHY LEIGH.

PROVERB. 1. 8. My sonne, heare
the instruction of thy father, and forsake not the lawe of thy mother.

Printed at *London* for *Iohn Budge*,
and are to be sold at the great South-
dore of Paules, and at Brit-
taines Burse. 1616.

2

MOTHERS BLESSING

1616

[sig. A2r]

TO THE HIGH
and excellent Princesse,
the Lady ELIZABETH
her Grace, daughter to the
high and mightie King of great
Brittaine, and Wife to the illustri-
ous Prince, the Count Palatine
of the Rhine:²

D.L. Wisheth all grace and prosperity here, and glory in the
world to come.

Most worthy & renowned Princess, I beeing troubled and wearied with feare, [sig. A2v] lest my children should not find the right way to heauen, thought with my selfe that I could doe no lesse for them, then euerie man will doe for his friend, which was, to write them the right way, that I had truely obserued out of the written word of GOD, lest for want of warning they might fall where I stumbled, and then I should thinke my selfe in the fault, who knew there were such downe-falls in the world, that they could hardly climbe the hill to heauen without helpe, and yet [sig. A3r] had not told them thereof.³ Wherefore I writ them the right and ready way to Heauen wel waranted by the scriptures of the olde and new Testament, which is the true word of God, and tolde them how many false paths they should finde, how they should finde them, and what care they should haue to shunne them: if they tooke a false way, what a trouble they should haue in turning againe, what danger if they went on: and of many doubts⁴ which the world would make with- [sig. A3v] out a cause, and how silent it would bee in danger. Thus when I had writtẽ vnto them of these things, I was at much peace, quiet and contentment.

But as no contentment in the world continueth long, so sodainly there arose a new care in my minde, how this scroule⁵ should bee kept for my children: for they were too young to receiue it, my selfe too old to keepe it, men too wise to direct it to,[6] the world too wicked to endure it. Then in great griefe I looked vp [sig. A4r] to heauen, from whence I knew commeth al comfort, and looking vp, I saw a most Angelicall throne of Princely Peeres and peerelesse Princes prepared for heauen, and yet by the appointment of God were heere to comfort vs on the earth: then I perceiued that this Throne was the ioy of England: then I considered that the highest blud had the lowest[7] mind: then I sawe humility looking downe-ward, while the sweet slips of her vertue grew vpward:[8] then, euen then, Princely Lady, I be- [sig. A4v] held your mild and courteous coũtenance, which shewed, your heart was bent to doe good to all: wherefore without feare, and with much faith, I aduentured to make your Grace the protectresse of this my Booke, knowing that if you would but suffer your name to bee seene in it, Wisedome would allow it, and all the wicked winde in the world could not blow it away. The Lord multiply his graces more and more on you, and vouchsafe vnto you a numerous posterity, in whom your [sig. A5r] Grace may receiue much ioy and comfort, and GODS Church, and true Religion continuall defence and propagation.

Your Graces, in all humble
and obseruant duty:
D.L.

[sig. A6r]

TO MY BELO-
ued sonnes, GEORGE,
IOHN, *and* WILLIAM
LEIGH, *all things*
pertaining to life and
godlinesse.

My Children, God hauing taken your Father out of this vale of teares, to his euerlasting mercy in CHRIST, *my selfe not onely knowing what a care hee had in his life time, that you should be* [sig. A6v] *brought up godlily, but also at his death being charged in his will by the loue and duty which I bare him, to see you well instructed and brought vp in knowledge,[9] I could not chuse but seeke (according as I was by duty bound) to fulfill his will in all things, desiring no greater comfort in the World, then to see you grow in godlinesse, that so you might meet your Father in heauen, where I am sure hee is, my selfe being a witnesse of his Faith in Christ. And seeing my selfe going out of the world, and you but comming in, I know not* [sig. A7r] *how to performe this duty so well, as to leaue you these few lines, which will shew you as well the great desire your Father had both of your spirituall and temporal good, as the care I had to fulfill his will in this, knowing it was the last duty I should performe vnto him. But when I had written these things vnto you, and had (as I thought) something fulfilled your Fathers request, yet I could not see to what purpose it should tend, vnlesse it were sent abroad to you: for should it be left with the eldest, it is likely the youngest should* [sig. A7v] *haue but little part in it. Wherefore setting aside all feare, I haue*

aduentured to shew my imperfections to the view of the World, not regarding what censure shall for
this bee laid vpon mee, so that heerein I may shew my selfe a louing Mother, and a dutifull Wife:
and thus I leaue you to the protection of him that made you, And rest[10] till death,

Your fearefull, faithfull,
and carefull Mother,
D.L.

[sig. A8r]

Counsell to my Children.

My Sonnes, the readers of this book,
   I doe you not intreate
To beare with each misplaced word,
   for why,[11] my paine's as great
To write this little booke to you
   (the world may thinke indeed)
As it will be at any time
   for you the same to read.

But this I much and oft desire,
   that you would doe for mee,
To gather hony of each flowre,
   as doth the labourous Bee.[12]
Shee lookes not who did place the Plant,
   nor how the flowre did grow,
Whether so stately vp aloft,
   or neere the ground below.

But where she findes it, there she workes,
   and gets the wholsome food, [sig. A8v]
And beares it home, and layes it vp,
   to doe her Country good,
And for to serue her selfe at need
   when winter doth begin:
When storm and tempest is without,
   then shee doth find within.

A sweet and pleasant wholsome food,
   a house to keepe her warme,
A place where softly she may rest,
   and be kept from all harme.

Except the Bee that idle is,
    and seekes too soone for rest,
Before she filled hath her house,
    whereby her state is blest.

And then as she did rest too soone,
    too soone she sorrow knowes:
When stormes and tempests are without,
    then she her selfe beshrowes.[13]
She looketh out and seeth death,
    ready her to deuoure:
Then doth she wish that she had got
    more of the wholsome flowre.

For why, within, her store is spent,
    before the winter's past.
And she by no meanes can endure [sig. A9r]
    the stormy winters blast.
Shee looketh out, and seeth death,
    and findes no lesse within,
Then too too late for to repent,
    you see she doth begin.

Therefore see you not idle be,
    this I would haue you know,
Be sure still that the ground be good,
    whereout the Plant doth grow:
Then gather well and lose no time,
    take heed now you doe see,
Lest you be vnprouided found,
    as was the idle Bee.

                                    D.L.

[TABLE OF CONTENTS ADDED TO THE 1618 EDITION.][14]

The Contents of this
BOOKE.

[p. 1]

The
MOTHERS
Blessing.

CHAP. I.

*The occasion of writing this Booke, was the consideration of the care of Parents
for their Children.*

My Children, when I did truely weigh, rightly consider, and perfectly see the
great care, labour, tra- [p. 2] uaile, and continuall study, which Parents take to
inrich their children, some wearing their bodies with labour, some breaking
their sleepes with care, some sparing from their owne bellies, and many
hazarding their soules, some by bribery, some by simony, others by periurie, and
a multitude by vsurie, some stealing on the Sea, others begging by Land
portions from euery poore man, not caring if the whole Common-wealth be
impouerished, so their children be inriched: for themselues they can bee content
with meate, drinke, and cloth, so that their children by their meanes may bee
made rich, alwaies abusing [p. 3] this portion of Scripture: *He that prouideth not for
his owne family, is worse then an Infidell:* {1. Tim. 5. 8.} euer seeking for the
temporall thinges of this world, and forgetting those things which bee eternall:
when I considered these things, I say, I thought good (beeing not desirous to
inrich you with transitory goods) to exhort and desire you to follow the counsell
of Christ: *First seeke the kingdome of God and his righteousnesse, and then all these things
shall be administred vnto you.* {Mat. 6. 33.}

CHAP. 2.

The first cause of writing, is a Motherly affection.

But lest you should maruaile; my children, [p. 4] why I doe not, according to the vsuall custome of women, exhort you by word and admonitions, rather then by writing, a thing so vnusuall among vs, and especially in such a time, when there bee so manie godly bookes in the world, that they mould in some mens studies, while their Masters are mard, because they will not meditate vpon them; as many mens garments moth-eate in their chests, while their Christian bretheren quake with cold in the street for want of couering; knowe therfore, that it was the motherly affection that I bare vnto you all, which made me now (as it often hath done heretofore) forget my selfe [p. 5] in regard of you: neither care I what you or any shall thinke of mee, if among many words I may write but one sentence, which may make you labour for the spirituall food of the soule, wch must be gathered euery day out of the word, as the children of Israel gathered Manna in the wildernesse.[15] By the which you may see it is a labour: but what labour? a pleasant labour, a profitable labour: a labour without the which the soule cannot liue. For as the children of Israel must needs starue, except they gath'red euery day in the wildernesse and fed of it, so must your soules, except you gather the spiritual Manna out of the word eue- [p. 6] ry day, and feed of it continually: for as they by this Manna cõforted their harts, strengthened their bodies, and preserued their liues; so by this heauenly Word of God, you shall comfort your soules, make them strong in Faith, and grow in true godlinesse, and finally preserue them with great ioy, to euerlasting life, through Faith in Christ; whereas, if you desire any food for your soules, that is not in the written Word of God, your soules die with it euen in your harts and mouthes; euen as they, that desired other food, dyed with it in their mouthes, {Num. 11. 3} were it neuer so dainty:[16] so shall you, and there is no recouery for you.

[p. 7]

CHAP. 3.

The best labour is for the foode of the Soule.

Oh my Children, is not this a comfortable labour? Our Sauiour Christ saith, *Labour not for the meate that perisheth, but for the meate that endureth to euerlasting life*: {Ioh. 6. 27.} and yet I see and feare, you shall see how many there bee that crosse Christ in these words: nay rather, crosse thẽselues: for, contrary to our blessed Sauiours counsell, they labour for the meats that perisheth, and in the meane time they lose the foode of euerlasting life. This (my beloued [p. 8] sonnes and deare children) this is the cause that maketh mee so much to feare you, and those who

hereafter shal come of you, because I see so many that regard not the words of our
Sauiour Christ, who came from the high Throne of God, and preached to vs, and
prayed for vs, and tooke our flesh vpon him, {Gal. 4. 4.}[17] and kept it without
sinne, refusing no company, healing euery sicknesse and disease, {Math. 4. 23} fed
the hungry, gaue pardon to euery sinner that would but aske it, dyed for vs, {Rom.
4. 25.} indured the paines of hell for vs, yea, more then this, euen in our owne
flesh hee ouercame sinne, death, and hel, yea, and more then that also, hee
carried our flesh in- [p. 9] to Heauen in the sight of many, and there keepes it, and
is become a Mediatour for vs in it; hee ioyned himselfe to vs in our flesh, as it is
written, *He tooke our flesh vpon him*: {Heb. 2. 14.}[18] he taught vs to ioyne our flesh
vnto him by faith, that *Where hee is, there wee might bee with him also*: {Ioh. 17. 24.}[19]
and if wee will not follow him, that hath done all this for vs, and much more then
I can write or declare, how vnthankefull shall wee shew our selues?

My deare Children, haue I not cause to feare? the holy Ghost saith by the
Prophet, *Can a Mother forget the child of her wombe?* {Es. 49. 15.}[20] As if he should say,
Is it possible, that shee, which hath carried her child [p. 10] within her, so neere her
hart, and brought it forth into this world with so much bitter paine, so many grones
and cries, can forget it? nay rather, will shee not labour now till Christ be formed in
it?[21] will shee not blesse it euery time it suckes on her brests, when shee feeleth the
bloud come from her heart to nourish it?[22] Will shee not instruct it in the youth,
and admonish it in the age, and pray for it continually? Will shee not be afraid, that
the child which shee endured such paine for, should endure endlesse paine in hell?
Could Saint *Paul* say vnto the *Galathians*, that were but strangers to him concerning
the flesh, [p. 11] only he had spent some time amõgst them to bring them to the
professiõ of the truth, from which hee feared they would fall: and could hee, I say,
write vnto them, *My little children, of whom I doe trauaile againe in birth, vntill Christ be
formed in you?* {Gal. 4. 19.} And can any man blame a mother (who indeed brought
forth her childe with much paine) though she labour againe till Christ bee formed
in them? Could S. *Paul* wish himself separated from God for his brethrens sake:
{Rom. 9. 3.}[23] and will not a mother venter to offend the world for her childrens
sake? Therefore let no man blame a mother, though she something exceede in
writing to her [p. 12] children, since euery man knowes, that the loue of a mother
to her children, is hardly contained within the bounds of reason. Neither must you,
my sonnes, when you come to bee of iudgement, blame me for writing to you, since
Nature telleth me, that I cannot long bee here to speake vnto you, and this my
mind will continue long after mee in writing; and yet not my mind, but I seeke to
put you in minde of the words of our Sauiour Christ, which saith, *Labour not for the
meate that perisheth, &c.* {Ioh. 6. 27.} where you see, that the food of the soule is to
bee gotten by labour. Why stand you here (sayth Christ?) {Mat. 20. 6.} here is no
time to be [p. 13] idle: they that will rest with Christ in heauen, must labour to
follow him here on earth. *Blessed are the dead, which dye in the Lord: for they rest from their
labour.* {Reu. 14. 13.} Thus you see, if you will goe to the place, which Christ hath

bought for you, you must labour to follow Christ: he labour'd to get it for you, or els all your labour would haue been as nothing; and now you must labour to lay hold on him, or els all your labour will bee worth nothing. Many there bee that labour the cleane contrary way; for they leaue Christ, and take hold of traditions: and a number loyter, and by that meanes neuer get holde on Christ.[24] And this [p. 14] is the cause why I write vnto you, that you might neuer fly from him with the one, nor yet loyter with the other, but that you might learne to follow him, and to take hold of him in the written Word of God, where you shall find him (as Christ himselfe witnesseth) and no where else. *Search the Scriptures*, sayth he, *for they testifie of mee.* {Ioh. 5. 35.}[25] Labour therefore, that you may come vnto Christ.

CHAP. 4.

The second cause is, to stirre them vp to write.

The second cause, my sonnes, why I write vnto you (for you [p. 15] may thinke that had I had but one cause, I would not haue changed the vsuall order[26] of women) is needfull to be knowne, and may doe much good. For where I saw the great mercy of God toward you, in making you men, and placing you amongst the wise, where you may learne the true written Word of God, which is the path-way to all happinesse, and which will bring you to the chiefe Citty, new Ierusalem, and the seuen liberall sciences, whereby you shall haue at least a superficiall sight in all things:[27] I thought it fit to giue you good example, and by writing to intreate you, that when it shall please God to [p. 16] giue both vertue and grace with your learning, he hauing made you men, that you may write and speake the Word of God without offending any,[28] that then you would remember to write a booke vnto your children, of the right and true way to happinesse, which may remaine with them and theirs for euer.

CHAP. 5.

The third cause is to moue women to bee carefull of their children.

The third is, to encourage women (who, I feare, will blush at my boldnesse) not to bee a- [p. 17] shamed to shew their infirmities, but to giue men the first and chiefe place: yet let vs labour to come in the second; and because wee must needs confesse, that sin entred by vs into our posterity,[29] let vs shew how carefull we are to seeke to Christ to cast it out of vs, and our posterity, and how fearefull we are that our sinne should sinke any of them to the lowest part of the earth; wherefore let vs call vpon them to follow Christ, who will carry them to the height of heauen.
[p. 18]

CHAP. 6.

The fourth cause is, to arme them against pouerty.

The fourth cause is, to desire you, that you will neuer feare pouerty, but alwaies know, it is the state of the children of GOD to bee poore in the world. Christ sayth, *Ye shall haue the poore with you alwaies.* {Ioh. 12. 8.} It may be he hath appointed you or yours to bee of this poore number: doe not striue against Christ. *It is as hard* (sayth he) *for a rich man to enter into heauen, as for a Camell to goe thorow the eye of a needle.* {Math. 19. 24.}[30] Saint *Iames* sayth, *Woe bee to you that are rich.* {Iam. 5. 1.} [p. 19] S. *Paul* sayth, *The desire of mony is the roote of all euill.* {1. Tim. 6. 10.} Which if it be true, as it is not to be doubted of, and you feare pouerty, then doth it necessarily follow, that you will desire the roote of all euil, which is money, and so become good for nothing. The feare of pouerty maketh men run into a thousand sins, which nothing els could draw them to: for many fearing the cold stormes of pouerty, which neuer last long, run on to the hot fire of hell, which neuer hath an end. This matter requireth many words, for it is hard to perswade the nature of man from the feare of pouerty: wherefore I wil speake more of that afterwards: onely I [p. 20] now say, Feare not to bee poore with *Lazarus*, but feare a thousand times to be rich with *Diues*.[31]

CHAP. 7.

The fift cause is, not to feare death.

The fift cause is, to desire you neuer to feare death; for the feare of death hath made many to deny the knowne truth, and so haue brought a heauy iudgement of God vpon themselues. A great reason, why you should not feare death is, because you can by no meanes shun it: you must needes indure it, and therefore it is meet that [p. 21] you should be alwaies prepared for it, and neuer feare it. *Hee that will saue his life,* sayth Christ, *shall lose it, and he that will lose his life for my sake and the Gospels, shall finde it.* {Math. 16. 26.}[32] Doe not feare the paines of death, in what shape soeuer hee come: for perhaps thou shalt haue more paines vpon thy bed, and be worse prouided to beare them, by reason of some grieuous sicknesse, then thou art like to feele, when God shal call thee forth to witnesse his truth. The only way not to feare death, is alwaies to be prouided to dye. And that thou mayest alwaies be prouided to dye, thou must be continually strengthening thy faith with the promises [p. 22] of the Gospell; as, *Hee that liueth, and beleeueth, shall not dye: and though he were dead, yet shall he liue.* {Ioh. 11. 25.26.} *Meditate in the lawe of the Lord day and night* {Psal. 1. 2.} (as the Psalmist saith) and then thou shalt be fit to bring forth fruit in due season:[33] then thou shalt bee fit to serue God, thy King and country, both in thy life and in thy death, and always shalt shew thy selfe a good member of IESVS

Christ,[34] a faithfull subiect to thy Prince, and alwaies fit to gouerne in the Christian common-wealth: and then thou mayest faithfully and truely say: *Whether I liue or dye, I am the Lords.* {Rom. 14. 8.} But without continuall meditation of the Word this cannot bee done. [p. 23] And this was one of the chiefe causes why I writ vnto you, to tell you that you must meditate in the Word of God; for many reade it, and are neuer the better, for want of meditation. If yee heare the Word, and read it, without meditating theron, it doth the soule no more good then meate and drink doth the body, being seene and felt, and neuer fed vpon: for as the body will dye although it see meate: euen so will the soule, for all the hearing & reading of the word, if that ye doe not meditate vpon it, and gather faith, and strengthen it, and get hold of Christ; which if ye doe, Christ will bring you to the kingdome of his Fa- [p. 24] ther; to which you can come by no meanes but by faith in him.[35]

CHAP. 8.

The sixt cause is, to perswade them to teach their children.

The sixt reason is, to entreate and desire you, & in some sort to commaund you, that all your children, be they Males or Females, may in their youth learne to read the Bible in their owne mother tongue; for I know, it is a great helpe to true godlinesse. And let none of you plead pouerty against this; for I know, that if you bee neither couetous, prodigall, [p. 25] nor idle, either of which sins will let no vertue growe where they come, that you need not faile in this: but if you will follow the commaundement of the Lord, and labour sixe dayes, and keepe the seuenth holy to the Lord, and loue him with all your heart, soule, and strength,[36] you will not onely be willing, but also able to see them all brought vp to read the Bible. *Salomon* that was wise by the Spirit of God, sayd: *Remember thy Creatour in the dayes of thy youth.* {Eccl. 12. 1.} And ye are also commanded, to *write it vpon the walls of your houses, and to teach it your childern.* {Deut. 11. 19.20.}[37] *I know* (sayth God) *that Abraham will teach his children, and his* [p. 26] *childrens children to walke in thy commandements.* {Gen. 18. 19} Also I further desire you, because I wish all well, and would be glad you should do as much good as could be in the wildernesse of this world, that if any shal at any time desire you to be a Witnesse[38] to the baptizing of their childe, that then you shal desire the person so desiring, to giue you his faithfull word, that the child shall bee taught to read, so soone as it can conueniently learne, and that it shall so continue till it can read the Bible. If this will not be granted, you shall refuse to answer for the child; otherwise doe not refuse to be a witnesse to any; for it is a good Christian duety. [p. 27] Moreouer, forget not, whether you answere for the child or no, to pray, that the child baptized, may receiue the holy Ghost, with all other children of the faithfull, especially when you are where a child is baptized; for it is your duty to pray for the increase of the Church of God. *Pray for the peace of Ierusalem* (saith the Psalmist) *let them prosper that loue thee.* {Psal. 122. 6.}

CHAP. 9.

The seuenth cause is, that they should giue their children good names.

The seauenth cause is, to entreate you, that though I do not liue to be a [p. 28] witnesse to the baptizing of any of your children, yet you would giue me leaue to giue names to them all. For though I doe not thinke any holinesse to be in the name, but know that God hath his in euery place, and of euery name; yet I see in the Bible, it was obserued by GOD himselfe, to giue choyse names to his children, which had some good signification.[39] I thinke it good therefore, to name your children after the names of the Saints of God,[40] which may bee a meanes to put them in mind of some vertues which those Saints vsed; especially, when they shal read of them in the Bible: and seeing many are desirous to name [p. 29] both their owne children and others after their owne names, this will be a meanes to increase the names of the Saints in the Church, and so none shall haue occasion to mislike his name, since hee beareth the name of such a Saint, as hath left a witnesse to the world, that hee liued and dyed in the true faith of IESVS Christ. The names I haue chosen you, are these; *Philip, Elizabeth, Iames, Anna, Iohn* and *Susanna.* The vertues of them that bore those names, and the causes why I chose them, I let passe, and only meane to write of the last name **Susan,* famoused through the world for chastity; {*The story of Susanna, though it be not canonicall, nor to be equalled to those books that are, yet it may bee true, and of good vse, as many other histories written by men are.}[41] a vertue which alwaies hath been, and is of [p. 30] great account, not onely amongst the Christians and people of God, but euen among the Heathen and Infidels: insomuch that some of them haue written, that a woman that is truly chaste, is a great partaker of all other vertues; and contrariwise, that the woman that is not truely chaste, hath no vertue in her.[42] The which saying may well be warranted by the Scripture; for who so is truly chaste, is free from idlenesse and from all vaine delights, full of humility, and all good Christian vertues: who so is chaste, is not giuen to pride in apparell, nor any vanity, but is alwaies either reading, meditating, or practising some [p. 31] good thing which she hath learned in the Scripture. But she which is vnchaste, is giuen to be idle; or if she do any thing, it is for a vaine glory, and for the prayse of men, more then for any humble, louing and obedient heart, that shee beareth vnto God and his Word: who sayd, *Six dayes thou shalt labour,* {Exod. 20. 9.} and so left no time for idlenesse, pride, or vanity; for in none of these is there any holinesse. The vnchaste woman is proud, and alwayes decking her selfe with vanity, and delights to heare the vaine words of men, in which there is not only vanity, but also so much wickednesse, that the vain words of men, [p. 32] and womens vainenesse in hearing them, hath brought many women to much sorrow and vexation;[43] as wofull experience hath, and wil make many of them confesse. But some wil say, Had they onely lent an eare to their words they had done well enough. To answere which, I would haue euery one know, that one sinne begetteth another. The vaine words of the man, and the idle cares of the woman, beget vnchaste thoughts oftentimes in the one, which may bring forth much wickednesse in them both.

Man sayd once, *The woman which thou gauest mee, beguiled me, and I did eate.* {Gen 3. 12.}[44] But [p. 33] wee women may now say, that men lye in waite euery where to deceiue vs, as the Elders did to deceiue *Susanna.*[45] Wherefore let vs bee, as she was, chaest, watchfull, and wary, keeping company with maides. Once *Iudas* betrayed his Master with a kisse, & repented it:[46] but now men, like *Iudas,* betray their Mistresses with a kisse &, repent it not: but laugh and reioyce, that they haue brought sinne and shame to her that trusted them. The only way to auoid al which, is to be chaste with *Susanna,* and being women, to imbrace that vertue, which being placed in a woman, is most commendable.

An vnchaste woman de- [p. 34] stroyeth both the body and the soule of him, shee seemeth most to loue, and it is almost impossible to set down the mischiefes, which haue come through vnchast women. *Salomon* sayth, that *her steppes lead to hell.* {Prou. 2. 18.}[47] Wherfore bring vp your daughters, as *Susanna's* Parents brought vp her: teach them the lawe of the Lord continually, and alwayes perswade them to embrace this vertue of chastity.

It may be, that some of you will maruaile, since I set downe names for the imitation of their vertues, that bore them; why I placed not *Mary* in the first place, a woman vertuous aboue all other women. My [p. 35] reason was this, because I presumed, that there was no woman so senselesse, as not to looke what a blessing God hath sent to vs women through that gracious Virgin, by whom it pleased GOD to take away the shame, which EVE our Grandmother had brought vs to: For before, men might say, The woman beguiled me, and I did eate the poysoned fruit of disobedience, and I dye. But now man may say, if he say truly, The woman brought me a Sauiour, and I feede of him by faith and liue. Here is this great and wofull shame taken from women by God, working in a woman: man can claime no part in it: the [p. 36] shame is taken from vs, and from our posterity for euer: *The seede of the woman hath taken downe the Serpents head*; {Gen 3. 15.} and now whosoeuer can take hold of the seed of the woman by faith, shall surely liue for euer.[48] And therefore all generations shal say, that she was blessed,[49] who broght vs a Sauiour, the fruit of obedience, that whosoeuer feedeth of, shall liue for euer: and except they feed of the seed of the woman, they haue no life. {Ioh. 6. 53.} Will not therefore all women seek out this great grace of God, that by *Mary* hath taken away the shame, which before was due vnto vs euer since the fall of man?

Mary was filled with the [p. 37] Holy Ghost, and with all goodnesse, and yet is called the blessed Virgin:[50] as if our God should (as he doth indeed) in briefe comprehend all other vertues vnder this one vertue of chastity: wherfore I desire, that all women, what name so euer they beare, would learne of this blessed Virgin to bee chaste: for though shee were more replenished with grace then any other, and more freely beloued of the Lord, yet the greatest title that she had, was, that shee was a blessed and pure Virgin; which is a great cause to moue all women, whether they be maids or wiues (both which estates shee honoured) to liue chastly, [p. 38] to whom for this cause God hath giuen a cold and temperate disposition,[51] & bound them with these words; *Thy desire shall be subiect to thy husband.* {Gen. 3. 6.}[52] As if God in mercy to women should say; You of your selues shal haue no desires, only they shall be subiect to your husbands: wch hath been verified in Heathen women, so as it is almost incredible to be beleeued: for many of them before they would be defiled, haue been carelesse of their liues, and so haue endured all those torments, that men would deuise to inflict vpon them, rather then they would lose the name of a modest mayd, or a chaste Matrone. Yea, and so farre [p. 39] they haue beene from consenting to any immodestie, that if at any time they haue been rauished, they haue either made away themselues, or at least haue separated themselues from company, not thinking themselues worthy of any society, after they haue once bin deflowred, though against their wils.[53] Wherfore the woman that is infected with the sin of vncleannesse, is worse then a beast, because it desireth but for nature, and shee, to satisfie her corrupt lusts.

Some of the Fathers haue written, that it is not enough for a woman to be chaste, but euen so to behaue her selfe, that no man [p. 40] may thinke or deeme her to be vnchaste. Wee read, that in the Primitiue Church, when there were warres betweene the Christians and the Pagans, if at any time the Pagans had gotten the victory, that then they would seeke to deflowre the Virgins: to the which sinne before the Christians would yeeld, they would continually laye violent hands vpon themselues; in so much that the Doctours of the Church were oftentimes constrained to make diuers Sermons and Orations to them, to disswade them from that crueltie, which they inflicted vpon themselues, rather then they would suffer them- [p. 41] selues to be deflowred:[54] such a disgrace did they think it, to haue but one spot of vncleannesse, and yet none of these were so holy as this *Mary*, this pure and vndefiled Virgin.

Some godly and reuerend men of the Church haue gathered this, that there were fiue women of great vertue in the time of the Lawe, the first letters of whose names doe make her whole name to shewe, that shee had all their vertues wholly combined in her, as namely;

Michal,
Abigail,
Rachel,
Iudith, &
Anna.

[p. 42]

She was as faithfull to her husband, as *Michal*, who saued her husband *Dauid* from the fury of *Saul*, although hee were her father and her King, not preferring her owne life before the safety of her husband. {1. Sam. 19. 12.}   She was as wise as *Abigail*, who is highly commended for her wisedome: {1. Sam. 25 .3.} amiable in the sight of her husband, as *Rachel*: {Gen. 29. 17} stout and magnanimous in the time of trouble, as *Iudith*: patient and zealous in prayer, as *Anna*. {1. Sam. 1. 10.11.}[55] Seeing then, that by this one name, so many vertues are called to remembrance, I thinke it meete, that good names bee giuen to all women, that they might call to minde the vertues of those [p. 43] women whose names they beare: but especially aboue all other morall Vertues,[56] let women be perswaded by this discourse, to imbrace chastity, without which we are meere beasts, and no women.

CHAP. 10.

Reasons of giuing good names to Children.

If ye shall thinke me too teadious about the naming your children, I tel you, that I haue some reason for it; and the first {1} is this, to make them reade in the Bible the things which are written of those Saints, and learne to imitate their ver- [p. 44] tues. Secondly, {2} because many haue made a God of the virgin *Marie*, the Scripture warranting no such thing, and haue prayed to her,[57] (though there they shal find that she was a woman, yea, and a comfort to all women, for she hath taken away the reproch, wch of right belonged vnto vs, and by the seed of the womã we are al saued) it was therefore fit I should speake largely of that name. Thirdly, {3} seeing many haue heretofore, and now doe make Images of Saints, to put them in minde of the Saints, and so by little and little haue at last worshipped the workes of their own hands, and for feare of forgetting the Saints, haue for- [p. 45] gotten the second Commandements;[58] I thought it better to haue you remember them, by bearing their names, and by reading what they taught vs in the Scripture, and how they led their liues, then by looking vpon a painted piece of Paper, or a carued stone. And this by the way may bee maruelled at, that they which loue to worship Images, neuer loue to name their Children after the names of the Saints; for if they had so done, by this time wee should haue had no other names but *Mathew, Marke, Iohn, Timothy*, and such as followed Christ faithfully. Then *Moyses* and his mildnesse would bee more talked of: [p. 46] *Samuel* and his obedience would bee more sought after: *Abraham* and his faithfulnesse, would be more followed. Lastly, {4} this I will tell you, that there is no man but wil be ashamed to do any thing, w[ch] shal disgrace the good name, after which [he] is called; as if one should say, Is this a *Moyses*? Is this an *Elias*, and haue such qualities as these?[59]

CHAP. 11.

Children to bee taught betimes, and brought vp gently.

I am further also to entreate you, that all your Children may be taught [p. 47] to reade, beginning at foure yeeres old or before, and let them learne till ten, in which time they are not able to do any good in the Commonwealth, but to learne how to serue God, their King & Country by reading. And I desire, intreat, and earnestly beseech you, and euery one of you, that you will haue your Children brought vp with much gentlenesse and patience. What disposition so euer they be of, gentlenes will soonest bring them to vertue; for frowardnes and curstnesse[60] doth harden the heart of a child, and maketh him weary of vertue. Among the froward thou shalt learne frowardnesse: let them therefore be gently [p. 48] vsed, and alwaies kept from idlenesse, and bring them vp in the Schooles of learning,[61] if you bee able, and they fit for it. If they will not bee Schollers, yet I hope they will be able by Gods grace to read the Bible, the lawe of God, and to bee brought to some good vocation or calling of life. *Salomon* saith, {Pro. 22. 6.} *Teach a childe in his youth the trade of his life, and he will not forget it, nor depart from it when hee is olde.*[62] [p. 49]

CHAP. 12.

Choyse of Wiues.

Now for your wiues the Lord direct you; for I cannot tel you, what is best to be done. Our Lord saith; *First seek the Kingdome of God, and his righteousnesse, and all things else shall be ministred vnto you.*[63] First, you must seek a godly wife, that she may be a helpe to you in godlinesse: for God sayd, *It is not good for man to bee alone, let him haue a helper meet for him*; {Gen. 2. 18.} and shee cannot bee meete for him, except she be truly godly; for God counteth that the man is alone still, if his wife bee not [p. 50] godly. If I should write vnto you how many the Scripture maketh mentiõ of, that haue beene drawne to sinne, because they married vngodly wiues, it would bee tedious for you to read.

The world was drowned, because men married vngodly wiues. {Gen. 6. 2.3.}[64] *Salomon*, who was not only the wisest man that euer was, but was also mightily indued with the Spirit of God, by marrying idolatrous women, fell for the time to idolatrie. {1. King. 11.4.} Neuer thinke to stand, where *Salomon* fell. I pray God that neither you, nor any of yours may at any time marry with any of those, which hold such superstitions, as they did, or as some doe [p. 51] now; as namely, to pray to Saints, to pray in Latine, to pray to go to purgatory, &c.[65] Let no riches or mony bring your posterity to this kinde of tradition. The beloued Apostle of Christ saith: *Loue not the world, nor the things that are in the world*: {1. Ioh. 2. 15} for he knew well that a little that a man loueth not, would suffice him:[66] a little with a godly woman is better then great riches with the wicked. *Rebecca* saith, *I shall be weary of my life, if Iacob take a wife of the daughters of Heth*;[67] as if she should say, If my Sonne marry an vngodly wife, then all my comfort of him and his is gone, and it will bee a continuall griefe to mee, to see him in league [p. 52] and friendship amongst the wicked. If such a shame and sin commeth vpon my Son, as can by no meanes be helped, nor I by no meanes comforted, what auaileth me then to liue?

Bee not vnequally yoked (saith the holy Ghost.) {2. Cor. 6. 14.} It is indeed very vnequall, for the godly and vngodly to bee vnited together, that their hearts must be both as one, which can neuer bee ioined in the feare of God & faith of Christ. Loue not the vngodly: marry with none, except you loue her, and be not changeable in your loue; let nothing, after you haue made your choise, remoue your loue from her; for it is an vngodly and very [p. 53] foolish thing of a man to mislike his owne choise, especially since God hath giuen a man much choyse among the godly; and it was a great cause that mooued God to commaund his to Marry with the godly, that there might be a continuall agreement between them.

CHAP. 13.

It is great folly for a man to mislike his owne choyse.

Mee thinkes I neuer saw a man shew a more senseles simplicity, then in misliking his owne choyse, when God hath giuen a man almost a [p. 54] world of women to choose him a wife in. If a man hath not witte enough to choose him one, whom hee can loue to the end, yet me thinkes hee should haue discretion to couer his owne folly; but if he want discretion, mee thinkes hee should haue policy, which neuer failes a man to dissemble his owne simplicitie in this case. If he want wit, discretion and policy, hee is vnfit to marry any woman.

Doe not a woman that wrong, as to take her frõ her friends[68] that loue her, and after a while to begin to hate her. If she haue no friends, yet thou knowest not, but that shee may haue a husband, that may loue her. If thou canst not loue [p. 55] her to the end, leaue her to him that can.

Mee thinkes, my sonne could not offend me in any thing, if hee serued God, except he chose a wife that he could not loue to the end: I need not say, if hee serued God; for if he serued God, he would obey God, and then hee would chuse a godly wife, and liue louingly and godlily with her, and not doe as some man, who taketh a woman to make her a companion and fellow, and after hee hath her, he makes her a seruant and drudge. If shee bee thy wife, she is always too good to be thy seruant, and worthy to be thy fellow. If thou wilt haue a good wife, thou [p. 56] must goe before her in all goodnesse, and shew her a patterne of all good vertues by thy godly and discreete life: and especially in patience, according to the counsell of the holy Ghost: *Beare with the woman, as with the weaker vessell.* {1. Pet. 3. 7.}[69] Heere God sheweth that it is her imperfection that honoureth thee, and that it is thy perfection that maketh thee to beare with her; follow the counsell of God therefore, and beare with her. God willed a man *to leaue Father & Mother for his wife.* {Gen. 2. 24.} This sheweth what an excellent loue God did appoynt to be betweene man and wife. In truth I cannot by any means set downe the excellency of [p. 57] that loue: but this I assure you, that if you get wiues that be godly, and you loue them, you shall not need to forsake me; whereas if you haue wiues that you loue not, I am sure I will forsake you. Do not your selues that wrong, as to marry a woman that you cannot loue: shew not so much childishnesse in your sexe, as to say, you loued her once, and now your mind is changed: if thou canst not loue her for the goodnesse that is in her, yet let the grace that is in thy selfe moue thee to do it; and so I leaue thee to the Lord, whom I pray to guide both thee and her with his grace, and grant that you may chuse godlily, and liue [p. 58] happily, and dye comfortably, through faith in IESVS Christ.

CHAP. 14.

How to deale with seruants.

Yet one thing I am to desire you to doe at my request, and for my sake: and though it bee some trouble to you to performe it, yet I assure my selfe you will doe it. If God shall at any time giue you or any of you a seruant or seruants, you shall aske them, if they can reade. If they cannot, you shall at my request teach them, or cause them to be taught, till they can reade the tenne Commaundements of almightie [p. 59] God: And then you shall perswade them to practise by themselues, and to spend al their idle time in reading, that so they may come the better to know the will of God written in his Word.[70] Remember, your seruants are Gods seruants as well as yours: if they be not, say as *Dauid* sayd: *There shall not an vngodly person dwell in my house, he that loueth or maketh lyes, shall depart out of my sight.* {Psa. 101. 7.}

It is not for you, by any meanes, to keep any vngodly, profane, or wicked person in your house; for they bring a curse vpon the place wherein they are, and not a blessing, neither will they bee taught any goodnesse: but you must keepe those [p. 60] that bee tractable and willing to serue God, that hee may blesse you and your houshold. For, God doth not delight in that Master, that will suffer his seruant to blaspheme his name, or to mis-spend his Sabbaoths: for God commaunded the master, {Ex. 20. 10.} that he should see his seruants to keepe holy the Sabbaoth day; and if hee keepe that day holy, he will learne to spend all the other dayes in the weeke well, in following the duties of his calling. I pray you keep the seruants of God, and then remember they are your brethren: vse them wel, and bee as ready to doe them good, as to haue their seruice. Be not chiding for e- [p. 61] uery trifle; for that wil hinder good liuing, and nothing enrich you. Be carefull that they be godly; for *Godlinesse hath the promise of this present life and of the life to come:* {1. Tim. 4. 8.} *godlinesse is great riches, if a man be contented with that hee hath: for wee brought nothing with vs into this world, neither shall we carry any thing out of the world, if wee haue food and rayment, let vs therewith be contented.* {1. Tim. 6. 6.7.8.} [p. 62]

CHAP. 15.

Patience is necessary for Gouernours of families.

Liue godlily and patiently in your house: if you cannot bee patient, neuer think to liue godlily; for if Sathan see you of a froward mind, he wil soon finde matter enough to set you on worke. Pray faithfully with your seruants twice a day, and liue so godlily, that you may be an example to them to follow you. Pray often priuately,[71] faithfully, and zealously vnto GOD, in the name of Christ, so as may bee well warranted by his Word; for [p. 63] that is a true marke of the childe of God. Many heare the Word, as our Sauiour witnesseth, but few follow it. {Mat. 22. 14.}[72] Many pray openly as the Pharises did, to bee seene of men; but Christ sayth, they haue their reward. {Mat. 6. 16.}[73] This was not because Christ misliked publike prayer, but because he sawe their hearts, and so knew that they praied more to be seene of men, then for any true faith they had in him. Christ sayth, *When two or three be gathered together in my name, I will be with them.* {Mat. 18. 20.} And this mercifull promise is enough to make any man pray: for though hee doe it very weakely and coldly; yet he sheweth his humility and obedience to God; and [p. 64] confesseth his owne weakenesse, and calleth to God for his assistance and grace to serue him. One is also helped by the prayer of another; and the weaker is made partaker of the praiers of the stronger; for Christ taught vs to pray one for another, Forgiue vs our trespasses. {Mat. 6. 12.} When Christ sayth, *If two or three be gath'red together in my name, I will be with them*; he doth not say, With some of them, but *I will be with them*, that is, with all of them that are ioined together in my name. Though some bee weaker, and some bee stronger, yet they all shew their obedient hearts, and God will accept them in Christ. And this is a great [p. 65] means to stir vp their hearts to praier; for it is the hardest thing that is, for any man to performe rightly, truely, and faithfully.

CHAP. 16.

Meanes to further priuate prayer.

Now all things are to bee vsed, that are meanes to stirre vs vp to priuate prayer, and all things are to be shunned, that hinder vs from it. Those things that may further vs to it, are hearing the Word, reading it, praying publikely, and being in company with others when they pray; for all these help to increase [p. 66] and strengthen faith, and without faith it is impossible to pray aright, either publikely or priuately, or to take hold of the promises of God in Christ, beleeuing that our prayers shall be accepted and granted, so far forth as shall bee to Gods glory and our good: and the true seruant of God will neuer desire more, then hee knoweth by faith in Christ (which hee hath learned by the promises of the Gospell) that he shall haue. [p. 67]

CHAP. 17.

Lets.[74]

There bee many things that will hinder both man and woman from this duetie. The diuell will doe what hee can to hinder vs: the world[75] is our hindrance continually: and a mans owne friends are oftentimes hindrances too: yea, a mans owne nature will neuer bee willing to talke with God; for by nature wee run away from him with *Adam*, and rather hide our selues with figge-leaues, and excuses,[76] then come to God and fall downe before him on our faces, confesse our sinnes, [p. 68] acknowledge our vnworthinesse, craue pardon for Christs sake of God, for all of our transgressions. Yet *Adam* had more cause to runne away, then we haue, and wee haue more cause a great deale to come to God, then hee had; for hee knew not then that God would call him backe againe, and giue him his pardon in Christ, who should tread downe the head of the Serpent, which beguiled him:[77] but we know that GOD hath called *Adam* and all his posterity, & giuen them pardon in Christ, if they wil come and ask it in faith and repentance. Hee therefore that doth not often and priuately fall downe and hum- [p. 69] ble himselfe before God, and confesse his owne sinnes, crauing pardon in Christ, & by faith applying the promises of God to himselfe, hath great cause to feare, that his heart is not true and right before God. And therfore if thou canst not pray priuately, or feelest thy selfe cold in prayer, for to helpe thy selfe, thus thou shalt do.

CHAP. 18.

Helpes against the former lets.

{1} Every morning, so soone as thou canst, (for the sooner, the better) before the world get hold on thee, either with [p. 70] profit or pleasure (for these are the diuels baytes) or before thou feedest thy bodie (for the body is a great deal more subiect to the Spirit, when it is not pampered nor fed at it owne will[78]) then I say, goe into some priuate place, and fall downe on thy face, as the Publican did, and see thy selfe a farre off, and say, *God bee mercifull to mee a sinner.* {Luke. 18. 13.}[79] O Lord, I acknowledge that I cannot pray: pardon mee, deare Father, for Iesus Christs sake, and quicken mee with thy holy Spirit; giue me faith to call vpon thee; and I beseech thee graciously to remēber thy promise, which sayest, *Come vnto me, all yee that labour, and be heauy laden, and I* [p. 71] *will ease you.* {Mat. 11. 28.}[80] O Lord, I am loaden with my sinnes, and against all reason they keep me from seeking pardon for them, and grace to shunne them. Good Father, for Christs sake, remooue my sins far from mee, and giue me faith in thy Sonne, which may assure mee, that thou doest accept of me, as of thy seruant in him. And though I bee most vnworthy in my selfe, yet by thy promises in Christ, which shall neuer faile, I pray thee accept mee.

{2} Furthermore, for the better stirring thee vp to pray, reade some Chapter of the Testament, as namely, the 6. of *Mathew*, or some other, wherein thou mayest heare [p. 72] the promises of GOD in Christ,[81] to strengthen thy faith.

{3} Take heede of idlenesse and slothfulnes, which is a great hinderance. I know that all sinnes are hinderances to prayer, but idlenesse, and following the world, either for profite or pleasure, are wonderfull mighty ones.

CHAP. 19.

To pray often.

Neuer make account of thy selfe as a diligēt seruant of God, if thou doest not twise a day (at the least) come priuately to God, and acknowledge thy infirmities, and confesse [p. 73] that thou canst not pray, and desire GOD to giue thee grace to doe it faithfully. When thou feelest a motion to pray, doe not ouer-slip it for any cause in the world; for thou knowest not what graces or blessings GOD meanes to bestow vpon thee at that time; for it is the Spirit of God calling thee; and therefore finde no delayes, but goe; for the nature of man, of it selfe will neuer be stirred to priuate prayer: But howsoeuer thou doest, be thou Master, or bee thou seruant, bee thou at home, abroad, or in what condition or place soeuer thou bee, doe not sleepe at night, till thou hast humbled thy selfe before God on thy knees in [p. 74] prayer; for night is a time when the world leaues a man (as it were) for a while, and when the world leaues him, the diuell hath not so much power ouer him; for the world is a great Instrument for the diuell to worke by. Therefore when the world is asleepe (as it were) the diuells power is weakened, and then bee sure thou prayest to God to deliuer thee from the diuell, and from the world. The world is like *Pharaoh*, which by no meanes would suffer the children of *Israel* to goe to serue the Lord;[82] so doth the world, if it know that thou goest to serue God, it will bring thee backe againe, if it bee possible: and there- [p. 75] fore it is best to pray priuatly, though thou doe it but weakely; for within a while this weake prayer wil strēgthen greatly thy faith. Pray when the world is asleepe, for assoone as it is awake, it will cry and call on thee (as *Pharaoh* did on the *Israelites*) to attend it: it will bring thee more worke still, as hee did to them. And as that Tyrant told the Israelites, that they should goe and serue their God; but when the time came, hee would not let them, but stil found imploimēt for them; euen so will the world doe by any that will beleeue it; it will promise, At such a time thou shalt goe serue God; and, When such a [p. 76] thing is done, thou shalt go pray; but when the time commeth, it will finde more worke for him still, and will not let him goe. *Pharaoh* is the very figure of the diuell, and the diuell calleth himselfe the god of this world.[83] And if the diuell hath to do with this world, as no doubt but hee hath, then it is certaine, that the world will neuer giue vs leaue to serue God. Our owne nature is as the nature of

the Israelites; for they had rather haue tarried with *Pharaoh*, {Num. 11. 5} who was the very image of the diuell, and haue been his slaues stil, then to haue gone thorow the red-sea, and the wildernes, to the promised land of Canaan, which was [p. 77] the figure of heauen:[84] and euen so had wee rather bee slaues and drudges to the world, which will take all from vs, and cast vs to the Diuell (as *Pharaoh* would haue done by the children of Israel) then we will leaue the world and all his baites, and goe to our God euery day, and humble our selues at his foote, and confesse our selues to bee weake in faith, and acknowledge our frailtie, and call earnestly for the helpe of God to ouercome the world for vs, and to strengthen vs by his power against the diuell, the world, and our owne frailty, and wicked fleshly lusts; and yet, except we doe call continually to God for his [p. 78] grace and helpe, we can no more ouercome these, then the children of Israel could ouercome *Pharaoh*, or goe thorow the red sea without drowning: for it was God that ouercame *Pharaoh* for them, and also all their enemies, & deliuered them out of the red sea: and so it must be God that must ouercome the Diuell and all thy enemies in the world, and deliuer thee, that thou sinke not in the sea of thy owne sinnes.
[p. 79]

CHAP. 20.

Not to neglect priuate Prayer.

Wherefore I desire you, and euery one of yours to the worlds end, that whatsoeuer seruice of God you omit, you doe not neglect priuate prayer; for many may heare the Word of God, as *Adam* did, and disobey it presently after: & some heare the Word of God, as *Adam* did after his fall, and had rather bee further off as hee had then.[85] But priuate prayer is, to offer thy selfe and thy seruice to God, confessing thy own imperfections, and to call [p. 80] to God for his assistance. Now when a sinner by himselfe calleth his owne wayes to remembrance, and confesseth his particular sinnes, then he seeth what sinne his owne nature is most subiect vnto, and prayeth earnestly against that sinne, wherwith he is most infected, and confesseth his owne weaknesse, and wondreth at himselfe that hee is not able to ouercome that one sinne, as well as some other sinnes of as great force. The reason is this, the nature of man is wholly corrupted with sin, and is good for nothing; as the earth is fit to bring forth nothing but weeds, except it bee digged and dressed, and continually laboured [p. 81] and weeded: yet one weed or other will grow in some part of the earth by nature, which will not grow in another part, though it be sowne there; but some other weed will grow there, that is as ill, and one weed ouergrowing the ground, is able to make it vnprofitable for any thing: so one sinne will rule where another will not, and that one ouerrunning thee, is able to make thee an vnprofitable member of the Church: therfore thou must labour by priuate prayer to ouercome it.
[p. 82]

CHAP. 21.

Men become worse for want of vsing good meanes.

Moreouer, as a garden, if it be twentie yeeres kept with digging, watering, and weeding, and then bee let but two yeeres alone, it will become vnprofitable, sauage, and of no respect; euen so, if thou dost in thy youth, or many yeeres vse priuate prayer, and hearing of the Word preached, and publike prayer and fasting, & all good means to keepe thy earthly body in subiection; yet if thou becommest negligent and carelesse but a while, it will soone be- [p. 83] come sauage and wilde, and consequently an vnprofitable member of Christ his Church, or rather manifest thy selfe to bee no member, as the earth will bee no garden; and therfore you must haue a cõtinual care of your selues. It is not for a smal matter that you must haue this care, but for a great & a most glorious kingdome, which lasteth for euer, where thou shalt enioy the sweete and louing presence of almightie God, and bee a member of Iesus Christ in the Kingdome of heauen for euer, world without end. Then neither Satan, nor the world, nor thy owne flesh shall bee able one minute to trouble thee, if through [p. 84] faith in Christ, by continuall prayer, thou once gettest thither. Neither is it to shunne a little danger, that you must bee thus watchfull and wary of your selues, as was drowning in the red sea, which was a figure of hell: but it is to auoid burning in hells torments for euer and euer, and being ioyned to the diuell and all his wicked spirits for euer, there to bee tormented, and neuer haue rest. And this will be more then a thousand millions of paines, to those that shall enter into these torments, to thinke that God hath offered so mercifull a meanes, as to send his owne Sonne to indure those paines for them, that they might ne- [p. 85] uer haue felt them, and sent them his Word, and willed them to follow that; and that should teach them to follow Christ, and Christ should bring them to heauen: and if that the diuell, the world and the flesh, did lay blockes in their wayes more then they could remoue, that then they should call vpon him, & he should helpe them ouer, and make the way in time more plaine and easie for them; and yet they would not take a little paines heere, to keepe them from endlesse paines of helfire. Oh, how will they bee tormented, whẽ they know that there neuer will bee an end of their perpetuall misery? What would they not [p. 86] giue? (nay, they haue nothing to giue; for the world hath deceiued them, and hath taken all things from them) but what paines would they not take to follow our Sauior now, if they might? paines? nay they would thinke it a great pleasure, and wonder greatly at themselues, that they euer could thinke it paines; when indeede it is the most pleasant, and most comfortable, the most profitable, and most delightfull, yea, and the most contenting thing in the world.
[p. 87]

CHAP. 22.

To lay holde on Christ, is the best thing in the world.

It is the most pleasing thing, because it brings so sweete contentment to the soule, minde, and conscience of man, that nothing can offend it. It is the most comfortable thing, in regard it so comforteth and strengtheneth the hart, that nothing can grieue it. It is most profitable, for it getteth an euerlasting kingdome to those that vse it. It is most delightfull, for it bringeth ioy to the whole man. It is most contenting, for no crosse in the world [p. 88] can discontent it; when as the world on the contrary side are neuer content, neuer quiet, neuer feele ioy in their hearts.[86] Though they laugh, their hearts are not quiet; for *there is no peace to the vngodly.* {Es. 48. 22.} And this is the cause that they seek so much for pastime, and sit vp in the night swilling and drinking, vntill they feele sleepe call them to bed, and then they lie downe like bruite beasts, neuer regarding the mispending of their time, nor calling for grace to spend the rest of their daies better. And yet for all this, in the darke they often feele discontent in their mindes, because they doe follow the diuell that wicked serpent, [p. 89] which will torment them, and hee begins to torment here, and yet they will serue him. On the contrary, those that serue God, and follow Christ, and euery night reconcile themselues vnto him, and confesse their own weaknesse, and pray Christ their Sauior to defend them that night and euermore, they feele much comfort in their hearts; for Christ begins the comfort heere. *I laid mee downe in peace and rose again* (saith Dauid) *and the Lord sustained mee.* {Psa. 3. 5.} So they which serue God, and follow Christ, are in peace; for the Lord sustaineth them.
[p. 90]

CHAP. 23.

What need there is to speake much of Christ.

It may bee you maruell my Sonnes, why I write so much of Christ. Maruell not why I write, for I wonder, that euery one which hath heard of him, doeth not write what Christ hath done for vs. For was it not a great wonder, that the onely begotten Sonne of God should come downe from heauen, and take our flesh vpon him, and keepe it without sin, and suffer himselfe to be buffetted, and also to haue his face spit in, and to bee most spitefully [p. 91] crowned with a crowne of thornes? And being without sinne, hee bare all our sins vpon him, and hauing neuer offended God, hee bare all the wrath of God, and indured the paines of hell for vs, which was due vnto vs for our sinnes, and hee hath ouercome sinne, death and hell for vs, and ascended into heauen to prepare vs a place there; & yet hee left vs not thus, but hee left his Wil and Testament, to direct vs the right way how to come vnto him;[87] and yet hee did more for vs then this; for hee taught vs in his Word, how wee should know when we were out of the way, and how we should returne into the right way [p. 92] againe. And yet he did more for vs then this, hee promised that hee would bee with vs vnto the worlds end, {Mat. 28. 26}[88] and whensoeuer wee wanted his helpe, do but call vpon him, and he would helpe vs. And yet hee did more for vs, hee sent preachers to call vpon vs, and put vs in remembrance of these benefits, and to direct vs the right way to heauen to himselfe. And what promises hee hath made to vs to intise and draw vs to come vnto him, and what threatnings and warnings hee hath giuen vs to shun hell, it is impossible for mee and all the Writers in the world to write. Saint *Iohn* saith, *If all things which Christ did were written, the* [p. 93] *world would not containe the Bookes.* {Iohn 21. 25.} But I am sure if all the Writers in the world, had written what Christ hath done for vs, they could not sufficiently declare it. If all the sea were inke, and all the iron in the world were pennes, and all the creatures writers,[89] they could neuer declare the great benefits, the great blessings, and the great mercies giuen vnto vs in Christ Iesus our Lord & Sauiour. What is man without Christ, more then a firebrand of hell?[90] and what an excellent creature a man is in Christ, can hardly bee expressed; and yet there are many that are angry, because there are so many bookes. Reading good [p. 94] bookes worketh a mans heart to godlines; for euen as the fire warmeth the wax, and maketh it fit to receiue a good fashion; euen so good bookes, written of the mercies of God in Christ, are the way to Christ, and teach vs how to shun the way that leads from Christ. But because I would haue you writers of the mercies of God in Christ, I will tell you what good writing of bookes doth. It maketh the way to Christ easie to those that desire to goe in it. And I will tell you who are they that are angry with writing of bookes: they are such as are ignorant, and the more ignorant they are, the more angry: they are [p. 95] those that loue the world so well, that they cannot finde leasure to read bookes. Saint *Iohn* saith, *Loue not the world nor the things that are in the world: for the loue of the world is an enmity to God.*[91] And here you see that they are enemies to God; for they loue not to haue him so much written of. And they that loue not many bookes, loue not many Sermons, neyther doe they care so much to know what Christ hath done for them, and how they should follow Christ: they are stalled[92] with it: they loue the earth, they can talke of it yeere after yeere, and they are neuer weary. In truth, it would weary a heauenly-minded Christian, to [p. 96] heare an earthly-minded man how continually hee will talke of the earth and earthly things; the very time that hee is in the Church, hee can hardly hold his peace from talking of some earthly thing or other, and the whole Sabbath which God sanctified, and rested himselfe, and in mercie to him commanded him to rest, that will neuer rest from these earthly and transitorie things, for heauenly rest hee neuer respecteth. Truely I thinke he meaneth to make himselfe sure of hell heereafter: for Christ saith, *Hee that loueth the world, is an enemy to GOD,*[93] And he that is an enemy to God, can neuer come to bee [p. 97] an inheritour of the kingdome of heauen, except hee returne, and reconcile himself to God through Christ: and hee cannot bee thus reconciled, except he leaue his

earthly affections and attend vpon Christ: for God loueth none but those, whom he
seeth waiting and attending vpon his Sonne; & then the Almightie God accepteth
him as his sonne, and bids him call him Father, and whatsoeuer hee needs, he is
ready to furnish and relieue him withall: but if hee be obstinate, and will not attend
vpon Christ, but attends his owne businesse and worldly affaires, GOD neuer
respecteth him, how many friends soeuer hee [p. 98] hath in the world, nor how
mightie soeuer they are, and then are his riches and his friends nothing worth,
neither can they doe him the least good as can be thought of. Now hee that loues
not writing of bookes, nor hearing of Sermons, hee hath little leasure, and lesse
desire to pray: this I assure you is true, and his owne conscience will tell him so
much, let him examine it when he will; for Sermons, and reading good bookes, are
the only means to bring a man to praier, and praier is the only meanes to helpe vs
to the mercies of God in Christ; for if we heare Sermons, and do not pray earnestly
to GOD, for Iesus [p. 99] Christs sake, to send the holy Ghost to inlighten our
vnderstanding, and to sanctifie our hearts, and follow that which wee heare, we are
neuer the better; for many heare and vnderstand not, and many vnderstand and
follow it not: but there is none that praieth faithfully to vnderstand, and for grace
to follow it, that obtaineth not, if hee continue in true praier. The holy Ghost saith,
Pray alwaies, and in all things be thankefull, {1. Thes. 5. 17.18.} and the promise is
made, *Aske and ye shal haue:* {Mat. 7. 7.} that is, whatsoeuer you goe about, pray to
God to blesse it, and thanke God in prosperitie and aduersitie, or howsoeuer it
pleaseth God to deale [p. 100] with you; for it commeth by his prouidence, &
therefore bee thankefull to God, what crosse soeuer it pleaseth him to lay vpon
thee. Doe not as they which rage and sweare at the losse of a few earthly things; but
thanke God againe and againe, that it is no worse. If it bee but for the losse of some
earthly thing, it cannot bee ill for the childe of God; for *Iob* neuer honoured God so
much, nor did so much good in the Church of God, while hee was rich, as when
hee was poore; for when hee was rich, the diuell himselfe told God, that *Iob serued
him not for nothing.* { Iob 1. 9.}[94] As if hee should say, Thou hast giuen him [p. 101]
many blessings, if he should not bee thankefull, it were a maruell.

CHAP. 24.

The vnthankefulnesse of rich men, a great sinne.

   Oh, this will bee a witnesse against many rich men, which receiue many great
blessings, and yet they bee vnthankefull: for the diuell thought, that he which
receiued gifts and blessings, could not chuse but bee thankefull: and yet when *Iob*
was rich, he neuer did God so much honour nor seruice in his Church, as when
his goods were gone: [p. 102] for before, hee was a rich man, and liued well, and
gaue somthing to the poor: what should hee haue done wth his goods else? & so
did many more besides him. But when all his goods were taken away, hee did not

as worldly men do: he did not say, I am bewitched; or, it is the negligence of my seruants; but he said, *The Lord giueth, and the Lord taketh, and as it pleaseth the Lord, so it commeth to passe; blessed be the name of the Lord,* {Iob 1. 9.}[95] And thus hee became thankefull for his losses. This is a thing that euery one cannot doe: and hee was so patient and thankefull, what crosses soeuer it pleased God to lay vpon him, that he glorified [p. 103] God in his obedience, and shewed that he loued God, and that his loue was not set on this worldly wealth. So he might haue God without the world, he cared not, hee was none of those that must needes haue God and the world together, or else they will none; but hee was one that left an example to the whole Church of God to be thankefull and patient.

CHAP. 25.

How to reade with profit.

I pray reade the story of *Iob*, and not onely reade, but gather some fruite out of it, and euer when you begin [p. 104] to read any part of the scripture, lift vp your harts, soules and mindes vnto God, and pray priuately or publikely; but of priuate prayer neuer faile, and desire God for Christs sake to inlighten your vnderstandings, to sanctifie your hearts, and to make them fit to receiue the good seede of his word,[96] and to giue you grace to bring forth fruite to Gods glory: for Christ saith, *In this is my father glorified, that you bring forth much fruite, and be made my Disciples.* {Ioh. 15. 8.} And againe he sayeth, *Let your light so shine before men, that they may see your good workes, and glorifie your father which is in heauen.* {Mat. 5. 16.} Here you may see you must glorifie God, and you must [p. 105] leaue an example to the Church, that you serue and loue God: this did *Iob*, and I pray God, for Christs sake that you may doe the like; and that you may doe it, you must pray to God continually, yea and in priuate for his grace and assistance.

CHAP. 26.

The preheminence of priuate prayer.

This is the most excellent vertue and happinesse, that belongeth to priuate prayer, no man by any meanes can depriue a man of it. Some haue had their Bibles taken away, that they [p. 106] could not reade: Preachers haue beene banished, that [they] could not heare: they haue beene separated from company, that they could not haue publike prayer, yet priuate prayer went with them:[97] thereby they talked with God, and made all their miseries knowne vnto him, and craued his assistance in all their troubles. And this is the greatest comfort that all good Christians haue, that no man can bar them from priuate conferêce with God. Then take heede you doe not barre your selues from it, since none else can doe it, and you know not what need you shall haue of it, nor what accident may happen to you in your liues, nor what need [p. 107] you shall haue of it in the houre of death. Therefore if you would alwaies haue it, you must alwaies vse it, and then you shall see what profit will come by it, and then you will bee humbly, faithfully, & familiarly acquainted with God.

CHAP. 27.

The benefit of acquaintance with God.

Oh heauenly and happy acquaintance! for the longer thou vsest it, the stronger will be thy faith, the humbler thy heart, the earnester thy zeale, & the holier thy life; and this makes [p.108] God accept you in Christ, and then thou art hee that Christ speaketh vnto; when he saith, *Aske what you will, and it shall bee done vnto you.* {Ioh. 16. 23.} Thy faith will be the stronger, because thou shalt see, that God heareth thy prayers, and granteth thy request. The more humble will thy heart be, because thou seest thine owne miserie and corruption, and that all grace and goodnes comes to thee from God: and this will make thee more earnest and zealous in prayer; and thy earnest and faithfull prayer will moue God, according to his promise, to giue thee grace and faith; for the Apostles prayed and said, *Lord increase our faith.* {Luk. 6. 25.}[98] And this grace and [p. 109] faith will worke in thee holinesse of life, and then shalt thou be able to fulfil Christs saying, *Let your light so shine before men, that they may see your good workes, and glorifie your father which is in heauen.* {Mat. 5. 16.}

CHAP. 28.

How long wee haue neede of priuate prayer.

Now that you and euerie one of you shall haue neede of priuate praier, from the very beginning of your life, to the verie last houre of your daies, my owne experience teacheth mee: and the word of God a true wit- [p. 110] nesse, affirmeth that we are wholly corrupted by the fall of *Adam* with sin, and therefore continually wee ought to suspect our selues, and to call vpon God without ceasing, for his helpe, grace, and assistance in all our actions: for wee know that our owne flesh is our owne enemie, and that it is made of the earth,[99] and is so heauie and earthly-minded, that it can neuer seeke for heauenly things, without the especiall grace of God; and the diuell hath made an entrance into this earthly bodie, by reason that our owne parents *Adam* and *Eue*, did take of the fruite of disobedience at his hands, and did eate at his appointment:[100] so that now he clai- [p. 111] meth such an interest in vs, that none but Christ can keepe him out: and therefore we haue no way, but to call continually on the name of God in Christ, to assist vs with his gracious spirit, which will keepe away the diuell, ouercome the world, and conquer our owne flesh for vs.

CHAP. 29.

Who pray priuately.

This is certain, that there are none godly, but those that pray priuately and truely to God according to his word; and there is no vngodly person, no swearer, no [p. 112] prophaner of the sabbaoth, no drunkard, no adulterer, no couetous person, no prophane person, nor none that is of a false religion, not warranted by the word of God,[101] that doth pray priuately, truely, and faithfully. By these considerations you shal find out the true markes of the children of God; for the wicked can heare the word, reade, come into publike assemblies of praier: the hypocrite wil talke of faith, as if he had come presently from heauen; but to goe into a priuate place, and lay open his heart before God, confesse his own imperfections, and pray that hee may not be an hypocrite, hee is farre inough from it. The [p. 113] swearer, the adulterer, the couetous, the idolater, nor no vncleane person dare come to God in the name of Christ except they leaue their wicked waies; and without they bring Christ with them they cannot come to God; and Christ delighteth not to goe with those that are continually breakers of his fathers commandements: for Christ himselfe telleth them, that *he that keepeth the commandements, and teacheth men so to doe, hee shall bee great in the kingdome of heauen*: {Math. 5. 19.} *and to him that ordereth his conuersation aright, will I shew the saluation of God*, {Psa. 50. 23.} saith God by the Psalmist.[102] Moreouer Christ saith, *Hee that will follow mee, let him forsake himselfe, and* [p. 114] *take vp his crosse, and follow me.* {Mat. 16. 24.} As if he should say, I am gone to heauen, and if you meane to follow mee thither, you must forsake your selues. I know this will bee a crosse vnto you, but you must take it vp and follow me, or else you may not come there.

CHAP. 30.

The way to rule our corruptions.

Againe, when the children of God, who would faine be with their father, see that they cannot rule their owne flesh, then with humble hearts they goe [p. 115] to God, and crie and call to him for helpe, that he would helpe to bridle their vnruly affections, euen but for that day, and at night they will waite vpon[103] his maiestie againe; and thus they will neuer leaue him, till they feele the spirit of God working in their hearts; and that will stirre them to continuall praier. But the wicked want faith to goe in the name of Christ, and this is the cause, there are so many wicked praiers in the world; for they that make them, haue no faith in Christ: and without him, they haue no promise to be heard; and therefore wanting faith to come to Christ, they goe to the Saints to pray for them; and yet [p. 116] the Saints did neuer promise them so to doe, neither doe they know whether the Saints heare them or no. Againe, some pray in latine, when they doe not vnderstand what they say, nor what they pray for; but the holy Ghost saith, *Pray with the spirit, and pray with the vnderstanding also.* {1 Cor. 14. 15.} Why say they, God knowes our harts; we pray with the heart. God knowes indeede that their hearts are vaine and foolish, because they doe not pray with vnderstanding, and therefore they haue no promise to be heard, & yet they will haue a paire of beades, and tell how many prayers they say, though they cannot tell what they say.[104] I dare [p. 117] vndertake, a parret might pray as well [as] they doe, if it could speake all the words. They pray while they liue, that they may goe to purgatory; and when they die, they giue much goods to others, to pray that they may come out of purgatorie againe:[105] these are most vaine praiers neuer warranted by the word of God. They pray also to our Ladie to helpe them, much as the Israelites praied to the Queene of heauen: and as the Israelites praiers were accepted, so are theirs.[106] But I pray God, for Christs sake, that you, nor none of yours may make such praiers. And I pray God to blesse his whole Church, that their praiers may bee right and [p. 118] faithfull, for prayer is the key which openeth vnto vertue. Oh Lord, let not our praiers be turned into sinne; for then the gates of thy mercy shall bee shut against vs.

Wherefore wee humbly beseech thee, giue vs the spirit of truth, that we may pray rightly, which if we doe, wee must needs search the scriptures, & see there how Christ teacheth his Disciples to pray. *When ye pray, pray on this manner. Our Father which art in heauen, &c.* {Mat. 6. 9.} And whatsoeuer praier is not on this manner is wicked and vngodly. And yet here you see, there is neither praying to Saints nor Angels, neither praying for the dead, nor to the dead: and therefore all [p. 119] such praiers are wicked, and are the ouerthrow of those that vse them.

But Christ saith, *When thou prayest enter into thy chamber, and when thou hast shut thy doore, pray unto thy father in secret, and thy father which seeth in secret, will reward thee openly: use no vaine repetitions, as the heathen doe: for they thinke to bee heard for their much babling,* {Mat. 6. 6.7.} *but whatsoeuer yee aske the father in my name, that will hee giue you.* {Ioh. 16. 23.} *Aske and you shall haue, seeke, and you shall finde, knocke, and it shal be opened vnto you.* {Mat. 7. 7.} *If your children aske you bread, will ye giue them a stone, or if they aske you fish, will you giue them a serpent? If ye which are euill, can giue your children good gifts, how much more shall* [p. 120] *your heauenly father giue the holy Ghost vnto them that aske it?* {Mat. 7. 9.10.11.}[107] And this was a great mercy in Christ, not onely to bid vs pray, but also to promise, that whatsoeuer we aske the Father in his name, wee should haue it, and hee appealeth to our consciences, how wee would deale with our children, if they aske vs any thing, and giueth vs warning wee should vse no vaine babbling, and telleth vs wee should aske in one word[108] the holie Ghost, without the which wee are miserable wretches: which if we haue, we inioy all happines and peace, for hee must bee our Comforter[109] and bring vs vnto Christ, and hee will bring vs vnto his Father. [p. 121] Christ also willeth vs to aske the Spirit of truth, because hee will inlighten vs, and shew vs the way of all

happinesse: {Iohn 16. 13.}[110] and because our faith should be strengthened to aske the holy Ghost, hee also promised vs to send him, to teach vs all things, and bring all things to our remēbrance, {Iohn 15. 26.}[111] without which we are like a house which is built faire on the outside: but there are no windowes to shew any light at all into it, and then the house is good for nothing, because there remaines nothing but darknes in it: euen so darke is the earth of *Adam*, which we are made of, that though wee seeme neuer so faire on the outside, yet if wee haue [p. 122] not the holy Ghost within vs, we can neuer see to finde the way to Christ: and then it is vnpossible to come vnto the Father; and so consequently wee must needs perish; for Christ saith, *No man commeth to the Father, but by mee.* {Mat. 11. 27.} And heere you see, that those that put their trust in Saints to pray for them, haue no promise to be heard, and it shewes that they are not inlightned by the holie Ghost, to see the way to Christ, and they themselues will confesse, that they dare not goe to Christ: which sheweth that they haue no faith to beleeue his promises, nor will to obey his Word. For Christ saith, *Come vnto mee* [p. 123] *all yee that labour, and are ladē, & I wil ease you.* {Mat. 11. 28.}[112] Here you see, that he leaues out none, but calls all sinners vnto him, and promiseth that he will ease them. I humbly beseech God to giue you and euerie of you, to the worlds end, grace to pray to God for the holy Ghost. And I pray you, let me request you to pray to God continually, to inlighten you with the holie Spirit, that the holie Ghost may bring you to Christ, so Christ to bring you to his Father; and then shall you raigne with them for euer and euer, world without end. Which God grant for Christs sake, our only Mediatour and aduocate.
[p. 124]

CHAP. 31.

The benefit of the holy Ghost.

Seeing some pray not at all, and others pray falsely, doe yee often and earnestlie pray for the holie Ghost; for I will tell you what hee will doe, hee will inlighten you, and vnite you to Christ, and giue you grace to rule ouer all your affections, and make you able to bee masters of your selues: where on the contrarie side, they which haue not the holie Ghost written within them, are mastered and ruled by their owne filthy affections,[113] and so become seruants to them; but [p. 125] if yee haue the holie Spirit, yee shall bee able to say to your selues, as the master saith to his seruants, Thou shalt doe this, and, Thou shalt doe that: Thou shalt not sweare, nor blaspheme thy God; Thou shalt not drinke and swill like a beast, neither shalt thou come in companie among such, &c. Reason thus, I will ouercome thee by Gods grace, thou earthen potsheard, which broughtest mee nothing,[114] and wouldst thou now confound all these excellent graces, which it hath pleased the almightie God to bestow vpon mee in Christ? no, by the grace of God, I will rule ouer thee, or else I will pine[115] thee. I [p. 126] may say with Saint *Paul*, These are *the messengers of Sathan to buffet mee,* {2. Co. 12. 7.} I will p[r]ay to my God to assist me, and *his grace is sufficient for mee.* {2. Co. 12. 9.} I knowe thy nature, thou art like an vnrulie colt, that if he be pampered, fed, and well kept, hee will throw his master vnder his feete, and cares not what become of him, so hee may be rid of him, and then hee runnes whither hee list himselfe, although hee fare much worse then he did before: euen so is it with those that become subiect to their affections, they are as hard to be ouercome, as a wilde colt, which manie times is like to be, and sometimes is, the vtter destruction of his [p. 127] master: therefore your resolution must bee, to deale with your stubborne and rebellious affections, as you will deale with a pampered wilde colt, and say vnto them, By Gods grace, I will not bee ouermastered by you, I scorne to serue so beggerly and so base a slaue as thou art, I will bridle thee, and thy headstrong, stout, proud, scornefull, and disobedient, vntemperate, vnholy, high-minded, froward, couetous, and idle disposition; for there is no goodnes in you by nature, but by Gods grace I will temper you, I wil make you humble, patient, chaste, quiet, and diligently to fall to some labour, you shall [p. 128] neuer be idle, for that will bring you to nought.[116] And this must be the victory betwixt your selues and your affections, and then the holy Ghost will teach you to master your selues, and not suffer you to bee subiect to euery filthy motion[117] of the flesh. Further, *hee will teach thee all things, and bring all things to thy remembrance;* {Iohn 14. 26.} as, *God resisteth the proud, and giueth grace to the humble.* {Iam. 4. 6.} *He that committeth adultery, sinneth against his owne body, and maketh the Temple of God, the temple of an harlot.* {1. Cor. 6. 18.19.}[118] *He that wil not worke, let him not eat.* {2. Thes. 3. 10} *He will giue thee faith to quench all the fiery darts of the diuel.* {Eph. 6. 16.} Therefore pray for the holie Ghost in all temp- [p. 129] tations, he will be with thee in them, & strengthen thee to ouercome them, hee will be with thee in the houre of death, when all thy friends, thy pleasures, and profits will forsake thee, and then he will bring thee to Christ; and therefore pray for him, and acknowledge his great mercy in Christ, who hath taught thee thus to pray, and whatsoeuer thou neglectest, neglect not priuate praier, and howsoeuer thou doest, seeke for continuall knowledge, that your praiers may be according to the Word of God; for if they bee not such, then are they turned into sinne, and then thou hast nothing to relieue, comfort, or reconcile [p. 130] thy selfe to God againe: for as concerning all the sinnes, that a man hath fallen into, through the frailtie of nature, he hath beene reconciled to God by faithfull prayer; but if your praiers be not at all, or not as they ought to bee, then all your helpe is in vaine.

CHAP. 32.

God accepts weake Prayers.

It is a very weake Prayer that God will not accept, if it be rightly made. I speake thus much, because I would not haue you discouraged, and thinke you had as good not pray at al, as pray weakly for the almighty God accep- [p. 131] teth your obedience and wel meaning, that you will prepare your selues to pray as wel as you can. But if thou see thy selfe neglect priuate prayer, be sure that satan hath somthing to worke against thee; and by this you may vnderstand, that there are none that euer did or shall perish, but it was, because either they did not pray at all, or else because they did not pray as God hath warranted them in his word.

Me thinks if I were a man and a preacher of Gods word, as (I hope) some of you shall be, and I pray God for Christs sake, you may, I surely perswade my selfe, that through Gods grace I should bring many to pray rightly, which now [p. 132] pray vnaduisedly or not at all. But those that haue gotten a custome to pray after the inuention of men,[119] and contrary to the word of God, as to pray to Saints, to pray to Angels, to pray to our lady, to pray in a tongue they vnderstand not, to pray to the dead, to pray for the dead, to pray to goe to purgatory; these, I say, you may pray for, that they may not vse such prayers any longer, but to perswade them, is almost as vain as their praiers. Yet once againe I say vnto you, Pray: for you haue no promise except you Pray. *Aske, and you shall haue* (saith Christ) {Mat. 7. 7.} *he* doth not say, you shall haue, whether *you* aske or no: but he saith, *Aske, and* [p. 133] *you shall haue.*

Was not this a great mercy of our Sauiour Iesus Christ to proffer vs, if we would but aske, we should haue. Surely, I thinke hee were a very vnworthy person, that would thinke much to aske a thing, for which he might be the better foreuer. If a master should say to his seruant, when such a lease comes out, aske mee for it, and I will let thee haue a verie good peniworth in it: because thou hast spent thy time in my seruice and in attending vpon me, therefore I would haue you get something to liue vpon hereafter to defend the world withall, that thou maiest not begge when thou art old: and this were a very reasonable thing. [p. 134] Now the Master being a worthy man, and fully resolued to do his seruant good, when the time comes, he considers with himselfe, at how easie rate hee may set the rent of his farme for him to liue vpon, and yet giue some attendance vpon him still. The time being come, he expecteth when he should aske; but if the seruant thinkes much to aske, it is tenne to one but his Masters minde will bee cleane altered, although he were neuer so fully bent to deale liberally with him, and saith to himselfe, If it be not worth the asking, it shall bee worth the keeping; or, If it be not worth the asking, it is not worth thanks: and very likely hee will thinke worse [p. 135] of his seruant, then euer hee did before, because he would not aske it, and thinke he is growne proud, and scorned his gentle offer.[120] Now if the Master will not giue his seruant the thing so promised, because he wil not aske him, although indeede he ought in conscience to giue him something; for God saith, *Let not thy seruant goe away a poore man;*[121] how dost thou thinke thou shalt receiue the thing which our Sauiour hath promised, vpon the same condition that thou shouldest aske, when thou hast deserued nothing at his hands, but he of his own free mercy hath bought thee, and paid a deere price[122] for thee, and thou hast done nothing [p. 136] for him, but for thy beggerlinesse he biddeth thee aske and thou shalt haue? What canst thou looke to obtaine, when our Sauiour Christ hath precisely told thee, thou must aske, & yet thou refusest to doe it?

Enter into thy chamber, saith he, *and shut thy doore.* {Mat. 6. 6.} Although euerie place will serue, yet it pleaseth Christ to name thy chamber, because he would haue a man without accumberances. Euery man findeth one place, or other to lodge in; let them then finde the same place, or some place else to pray priuately in. *Shut the doore* (saith Christ) as if he should say, shut thy selfe from the world, and shut the world from thee; it may bee [p. 137] thou hast some thing to say to mee, that thou wouldest not haue the world to heare. Oh the mercy, the wonderfull mercie of Christ to man how hee became man for man. And hee knew the nature of man, that hee would bee loath that euerie one should know the corruption which was in him, and therefore said, come to me alone, & shut the doore, no body shall know, what is betwixt thee and me. I know thy sinnes alreadie, but I would know whether thou knowest them or no; for manie a man sinneth and knoweth it not, because hee knoweth not my word: but if thou knowest them, confesse them to mee and I will giue thee [p. 138] pardon for them: and if thou wilt leaue them, & canst ask helpe of me, I will giue thee grace to ouercome thẽ; for I haue ouercome them all for thee, euen in thine own flesh, and thou through mine help shalt doe a greater worke; for thou being a sinner, shalt ouercome in thy self, which is a greater worke then for me, which am God, and without sin to ouercome sin:[123] and yet not you, but I your Sauiour, who dwell in all those, that lay hold of me by true faith, for without me yee can doe nothing; & therefore come to me, follow my counsell, come secretly, let no body know of it for hindring you, or for feare vaine glorie should follow you, no man [p. 139] shall neede to know of it, for I wil reward you openly.[124] Oh the wonderfull mercies of Christ to man, neuer able to be set out! he knew that man would be desirous to haue it known that he serued such a worthy master, as none could serue a better, that euery one shold say he serued Christ, he serued the son of God, who will bring him to prefermẽt.[125] Euerieone desireth to haue it knowne, that hee serueth a noble master, and therefore he will weare his cognisance vpon his sleeue;[126] that it may be knowne what an excellent man hee serues; for it is a great credit to serue a worthie master, and a man shall bee verie well accounted of for his sake: but he that ser- [p. 140] ueth a wicked and vngodly man, shall neuer bee so well thought of, because his master is wicked, & he is oftentimes ashamed of his masters doings, so that he will neuer bee a credit vnto him; and therefore neuer serue a wicked man, although hee bee neuer so rich; for the desire of man is to serue a master of credit, and that Christ knew: he knew also that man was loath to haue his sinnes openly knowne; and therefore out of his great mercie and wonderfull wisdome, he appointed man to confesse his sinnes priuately, without which there can be no good praier.

{The rewards of Christs seruice are heauenly.} He told man, that he should not neede to make shew of it vnto the world; for [p. 141] he would reward him openly, and make it knowne, that he serued a good master indeede; for hee would giue him such graces and blessings, as all that knew him, should perceiue that he had them neither of the world, the flesh, nor the diuell, nor of his owne nature: but it should appeare, they were onely the gifts of the almightie God. Hee did not promise earth and earthly things, you may see; for euery venemous earthworm,[127] is full of these: the vsurer that is as farre from heauen as it is to hell, where if hee take not heede, in time hee may finde his part, he (I say) may bragge of his gold: the extortioner, whom God ha- [p. 142] teth, may bragge of his siluer: the couetous person, whom God abhorreth, hee may bragge what a deale of earth and earthly durt hee hath purchased, as the Prophet saith, *they loade themselues with clay*: {Hab. 2. 6.} he doth not say, God giueth it them; but *they loade themselues*.

Among these foolish and abominable people, whom the scripture speaketh so much against,[128] as against no man more, nor so much, I thinke, strumpets and whores, who for couetousnesse sake sell their soules and bodies, and make themselues such filthie vessels in this earth, that it is most loathsome to thinke of, may bragge as well of their iewels and costly appa- [p. 143] rell that the world bestoweth vpon them, as anie other of these couetous wretches, whom God abhorreth, and giueth warning that no man shall speake well of them, for the holy Ghost saith, *Speake not good of the couetous whom God abhorreth*.[129] And that thou maiest know it is no worldly trash that God bestoweth on thee: know, that the diuell calleth himself the prince of this world:[130] and so one would think he were; for these outward things are most commonly bestowed vpon the wicked; but that which God will bestow on thee, is a treasure which the wicked ones haue not, nor are neuer like to enioy, except they leaue their wicked waies, and goe [p. 144] priuately to the Lord Iesus Christ, and lay open their miserable estate to him, and craue his pardon and grace to liue a new life, and then he will giue thee the greatest treasure that man can imagine, euen a most heauenly treasure: hee will giue thee faith, which will bring thee to the euerlasting kingdome of heauen: he will giue thee patience, to beare al the crosses & troubles in the world: hee will giue thee humilitie, which will fill thee full of grace, and make thee in fauour with God and man: he will giue thee his grace so plenteously, that thou wilt speake alwaies the truth, and keepe thy promises, though it bee neuer so much to thy [p. 145] hinderance in the sight of the world. Nay, in the sight of the world it must needs be a praise to thee, for the world seeth that euery earth-worm can breake their promise or turne it so,[131] that it is worse then a promise-breaking; for it sheweth that they are full of hypocrisie, dissemblers, and would serue the world, and would not haue the Diuell know it: but the diuell will not bee so deceiued, hee maketh account the world is his, and hee hampereth all those that loue it, in chaines, and hee will haue the world know it, that it may bee a witnesse on his side at the day of Iudgement.

{The danger of breaking promise.} Nay, his owne conscience will bee a witnesse against him [p. 146] at the day of iudgement, that breaketh his word, euen at that dreadfull day, when the trash, for which hee so lightly regarded his promise, shall bee consumed with fire & brimstone,[132] then will hee wonder, hee could thinke it would bee so long before that day would come, and now seeing it is come, hee fully perswadeth himselfe, that his paine will neuer haue an end. If thou thinkest, that breakers of their word haue a roome in heauen, reade the fifteenth Psalme.[133] But what should I speak of a roome in heauen, when indeede they ought to haue no roome amongst ciuill men[134] on the earth: nay, nor yet among the heathen? [p. 147] for it hath beene accounted so great a shame for a man to breake his promise, that hee would rather die, then it should be sayd that he were one of those. But pray thou priuately and faithfully, and God will not onely giue thee power to keepe thy promise with men; but thou shalt also haue grace to keepe thy word and promise thou hast made to Almighty God, to forsake the diuell, the world, and thine owne filthy affections: Which will shew openly that thou art the seruant of God, and that God hath bestowed his manifold graces and blessings vpon thee, as Christ sayd vnto *Peter, Flesh and bloud hath not taught thee these things, but my* [p. 148] *Father which is in heauen.* {Matth. 16. 17.} So euery one that beholdeth thee, will know, that neither the diuell, the world, nor thine owne flesh hath bestowed these gifts on thee, but the Father which is in heauen. Blessed be the name of Christ for his bountifull goodnesse bestowed vpon mankinde; he did not onely bid men pray, and promised they should bee heard, but also told them to whom to pray; and because men durst not goe to God alone, hee bad them goe in his name, and promised that he would be there with them, and hee would be a Mediator, which none else could doe, and hee would make peace betweene God and them, and therfore [p. 149] any might boldly come to him; hee teacheth them where to aske: priuately: and what to aske: the Holy Ghost, without the which, we are fire-b[r]ands of hell: but if we haue him, we are Saints in heauen, euen ioyned to Christ and as his members; and yet hee fearing all this would not serue, it was his greatest mercy to shew vs more concerning two men, which were praying, and made vs acquainted how they prayed, and how they sped. {Luk. 18. 10.} Christ saith, *There was a Pharisie and a Publicane went into the Temple to pray.* The Pharisie was one that thoght himselfe a iust man, and despised others. The Publican accounted himselfe a sinner [p. 150] openly knowen. *The Pharisie stood vp and prayd, and sayd, I thanke thee, oh Father, I am not as other men are, nor like this Publican: I fast twice in a weeke: and giue tithe*[135] *of all that I haue.* Now you may see who they bee, that say I fast, or we fast: as if they should say, I feare it shall neuer bee known that it is I, or we that fast and pray, and pay tithe of all that we haue, and that we deale iustly and keep the commandements. *But the Publican stood afarre off, and durst not looke vp to heauen, but smote on his breast, and sayd, Lord, be mercifull to mee a sinner.* Heere you see wee must humble our selues, and confesse our sinnes; for Christ saith, *Hee went away iustified* [p. 151] *rather then the other: for hee that humbleth himselfe shall be exalted; and hee that exalteth himselfe, shall bee brought low.*[136]

Also hee willeth alwayes to pray, and not to waxe faint, saying: {Luk. 18. 2.} *There was a certaine Iudge in a city, which neither feared God, nor reuerenced man, and there was a widdow in the city which sayd, Doe me iustice against mine aduersarie; but he would not for a time; yet afterwards hee sayd, Although I feare not God, nor reuerence man, yet will I doe her iustice, lest at the last shee chance to weary me, And the Lord sayd, Heare what the vnrighteous Iudge saith, And shall not God auenge the cause of his Elect, which cry and call day & night vpon him?*[137] And therfore pray [p. 152] continually. And doe not thinke (my sonnes) that I haue spoken too much of prayer; for as I sayd before, without it wee haue no promise to obtaine any fauor of God, nor yet to be kept frõ any euill by God, and therefore doe it. You must needes also bee thankefull to God for his mercies in Christ, & most humbly thank Christ, who hath thus mercifully taught you to pray, and giue God thankes who hath brought you into the world in such a time, when as you may bee taught to pray according to his word; and I beseech him, that you may pray according to his counsell. [p. 153]

CHAP. 33.

No certaine rule for priuate prayer.

Now I would haue you know, that priuat praier is for euery mans priuat vse; and therfore there is no certaine rule, neither can words be set downe what ye should say: for though we be all sinners, yet some are more troubled with one sinne, some with another, and some are troubled because they cannot bee troubled so much with their sinnes as they desire, which sort Christ calleth vnto him, saying, *Come vnto me, all yee that labour and are laden, and I will ease you.* {Matth. 11. 28.} [p. 154] But although all sinnes dwel in vs, and wee are subiect to them (wherfore Christ saith, *Yee had neede watch and pray* {Matth. 26. 41.}). Yet there is in euery one of vs, some one sinne, that will draw to a head, & beare som rule in vs,[138] and will not bee subiect nor subdued to the Spirit, as the childe of God would haue it: but then hee goeth to Christ, and craueth his assistance, and yet sometime the sinne wil ouercome him, and then he goeth and confesseth his sinne againe, and craueth pardon, confessing withall his owne weakenesse, that hee should bee ouercome of so vile and base an affection. And thus euery one ought to seek by praier to God, to get victory of [p. 155] that sinne, which otherwise would ouercome, and destroy him body and soule for euer and euer.

CHAP. 34.

Diuers men troubled with diuers sinnes.

Some are troubled most with enuie, some with pride, some with anger, some with couetousnesse, and some with sloth, &c. All these with a companie that attend on them, set vpon euerie man, but one must be captaine; then ouercome the captaine, and all the army will be discomfited.[139] In warres, if the Captaine pre- [p. 156] uaile, the souldiers will ruinate the Cittie: euen so it is with sinne, if the chiefe sin getteth the victorie, it will let in a great number of enemies that wil neuer leaue, vntill they haue vtterlie ruinated and brought to confusion the whole bodie and soule of a man; and therefore euerie one ought to pray to God, for helpe and assistance against his greatest temptation; for if we ouercome that, the rest will flie, as S. *Iames* saith, *Resist the diuell, and he will flye from thee.* {Iam. 4. 7.} And this will be a great comfort to any man, when hee seeth his enemy cannot triumph ouer him: then the diuell shall haue no cause to laugh in his face, nor the [p. 157] world to iest behinde his backe, neither can his owne affections braue nor vpbraid[140] him: but hee shall haue a greater comfort then this; for by obtaining this victorie, he shall bee sure to bee seruant and souldier to the most worthy Captaine that euer was. Yet hee must acknowledge that hee got the victorie by the helpe of his Captaine; and so long as hee is a souldier vnder him, hee shall alwaies haue the victorie: for the diuell himselfe is afraide of this Captaine, the world will flie at his presence, and thine owne affections will fall downe before thee, if hee come. [p. 158]

CHAP. 35.

Be not hurt by a little temptation.

There is another thing, which I must admonish you of, that ye be not ouercome of a little temptation; for that is the basest thing in the world: euen as if a great Captaine should bee ouercome of a meane souldier, that had neither might nor policy, which must needes returne with shame to the Captaine. But it is much more shame for a Christian, that hath vowed to forsake the diuell, the world, and his owne affections, to bee ouercome by the weakest [p. 159] of them all. There be many that thinke, if the diuell ouercome them not in a great sin, all is well, though that indeede he set them on work continually on trifles, and by this meanes keepe men in some deuice[141] or other. Hee cares not what they doe, so they serue not God, and so he may blindfold them that they cannot see their owne sinnes. And thus they are in a very dangerous and euill case, and know not what they doe; yet they shadow their folly, that the world may not perceiue it, & then they thinke it is well enough.

Thus the diuell leads them quietly to hell, and they neuer know whither they are going, till [p. 160] they come there; euen as a winde carrieth a ship, and they that are in it, know not where they shall bee set on shore[.] For the diuell is a cunning fowler,[142] he will neuer lay a great baite, where hee knowes, a little one wil serue the turne; and hee is so full of policy, that hee seeth a great baite would make the partie afraide to come neere it: but thus doth the diuell, first hee giueth a little baite, and saith to him whom hee meaneth to catch, I warrant thee, thou maiest take this, goe neere it, taste of it, it will not hurt thee, many swallow a greater baite then this, and thou seest no hurt come of it: as hee said to *Eue*, It is but an apple, it [p. 161] may doe thee much good, to bring thee to knowledge, and make thee like a God.[143]

And therefore now wee see, wee had neede set a speciall watch ouer our selues, that we may spy the diuel, when hee goeth about thus to intrap vs in his engines,[144] with his alluring baits, and returne his baits againe, and when hee offereth vs any of them, may say: I defie thee, Sathan, and by Gods grace haue knowledge that thou art a wicked serpent, and diddest deceiue our first Parents with an apple. I will not play with thy baits, bee they neuer so sweete, pleasant, or beautifull. I know thy subtiltie, and I know that I serue a Captaine, [p. 162] Christ, that thou art afraide of, and he will bring vs to a happier Paradice, then thou didst put vs out of, and hee will make mee like a God, and renue the image that thou didst decay in vs.[145] Thou didst scoffe at mee, and saidst, I should haue knowledg, when thou wouldest haue vtterlie ouerthrowne mee; yet I haue this knowledge (I thanke the almightie God for it) that now I can see thy policy, and how thou camest to our Parents, when they were alone; thou thoughtest they could not stand by themselves: but thou shalt neuer finde mee alone; I know I cannot stand by my selfe, and therefore I draw [p. 163] neere vnto my Lord and Sauiour Iesus Christ by faith, and I will attend vpon him, and will not leaue his Commaundement vndone, for all thy baits and alluremĕts thou canst shew mee in the world, where thou callest thy selfe Prince: but thou gettest it by wicked policy, and thou rulest it by a wicked tyranny, destroying the good, and maintaining the wicked, & bestowest thy trash on them not for any loue thou bearest to them, but to make them thy wicked instruments, that thou maiest doe the more hurt by them. And as soone as they haue serued thy turne a while, thou wilt bring them to [p. 164] shame in this world, and euerlasting destruction in hell fire. And therefore now I would haue thee know, that I haue knowledge, and perceiue that all these vsurping tyrants haue learned all their mischieuous policies of thee, vsing all meanes they can possibly, to destroy the good, and with their paltrie trash, which they call their wealth, they winne the wicked to their wils; and when they haue their purpose a while, they will picke some quarrell against them, although they haue no reason for it, and although they follow their wicked wils neuer so much, yet in the ende they will ouercome them.

And so, [p. 165] Sathan, dost thou deale with all that serue thee; and therefore thou art an vsurping tyrant: for the earth is my Lords, who hath made it, and all that is therein; and that which belongeth vnto thee, is nothing but that trash, that he careth not for: it is like tares,[146] and the worser sort of graine, more fit to feede swine, then for the children of so mightie a King as my Lord is, who hath such treasure for those that belong vnto him, as thou shalt neuer come neere. Yet this is thy despight and enuie, because thou canst get none of it thy selfe, thou wouldest haue mee haue none of it neither. But thou shalt not [p. 166] deceiue me with these earthen baits, which one day my almightie God shall set on fire about their eares that loue them so well, when themselues shall be suddenly strangled with the smoak thereof: and it makes mee maruell, how thou shouldest deceiue so many as thou dost with them; for once my gracious Lorde drowned them[147] & all that loued them, & many times he sinketh very much trash in the sea, that Pirats might see they shall sinke one day, and all those that sell their soules for such trash, except they turne speedily vnto my Lord and Sauiour Iesus Christ, who is a Sauiour, and will saue all sinners that [p. 167] turne vnto him. But thou art a destroyer, and wilt destroy all those that follow thee: thou knowest my Lord burnt *Sodome* and *Gomorrha*, with other Cities, which were full of the glistering drosse, to shew that hee cared no more for it, then Kings do for counters:[148] for if he had respected it, he would neuer haue burnt it, and consumed it with fire: Yet thou, Sathan, doest deceiue worldly wise-men, giuing them drosse for gold, which is no better then copper counters, and in the mean time thou makest thẽ deceiue themselues of an euerlasting treasure. Earthly treasure may bee compared to glasse, which is so [p. 168] brittle a metall, it can neuer continue long; for as it might bee, now a man hath it to doe him good, and in the turning of a hand it is broken and worth nothing. Euen so it is with the trash and pelfe of this world, and the life of man which is but a breath, and what can be of lesse power then a breath.

The Scripture saith, *it is like a vapour, which appeareth suddenly, and is as suddenly gone againe*; {Iam. 4. 14.} Christ saith, *Thou foole, this night shall they take away thy soule from thee, and whose things shall these bee that thou hast gathered together?* {Lu. 12. 20.} If our Sauiour Christ calleth him a foole, that careth for earthly things, I know he is a foole, and ther- [p. 169] fore thou shalt not make me so simple, but thou shalt make mee wise; for I will euer be watchfull, and wary in all my waies, continually attending vpon the Sonne of God, Christ Iesus, my Lord and Sauiour, that thou maiest not finde mee alone. I will also keepe company with the godly, by which meanes the way of my Sauiour will bee made more easie for me; for when many godly men are together, they incourage one another to that which is good.
[p. 170]

CHAP. 36.

Idlenesse and couetousnesse to be auoided.

Now though euery sinne bee a great hinderance to praier, yet idlenesse and couetousnesse are two of the greatest; and therefore wee ought most earnestly to pray against these sins, and to take heed of such sports and recreations, which haue no warrant in the Word of God:[149] for many are so carried away with idlenesse and pastimes, that they can find no time to pray; and therefore we had need to be very circumspect, and watchfull ouer our selues, lest wee bee [p. 171] snared with this part of the diuels policy: for if a man take not heed, Sathan will fill his heart so full of these vaine and idle pastimes, that hee shall neuer haue any regard of preparing himselfe to pray. GOD saith, *Six dayes thou shalt labour, and doe all that thou hast to doe*; {Exo. 20. 9.} and therfore be sure there is no time appointed in these six dayes to follow your idle pleasures and sports; *and the seuenth day, we must keepe holy*. The holy Ghost saith, *Whatsoeuer is not of faith is sinne*; {Ro. 14. 23.} and thou canst do nothing of faith, except thou hast good warrant for it in the Word of God: and the Word of God saith, *Redeeme the time, for the dayes are e-* [p. 172] *uill*. {Ephe. 5. 16.} And thou canst not redeeme the time with vain recreations. I speake not to bar anie from lawfull recreation, but to warn you to take heed that for a little foolish and idle pleasure, which presently commeth to an end, you lose not a glorious kingdom which endureth for euer. And this Kingdome can neuer bee gotten without priuate, true and faithfull praier; for although Christ hath alreadie obtained it for vs, yet we haue no promise of it, except wee lay hold on him by faith, which faith wee can neuer haue, except wee pray for the holie Ghost to enlighten vs, and teach vs to laie held on Christ. You must continually call for [p. 173] mercie and grace; mercie for thy sinne, and grace to serue God. And this I am well assured of, that hearing of the Word preached, is the verie meanes that God hath appointed for obtaining of faith, and by no means may wee neglect that, except you will contemne the counsell of the Holy Ghost, which I pray God for Christs sake you may neuer doe. The holie Ghost telleth you, that *Paul planteth, and Apollo watereth, but God giueth the encrease*. [1. Cor. 3. 6.] So you must alwaies haue your praiers ascending to the Almightie God, to desire him to send the showers of his grace into your hearts, that the seede of his Word may grow, and bring foorth [p. 174] fruit to euerlasting life.

CHAP. 37.

A dangerous let of prayer.

I will let you vnderstand in my iudgement, what is one of the greatest hinderances vnto prayer that can be, but it is so close and subtil an enemy vnto mankind, that I can by no meanes discouer[150] it so well as I would; for it is so cunning, and so forcible an allurance of the Diuell, that it draweth many more from true & faithful prayer, then any net that euer hee layd: but I cannot well tell, which way to describe it vnto you. I cannot [p. 175] say, that it is altogether couetousnesse: for as *Dauid* saith, *If it had beene an open enemie, that had done mee this dishonour, I could haue borne it*; {Psal. 56. 12.}[151] So I may say, If it were an open sinne, which would depriue you of this benefit of prayer, peraduĕture I should finde some way to disgrace it vnto you; but it is a thing that carrieth some colour of goodnesse, euen amongst them that thinke themselues good, and yet indeede it is starke naught, and deceiueth a multitude, & it frequenteth euery place, city and towne, and among all sorts of people, husband-men, trades-men, and all kindes of arts and professions in the world: so that I cannot, as I would, [p. 176] tell you which way to shun it: I would to God it were not amongst Preachers.

Now as well as I can I will explaine it vnto you: it is an ouer-much care of those things which a man may lawfully vse. For man being earth, those earthly things beare much sway in his mind, and especially because they carry the name of lawfull: and so they make a man forget the Law of God, and neglect the duty of Prayer; the which two things being ouerslipped, hee loseth the promise of the gospel, which is an euerlasting kingdome. And that it is thus, I will make it more plaine vnto you, because I hope God wil giue you grace to shunne it, [p. 177] which I desire you may for Christs sake. Man beeing earth, and Sathan being the Prince of this earth, hee labours to set mens earthen mindes altogether on this earthen world, which he may easily doe: for man beeing earth by nature, & naturally enclined to loue earthlie things, he is the more easilie drawen vnto this ea[r]thlie affection. It is euen as if a man should runne downe a steep hill, hee can more easilie run downe, then goe vp softlie: euen so man can easier run after these earthlie thinges, then stay himselfe in a mean.[152] He hath nothing to help his earthly nature, but grace; which hee must needes pray for, or els he can neuer haue [p. 178] it; yet doth hee follow the things of the earth so much, that hee hath no leasure to pray for it. In the night, when he should meditate on the Law of God by the appointment of the H. Ghost, he is thinking of some earthlie thing or other, either of this bargaine, or that purchase, or such like; when oftentimes hee might be much more happie to bee without it. And mee thinkes, hee that can think of heauen & haue it, is well enough: but these kinde of people would haue heauen and earth too. It is sayd, *It is as hard a matter for a rich man to be saued, as for a Camell to creepe thorow the eye of a needle.* {Matth. 19. 24.}[153] And this is the cause of it, his head is so bu- [p. 179] sied about earthlie thinges that be lawfull, that hee forgets to meditate of the Law of God in the night. And in the morning when he should pray, before hee can settle himselfe to it, his earthly busines is so much, & requires so great haste, that then hee cannot stay to pray; but if hee doe, they are such prayers as some offer to their Saints: they speake of God, but their hearts are on the world: some are troubled with their marchandize, som with buying & selling, some coueting to grow rich, some casting[154] to maintain their families, but their riches are so vnlawfully vsed, and so hard a matter it is for them to vse them lawfully, that it cannot [p. 180] by any meanes be expressed.

But the most mercifull and mighty God hath taught man what to doe in such a case, which is to meditate in his lawes day and night, & then he shall bring forth his fruit in due season, and shall know when to serue God, and when to deale in the world. Take heed therfore: you see what danger you are in, whilest you are heere on earth; for this is a dangerous disease, and many die of it; and therfore cleaue to the mercies of God in Iesus Christ, which hath giuen you such warning of this desperate disease, saying, *Labor not for the meat that perisheth, but for the foode of euerlasting life.* {Ioh. 6. 27.} Thus you see, what Christ [p. 181] saith, hee biddes you not *labour for earthly things*, he tels you, *they perish*; he bids you labour for the food of the soule, which shal neuer haue end. The holy Ghost saith, *Bodily labour profiteth little; but godlinesse is profitable to all things, which hath the promise of the life present, and of that which is to come.* {1. Tim. 4. 8.} Heere you see, godlinesse hath the promise of the life present, and therefore I maruell men should refuse to be godly: it hath the promise of the life present, and of the life to come; whereas worldlinesse hath not so much promise, as of the life present. *Godlinesse is great gaine.* {1. Tim. 6. 6.} Would you haue gaine? then embrace godlinesse; so shall you haue [p. 182] your desire: for that purchaseth a Kingdome, and it is profitable for all things. *Seeke first the Kingdome of God, and all things else shall be ministred vnto you.* {Mat. 6. 33.} Heere Christ promiseth, that if you will serue God, all worldly things shall bee giuen you. Christ saith, *Care not for to morrow; let to morrow care for it selfe, the day hath enough with his owne griefe.* {Mat. 6. 34.} Heere you see, Christ would not haue you care so much for these earthly things, as you doe. *Cast all your care vpon God; for hee careth for you.* {Psal. 37. 5.}[155] Heere you see, that God dischargeth you of all your earthlie cares, and telleth you, that he taketh care for you, as if he should say, Your [p. 183] care can doe you no good, and therefore take none: serue mee, and I will take care for you: as if a father should say to his sonne, Goe to the schoole of learning, study to serue God, your King and Countrie, and I wil prouide you all things necessarie, and you shall want nothing.

Labour for learning, or else you can neuer get it; that is a thing, which I cannot buy for you; you must get it by your owne industrie and diligent studie, if you will haue it: but when you haue it, it is more worth then all I can leaue you besides. It will be a wise master to teach you, a diligent seruant to attend you, a discreet Counsellour to admonish [p. 184] you, a witnesse of the well spending of your time, a faithfull friend, and of great account, able to credit thee euen with Princes: and these things cannot by anie means be gotten without thine own diligent study. Euen so our louing father in Christ tels vs by the mouth of his Son our Sauiour, that we should not care for these earthlie things, for they shall bee giuen vnto vs: but wee must care for the Kingdome of heauen; for that cannot bee gotten without care and labouring for; and this is a thing worth our labour, this is a kingdome, and lasteth for euer; it will bring comfort to your hearts, euen in this life, and bring you in fa- [p. 185] uour with God and all good men, and euerlasting happinesse without woe, want, or end.

Furthermore I will tell you, what cause you haue to take care for this kingdom: if you lose it, you fal into a pit of euerlasting destructiõ, where you shall be tormented with fire and brimstone for euer and euer, where no man shal euer come out againe;

for there is no redemption: and therefore by all meanes possible I aduise you to take heede. Christ endured the pains of hell for you, because he pittied you, & knew you were not able to ouercome them. Therefore you may beleeue mee, if you could beare al the pains of hel one houre, and then could bee [p. 186] deliuered, you would neuer come there againe for all the world, nay you would neuer loue the world, nor anie thing that is in it, because they are nothing but baits to draw men to destruction. But if the Diuell get you once there, you can neuer come backe againe, & Christ will neuer fetch you from him; for the Diuell and hee are enemies, and he is able to liue without anie of his seruants: for those that will serue him, shall haue an euerlasting Kingdome, and liue in ioy and happinesse: and those that will serue the diuell, he will torment them in fire and brimstone for euer.

Now if Sathan can get anie to serue him, hee is wor- [p. 187] thy to haue them; for Christ will none of them: and therfore I tell them now, if they come once in hell with the diuel, they shall neuer come in heauen with Christ; for he is iust, and will not meddle with the seruants of another. But if anie see his filthie and base waies, and consider the miserable and wretched estate it will bring him vnto, and then turne to me (saith Christ) and defie the Diuell and all his workes, and serue me, I will saue him; for I am a Sauiour, and that is my name, and my glorie: for there is no Sauiour but my selfe, *I came into the world to saue sinners*,[156] but not such sinners as will serue the Diuell; for though there be none in [p. 188] the world but sinners, yet those that loue me, and keep my commandements, them will I saue; but them that serue the Diuell, I will destroy and torment them. Although all are sinners, yet those sinners that plucke vp their sinnes, as a Gardiner pulleth vp his weedes, and cast them behinde them, and follow me; although they be weake, and feare that they cannot ouertake[157] mee, yet I will put forth my hand, and take hold of them, they shall not need to feare. *The bruised reede will I not breake, and smoking flaxe will I not quench:* {Matth. 12. 20.} *I came to binde vp the broken-hearted, to preach liberty to the captiues, & to côfort them that mourne: let all that labour and* [p. 189] *are heauy laden, come to mee and I will ease them;*[158] but those that follow their sinnes, and are merrie and ioyfull, and carrie them lightlie, and neuer feele any waight in them, they neuer call for helpe to beare them, they carrie them well enough, they dance after the Diuels pipe, they follow the diuell more swiftlie, then my seruants follow mee: for they follow nature,[159] and the Diuell helpeth them forward, and the world is a friend to them both, and they like laden asses follow the Diuell with his treasure, and make him their Lord and Master; and yet some of them will not sticke to say, they hope, I will saue them, though I haue often [p. 190] told them, I will saue none but my seruants, and I will not meddle with them; for if they will serue mee, they must cleane forsake mine enemy the diuell: for hee is an enemy to me & all mine, and doth all the despight against vs, that hee can; and I will not saue him that will serue mine enemy; & therefore let them neuer presume vpon my mercy: for I haue told them, that *the hope of the vngodly shall perish.*[160] Hee that is an vngodly person, a swearer, a drunkard, a prophaner of the Sabbaoth, false in religion, carelesse in life, and yet hopes to be saued by me, his hope is in vaine, and grounded vpon no foundation; for I ne- [p. 191] uer made promise to saue any such: and therefore they haue no reason to say, they hope I will saue them, except they speedily returne from the diuell, and his wayes, and follow mee and my waies; for I haue plainely told them, *He that will be my Disciple, must forsake himselfe, take vp his crosse and follow mee, and assuredly I will saue him.* {Mat. 16. 24.}

Now tell mee, how would a man like one that should serue his vtter enemy, and doe what his enemy could deuise to hurt and grieue him, and then when hee had done all the hurt, that hee could against him, when he could do no more then hee would come to him, and thinke to haue a [p. 192] great blessing and a great benefit of him? hee should surely bee deceiued. Then with what face can a sinner goe to Christ to saue him when hee dieth, who would neuer serue Christ while he liued? Though God had commanded him to cast all his care vpon him, for hee would care for him, yet hee hath spent almost all his time in seruing the world, the flesh, and the diuell.

CHAP. 38.

Reasons of casting our care vpon God.

{1} I wil tell you great reason, why you ought to cast all your care vpon God, and [p. 193] none vpon the world; for God is our Father, our Maker, and gouernour, and our feeder: Christ is our Sauiour. Now the father and gouernour knoweth, what is fit for the childe, better then the childe; for the childe would surfet, if hee might haue his owne will; therefore let him be content with that which his gouernour will giue him.

{2} Another great reason why wee should cast all our care vpon God, is, because when the diuell maketh all his poysonous baits, wherewith hee draweth an innumerable company of soules to hell, hee couereth them all with some worldly thing or other, that they may not see [p. 194] the hooke; some hee couereth with gold, some with siluer, some with earth, some with clay, some with honour, some with beautie, some with one thing, and some with another. Hee will not lay all his baits alike; for hee is cunninger then a fisher: hee knoweth a little bait, will serue for a little fish, and a great bait for a great fish; for a great bait will not serue to catch a little fish, nor a little bait will not serue to catch a great fish. And besides this, hee must haue the alteration of baits, as the cunning fisher well knoweth; but with these baits hee must haue a sharpe hooke to take them, and a long line to draw them to [p. 195] himselfe. So soone as hee seeth they haue swallowed the sweet bait, hee lets them play a while with it, but before it be long, hee draweth them out of the sweete streame, the water of life, and throweth them into a panne of boyling liquor: and as sometime the fisher is faine to intangle the fishes with his nets, and so take them: euen so Sathan findeth the humour of euery man, and then he searcheth in the world to finde a bait fit for him, & hauing found the bait he presently poysoneth it: then hee puts in a hooke and a line, to draw him from the pure sweete streame, the water of Life, the Word of God: and then [p. 196] hee lets them play a while with the poysoned baits of the world, and so drawes them to him, and throwes them into a furnace of boyling brimstone, whose boyling shall neuer end.

Now there is none that can keepe vs from the baits of the diuell, but onely God our Father, our gouernour, our Sauiour, our sanctifier; and had wee not neede then cast all our care vpon God, since we are in so great a danger, and none can keepe vs from the diuell but hee? We cannot keepe our selues from the baits of the diuell, no more then children can guide themselues in all their wayes, to feed, learne, gouerne, & clothe themselues, [p. 197] without the helpe of their father and gouernour. Shall the children depend onely vppon their father and gouernour, and shall not wee depend only vpon our God, that is our Maker, our Father, and our gouernour? and who, when wee fell from him, and followed the counsel of the diuel, sent his onely Sonne to die for vs, and to indure the paines of hell for vs? the holy Ghost saith: *If hee hath giuen his sonne for vs, will hee not with him giue vs all things also?* {Ro. 8. 32.} And yet shal we not dare to depend vpon him? Is he not able to dry vp the waters of the red Sea, that thou mightest goe on foot dry-shodde thorow? Cannot hee raine [p. 198] thee Manna, that thou needst not starue? Cannot our God giue thee water out of the rocke? He giueth thee water out of the rocke Christ euery day: Oh that thou wouldest receiue it! But I know what thou wouldest haue; thou wouldest haue Quailes to fulfill thy lusts:[161] for *lust when it conceiueth, bringeth forth sinne, and sinne when it is finished, bringeth forth death.* {Iam. 1. 15.} Then maist thou cry, *Oh wretched man that I am, who shall deliuer me from the body of this death? I thanke God through Iesus Christ our Lord, it is hee that must deliuer me from this body of death.* {Ro. 7. 24.}[162] And yet thou wilt not follow him, nor depend vpon him.

[3?] Another [p. 199] reason why thou shouldest follow Christ and depend vpon him, is, because if the diuell finde thee at any time alone, thou canst not escape his hands: and therfore my greatest desire is, that I might perswade you to cast all your care vppon God, and none vpon the world: nay, I pray God, that Christ may preuaile with you, {4.} for hee hath gone about to perswade you already, and told you a reason, for hee careth for you: and if hee careth for you, you need no more care, for you shall bee well prouided for: therefore obey him, cast all your care vpon him, and care not for this world; liue as hee hath appointed you, labour in [p. 200] your vocation six dayes, and keepe the seuenth holy to the Lord, and in all your labour vse no kinde of deceit, nor desire to bee rich. Doe you labour in your vocation, and be sure you pray morning and euening, and at noone, and at all

times, & heare and read the Word of God, & meditate on that day and night, and follow Christ and take holde on him by faith; let that be all your care, and for your bodily goods take no care. If you dare not trust God with your bodies, who feedeth them as you see euery day, how dare you trust him with your soules, which you cannot well discerne by reason of your earthly nature? [p. 201] You haue a promise for your bodies, if you wil serue God and keepe his Commandements; and yet many dare not trust him, they would serue him with all their hearts, if they durst trust his Word. If they should loose their mortall bodies, it were but a small matter, for they must haue an end. And for your soules you haue but his Word and promise, vpon condition that you follow Christ, and take hold of him by faith: now if you neglect the condition, the promise is void: and yet you say, you durst trust God with your soules, when you neuer goe about to keepe his Commaundements: you neuer follow [p. 202] Christ, nor take hold of him by faith, nor haue you any experience by your bodies,[163] for you neuer durst trust Christ. *Dauid* saith, *I haue killed a Lion & a Beare, and therefore I dare venture on this vncircumcised Philistine.* {1. Sam. 17. 34.35.} If he had suffered the Lion and the Beare to haue ouercome him, hee had neuer ouercome the Giant, & then had he neuer bin made the Kings sonne.[164] So if thou wilt ouercome that great Goliah, thou must first kill the Lion and the Beare: thou must first ouercom the temptations of the world, if thou meanest to ouercome the diuell, and so bee made the Kings sonne of heauen.
[p. 203]

CHAP. 39.

Against immoderate care.

Our Sauiour saith, *Care not for to morrow, let to morrow care for it selfe; the day hath enough with his owne griefe.*[165] Heere you see, that our Sauiour pitties you, that you will take such care, and willeth you that you should not take care for the next morrow, because you do not know, whether you shall liue till then or no; for Christ saith, *Thou foole, this night will they take away thy soule from thee.* {Lu. 12. 20.} As if Christ should say, I[f] thou dyest with taking care for this world, thou losest the king- [p. 204] dome of heauen, and thou shalt lye burning in hel fire. Then doest thou not shew thy selfe a foole, to take so much care for this world, since thou knowest that hell fire is before thee, and thy goods are behinde thee, and thou knowest not who shall inioy them? {Psal. 39. 6.} If thou thinkest thy children shall, thou knowest not whether they shall liue or no, or spend and waste them wickedly, as thou perhaps hast gotten them, or whether they shall bee other waies depriued of them or no.

A thousand wayes may separate thy sonnes and their goods asunder: thou knowest not but that the world may end: thou knowest not what shall become of [p. 205] thy goods, or whether any body shal inioy them or not: and to say the truth, some of you make sure worke that none shall inioy them; for whosoeuer getteth thẽ, were better bee without them, if they bee not gotten in the feare of GOD, and then they cannot bee enioyed in the faith of Christ; for it is unlawfull to haue stolne goods in thy house, and thy goods may bring a punishment vpon thy children, and therefore thou art a foole, to take any care at all for or about these things, and thou art a foole because thou doest care, yea and spend all thy care about these things. Thou knowest, if thou doest not spend [p. 206] thy time in the feare of God which is but *the beginning of wisedome*, {Prou. 1. 7.} and in the faith of Christ, which is the end and finishing of wisedome; thou thy selfe, thy body, and thy soule shal lye burning in hel fire for euer and euer, and there is no meanes for thee to be deliuered. Thou maist turne thee and tumble thee in the fire of hell, and canst neuer get out, & wonder at thy selfe, that thou wert such a foole to take care for those things which thou shouldest neuer know what became of them, and take little or no care for thy self, when thou knewest, thou shouldest come to this miserable and wretched ende, that should neuer ende.

[p. 207]

Here in the world none dare call a rich-man foole: but Christ saith, he is a foole that setteth his heart on these worldly things.[166] But if by taking care for worldly things, he misse heauen, & fall into hell; hee will call himselfe a thousand millions of fooles, that omitting better things, he would take care for this world, which is worth nothing: nay, it is worse then nothing; for his own conscience will tel him, if he had had nothing, hee should haue cared for nothing, and so hee might haue serued GOD and gone to heauen: and hauing something, his care was so much to compasse more, [p. 208] that indeed he had gotten nothing but euerlasting torment.

And now he knoweth not what to doe: sometimes he thinkes, I would I might creepe thorow tenne thousand hells, and bee ten thousand millions of yeares in crawling thorow them, to go to Christ, and then get faith, & take hold on Christ: for he knoweth now, that none can come to God, but by faith in his sonne, for the which hee would now take all the paines that could euer bee deuised, to obtaine that faith in the end, and yet he thought, whilest he was in this world, that one Sermon in a moneth would haue serued him to haue gotten that faith; but hee [p. 209] seeth he would not beleeue the word of God, for Gods owne word willed him, that he should not *labour for the meate that perisheth*, but for *the foode of euerlasting life*; And least hee should doubt of these things which God saith, Christ saith, *Consider the Lillies of the field, they labour not, neither spinne they: I say vnto you, that Salomon in all his glory was not cloathed like one of these. If God so cloath the grasse, which is here to day, and to morrow is cast into the furnace, will hee not do much more for you, Oh yee of little faith?* {Matth. 6. 28.29.}[167] Heere Christ tels them that will not beleeue his promise, and follow his counsell, they are of little faith. And the holy Ghost [p. 210] telleth vs that *faith commeth by hearing* {Ro. 10. 17.} of the word preached: and, *Without faith it is impossible to please God:* {Heb. 11. 6.} and there were neuer any saued but by faith, nor there were neuer any damned, but for want of faith. For the holy Ghost saith, *Hee that commeth to God, must beleeue that God is, and that he is a rewarder of them that seeke him.*[168] He did not beleeue that God would prouide for him in this world, and saue him in the next, because he wanted faith. And he wanted faith, because his delight was not as *Maries* was, to leaue his worldly affaires, & to heare the Word preached.[169] Hee could not pray, that hee might profit by the Word [p. 211] preached, because hee had no knowledge by the word to see his wants. He had no knowledge, because hee did not continually heare and read the word, which would haue taught him to haue knowne God and himselfe. If hee prayed sometimes without knowledge and faith, his prayers were vaine and friuolous.

And thus he seeth, it was his owne negligence that brought him to hell, because hee would not labour for the meat that perisheth not, and now hee is so vexed at himselfe because he did not follow the counsell of our blessed Sauiour Christ, that took such paines for him, and gaue him so many warnings, and told [p. 212] him how hee should finde it, if he would follow his counsell, that hee would now, if it were possible, bee reuenged on himselfe, as Iudas, {Mat. 27. 5.} whẽ he had done that which Christ had warned him of, and saw that now it could not be vndone, hee laid violent hands on himselfe to be reuenged vpon himselfe. But when they see they cannot bee reuenged on themselues, nor no way can mitigate their torment, then they are ten thousand times more tormented with torments, which cannot bee expressed; then they will defie Sathan, & crie out against the world they loued so well, and say, Sathan laid all his baites by the things which are in the [p. 213] world, yea manie baits hee laid, and tooke manie euen with things that were lawfull to bee vsed in the world, by the appointment of God, as you shall see. Meat is ordained of God for the nourishment of man; and yet how manie doth Sathan take with the sinne of gluttonie; and therefore take heede that thou eatest temperatelie. *Meat is ordained for the belly, and the belly for meat, but God will destroy both them and it.* {1. Cor. 6. 13.} Drinke is verie lawfull; yet how manie doth Satan take with the sinne of drunkennesse? and therefore Christ saith, *Take heede, lest at anie time your hearts bee ouercome with drunkennesse and surfetting, and cares of this world.* {Luk. 21. 34.} [p. 214] Mark this counsel of Christ, *Lest at anie time.* As if hee should say, bee continuallie carefull, lest thou art ouercome with surfetting and drunkennesse, and cares of this world; for thou mayest surfet and bee drunken with anie thing thou takest care for in this world.

And therfore Christ saith, *Take no care and doe not say; What shall wee eat, and what shall we drinke? and wherewith shall we bee clothed? for after these things seek the Gentiles. And your heauenly father knoweth, you haue neede of these things. But first seeke the Kingdome of God and his righteousnesse, and all these things shall bee ministred vnto you.* {Mat. 6. 31.32.}[170] Oh the mercie of God, which would tell you, that [p. 215] your heauenly Father knew, that you had neede of these things, and hee would giue you that he knew sufficient? *Seeke ye the Kingdome of heauen, and these things shall bee ministred vnto you.* Seeke yee the heauenly treasure, and a little of this earthly trash wil serue the turne. And if you knew all, and how Sathan hath poysoned most of it, you would be afraid to take anie of it. But if you take nothing but at my hands (saith Christ) Sathans poison shall neuer hurt you:[171] but if you beginne to bee your owne caruers, Sathan will so sawce it with sweet poison, that hee will deceiue the wisest worldling in the world. And therfore see you take nothing [p. 216] but at the hands of the Lord; for Sathan hath spred his net, as the spider doth her webbe. Now the spider lieth close hidden in a darke hole, vntill the sillie[172] flie bee entangled, and then hee comes and taketh her as his owne: and euen so Sathan lieth close, vntill hee see you entangled within the things of this world, and then hee claimeth the world, and you and all, for his owne.

CHAP. 40.

The poyson of outward things.

See how Sathan hath poysoned all things in this world, as apparel with pride, [p. 217] honour with haughtinesse, beauty with vanity, recreations with swearing, riches with couetousnesse: a thing clean against reason: for the naturall man[173] would thinke, that hee which is rich, neede not be couetous; and yet it is commonly seen, the more rich, the more couetous. Yea, and euen our vertues, how doth Sathan seeke to poyson them? as for liberality, how doth hee seeke to poyson it with prodigalitie, and honest labour with carefulnesse?[174] And therefore S. *Iohn* saith, *Loue not the world, nor the things that are in the world: for the loue of the world is enmity to God.* {1. Ioh. 2. 15.}[175] Then some worldly man will say, What? shall we doe nothing? Yes: [p. 218] but see how soone the Diuel will lay a snare to entangle the[e] withal, that thou maist be idle; the verie bait with the which hee catcheth all: for many desire goods, that they may bee idle, and the Diuell hath most leisure to talke with a man, when he is idle; and idlenesse bringeth a man to manie vaine recreations, and so to much eating and drinking, and to manie wicked sinnes. The holy Ghost saith, that *we shall giue account for euery idle word that wee speake*: {Matth. 12. 36.} and therefore thou maiest not bee idle by anie meanes. Thou must labour sixe daies, for GOD hath commanded thee so to doe; and thou must doe it, not for anie care thou hast of the [p. 219] world, but because GOD commanded thee: and thou must shew thy selfe obedient to him, and all thy care in thy labour must bee how to please him, and leaue the successe of thy labor to him, and thou must be carefull in thy labour, that thou takest no care for thine owne profit, nor thine owne pleasure, but how to please God, and then let it please thee: but be sure it please not thee and offend God. And thus thou must labour sixe daies; and follow the commandement of God, and his example, after whose image thou wert made, and whom thou art to imitate: hee laboured and made in sixe daies these things for thee, labour thou [p. 220] to obey him: hee laboured and looked ouer his worke, and saw it was good.[176] So thou must labour, and looke ouer thy worke, and see that it bee good before God. Though there are manie imperfections in thee, yet because thou art reconciled to GOD in Christ, and now shewest thy humble obedience to his commandement, that thou wilt neither bee idle, nor yet labour for thine owne profit nor pleasure, nor doe thy owne wayes, but see that thou dost those things that hee hath appointed thee, taking hold of Christ by faith; hee accepteth them for good through Christ, who hath fulfilled all for thee: for *obedience is better then sacrifice.* {1. Sam. 15. 22.}

[p. 221]

Then also thou must rest the seuenth day, for so for thy ensample he rested, & commanded thee to rest that day, and to keepe it holy to the Lord.[177] Now he commandeth thee to leaue all earthly businesse, and attend vpon him, and heare what further instructions hee hath for thee, how to strengthen thy faith, how to take hold on CHRIST, and how to come to his kingdome.

Now thy care must be, how to learne at his mouth to keepe his commandements. Now hee will shew thee the figure of that euerlasting rest, which hee will bring thee to through Christ. Now if thou beest not very ready and diligent to attend [p. 222] vpon him the seuenth day, thou shewest, that all thy labour on the six daies was for thine own pleasure or profit, more then for thy obedience toward the Lord thy God: for if thou wouldest haue obeyed him in thy labour in the six dayes, thou wouldest haue obeyed him in thy rest the seuenth day also. This shal be a witnes to thine own conscience, least that thou bee deceiued, as many bee, who thinke that they labour all the weeke to please God, when indeede they labour to please themselues, because that commandement pleaseth their humour better, then to keepe holy the Sabbath: and they will bee willing to take [p. 223] one houre from the Lord in the morning, and another in the afternoone, or two it may be, which sheweth that their mindes and affections are more on the world, then on the true seruice and obedience they owe to God.

CHAP. 41.

Prodigality set out.

Some think, that the prodigal man taketh too little care for the world: but I say, he is a wicked man, and taketh too much care for the world, and too little care to please GOD. Hee is an idle man, and will not labour 6. dayes. Hee is a disobedient man, and wil not keepe holy the seuenth day. He is a wastfull man, he wil spend wast- [p. 224] fully for the vaine-glory of the world, which some say they care not for, he leaueth those things wch God hath giuen him and his family without care. Yea, he is a couetous man, for he will borrow of others, and spend it wastfully, and neuer pay it againe. He breaketh the cõmandement, which saith, *Owe nothing to any man, but this, that you loue one another,* {Ro. 13. 8.} for the holy Ghost saith, *The vngodly borroweth, and paieth not againe, but the mercifull man is liberall and lendeth.* {Psa. 37. 21.}

Some will say, they would pay if they had it: but indeede they will not haue it, because they will not obey God, and liue as hee hath appointed them. They are [p. 225] proud, and will spend so far beyond their calling,[178] that they haue nothing to lend to the poore children of God, because they spend either vpon the wicked, or in excesse when there is no neede, or vppon those that haue as little, or lesse neede then thẽselues. *Such a person is worse then an Infidel, because he prouideth not for his owne houshold.* {1. Ti. 5. 8.} God doth not say, Because hee taketh not care for his owne houshold; for all his care should bee to please God: but hee careth not to please God, neither doth he obey God, to labor 6. daies, and to see his houshold labour; for whilest he is idle, or vsing some vaine pastime out of his calling, [p. 226] his children & seruants disobey GOD, and mispend their time, and weaken his estate, and all through his owne carelesnesse to please God. Hee sheweth himselfe no good Christian: for a good Christian life is a carefull life, not carefull of the world, but carefull least the world should hinder him any way frõ seruing of God, either in being too negligent in his calling, and so prouide not for his houshold, & become worse then an Infidel; or lest hee should bee couetous, and become the man whom God abhorreth.

And yet there bee some so ignorant, that they will say, The prodigall man beareth a noble mind, But hee beares a [p. 227] wicked mind, & they know not what a noble minde is, that say so. Our Peeres and Princes are called Noble men, because they beare noble mindes, that is, they are vertuous and temperate, & discreet,[179] gouerning the Cõmon-wealth, according to their calling, regarding the vertuous, & keeping vnder the vicious, holding in the prodigall, who would run away with a whole kingdom, if they might haue it: nay, no kingdome is able to satisfie prodigal persons; for their disobedient humour wil neuer be satisfied, because they doe not labour to keepe the commandement of God. Some are more infected wth this sin, then others, but all [p. 228] that are not infected with prodigalitie, haue a disobedient humour, they are vndiscreet because they cannot spend whẽ they should, and spare with discretion when the time is.[180] They are vnthankful because they do not heartily thank God for his blessings, but wish they were more. Neither wil they bee thankefull to the King, nor a worthy noble Prince or Peere; for if they spend a little prodigally in their seruice, they will thinke they are indebted to thẽ, though all of it were by the Prince liberally bestowed on them: but indeede such are not to be about Princes or Peeres, no more then the couetous. Some wise and learned men [p. 229] haue disputed, whether the couetous or the prodigal be the worst member in the Common-wealth; but I pray God you nor yours be none of both: but here what the holy Ghost saith, The couetous is the man whom God abhorreth:[181] The prodigall is worse then an infidell. And thus I leaue them, and pray to God for Christs sake, they and wee may leaue both those and al other sins, and take hold of Christ by faith, and liue through him with God for euer and euer.

CHAP. 42.

Difference betweene an act & habite of sinning.

Now you must know this, that the deare [p. 230] children of God, for want of discretion, doe sometime an act, wch may be called couetous, & yet not vpon a couetous humor;[182] and an act, that may be called prodigall, and yet not vpon a prodigall humour, but for want of discretion at that time: for there is none so discreet at all times, that is not somewhat infected with either of these sins; for wee are infected with all sins; and therefore God, in great mercy to man, made the Sabbath, or Lords day, so that if a man did in sixe dayes ouerslip himselfe, as indeed we all do, and did not reconcile himselfe to God euery night, as we ought to do; yet on the Sabbath day, the Lord calleth him to him, [p. 231] and sheweth him his faults, and wisheth him to bee reconciled vnto him through Christ, and breatheth into his face the breath of life again, and renueth in him the image of God again, that was decayed by his sin, and so he goeth home a renued man.

And therfore I say, & say truly, that all the writers in the world cannot expresse, what hurt that man, woman or childe doeth himselfe, that doth not attend on the Lord on the Sabbath day, neither can any man or woman doe their seruants more hurt, thẽ to keepe them frõ the Lords house that day. The Lord hath charged thee, that thou (if thou hast any vnder thee) shalt see thẽ come, [p. 232] and come thy selfe, as thou wilt answere it: for the Lord himselfe is now there prepared to teach thee and thine; and therfore go to him, and go prepared, *clense thy heart of all earthly things*, {Iam. 4. 8.}[183] & know that hee is there to see thine heart, and all thine affection and behauior. Some wil say, I would goe to the Church, but there will be little: but I say vnto thee, I feare that thou wilt not learne that little. If God, for thy disobedience, wil speak but a little to thee that day, yet thou hast a great deale to say to him; confesse thy sins, shew thine obedience, be an example to them, which would stay frõ the presence of God, pray for his grace vpon thee and [p. 233] them, & the whole Church, & appeale to the promise of God; *When two or three be gathered together in his name, he will be with them*: {Mat. 18. 20.} pray that GOD may send his word plentifully for Christs sake, although our sinnes deserue to haue it taken away altogether; seek to doe some good to the poor, although there be but a poore company of you gathered together. Moue the people to prouide themselues a Preacher, tell them of their wants, speake to the Magistrates, mourne to see the Alehouses full, and the Church of God emptie.[184]

CHAP. 43.

The seruice of the Sabbath ought to be publike.

Some will goe to the Church of God in the [p. 234] forenoone, and in the afternoone they will serue God at home; but thou canst not doe God so great seruice at home: serue him six daies at home, and the seuenth go to the Church of the Lord, if God bee truely worshipped there, as I pray God he euer may bee in our Churches to the worlds end; and I pray God you may bee true worshippers of God. And alwaies in the Church of God, both forenoone and afternoone, let there be one the more for thee.[185] But of this I warn you, for the loue I beare to your soules & bodies; if you cannot get the people to prouide a Preacher, wch may dispēce the Word truly & sincerely, remoue you, where you may [p. 235] haue and heare the Word so preached; for *where the Word of the Lord is not truly preached, the people perish for want of knowledge.* {Prou. 29. 18.}[186] But if you can get a Preacher where you dwell, and doe good both to your selfe and others, I thinke it better so; for *the haruest is great, but the laborers are few; therefore pray the Lord of the haruest to send forth labourers into his haruest*: {Matth. 9. 37.38.} for the true laborers indeed are not few, but verie few: for as the holy Ghost saith, *All seeke their own, and not that which is Iesus Christs.* {Phil. 2. 21.} *All* is taken heere, as it is in many other places, for the most part;[187] for the most seek their own: nay, it would seeme well, if some would be contented with their owne; [p. 236] but they seeke more then their owne: if they examine themselues well, they shall find it so; whereas the true Preachers of Gods word will be contented with lesse then their owne; so they may win soules vnto Christ they care not. They count al the world dung, as indeede it is, so they may bee Christs, and draw many to him.

I hope in God, that through his grace som of you wil be preachers.[188] I pray God, for Christs sake, to enlighten you with his Spirit, and giue you grace, that you may be truly godly, and very zealous for the glorie of God, labouring by all meanes possible to encrease the glorious kingdom of Christ. And of this bee [p. 237] sure, if you will lose nothing of your own, you will neuer winne manie to Christ: and marke how the holie Ghost saith, *They seeke their owne.* He doth not say, They seeke more then their owne: but, *They seeke their owne.* As if he should say, as indeede hee meaneth; They busie themselues about seeking their owne, but in the meanetime they neglect the great worke and the great businesse that I haue set thē about, to gather together the souls that Iesus Christ the Son of God shed his heart bloud for; & contrarie to all reason, they look for their wages, before they haue done their work. S. *Paul* which was called to be a Preacher of the Word of God, [p. 238] saith, *Woe be to me, if I preach not the Gospel.* {1. Cor. 9. 16.} But hee doth not say, Woe bee to mee, if I seek not goods. He saith, *Necessitie is laid vpõ me to preach the Gospell.* But he doth not say, Necessitie is laid vpon me to get goods. Yet some of

them will say, they must not lose their goods & right: rather they must go to law for them: but contrary to the Law of God, they neglect their duty in his Church, they doe not studie how to diuide the word of God aright, & to giue to euery one that which is fit for him. What doth the holie Ghost call negligent Preachers, but *dumb dogs that will not barke?* {Esay. 56. 10.11.}[189] The dog will barke and giue warning to the whole house- [p. 239] hold within, if anie danger be neere: but those that shold deliuer my message vnto the people, they busie themselues about their owne affaires, they slumber and delight in sleeping: they will not call out to the people, and giue them warning of the danger that is neere them. I pray tell me, or let any man tell me, if he be a good seruant, which will goe about his owne busines, and neglect his masters or no? no man will account of such a seruant, but will cast him off for naught: euen so God will cast them off for naught, that seek their owne, & neglect the diligent seeking of that which is Iesus Christs.
[p. 240]

CHAP. 44.

The honourable calling of Ministers stained by worldlines.

I must needs say, I haue bin verie desirous, and haue often begged of GOD, that some of you might be Preachers, yea and all of you and yours, if it might please his diuine Maiestie to bestow such graces vpõ you, as were meet for so high a calling. But God knowes, I neuer desired it, because you should get any thing in the world, but because you should get seruants to God, and soules to Christ, and because you might be so enlightned with the Word through the holy Ghost working within you, that you might make no ac- [p. 241] count of the world, as indeede it is nothing, nay, it is worse then nothing; for nothing doth no hurt, and the world doth much hurt. *I pray not for the world*, saith Christ, *but for those thou hast giuen mee out of the world*: {Ioh. 17. 9.} those, that though their bodies be in the world, yet their hearts, their minds and their affections are as high as heauen. *If you be risen with Christ seeke those things which are aboue, where Christ sitteth at the right hand of God: set not your affections on things which are on the earth, but on things which are in heauen.* {Col. 3. 1.}[190] I pray GOD for Christ his sake, you may bee of those, which Christ prayed for, those which haue their [p. 242] mindes and hearts busied about heauenly things, & neuer taking care for the things of the world. Woe is mee, which feare, lest anie of you or yours should loue this world: but if it please God that anie of you heereafter should bee a Preacher, and loue the world, I cannot expresse the greefe it would be to me, euen so long as I were in the world. If anie of you should aske me, if it were not as euill in another man, as in a Preacher? I answer, no; for it is a very dangerous and indeede a damnable estate to loue the world. I know what I say; I doe not say, to be couetous, or desire to bee rich, wherby one is moued to vse vnlawfull meanes to get [p. 243] goods: but I say, to loue lawfull goods which God hath giuen thee, and to neglect the seruice of God about them, if it be but in thinking of them, and to bee at anie time more loth to lose thy lawfull goods, then to go to law to the hurt of thy brother whom Christ died for, it is a wicked sin in anie man. To set a rent or price of any of thy lawful goods or lands, more then thou in such a case wouldest bee willing to giue, it is a wicked sin.

{The danger of dealing with wicked men.} To let or sell any thing to any man, for sinister respects, that thou doest not thinke to be the true and faithfull seruant of God, if thou maist let it well to those that are, is a sin.[191] But to let a Farme to anie [p. 244] that thou doest not think to bee the true seruant of God, but because he is richer, or is better able to pay thee, or wil giue thee more for it, is a great sin: *For the earth is the Lords, and all that is therein,*[192] & he hath set thee as a steward ouer some part of it, and thou art by his appointment to let it to his children & seruants that loue him; and because many things haue many prices, he bids thee deale in all his businesse, as thou wouldest bee dealt withall in such a case. Hee biddes thee *deale liberally with thy brother, that his soule may blesse thee:* {Iob 31. 29.}[193] yet thou wilt neglect thy brother, whõ thou seest carefull to serue God in Christ, & let it to one that hath little [p. 245] or no Religion in him, because thou seest that hee can deale more warily in the world, or more wisely, as the world cals it, though indeed it bee more wickedly before God: yet because thou seest he is more able to pay thee thy rent, thou wilt let it to him, who is indeed Gods enemy, and for whõ God neuer made it: for God made these things for his children and seruants, & he doth neither loue God as his Father, nor obey him as a seruãt: neither will he more becom obedient to God, & seruiceable to his Church, if thou let him a good peniworth;[194] whereas if he thriue not of it, he will raile on thee, and on thy religion, which is indeede a- [p. 246] gainst God; for he knoweth not, that it is God that giueth power to get goods, and that it is God again, that keepeth men short: althogh sometimes with his mouth he speaketh it, yet the true knowledge of it dwels not in his heart; and if he grow rich vpon it, he will not bee liberal to the poore children of God, considering their wants as if they were his owne: for he hath no naturall affection towards them, because they are not his brethren.

Loe, heere thou seest what to do with thine own, or, as some say, Gods and thine owne; or, as the truth is Gods, and not thine own; and therfore thou maist offend God in it: for thou art [p. 247] but a tenant at the wil of the Lord, and art to depart at an instant; yet thou hast a great title[195] vnder God for thy time and thy title is good, & lawfully thou maist inioy them, yet the loue that thou bearest vnto them is vtterly vnlawfull; for it is the loue that thou bearest to these worldly goods, that maketh thee to let them to such a tenant, as wil neither serue God, nor doe good to the poore seruants of God. The man to whome thou lettest it, may be a ciuill honest man in the world: for among the heathen, yea, among the Iewes that would kil Christ again, if they had him, & hate the children of God;[196]

there are such as in the world wil deale [p. 248] ciuilly, and pay at their day, perhaps, better then some Christian. But if thou beest the true childe of God, thou must haue a discerning eye of faith, wch euery one hath not, and know the childe of God from a ciuill man:[197] neither maist thou iudge the other for all that, but pray for him, and hope that though he be not the true seruant of God now, yet in good time, by Gods grace he may bee. Thou maiest not impart the benefits of God, as neere as thou canst, but to those whõ thou knowest to be the lords true seruants, and thou must do it for the loue thou bearest to God.

Why shouldest thou not loue Gods childrẽ much more then any goods [p. 249] thou hast? There is great reason to doe it, able to perswade any man, if his heart be not of stone. For GOD made vs most excellẽt creatures, according to his owne image. Satan came by stelth and subtiltie, & through enuy stole away that excellent image from vs, and made vs most ougly persons, deformed diuels, so that we were ashamed of our selues, ran away and hid our selues, and wee were good for nothing, but euil for all things, fit for nothing but firebrands of hell, into the which we were ready euery houre to fall, & God had said, that if we suffered the diuel to deceiue vs, hell should bee our portion, the diuel stood gaping to re- [p. 250] ceiue vs: wert thou not in a miserable case then? I tell thee, we were all in this miserable case. And I tell thee true, I am sorry at the heart, when I see any that doth not consider the case wherin he was, and I am afraide, lest any of you should forget the state wherein ye were, and so become vnthankefull, and fall into it againe. Oh, the danger is great! But tell me, wouldest thou not loue him, that would come and make thee like a God againe, and wash away al thy filthy poyson, and deliuer thee frõ the slauery of the diuell, & from the fire of hel, and set thee in Paradice againe, yea in such a Paradice as the diuell can neuer haue power to deceiue [p. 251] thee? and for thy better assurance bids thee hold thee by him, and thou shalt neuer need to feare? If thou shouldest not loue him and al his, thou wert greatly to blame.

But I know now in thy distresse thou dost not make so much question, whether thou shouldest loue him or no; for thou thinkest it vnpossible but that thou shouldest loue him and all his, & do whatsoeuer he would bid thee. If thou wert once in Gods fauour againe, thou wouldest not disobey him for all the diuels and worlds that euer were. But ôh the misery! heere is the thing: how is it possible that thou shouldest be helped? God is thine enemy, the diuell is [p. 252] thine enemy, the world can doe thee no good, nor make thee cleane: for al the bloud within thy veines is corrupted, thy hart bloud is becom most filthy poyson, & thou art become most vgly deformed like the diuell, and thou art a shame to thy self, although no body see thee but thy selfe, and hell fire is so bigge, that all the water in the world cannot quench it. Thus beginning to despaire, thy torments beginne to increase, whẽ thou couldst see no way to escape it: but ôh the loue of God, the wonderful loue of God toward thee neuer to be expressed, not for any goodnesse that is in thee; for behold here what a filthy creature thou art; but [p. 253] for the euerlasting goodnes, that was in himself, his great mercy and wonderfull wisedome he found a way, euen for his own sake; or else man and his posterity had beene burning in hell fire for euer and euer. How did he find a way? he sent his only Son to wash this filthy creature mã, his only Son, I say, the Son of God. And how did hee wash him? No water would make him cleane: hee washed him with his owne bloud, & he sweat water and bloud with washing of him, yea, he shed his hart bloud, & gaue it man to drinke, {Mat. 26. 27.} that it might enter into his heart, and so run through all his veines, & so cleanse him indeed. *Mans flesh was corrupted.* {Gen. 6. 12.} *The Sonne* [p. 254] *of God brake his body, & gaue them his flesh to eate,* {Mat. 26. 26.} that it might renue their flesh, and that their leprosie might be healed: and the Son of God did this indeed; he brake his body, and gaue it vs to feed on; hee shed his bloud, and gaue it vs to drink, or else we could neuer haue bin clensed.

But woe is me, God wold not accept him, he said that man for his disobedience to him, and obeying the diuell, must goe to hell and burne there. Oh the mercies of the Sonne of God, how is it possible they should be shadowed[198] out! for no body can expresse the depth of it, {Eph. 3. 18.19.}[199] that he would indure the paines of hel for vs: {Gal. 3. 13.}[200] he being man, indured them; and being [p. 255] God, ouercame them: hee stopped the mouth of the diuell, shut the gates of hel, tooke man by the hand, hee hauing washed him and indured the paines of hell for him: hee takes him by the hand I say, and leads him to his father, {Iohn 14. 7.}[201] hee accepts him in Christ. {Iohn 8. 36.}[202] Oh the mercies of God in Christ, that are neuer able to bee set out by man! Man throgh his fal wrought his vtter ruine alone by himself; {Eccl. 7. 29.}[203] Christ the Son of God, hath wrought his recouery alone by himselfe, without the helpe of any, {Iohn 3. 16.}[204] and set man in a far better estate, then he was before; for now hee hath giuen him the hand of faith to hold on him, that he may neuer fall: {Ioh. 11. 25.}[205] [p. 256] before, man was alone, but now hee is ioyned fast vnto Christ by faith. Now what hath man to do, To follow Christ, & take hold of him by faith. {Mar. 16. 16.} Not that man deserueth heauen by following Christ, no nor by his faith; but he taketh hold of him, which hath deserued heauẽ for him, and bringeth him thither, and setteth him in a glorious place by God his Father, and God accepteth him in Christ, & taketh him at his hands. *No man cõmeth to the Father, but by me* (saith Christ.) {Mat. 11. 27.}[206]

Now oughtest not thou in conscience to loue, obey, and follow his counsell, that hath done all this for thee? & to loue his children & seruants, better then [p. 257] the children and seruants of thy vtter enemy the diuell? who was not only enemy to thee, then when he first corrupted thee & thy seed, but hee is vtter enemy to thee still, & not only an vtter enemy to thee, but also to christ thy Sauiour, and will by all meanes hinder him, and impouerish his kingdome, & if he can possible he wil bring thee frõ Christ to hel again? And wilt thou inrich his kingdome for a little goods (wᶜʰ Christ neuer bid thee get) who is an vtter enemy to thy Sauiour, and seeketh by all meanes to impouerish his kingdome, to speake against his Word, to scoffe at them that follow him, yea, oftẽ stoppeth their mouthes [p. 258] that would gladly speake on Christs side, saying, If thou art altogether on Christs side thou art not *Cæsars* friend, {Ioh. 19. 12.}[207] & wilt not inrich his kingdom? Thou knowest when thou inrichest Satans kingdome, thou weaknest the kingdõe of Christ, in that thou weaknest thy faith; for thou canst not in faith part with any of thy goods, to one whõ thou dost not think the seruant of God in Christ; and *whatsoeuer is not of faith, is sin.* {Ro. 14. 23.}

And I prooue this vnto thee thus. When thou losest the fauor of God, and becommest a bondslaue of the diuel, thou losest all the blessings, which God in mercy hath made for thee, and bestowed on thee. But they did not then fall to [p. 259] the diuell, but did fall to the Lord, whose they were; for they were not thine before, but the Lords, and therefore thou couldest not lose them, nor forfet them to the diuel: yet thou hast lost thẽ frõ thy selfe, & they fell to the Lord, who lent thee them so long as thou didst serue him: but the Diuell finding thee possest of them, claimeth them now, not that hee hath any right to them, but like an vsurping Tyrant, and it was thy fault in yeelding thy obedience to him, which maketh him to claim thee as his bond-slaue, & all thy goods to be at his commandement; but thou hadst nothing to lose but thy selfe, and that thou losest, but Christ redee- [p. 260] med thee. Take heed therefore, for as an vsurping Tyrant, who hauing gottẽ once possession of a kingdom, will euer after lay claim to it, and will vse all the means he can to get it againe; and the first possession is not only a great light to make him get it the easier, but also it maketh him if he get it againe, to keep it more strongly, and fortifie it with a mighty power, & keep watch and ward in it,[208] that he will neuer lose it againe: So will the Diuell; & therefore take heed thou deal not with any of the seruants of the diuell, nor by no means inrich his kingdome.

If a noble and worthy-minded man, who hath great possessions, passe by some puddle,[209] where hee [p. 261] should see a harlot casting away her own son, if he should inquire for the father, & find that contrary to nature, hee were run away from his own child, leauing it to vtter ruine & destruction; if this noble-minded Gentle-man should take vp the childe, and cause it to be washed, clothed & fed, and cause it to be instructed, & taught those things which it were fit it should learne, & when he came to be a man, hee should say, I found thee thus and thus, and seeing no body had care of thee, I tooke thee vp, and euer since maintained thee in good estate; & now I would haue thee acquainted with my affaires & busines; for I meane to trust thee with those things that I [p. 262] haue: for so it is, my King calleth for me, & the affaires of my Country require that I should neglect mine owne busines & attend vpon them; wherefore I leaue my Lands, Lordships and Tenements with you in trust, till I come again: let thẽ to my friends, & let thẽ such pennyworths, that they may well liue vpon them: let your owne friends some part of them; deale so in it, as at my cõming home I may finde you faithfull.

Now if this seruant should neglect his charge, neglect his owne friends and his masters, and go for a little more rent, which his master cared not a whit for, & let his lands and tenements to his vtter enemies, who growing rich [p. 263] with the Lands and goods of this noble Lord, would bee ready to bidde him battle at his returne home, & to strike at him with his owne sword; iudge you, would not this Lord think, he had dealt very euill with him? nay, would not euery honest man that should but heare of it, thinke & say that he had dealt most vildly[210] with so good a Lord and Master, and that he were neuer meete to come in the company of an honest man againe?[211]

Thus hath Christ dealt with vs; When our wicked father and vngodly mother, *Adam* and *Eue*, cast vs into the puddle of sin, & ran away, & left vs there, where we should neuer haue beene able to haue gotten out, Iesus [p. 264] Christ, the onely Son of the high and mighty God, our mercifull Lord and Sauiour, came by, and washed vs, and brought vs vp at his own cost & charges, and we haue nothing but frõ him; he taught vs himselfe in all good doctrine; and being gone to ouercome the enemy of his King and Country, he hath left his goods with thee, bids thee to deale well with his seruants, and let them good penny-worths, and deale not with his enemies, neither make any mariage with thẽ: {2. Cor. 6. 14.} yet thou for a little money wilt buy and sell, marry and giue in marriage with them, yea & thinkest, because thou findest thẽ more rich in the world, they are better for [p. 265] thee to deale withall; & yet they are the vtter enemies of thy Lord, and will bee ready at his comming to bid him battle, and strike at him with his owne sword.

CHAP. 45.

The right vse of goods.

Heere thou seest, what cause thou hast to loue Christ and his seruants, and how thou oughtest not to loue thine own; but to vse it, as the Lord hath appointed thee, whose indeede it is. If thou dealest not with thy Lords goods and lands, as he hath appointed thee, art thou not in a great fault? Surely thou hast nothing to say for thy selfe, saue to appeale to his mercy, confesse thy sinnes, & amend thy life. [p. 266] But if a Preacher, whõ God hath enlightned to see, what he was out of[212] Christ, & what he is in Christ, and hath willed him to tell the people from his mouth, how he and they should now behaue themselues inwardly in their hearts, & outwardly in their goods and substance; {Tit. 2. 1.}[213] if he, I say, Whom God hath set vpon a hill to giue light to many; {Mat. 5. 14.} if he I say, whom God hath giuen much vnto, and of whom much shall bee required;[214]

{Luk. 12. 48.} if he, I say, whom the sunne of vnderstanding should arise vpon; nay, if he, I say, in whose heart the glorious Sonne of God should shine, will darken his glorie with the thicke clouds, or rather thicke clods of this ear- [p. 267] then world, his sin is great: but what did I say, darken their light? nay, they darken the light of the Gospell, that all should see to goe by: nay, they darken the glorious light of the Son of God, & ecclipse his glory: wheras they should draw many vnto Christ by their liberalitie and true preaching, {1. Tim. 4. 16.}[215] they driue many from Christ by loue of their owne (as they say) & by their idlenes & negligence in preaching (as I say) & I say, this loue of their own, as they call it, is a thousand times worse in them, & doth a multitude more of hurt, then in other ordinarie men, who loue the world as well as they; but there are not so manie that looke on them, [p. 268] and God hath not set them for a light, as hee hath done the Preachers.

And the reason why the Preachers are many times ouercom, is this, because the enemie doth bend all his forces against them, not vnlike the enemy to the Israelites, who sayd, *Fight neither against more nor lesse, but against the King of Israel.* {1. King. 22. 31.} So doth our enemy the Diuell, hee fighteth neither against more nor lesse, but against the Captaines of the Church, namely the Preachers; for he knoweth, that if they bee once ouercome, then the whole armie will soone bee confounded and brought to nought. Bee you all vpholders of them, which by no meanes can bee done [p. 269] but by prayer; for as our preachers should pray for al, so all should send vp their praiers to Almightie God, in the name of his Sonne, to send his holie Spirit into the hearts of the Preachers, to sanctifie them throughout, that they may be holy in bodie & minde, following the exãple of our Sauior Christ, who said to *Peter* his Apostle, whom he had appointed to be chiefe Preacher to the Church of the Iewes, *Peter, Peter, Sathan hath sought to winnow thee like wheat, but I haue praied that thy faith faile not.* {Luk. 22. 31.}[216] Againe, S. *Paul* appointed by the Son of God to bee cheefe Preacher to the Church of the Gentils, witnesseth of himselfe, saying, [p. 270] *The messenger of Sathan was sent to buffet me, but I besought the Lord Iesus, that hee might depart from mee.* {2. Cor. 12. 7.8.}

Now in these two great combates made between the diuell & the deare children of God, ye see, that praier is the weapon whereby the Tempter is ouercome. Wherefore I earnestlie entreat you, let your praiers alwaies be sent vp to God, through Christ, for the Preachers, & all such as are in high places, that so they continuing firme and stedfast, your faith may by thẽ be more confirmed. And the blessing of God Almightie, the Father, the Sonne, and the holy Ghost be with you all from this time, euen to the worlds end. Amen.

FINIS.

Notes

1. *But especially for those . . . Instruction*: omitted in later editions.

2. *Elizabeth*: eldest daughter of King James I of England. She married Count Frederick, Elector Palatine, on St Valentine's Day 1613.

3. Imagining one's progress towards heaven as a journey was commonplace, cf. Arthur Dent's extremely popular *Plaine mans path-way to Heaven*, first published 1601.

4. *Doubts*: fears, apprehensions of danger.

5. *Scroule*: a piece of writing, especially a letter.

6. *Men too wise to direct it to*: learned men might scorn to receive or patronize it. Cf. below *Wisedome* stands metonymically for the 'learned'.

7. *Lowest*: most humble.

8. *Slips*: offshoots or cuttings from a plant; figuratively, offspring. By 1616, Princess Elizabeth had had one child, Prince Frederick Henry.

9. *Knowledge*: here means particularly religious knowledge or knowledge of the gospel, as in James 3:13: 'Who is a wise man & endued with knowledge among you? let him shew by good conuersation his workes in meeknesse of wisdome.'

10. *Rest*: remain.

11. *For why*: because.

12. Bees are proverbially industrious (Tilley B202). They were also an emblem of the humanistic reading practice of gathering sententious wisdom from a wide range of sources.

13. *Beshrowes*: curses.

14. The 1618 table of contents merely collects the chapter headings of the first edition. The heading of Chapter 23, '*What neede there is to speake much of Christ*' is transposed to: '*What neede is there . . .*'

15. The Israelites had to gather manna every day because it would not store. Exodus 16:20–21.

16. The scriptural reference is probably misprinted. Numbers 11:33 refers to the wrath of the Lord, kindled against the Israelites who were not satisfied with the manna in the wilderness, but lusted after flesh. The Lord then sent quails, but while 'the flesh was yet betweene their teeth . . . the Lord smote the people with an exceeding great plague'.

17. Galatians 4:4: 'when the fulnesse of time was come, God sent forth his Sonne made of a woman'.

18. A paraphrase of Hebrews 2:14: 'Forasmuch then as the children are partakers of flesh and blood, hee also himselfe likewise tooke part with them'.

19. Jesus says in John 17:24: 'Father, I will that they which thou hast giuen me, be with me euen where I am'.

20. Isaiah 49:15: 'Can a woman forget her child, & not haue compassion on the sonne of her wombe?' Authorship of the scriptures was conventionally attributed to the Holy Ghost.

21. Leigh adapts Galatians 4:19, which she quotes below.

22. Mother's milk was literally thought to be sublimated blood. Leigh also alludes here to the pelican: believed to feed its offspring from a wound in its breast, and hence a symbol of the self-sacrificing Christ.

23. In Romans 9:3, Paul wishes himself 'separate from Christ' for the sake of his brethren, the Jews. According to the Geneva note, this shows that Paul loved his kinsmen 'so entirely, that if it had

bene possible, he would have bene readie to haue redeemed the casting away of the Israelites, with the losse of his owne soule for euer'.

24. *Traditions*: purely human (as opposed to scriptural) beliefs and practices; often used to refer to Roman Catholicism or its 'remnants' in English Protestantism. *Loyter*: waste time.

25. In fact, John 5:39, compressed: 'Search the Scriptures: for in them yee think to haue eternall life, & they are they which testifie of me.'

26. *Order*: appointed place or role.

27. At the time of the composition of her legacy, Leigh's sons were either at school or university, evidently learning the original languages of the Bible (Greek and perhaps Hebrew). Compare her sons' learning of 'the true written Word of God' with her insistence that all children, female as well as male, learn to read the Bible 'in their owne mother tongue' (beginning ch. 8). For the seven liberal sciences (or arts), see Joscelin, 'Introduction'.

28. Because they are men, not women bound by the imperative to keep silence, they need not fear to offend by their writing and speaking.

29. Eve was the first to sin by tasting the forbidden fruit in Eden (Genesis 3). As well, the unborn child was thought to inherit original sin at the moment of conception in the mother's womb.

30. The Geneva version of Matthew 19:24 has: 'It is easier for a camel to goe thorow the eye of a needle, then for a rich man to enter into the kingdom of God.' In fact, all of the early English Bibles (Tyndale, Great, Bishop's, and King James) make it 'easier for the camel' etc. Shakespeare, however, uses the same formula as Leigh in *Richard II* (5.5.16): 'It is as hard to come as for a camel / To thread the postern of a small needle's eye.' Both Leigh and Shakespeare may be using a proverbial version of this verse. See Tilley C26.

31. When Lazarus the beggar dies, his soul is carried into the bosom of Abraham. The rich man at whose gates he begged is, however, sent to hell. Luke 16:19–26. *Dives* is 'the rich man' in the Vulgate, thence entering into popular usage as the proper name of the man in the parable, or a generic name for any rich man.

32. Matthew 16:25: 'For whosoeuer will saue his life, shal lose it: and whosoeuer shall lose his life for my sake, shall finde it.' . . . *and the Gospels* is Leigh's addition.

33. Psalm 1:3.

34. Romans 12:4–5: 'For as we haue many members in one body, and all members haue not one office. So we being many, are one body in Christ.'

35. An allusion to the words of Jesus in John 14:6: 'No man commeth vnto the father, but by mee.'

36. Deuteronomy 6:5: 'thou shalt loue the Lorde thy God with all thine heart, and with all thy soule, and with all thy might.'

37. Deuteronomy 11:20 has 'vpon the posts of thine house, and vpon thy gates'. Leigh may have been thinking of the godly broadsides printed to adorn the walls of a house and instruct its inhabitants. See Tessa Watt, 'Godly Tables for Good Householders', in *Cheap Print and Popular Piety 1550–1640* (Cambridge University Press, 1991).

38. *Witnesse*: godparent. Leigh's usage is distinctively Puritan (s.v. *OED* 'witness' sb. 5b).

39. On the significant names of God's children (the Jews), see note 59 and Joscelin, note 12.

40. *Saints*: Leigh refers not to the canonized saints of the Roman Catholic Church, but rather to God's chosen or elect, especially those whose stories are told in the Bible.

41. *Famoused*: celebrated. For the stories and virtues of Elizabeth, Anna, and Susanna, see Joscelin, note 54. Philip, James, and John were Christ's disciples – the last singled out as the disciple 'whom hee loved' (see, for example, John 19:26).

42. Pagan and Christian strictures regarding female chastity are summarized in the popular English translation of Vives' manual on female education, especially the chapter 'Of keeping of virginitie and chastitie'. 'Take from a woman her beautie, take from her kindred, riches, comleynesse, eloquence, sharpenesse of witte, cunning in her craft: giue her chastitie, and thou hast giuen her all things. And on the other side, giue her all these thinges, and call her a naughtie packe, with that one word thou hast taken all from her.' Juan Luis Vives, *Instruction of a Christian Woman*, trans. Richard Hyrde (London, 1592), sig. E4v.

43. Leigh is punning on two senses of *vain* in this passage: (1) worthless or idle (2) conceited, desiring admiration.

44. The form of words is in fact that used by Eve rather than Adam in Genesis 3:13: 'The serpent beguiled me, and I did eat.'

45. See Joscelin, note 54.

46. Luke 22:48. For Judas's repentance, see p. 64.

47. Proverbs 2:18: 'her house tendeth to death, and her paths vnto the dead'. The 'dead', as the Geneva note explains, are 'them that are dead in body and soule' – fit inhabitants for hell.

48. Gen 3:15 is God's curse on the serpent in Eden: 'I will also put enmitie between thee and the woman, and betweene thy seed and her seed. He shal breake thine head, and thou shalt bruise his heele.' It is taken as a prophecy of Christ (the seed of Eve by being born of her descendant Mary) who will break the head of the serpent (the devil).

49. From Mary's 'Magnificat': 'henceforth shall all ages call me blessed' (Luke 1:48).

50. Mary's conception of Jesus was by the Holy Ghost (Luke 1:35).

51. Woman's disposition was thought to be governed by her predominant humours, which were cold and moist. Temperance, however, was not one of her more usual attributes. See Sara Mendelson and Patricia Crawford, *Women in Early Modern England 1550–1720* (Oxford, Clarendon Press, 1998), pp. 19–20.

52. Genesis 3:16.

53. Instances of the incredible chastity of heathen women are numerous. Valerius Maximus, for instance, collected examples in *Factorum et Dictorum Memorabilium Libri*, including the story of the Greek woman who drowned herself to avoid rape, and of the wives of the conquered Teutons, who when they were refused their request to become vestal virgins, committed suicide *en masse*. [For a seventeenth-century translation, see Q. Valerius Maximus, *Collections of the Memorable Acts and Sayings of the Antient Romans* (London, 1684), Lib. VI. Chap. I, 'Of Chastity'.] The most famous example is of course the Roman matron Lucrece, who committed suicide after she had been raped. Vives mentions her example, not 'because others shoulde followe the deede, but the minde' (*Instruction of a Christian Woman*, sig. E4r).

54. In his *Christiani Matrimonii Institutio*, Erasmus approvingly reports Caesar's repudiation of his wife for merely *appearing* unchaste. *Opera Omnia*, ed. J. le Clerc (Leiden, 1703–6) V, 660. St Augustine reasoned against the suicide so often resorted to by the virgin martyrs. See *Of the Citie of God*, trans. J[ohn] H[ealey] (1610), Chapter 17.

55. *Michal*: with a rope, she lets down her husband David from a window so that he can escape the wrath of her father, Saul. *Abigail*: a woman 'of singular wisedome' who, while married to her churlish first husband, gives David good advice. She later becomes another of his wives. *Rachel*: 'beautifull and faire,' she is chosen by Jacob for his wife, over her elder sister Leah. *Judith*: heroine of the apocryphal book of Judith. While her city is under siege by the Assyrian general Holofernes, Judith not only encourages her people but manages to bring back Holofernes' head, which she has cut off after he has been lulled by wine and her deceiving words. *Anna*: or Hannah. She is a barren woman who prays and weeps for a son in the Temple – to the point where she is mistaken for a drunken woman by the Temple priest Eli.

56. *Morall vertues*: qualities of moral excellence which could be obtained without the help of religion (by virtuous pagans, for example); often opposed to the Christian virtues of faith, hope, and charity.

57. Leigh is alluding to Catholic devotion to the Virgin Mary. Prayers, especially the 'Ave Maria', were addressed directly to her.

58. Another criticism of 'papistical' religious practices. Puritans were distressed at the persistence of images or statues of saints in Jacobean churches; they regarded this as a violation of the Second Commandment (Exodus 20:4–5).

59. *Mathew, Marke, Luke, Iohn* were the four evangelists, and *Timothy* the apostle Paul's companion and helper. *Moses*: 'Moses was a very meeke man aboue all the men that were vpon the earth' (Numbers 12:3). *Samuel*: as child serving in the Temple, Samuel showed his obedience by responding repeatedly to a call which he thought was from the priest Eli, but which was in fact from God (1 Samuel 3). *Abraham*'s faithfulness was tested when God asked him to offer his son Isaac as a sacrifice. *Elias*: the Old Testament prophet Elijah.

60. *Frowardnes and curstnesse*: perverse ill temper.

61. *Schooles of learning*: presumably Leigh is thinking of grammar schools here, and so primarily of the education of boys.

62. Proverbs 22:6: 'Teach a child in the trade of his way, and when he is old he shall not depart from it.'

63. Matthew 6:33.

64. The flood in fact happens in Genesis 7.

65. Leigh does not want her sons to marry Catholics or Protestants who retain pre-Reformation practices and beliefs, such as the belief in purgatory as a place of penitential punishment intermediate between life on earth and heaven.

66. In other words, if a man does not love worldly goods, he will find a small amount sufficient for his needs. John is the 'beloued Apostle'. See note 41.

67. Rebecca says to her husband Isaac in Genesis 27:46: 'I am wearie of my life for the daughters of Heth.' They were living amongst the Canaanites, and Rebecca did not want her younger son to intermarry like his brother Esau, who had married a 'daughter of Heth', a Hittite.

68. *Friends*: in seventeenth-century usage, included relatives.

69. In the Geneva version, 1 Peter 3:7 advises husbands to give 'honour vnto the woman, as vnto the weaker vessel'. Leigh may have derived *beare with the woman*, and her thoughts following from the commentary on this passage: 'The more wisdome the husband hath, the more circumspectly hee must behaue himselfe in bearing those discommodities, which through the womans weakenesse oft times cause trouble.'

70. Leigh's emphasis on literacy for servants goes further than the advice given in Robert Cleaver's *A Godly Form of Household Government* (1598), which recommends that servants be catechized by their masters rather than taught to read scripture for themselves (p. 379).

71. See Joscelin's distinction between public and private prayer, note 61. In this chapter, Leigh is mostly concerned with the former.

72. Matthew 22:14: 'For many are called, but few chosen.'

73. Matthew 6:16 denounces the hypocrites' practice of disfiguring their faces to show they are fasting. Matthew 6:5 is in fact the more applicable verse: 'And when thou prayest, be not as the hypocrites: for they loue to stand, and pray in the Synagogues, and in the corners of the streets, because they would bee seene of men. Verely I say vnto you, they haue their reward.'

74. *Lets*: hindrances, obstacles [to prayer].

75. *World*: usually collocated with the flesh and the devil: the three things which seduce believers away from following God's commandments.

76. After their disobedience, Adam and Eve cover themselves with fig leaves and hide (Genesis 3:7–8). The doctrine of original sin deems that we inherit Adam's now fallen 'nature'. (Leigh lays out this doctrine fully in Chapter 28.)

77. See note 48.

78. On the Holy Spirit's part in self-mastery, see Chapter 31. *At it owne will: it* has possessive force here, cf. *Winter's Tale* 2.3.176–7, 'leave it, / Without more mercy, to it own protection'.

79. The Publican (who utters these words) shows his humility by 'standing a farre off' (which the Geneva notes gloss as 'Farre from the Pharise in a lower place').

80. Leigh's quotation is not from the Geneva Bible, which has: 'Come vnto me, all yee that are weary and laden, and I will ease you.' She is more likely making a composite of more than one translation. See Leigh, 'Introduction'.

81. The promises in Matthew 6 include forgiveness if we forgive others (verse 14), as well as provision of all earthly things – food, drink, and raiment – if we seek first the kingdom of God (verse 33).

82. See Joscelin, note 24.

83. The devil offers Jesus all the kingdoms of the world if he will bow down and worship him. Matthew 4:8–9.

84. In Numbers 11:5, the Israelites, who have escaped Egypt and are on their way through the wilderness to their promised new land, complain: 'We remember the fish which we did eate in Egypt for nought. . . .' *Figure*: symbol, typological representation.

85. Adam hears and hides from the 'voice of the Lord God' in the garden of Eden in Genesis 3:8 (see note 76). The Geneva commentary glosses this verse with the reflection that the 'sinfull conscience flieth Gods presence'. *Presently*: immediately.

86. *The world*: the ungodly, compare previous definition at note 75.

87. *His Wil and Testament*: the gospels.

88. Matthew 28:20.

89. Leigh seems to be recalling the nursery rhyme (well known, according to Iona and Peter Opie, in the time of Charles I):

> If all the world were Paper,
>
> And all the sea were Ink;
>
> If all the trees were bread and cheese,
>
> How should we doe for drink.

See *The Oxford Dictionary of Nursery Rhymes*, eds. I. and P. Opie (Oxford University Press, 1997), p. 525.

90. *Firebrand of hell*: one who is doomed to burn in hell.

91. A conflation of 1 John 2:15, quoted previously (see p. 31) and James 4:4: 'know yee not that the amitie of the world is the enimitie of God? Whosoeuer therefore will be a friend of the world, maketh himselfe the enemie of God.'

92. *Stalled*: brought to a standstill; or possibly glutted, satiated (*OED* s.v. 'stalled', a. 6).

93. James 4:4 (see note 91).

94. The devil suggests that the rich and faithful Job would curse God if his prosperity were taken away. But although God allows him to suffer affliction after affliction, Job persists as an example of righteousness and in the end is given twice as much as he had before.

95. Job 1:21. Leigh adds: *and as it pleaseth the Lord, so it commeth to passe.*

96. An allusion to the parable of the sower in Matthew 13: 'But he that receiued the seede in the good ground, is he that heareth the word, and vnderstandeth it, which also beareth fruit' (verse 23).

97. *That [they] could not heare*: 'they' added in the 1618 edition.

98. Luke 17:5.

99. Adam is created out of the 'dust of the ground' (Genesis 2:7).

100. *Appointment*: decree, dictation.

101. *A false religion, not warranted by the word of God*: Christianity which is not scripturally based. For Leigh, this seems to refer not only to Catholicism, but to 'profane' Protestants who may thereby be distinguished from the true 'children of God' (see below).

102. *The Psalmist*: the author of the Psalms, presumed to be King David. This quotation from Psalm 50:23 corresponds exactly to the King James version rather than to the Geneva.

103. *Waite vpon*: attend to; place their hope in (*OED* s.v. 'wait' v. 14h).

104. Leigh criticizes the Catholic praying of the rosary, in which the devotee keeps track of a set cycle of prayers with the mnemonic aid of a string of beads (formerly called 'a pair of beads').

105. The practice of endowing masses for the dead was believed to shorten the soul's time in purgatory. See note 65.

106. Catholic intercessory prayers to the Virgin Mary ('Our Lady') are compared to the Israelites' idolatrous worship of 'the Queene of heauen' (Geneva gloss: the 'Sunne, Moone and starres') which angers God in Jeremiah 7:18.

107. Matthew 7:11 has 'good things' rather than *holy Ghost*.

108. *In one word*: briefly.

109. The *Comforter* is explicitly equated with the Holy Ghost or Spirit in John 14:26 and 15:26 (see marginal note – probably misplaced – below).

110. John 16:13: 'when he is come which is the spirit of trueth, he will leade you into all trueth'.

111. John 15:26: 'But when that Comforter shall come whom I will send vnto you from the Father, euen the Spirit of trueth, which proceedeth of the Father, he shall testifie of me.'

112. The wording of both Tyndale's translation and the Great Bible.

113. *Affections*: passions, desires.

114. *Potsheard*: a broken piece of pot is both insignificant and a made thing; thus, insignificant man made by his Creator. For example, Isaiah 45:9: 'Woe bee vnto him that striueth with his maker, the potsheard with the potsherds of the earth: shal the clay say to him that fashioneth it, What makest thou?'

115. *Pine*: starve.

116. *To nought*: to nothing, to no good.

117. *Motion*: prompting, impulse.

118. *The temple of an harlot* is Leigh's own addition here, probably glancing at 1 Corinthians 6:16: 'Doe ye not know, that hee which coupleth himselfe with an harlot, is one body?'

119. *Custome*: see note 24 on *traditions*.

120. A parable of Leigh's own making. A master offers his servant a good pennyworth (or profit) from the renting of some of his land; but the servant must ask for it once the present lease expires. When the servant fails to do so, the master thinks better of his generosity.

121. Not a direct biblical quote, as far as I have been able to tell. Leigh could be alluding to any one of a number of biblical exhortations not to forget the poor.

122. *A deere price*: a high price; Christ 'buys' the sinner at the cost of his own life.

123. With divine help, the believer will be able to do something which the sinless Christ himself did not need to do; that is, overcome sin in his or her own self. In the next passage, Leigh quickly qualifies this: it is fact Christ who ultimately overcomes sin, even in oneself.

124. An allusion to Matthew 6:6, which Leigh quotes on p. 45.

125. *Preferment*: promotion.

126. *Cognisance*: a badge worn by the retainers of a noble house.

127. *Venemous earthworm*: for the (largely seventeenth-century) disparaging usage of *earthworm*, see *OED* s.v. 'earthworm' 2, which cites *De La Primaudaye's French Academie*: 'This generation of earth-wormes, which place nature . . . in the roome of the Creatour.'

128. As in 1 Corinthians 6:9–10. The remainder of the chapter speaks against fornication and the harlot (verses 15–16), which perhaps informs Leigh's criticism of 'strumpets and whores' below.

129. Psalm 10:3.

130. See note 83.

131. Leigh's own rendering of the proverbial 'Tread on a worm and it will turn' (see Tilly W909). (It is usually taken to mean that even the lowly resent ill-treatment.)

132. As the wicked cities of Sodom and Gomorrah were consumed with fire and brimstone in Genesis 19:24, so the earth and the wicked will be purged in the last days (see Revelations 8:7, 9:17–18).

133. Psalm 15:1–2: 'Lord, who shall dwel in thy Tabernacle? who shall rest in thine holy Mountaine? He that walketh vprightly and worketh righteousness, and speaketh the truth in his heart.' The Geneva commentary notes here that God requires 'trueth and simplicity in our words'.

134. *Ciuill men*: virtuous but unregenerate men; as opposed to the Saints (see note 40).

135. *Tithe*: a tenth part; given to the Lord, and for the maintenance of priests, as ordained by Mosaic law.

136. Luke 18:14: 'I tell you, this man departed to his house, iustified rather then the other: for euery man that exalteth himselfe shalbe brought low, and hee that humbleth himselfe shalbe exalted.'

137. Luke 18:2–7. The passage is closest to the Geneva version, but Leigh has probably reconstructed it from memory.

138. *Draw to a head*: the metaphor alludes to the maturation of a boil or abscess as well as to the emergence of one sin as 'leader' (*OED* s.v. 'head' sb. 14 and 25).

139. *Companie*: a military company. *Discomfited*: routed, defeated in battle.

140. *Braue*: defy, threaten. *Vpbraid*: reproach.

141. *Deuice*: (1) a trivial occupation or inclination; (2) a trap.

142. *Fowler*: a hunter of wild birds. Fowlers used nets and (evidently from Leigh's analogy) bait.

143. In Genesis 3:5 the serpent tempts Eve with the fruit of the forbidden tree, promising her, 'ye shall be as gods'. He does not, however, say, 'It is but an apple.'

144. *Engines*: nets or traps.

145. Adam and Eve are created in God's image (Genesis 1:27).

146. *Tares*: worthless and harmful weeds which grow among corn. For the parable of the tares, see Matthew 13.

147. *Drowned them*: that is, the 'earthen baits'. They were drowned in the flood announced in Genesis 6:17.

148. For the destruction of Sodom and Gomorrah, see note 132. *Counters*: imitation or debased coins (see *copper counters* below).

149. Puritan disapproval of secular recreation was expressed most strongly through rigid sabbatarianism, which included the prohibition of all Sunday pastimes unconnected with religious worship. In 1618, it was enough of a problem for James I to issue his 'Book of Sports', which declared unscriptural recreations such as church ales, morris dancing, and archery to be entirely lawful.

150. *Discouer*: reveal, expose.

151. Not the verse cited, but Psalm 55:12.

152. *Softlie*: easily, without strenuous effort. *Stay himselfe in a mean*: restrain himself with moderation.

153. See note 30.

154. *Casting*: calculating, scheming.

155. Not the verse cited, but 1 Peter 5:7.

156. 1 Timothy 1:15.

157. *Ouertake*: catch up with, reach.

158. Luke 4:18 and Matthew 11:28 put together. For the latter, see note 80.

159. *Nature*: that is, corrupt human nature. See note 76.

160. Psalm 1:6: 'the way of the wicked shall perish'. (The King James Bible has 'the ungodly'.)

161. Leigh alludes to miracles done by God for the Israelites: the parting of the Red Sea, so they could escape from pursuing Egyptian troops on dry land (Exodus 14:22), as well as manna and water miraculously appearing in the desert to feed them (Exodus 16:15, 17:6). For quails, see note 16.

162. The quotation includes the first half of verse 25 as well as Romans 7:24; but Leigh herself (and not scripture) provides the answer to the question: '*it is hee that must deliuer me from this body of death*'.

163. *Experience by your bodies*: venturing to trust God with the body; physical or emotional signs or states which confirm or give proof of faith (see *OED* s.v. 'experience' sb. 4b).

164. David tells the story of having killed a lion and a bear who were preying on his father's sheep in order to convince King Saul to allow him, a mere youth, to fight the Philistine giant. David's success leads to his marriage to Saul's daughter Michal. 1 Samuel:17–18.

165. Matthew 6:34 (as above at p. 58).

166. Luke 12:20.

167. *Labour for the meate* . . . : John 6:27, quoted by Leigh more than once. In the 1616 edition, the marginal citation of Matthew 6:28–9 is placed beside this quotation, but refers to the next: *Consider the Lillies* etc. (actually Matthew 6:28–30).

168. Hebrews 11:6.

169. To the annoyance of her sister Martha, Mary neglected the housework; instead she 'sate at Jesus feet, and heard his preaching' (Luke 10:39). Leigh continues to hypothesize about the man who sets his heart on worldly things.

170. The quotation extends to Matthew 6:33.

171. Perhaps an oblique reference to the promise of Mark 16:18, that believers will be able to take up serpents and drink poison without harm.

172. *Sillie*: defenceless, weak.

173. The *naturall man* does not have the benefit of divine revelation but can use his innate reason. Cf. 'civil man', note 134.

174. *Carefulnesse*: too much worry (or care) for the things of the world, as is warned against at length in the previous chapter.

175. '*For the loue of the world is enmity to God*' is Leigh's addition. The Geneva note to 1 John 2:15 could very well be at the back of Leigh's mind: 'The world which is full of wicked desires, lusts or pleasures, and pride, is vtterly hated of our heauenly Father. Therefore the Father and the world cannot be loued together: and this admonition is very necessary for greene and flourishing youth.'

176. Genesis 1:32.

177. Exodus 20:10–11.

178. *Beyond their calling*: beyond their means; or beyond what is appropriate to their rank.

179. *Discreet*: prudent; used also in this sense at the opening of Chapter 42.

180. *They cannot spend . . . when the time is*: they can neither spend nor save when they should.

181. Psalm 10:3.

182. *Humour*: disposition, character.

183. James 4:8: 'Draw neere to God, and he will draw neere to you. Clense your hands, ye sinners, and purge your harts, ye double minded.'

184. Leigh aligns herself with Puritan social and religious concerns and advocates activism: to address, for instance, the shortage of preaching ministers. For the reasons behind this shortage and for local Puritan solutions (such as the establishment of lectureships), see Christopher Hill, *The Century of Revolution 1603–1714*, 2nd edition (London, Norton, 1980), pp. 73–5.

185. *Let there be one the more for thee*: let your presence add one more true worshipper of God.

186. Proverbs 29:18: 'Where there is no vision, the people decay.' The Geneva note glosses: 'Where there are not faithfull ministers of the word of God.'

187. Here Leigh may have the Geneva Bible open before her. Not only does her quote correspond

word-for-word to its translation of Philippians 2:21, she also seems to be referring directly to the Geneva note which glosses *all* as 'The most part'.

188. Her son William did become a preacher and got into trouble for nonconformity in the 1630s. See Tom Webster, *Godly Clergy in Early Stuart England: The Caroline Puritan Movement* c. *1620–1643* (Cambridge University Press, 1997), pp. 208–9, and Leigh, 'Introduction'.

189. Isaiah 56:10–11: 'Their watchmen are all blind: they haue no knowledge: they are all dumbe dogs: they can not barke: they lie and sleepe, and delight in sleeping. And these greedy dogs can neuer haue enough: and these shepherds cannot vnderstand: for they all looke to their owne way, euery one for his aduantage, and for his owne purpose.' According to the Geneva note, this passage refers to 'the gouernours, prophets, & pastours, whose ignorance, negligence, auarice, and obstinancie prouoked Gods wrath against them'.

190. Colossians 3:1–2.

191. *For sinister respects*: for dishonest or malicious motives. Leigh seems to be thinking of her sons as potential landowners as well as potential preachers.

192. Deuteronomy 10:14.

193. Not this verse.

194. *A good peniworth*: see note 120.

195. *Title*: a legal right to possession.

196. Christian anti-semitism was underpinned by the charge that the Jews had been responsible for Christ's death.

197. *Ciuill man*: see note 134.

198. *Shadowed out*: represented, perforce imperfectly.

199. Ephesians 3:18–19: 'That yee, being rooted and grounded in loue, may be able to comprehend with all Saints, what is the breadth, and length, and depth and height: And to know the loue of Christ, which passeth knowledge, that yee may be filled with all fulnesse of God.'

200. Galatians 3:13: 'Christ hath redeemed vs from the curse of the Law, made a curse for vs, (for it was written, Cursed is euery one that hangeth on tree)'. The Geneva note explains: 'Christ was accursed for vs, because he bare the curse that was due to vs, to make vs partakers of his righteousness.'

201. The marginal citation is placed next to the first instance of the phrase '[he] tooke man by the hand', above. John 14:7: 'If yee had knowen me, yee should haue knowen my Father also: and from henceforth ye know him, and haue seene him.'

202. John 8:36: 'If that Sonne therefore shall make you free, yee shall be free indeed.'

203. Ecclesiastes 7:29 in the King James Bible: 'Lo, this only have I found, that God hath made man upright, but they have sought out many inventions.' Leigh is evidently *not* citing the Geneva Bible in this case, where the verse is numbered 31, nor the Great Bible, where it is 27.

204. John 3:16: 'For God so loued the world, that hee hath giuen his onely begotten Sonne, that whosoeuer beleeueth in him, should not perish, but haue euerlasting life.'

205. In John 11:25, Jesus says to Martha, who is sceptical that he will be able to raise her brother Lazarus from the dead: 'I am the resurrection and the life: he that beleeueth in mee, though he were dead yet shall he liue.'

206. The exact scriptural quotation is in fact from John 14:6. John 11:27 is similar: 'no man knoweth the Sonne, but the Father: neither knoweth any man the Father, but the Sonne, and he to whom the Sonne wil reueale him.'

207. In John 19:12, the Jews warn Pilate that if he releases Jesus, 'thou art not Cesars friend'.

208. *Keep watch and ward*: guard, exercise surveillance.

209. *Puddle*: pond.

210. *Vildly*: vilely.

211. See note 120 for a parable similar to this one, also of Leigh's own making. It is striking that she chooses to invent parables, taking her material from contemporary land ownership and patronage relations, rather than, for instance, making her points with very similar biblical parables (e.g. Matthew 24:48–51, 25:14–30).

212. *Out of*: without.

213. Titus 2:1: 'But speake thou the things which become wholesome doctrine.' The Geneva note comments that doctrine should not only be pure, but must be 'applied to all ages & orders of mē, according to yᵉ diuersity of circũstances'.

214. The 1616 text has 're | required' – evidently a printer's error.

215. *Liberalitie*: generosity. 1 Timothy 4:16: 'Take heede vnto thy selfe, and vnto learning: continue therein: for in doing this thou shalt both saue thy selfe, and them that heare thee.'

216. Luke 22:31–2.

Part II

ELIZABETH JOSCELIN

ELIZABETH JOSCELIN

Introduction

ELIZABETH JOSCELIN'S LEGACY TO HER UNBORN CHILD, 1622

S hortly before she died in childbed in October 1622, Elizabeth Joscelin wrote a 'letter' to the child she was carrying, in which she remarked: 'it may . . . appear strange to thee to receyue theas lines from a mother that dyed when thou weart born'. Joscelin's words do indeed seem strange and poignant to us – not only because her premonitions of dying in childbirth turned out to be true, but because she tried to embody her maternal advice and care in a text which would speak for her after her death. Reading Joscelin's legacy is like listening to a voice speaking from the grave.

The fear which impelled Joscelin to write was certainly not unrealistic. A recent study by Roger Schofield suggests that maternal mortality would have been most 'visible' to women in the twenty-five to thirty-four age group, in which one out of five deaths was related to childbearing. Elizabeth Joscelin was in the most risky group: aged twenty-six, expecting her first child. Although Schofield also suggests that maternal mortality in pre-industrial England was in fact lower than once thought (overall, a 6 to 7 per cent risk of dying in childbirth), Linda Pollock rightly points out that early modern women's *attitudes* to childbirth were shaped not so much by statistical risk as by the knowledge that any problem would almost certainly lead to a painful death.[1] Preparing spiritually for the possibility of death was therefore as much a part of a woman's pregnancy as taking physical care of herself and her unborn child. Women were advised to meditate and pray, and themselves solicited the prayers of others for strength and preservation during their time of trial.[2] While Joscelin's fear of death was not in itself unusual, then, her strong sense of its inevitability was. Although she assures her husband Taurell, 'my deare I dispayr not of life nay I hope and dayly pray for it if so god will be pleased', the greater part of the letter to him which prefaces her legacy is pervaded by grim resignation rather than hope. Its final words read like a deathbed blessing.

In the shadow of death, Joscelin sets about writing to the child she thinks she will not live to speak to, creating in her text a kind of surrogate mother who will be able to instruct her child after she is dead: 'a deputed Mother for instruction' as her first editor, Thomas Goad, called it.[3] Joscelin fears 'the losse my littell one should haue in wantinge mee': a deprivation not only material and emotional, but more seriously in her eyes, moral and spiritual. She is particularly afraid that her child will miss the 'religious trayninge' which it was both parents' duty to provide, but which was a mother's particular job in the child's first years. Male and female children alike were under the care and instruction of the mother until about the age of seven.[4] Puritan authors in particular stressed the importance of beginning religious training at this early impressionable age, for children were 'like vnto vessels which sauour of the liquor, wherewith they are first seasoned'.[5] In his *Domesticall Duties*, the Puritan preacher William Gouge wrote that mothers especially should note this 'point of *timely nurture*, as a point in peculiar appertaining to them', adding that experience confirms the mother's formative influence, as most children will follow the mother if mother and father differ in religion.[6]

Joscelin tells us it was a sense of 'motherly zeale' to fulfil this particular duty, in combination with her premonitory fear of death, that resolved her to leave her instruction as a written legacy – even though she declares she was 'ashamed' by the weakness of her writing. Yet her letter to her unborn child (or 'treatis', as she also calls it), holds its own against the 'public' treatises – like Gouge's treatise on the duties of children, the fifth of his *Domesticall Duties* – which Joscelin might have encountered. Joscelin's legacy is more concise, her advice more pithy, and her voice more eloquent. She gains authority through her proximity to death; as Gouge writes, the 'words of a dying parent are commonly most regarded' and 'doe make a deep impression'.[7] But she also calls upon the authority, as well as the intimacy, with which a mother addresses her child. Although she confesses there are 'many excellent books' in the world, she declares that she writes, 'not to the world but to mine own childe. whoo it may bee will more profit by a few weak instructions cominge from a dead mother (whoo cannot euery day prays or reproue it as it deserues) then far better from much more learned'. The particular eloquence of Joscelin's testament derives from its reproduction of the intimate speech act of maternal praise or reproof, which conveys to the reader the immediacy of a spoken exhortation.

But we gain this sense of immediacy only at a price. We are able to read Joscelin's legacy because she feared, and correctly predicted, that her actual spoken exhortations would be cut off by death. It is an irony that Joscelin's preventive measures, her laying up of her exhortations in written words, made her text available not only to her child, but to the world.

JOSCELIN'S LIFE AND DEATH

Elizabeth Joscelin was born Elizabeth Brooke in 1596, the only child of Richard Brooke and Elizabeth Chaderton. Richard Brooke was the eldest son of Thomas Brooke, Esquire, of Norton in Cheshire. In marrying Elizabeth Chaderton, he had done well for himself, for she was an heiress, the only child of William Chaderton, Bishop of Chester.[8] The Brooke family themselves came from Cheshire: the family seat was at Norton, north-east of Chester in the Bucklow Hundred.[9] It may be that the daughter of the local bishop and the local gentleman first met while Chaderton was busy pursuing Catholic recusants and nonconforming Puritans throughout his diocese – both of which groups he energetically sought to bring to conformity.[10] The marriage between Richard and Elizabeth, however, was clearly not a happy one. Three years after their only child, also named Elizabeth, was born, Richard Brooke was in Ireland, being knighted by the Earl of Essex and likely already separated from his wife.[11] Sir Peter Leycester reported, writing about the families and the history of Cheshire in the latter half of the seventeenth century, that 'through some dislike after Marriage, Sir *Richard* and . . . his Wife lived asunder'.[12] This may explain, as Leycester also reports, why Elizabeth 'had all her Mothers Lands' (her grandfather ensuring that his grand-daughter inherited rather than granting Sir Richard a life interest), as well as why she was raised in her grandfather's household. Still, Elizabeth's estrangement from her father was not complete. In her legacy, she recommends to her husband that their child, if a daughter, might be sent to live with her father and his second wife Katharine, to be educated with their daughters, her step-sisters.

In April 1595, Chaderton was elected to the Bishopric of Lincoln. He therefore moved east and took up residence, not in the episcopal palace at Buckden, but in an estate he had purchased about a mile away, at Southoe. It is here that Elizabeth must have received her education. It may have been here too, when she was only six years old, that she witnessed the death of her mother. With her last words, Elizabeth Brooke urged her daughter to obey and reverence both her father and her grandfather. Thomas Goad, who not only took charge of the editing of Elizabeth Joscelin's legacy but claimed to have known her personally, wrote of the deep impression her mother's deathbed scene made on her: an impression which may very well have helped her form the resolve to leave her own last words to her unborn child.[13]

At Southoe, Elizabeth seems to have been educated early and more learnedly than most girls of her class. Bishop Chaderton took an active part in her lessons. Goad tells us that it was 'by and vnder' him that 'shee was from her tender yeeres carefully nurtured, as in those accomplishments of knowledge in Languages, History, and some Arts, so principally in studies of piety'. As Chaderton had been successively Lady Margaret and Regius Professor of Divinity at Cambridge, as well as president of Queen's College, Elizabeth could hardly have had a more learned man to oversee her studies. Chaderton had also, as a young man, written Latin verses which were printed in Barnaby Googe's translation of Palingenius, the *Zodiake of Life*, in 1561.[14] As part of her training in languages, Elizabeth evidently learned Latin, for Goad praises her ability to memorize Latin as well as English poetry, 'enabling her vpon the first rehearsall to repeat aboue 40. lines'.[15]

Elizabeth's early education was closer to that a boy would have received, particularly in its attention to languages (especially Latin), history, and 'some Arts'; that is, the liberal arts, traditionally, grammar, logic, rhetoric, arithmetic, geometry, music, and astronomy. This may have been a consequence of her mother's relatively early death and the part her grandfather had in her studies. Ordinarily, a

looking glasse whearin to
see when J am too seuear
when too remiss and in
my childes fault thorough
this glass discern mine own
error, and J hope god wil
so giue me his grace that
J shall more skillfully act
then apprehend a mothers
duty: my dear thou
knowest me so well J shall
not need to tell thee J haue
written honest thoughts in
a disordred fashion not
obseruinge method for thou
knowst how short J am of
learninge and naturall
endowments to take such
a cours in writinge, or if
that stronge affection of thi
haue hid my weaknes from
thy sight J now professe

The conclusion of Elizabeth Joscelin's epistle to her husband Taurell. Additional
Manuscript 27, 467, fols. 5v, 6r. (*By permission of the British Library*)

seriously my own ignoranc
and though I did not, this
following treatif would
betray it, but I send it only
to the eys of a most louing
houfband and a childe ex
ceedingely beloued to whom
I hope it will not be all togethe Un
profitable Thus humbly de
siringe god to giue thee all
comfort in this life and hap
pines in the life to com I
leaue thee and thine to his
most gracious protectyon :

Thine inviolable

Eliza Jofcelin

girl of her class would have spent most of her time on needlework, learning the skills she would need to manage a household, and reading the Bible.[16] She would, in fact, have received the sort of education that Elizabeth Joscelin's step-sisters received: 'learninge the Bible . . . good huswifery, writing, and good work'.

Given her own relatively liberal upbringing, it is perhaps surprising that this is exactly the education Joscelin recommends in her legacy for her own daughter: 'other learninge a woman needs not'. But it is also notable that she hedges on the question, admitting her admiration for learned women 'whom god hathe blesst wth discretion' and declaring that a woman who manages to be learned, wise, and virtuous is 'the fittest closet for all good∧⌐nes⌐'. Joscelin's vacillation at this point in the legacy, and her evident self-consciousness when contemplating the virtuous learned lady – '. . . she is; indeed I should but shame my selfe if I should go about to prays her more' – suggest that she was troubled about the compatibility of learning with female virtue not just in her daughter's life, but in her own. Her training in her grandfather's household still left her with conventional fears about women being spoiled by learning: sinking under its burden like a small boat driven underwater by too large a sail. Joscelin uses this very image when discussing the education of a daughter, and likely borrowed it from Sir Thomas Overbury's immensely popular characterization of an ideal wife. As far as knowledge and understanding go, Overbury is clear about where he draws the line in a woman:

> A *passive vnderstanding* to conceiue,
> And *Iudgement* to discerne, I wish to find,
> Beyond that, all as hazardous I leaue,
> *Learning* and *pregnant wit* in Woman-kind,
>   What it findes malleable maketh fraile,
>   And doth not adde more *ballaste*, but more *saile*.[17]

Nonetheless, later in her legacy, Joscelin suggests that it is the 'wise or learned or religious woman' who is most worthy of commendation. Here, her less unequivocal endorsement of women's learning is too much for the editor of the first printed version of her legacy, who changes 'learned' to 'honest' (that is, 'chaste').[18]

As her mother's death deeply impressed her when she was six, so too must have her grandfather's death when she was about twelve. William Chaderton died suddenly at Southoe in the spring of 1608, leaving Elizabeth as his heir. It is not known where she spent the next eight years, between the death of her grandfather and her marriage in 1616. It may be that she was with her father, Sir Richard, now Lord of the Manor in Norton, his father having conveyed the family seat to his son and heir for life in 1607.[19]

With all her mother's lands, Elizabeth Brooke would have been an eminently marriageable woman. In 1616, at the age of twenty, she married Taurell, son and heir of Sir Thomas Joscelin of Willingale, Essex.[20] The unusual first name commemorates inherited wealth: Taurell's paternal grandfather Henry married Anne Torell, daughter and heiress of 'Humfridus de Torell'. As well as wealth, Taurell also had at least one eminent scholar in his family: the brother of the same paternal grandfather Henry, and so Taurell's great-uncle, was John Joscelyn the Anglo Saxonist.[21] Taurell himself matriculated in 1606 as a 'fellow-commoner' of Jesus College, Cambridge. The date of Taurell's matriculation suggests that he must have been about six or seven years older than Elizabeth, a usual age for going up to university being sixteen or seventeen. Two years later, following a typical path for young men of wealth and station, he was admitted to Lincoln's Inn.[22] By the 1620s, he held an estate called Crowlands in Oakington, a village four miles north-west of Cambridge.[23] It is here that Elizabeth must have composed her mother's legacy.

Elizabeth Joscelin's marriage was clearly much happier than her own parents' had been. Unlike Sir Thomas Overbury, Taurell must have been tolerant of the idea of a learned wife, perhaps even sympathetic, for Elizabeth continued her studies after her marriage. Goad writes that, beside 'the domestique cares pertaining to a wife', she spent the first years after her marriage studying 'morality and history, the better by the help of forraine languages'. He also tantalizes us with the information that she was helped in her studies by her 'taste and faculty in Poetry'. Goad says no more than this, but his words suggest that Joscelin might have been reading long didactic poems like du Bartas' *La Sepmaine*, or, even more aptly, the Latin *Zodiacus Vitae* of Palingenius, for whose English translation her grandfather had composed Latin verses.[24] Most tantalizingly of all, Goad tells us that she did leave behind 'some essay' in poetry, which he characterizes as 'ingenious, but chaste and modest, like the Author'.[25] Unfortunately, Goad did not see fit to preserve the poems as he did the legacy. Whether they have survived somewhere, and could be found, is an open question.

Goad also notes that Joscelin made very little reference to her considerable knowledge in conversation. This modesty or reticence carried over into her writing. With the exception of a brief, commonplace reference to Aeneas, and the possible allusion to *A Wife*, one would not guess from Joscelin's legacy that she had any interest in poetry, any knowledge of a language other than English, any interest in any study except piety. Another detail supplied by Goad suggests an explanation. In the years before her death she gave up all studies except divinity.[26] Divinity is also the principal study she recommends to her child. Perhaps she felt that her laboriously acquired and, for a woman of the time, exceptional knowledge was tempting her to pride – a sin against which she warns at some length in her legacy. Certainly in dedicating herself to a single-minded study of the things of God, Joscelin made a self-denying decision, performed an act of mortification which anticipates the rhetorical self-abnegation of her legacy. The decision must not have been an easy one, judging from the sustained ambivalence of her writing on the subject of 'a learned daughter'.

For her study of divinity, Joscelin almost certainly made a close study of the Geneva Bible, whose translation and annotations were favoured by the more godly sort of Protestant. Joscelin's biblical quotations and even her spelling of biblical names (as, for example, 'Jaakob') correspond most closely to the Geneva version.[27] Her 'near misses' suggest some interesting possibilities for her reading and writing practices. She *nearly* quotes Luke 14:11, for instance. Her rendition of the verse – 'whoosoeuer exalltethe himselfe shall bee humbled' – is an effective compression of the Geneva version: 'For whosoeuer exalteth himselfe, shall be brought lowe, and he that humbleth himselfe, shall be exalted'. Joscelin's compression, and her retention of the essential Geneva vocabulary, suggests that she was working from memory. The fact that she added the scriptural citation '{Lu 14 11}' in the margin, seemingly after writing her version of the verse, strengthens the memory hypothesis: either she retained chapter and verse in her memory as well (as Dorothy Leigh seems routinely to have done), or she looked them up afterwards to verify what she had written. Often she gets the Geneva wording exactly right, but uses her own idiosyncratic spelling – again suggesting that she did not ordinarily write with a Bible open in front of her, but that she had an extraordinarily rentetive memory, as Goad attests. It is clear from her legacy that she had absorbed large parts of the Bible. Biblical language is woven into her text: not just quotations and near quotations, but biblical paraphrases, pastiches, and metaphors. The endnotes document some of this intertextual play, but it is impossible to do justice to the full extent of Joscelin's immersion in the rhetoric of the Bible, as well as its teaching.

Joscelin writes of there being 'so many excellent books' that her own treatise might seem unnecessary, were it not for the unique and intimate relationship between its author and intended reader. As part of her study of divinity, Joscelin evidently continued to read some of these 'excellent books' of godly devotion or instruction. An author whom she certainly knew and used daily was Henry Smith, a Puritan preacher who died in 1591, but whose works were still being reprinted in the 1620s and 1630s. In her legacy, Joscelin recommends Smith's morning and evening prayers for daily use, and probably did not do so unadvisedly: they are both long, dwelling on the corruption of the will and the inescapable burden of sin – relieved only by divine grace (see notes 59 and 96). Joscelin's characterization of these prayers as 'for a family' suggests that she was reading the issue of the prayers which was appended to *A Preparatiue to Mariage* (1591).[28] Because Joscelin, then, almost certainly owned a copy of *A Preparatiue*, I have used it for some of the contextual notes to her legacy, in addition to William Gouge's *Of Domesticall Duties*, which was published in 1622, the year in which she was writing the legacy – also the year of her pregnancy, and her death.[29]

The most immediate influence on her writing, however, may have been another woman. Dorothy Leigh's *Mothers Blessing* was first published in 1616, the year of Joscelin's marriage. More than the treatises of Smith or Gouge, Leigh's mother's legacy may have been the model upon which she based her own text.

There are numerous similarities between the two legacies which argue influence and perhaps emulation.[30] I note some of them in the endnotes to Joscelin's text.

Occupying herself with study and housewifely duty, Joscelin seems also to have had the sort of godly companionate marriage recommended by Smith in his *Preparatiue to Mariage*. This model emphasized the spiritual and emotional dependence of the married couple and their equality as co-governors of a Christian family – although in the relationship of husband and wife, the former remained the head of the latter.[31] True to the nature of their spiritual partnership, Elizabeth makes Taurell the 'ouerseer' of her legacy. She addresses him affectionately in her prefatory letter as 'my truly louinge and most Dearly loued husband', and later as 'deare loue' and 'dear hart'. Although she maintains a posture of humility (especially about the quality of her writing) and of wifely deference (in leaving Taurell the final decision on a daughter's education), it is also worth noting that Elizabeth's prefatory letter gives detailed, firm, and authoritative advice to her husband about how their child ought to be raised. It appears that she was used to sharing her thoughts with Taurell. She writes, towards the end, 'I know thou wonderest by this time, what the caus should bee that wee too continually vnclaspinge our harts one to another I should reserue thi[s] to write.' To explain, she asks him to 'remember how greeuos it was to thee but to hear me say I may dy'. Taurell Joscelin also seems to have been troubled by the dangerous time approaching for his wife.[32]

The usual fears associated with childbirth may have been exacerbated by the lateness of this first child. Elizabeth and Taurell Joscelin had been married six years: in most cases conception occurred within ten months of marriage.[33] Joscelin begins her legacy by recalling how 'longe often and earnestly' she had prayed that she might become a mother. Once she did diagnose the signs of pregnancy, her reaction, as recounted by Goad, was to prepare herself for the worst. In this 'later time', Goad writes,

> the course of her life was a perpetuall meditation of death, . . . euen then when she had not finished the 27. yeere of her age, nor was oppressed by any disease, or danger, other than the common lot of child-birth, within some months approaching. Accordingly whẽ she first felt her selfe quicke with childe (as then trauelling with death it selfe) she secretly tooke order for the buying a new winding-sheet.[34]

Buying one's own winding-sheet or shroud seems to us an excessively morbid gesture, but such gestures were far from uncommon in a religious culture which taught that preparation for death was a lifelong process, a 'perpetuall meditation'. Joscelin used her shroud as a *memento mori*, much as John Donne would use his as both prop and reminder in his own preparation for death a decade later. Donne had himself drawn: eyes closed, standing on an urn, wrapped in his burial sheet.

The drawing was used for his funeral monument in St Paul's, but Donne himself (in a gesture that Joscelin also anticipates, as we shall see) kept it at his bedside during his last illness.[35] Joscelin's other tangible demonstration of her preparedness for death was of course the writing of the legacy itself – which Goad suggests she began about the time she ordered the winding-sheet.

Joscelin never finished her legacy. Goad speculates that she was prevented from doing so either by miscalculating the time of her delivery or because of 'some troubles befalling her about a moneth before her end'.[36] Did she now have surer signs of approaching death, in the form of sickness? On 12 October 1622, she gave birth to a daughter. The child was baptized Theodora, 'gift of God', after the child's grandmother, Taurell's mother.[37] As soon as her daughter had been baptized, Joscelin called for the winding-sheet to be brought out and laid upon her. Like Donne, she may have been certain now that she was enduring her last illness. She died after a 'violent fever' lasting nine days, giving, as Goad reports, 'a comfortable testimony of her godly resolution' at the end. She was buried in the church at Oakington on 26 October.[38]

THE AUTOGRAPH MANUSCRIPT AND EDITORIAL INTERFERENCES

Elizabeth Joscelin's legacy is most often read in the version which was printed two years after her death as *The Mothers Legacie, To her Vnborne Childe* (London, 1624). This version, however, differs significantly from Joscelin's own manuscript of the legacy, now in the British Library (Additional Manuscript 27,467).

The text which follows is that of the British Library autograph. It is signed 'Eliza Joscelin' and uses the same practised italic hand – of the sort usually taught to women – throughout. (See Plates, pp. 94–5.) The manuscript contains a number of suggestive authorial revisions and self-corrections, which are also reproduced in the following text. These revisions are traces of the process of writing, and often of choice and struggle in Joscelin's attempt to voice authoritative maternal instruction. Revisions often occur at points where Joscelin is referring to her own writing or writerly ability: where she hopes, for instance, that her legacy will 'not be vnprofitable' (revised to the hope that 'it will not be ∧[alltogether] vnprofitable'). Similarly, her wish for 'eloquence' is revised to a wish for 'skill to write'.

Also reproduced in the following text (as footnotes) are the substantive changes which the first printed edition of 1624 made to Joscelin's legacy. This first appearance of Joscelin's writing in print – and presumably the interference with her text – was supervised by Thomas Goad, whose introductory 'Approbation' to the 1624 *Legacie* has been referred to several times in the section on Joscelin's 'Life and Death'. Goad evidently knew Joscelin, perhaps from her childhood, and if not present at her death, certainly had an account of it from an immediate witness. In his 'Approbation', Goad declares he has 'heretofore bin no stranger to the Testators education and eminent vertues'. For this reason, and because, as he puts it, he felt himself 'bound to do right vnto knowne vertue', he 'vndertooke the care of the publication thereof'.[39] Goad might have come to know Joscelin and to be interested in her posthumous legacy through their respective connections to the Church hierarchy. Goad was ordained a minister in 1606, and became a Bachelor of Divinity in 1607, the year before Bishop Chaderton died. In subsequent years, Goad rose quickly in the hierarchy, holding livings in Cambridgeshire, Suffolk, and Essex, and becoming domestic chaplain to George Abbot, the Archbishop of Canterbury, in 1611. As chaplain to Abbot, Goad had an additional interest in Joscelin's legacy: archepiscopal chaplains had the job of licensing works for the press, and Goad did in fact license Joscelin's work, as the entry in the Stationer's Register for 12 January 1623/4 shows.[40] He refers obscurely to his part in licensing Joscelin, punning on the two senses of his 'Approbation': 'vpon the very first view, I willingly . . . subscribed my *Approbat* for the registering this *Will* among the most publique Monuments'.[41]

Whether Thomas Goad was the sole source of the changes, or whether he worked as editor in collaboration with a copyist, is impossible to verify without further evidence. The changes made in the 1624 *Legacie* are generally additions and expansions, suggesting that Goad made or was working from a copy of Joscelin's autograph – he or the scribe (or both) adding to Joscelin's words, less frequently substituting another word for one of hers, and, least frequently of all, cutting a word or phrase. Sometimes the changes seem entirely gratuitous – particularly towards the end of the legacy. Why replace 'force' with 'inueigle', for instance? Some of the changes certainly suggest a proprietorial care for the duties and privileges of the ministry. Others – like Joscelin's commendation of the 'learned' woman, changed to 'honest' – bring Joscelin's words more strictly in line with conventional gender expectations. Still others moderate Joscelin's zeal where it verges too close to outspoken Puritanism: where she advises an extremely rigorous observation of the Sabbath, for instance.[42]

Editorial interference with Joscelin's text did not end with its publication in 1624. Sixty years later, in 1684, an edition of Joscelin's legacy printed at Oxford excised her recommendation of the Puritan Henry Smith's prayers, replacing them with *The Book of Common Prayer*.[43] Joscelin was re-appropriated for post-Restoration conformity, just as she had been appropriated by Goad's edition as an approved model of feminine piety, of 'knowne vertue'. Some of the seemingly unmotivated changes of the first edition may have been made, then, just for the sake of sealing this appropriation: interference for the sake of interference.

THE TEXT OF ELIZABETH JOSCELIN'S LEGACY

In editing Additional Manuscript 27,467, I have tried to make a representation of the manuscript which is both readable and as faithful to the original as possible, without being a full diplomatic transcription. Editing inevitably involves transformation, however, and I shall here outline my transformations of the original copytext, and the thinking behind them.

Add MS 27,467 is a small duodecimo volume, with trimmed pages measuring 7 cm x 12 cm. It was rebound in blue velvet some time in the nineteenth century. It consists of sixty folios, numbered as follows: 2 blanks, fols. 1–6, 3 blanks, fols. 7–8, 6 blanks, fols. 9–44, and 5 blanks. In addition, two extra leaves were added both at the beginning and at the end when the manuscript was rebound.[44]

Because Joscelin's text is written on such tiny pages, she normally averages only about six or seven words per line, and between about twenty and twenty-five lines per page. Joscelin uses punctuation sparsely; sometimes her line breaks work as marks of punctuation, breaking up the sense of long lines of thought or forcing a pause. I represent line breaks with four spaces: this should allow continuous reading, while still indicating the breaks in the copytext. Joscelin sometimes marks the end of a page with a double vertical slash ||, and in one instance, brings a passage to an emphatic close with a series of colons, one curly bracket, and a dash (see p. 120). All such marks are reproduced in the text. Joscelin's own paragraphing (such as the beginning of a numbered section or chapter) is indicated by an indentation. In the interests of readability, I have sometimes broken up long blocks of texts by interposing a blank line, but no indentation. I have done so, however, only where the text seems to allow such a break. For instance, where Joscelin ends a line short and begins the next with a fresh thought, I leave a blank line between the two.

As with the texts of Leigh and Richardson, my interpolations are enclosed by square brackets [ ], material written in the margin is enclosed in curly brackets { }, and revisions inserted over the line are enclosed in half-square brackets ⌈ ⌉.

Endnotes provide further information about the appearance of the manuscript, as well as providing the usual glossarial and contextual notes. Footnotes reproduce substantial changes made in the 1624 edition, but do not note minor changes of spelling or punctuation. This should allow readers to see, quickly and easily, which parts of Joscelin's text attracted editorial interference.

In editing Joscelin's legacy, my intention has been in some sort to reverse the historical fate of much religious writing by early modern women: its marginalization, as well as its appropriation by seventeenth-century male editors for the purposes of edification and exemplarity. Here I have made the woman's text, with its own uncertainties and self-contradictions, central. Subsequent editorial interference is documented, but is placed at the margins.

Notes

1. R. Schofield, 'Did the Mothers Really Die?', in *The World We Have Gained: Histories of Population and Social Structure*, eds L. Bonfield *et al.* (Oxford, Basil Blackwell, 1986), pp. 255, 259. Linda A. Pollock, 'Embarking on a Rough Passage: The Experience of Pregnancy in Early Modern Society', in *Women as Mothers in Pre-Industrial England*, ed. Valerie Fildes (London, Routledge, 1990), pp. 47–8. Pollock quotes Joscelin's apprehension of 'the paynfullnes of that kinde of death' from her prefatory letter to her

husband. For the fear with which women approached childbirth, see also Patricia Crawford, 'The Construction and Experience of Maternity in Seventeenth-Century England', in Fildes (ed.), p. 22.

2. Pollock, pp. 47–8. In *The Monument of Matrones: The Fift Lampe of Virginitie* (1582), Thomas Bentley provides numerous prayers for a woman with child or 'in trauell', as well as a morbid series 'if the partie be in long and sore trauell, and in danger of death' or when 'she is departing and yeeldeth vp the ghost'. Sigs. O5v–O6r.

3. 'The Approbation', *The Mothers Legacie, to Her Vnborne Childe* (1622), sig. a6r.

4. At seven, girls and boys were separated, the latter now dressed in breeches and placed under the care of their fathers. See Ralph Houlbrooke, *The English Family 1450–1700* (London, Longman, 1984), p. 150.

5. Francis Dillingham, *Christian Oeconomy, Or Household Government* (1609), p. 37. See Joscelin's *Legacy*, note 31.

6. Gouge, *Of Domesticall Duties* (1622), p. 546.

7. Gouge, p. 568.

8. Richard Brooke's first wife is identified in his funeral certificate as 'Elizabeth, daughter and heyre to William Chatterton, Bushop of Chester'. J.P. Rylands (ed.), *Cheshire and Lancashire Funeral Certificates A.D. 1600 to 1678*, Record Society of Lancashire and Cheshire, VI (1882), p. 43. A Visitation of 1613 confirms 'Elizabeth' (contrary to Chaderton's *DNB* article, which has 'Joan', and Sir Peter Leycester's *Historical Antiquities*, which has 'Jane'). G.J. Armytage and J.P. Rylands (eds), *Pedigrees Made at the Visitation of Chesire. 1613*, Record Society of Lancashire and Cheshire, LVIII (1909), 45.

9. Sir Richard's grandfather (another Richard, the younger son of Thomas Brooke of Leighton) purchased the manor of Norton from Henry VIII in 1545. It included a dissolved priory (which thenceforth became the seat of the Brookes of Norton), as well as all the property in the town. P. Leycester, *Historical Antiquities* [Chester] (1673) II, 326. *The Victoria History of the Counties of England: A History of the County of Chester* (Oxford, 1950) III, p. 169.

10. *Victoria History: Chester*, III, pp. 23–5.

11. The Earl of Essex knighted 'Robart Brooke' in Dublin on 10 Sept 1599 – just before returning, against the Queen's orders, from his disastrous Irish campaign. W.A. Shaw, *Knights of England* (Baltimore, Genealogical Publishing, 1971), II, p. 97.

12. Leycester, II, 327.

13. 'Approbation', sig. a2r. Goad's 'Approbation' – his introduction to the 1624 edition of Joscelin's legacy – is an important source for biographical details about Elizabeth Joscelin, particularly concerning her education and death. Goad provides a level of detail not usually available in comparable texts, like women's funeral sermons; his very specificity credits his details. Nonetheless, it is important to remember – particularly where it is not possible to corroborate Goad – that his purpose is 'approbation'. (See 'The Autograph Manuscript and Editorial Interferences' below.)

14. 'In Gogaei aeditionem', *The Firste Syxe Bokes of the Mooste Christian Poet Marcellus Palingenius, Called the Zodiake of Life*, trans. Barnaby Googe (London, 1561).

15. 'Approbation', sigs. a1r, a3v.

16. Sara Mendelson and Patricia Crawford, *Women in Early Modern England 1550–1720* (Oxford, Clarendon, 1998), pp. 90–1.

17. *A Wife Now the Widdow of Sir Thomas Ouerburye* (1614), sig. C1r. (See Joscelin's *Legacy*, note 8.)

18. See p. 116 footnote a.

19. R. Stewart-Brown (ed.), *Cheshire Inquisitions Post Mortem, Stuart Period 1603–1660: Vol. I, A–D*, Record Society of Lancashire and Cheshire, LXXXIV (1934), 86.

20. A pedigree of 1627 (added to the manuscript of the 1612 Visitation of Essex; see Harl. Soc., XIII, 226–30) gives the surname of the family as 'Josselyn' or 'Jocelin' and latinizes Elizabeth's husband as 'Torrellus'. Elizabeth signs herself, however, as 'Elizabeth Joscelin' and writes to her husband as 'Taurell' in the autograph manuscript which I have used as the copytext for her legacy. I adopt these last spellings as my standard.

21. Harl. Soc., XIII, 229–30.

22. 'Torrell Joselin', *Alumni Cantabrigienses*, Part I (Cambridge University Press, 1922). Fellow-commoners were privileged undergraduates, ordinarily the sons of wealthy gentlemen. The name derives from one of their perks: they dined at a common table with the fellows of the college. Houlbrooke notes that the median age of entry at Oxford was sixteen-and-a-half in 1600. *The English Family*, p. 167.

23. William Chaderton's old college of Queen's, Cambridge had purchased the estate of Crowlands in 1560. Perhaps helped by his wife's connections, Taurell obtained the manor under a beneficial lease; that is, he could use and profit from the estate, but not pass it on. *The Victoria History of the Counties of England. A History of the County of Cambridge and the Isle of Ely* (1989) IX, p. 195.

24. Du Bartas' epic account of the seven days of creation (translated into English by Joshua Sylvester 1592–1608) was favoured by well-educated women of the period. Anne Bradstreet, for instance, composed a poem in praise of Du Bartas, and Lady Anne Clifford included 'All Du Bartas his Workes' as one of the painted background books in her autobiographical triptych. Richard T. Spence, *Lady Anne Clifford: Countess of Pembroke, Dorset and Montgomery (1590–1676)* (Stroud, Sutton, 1997), p. 188. Palingenius' *Zodiacus Vitae* was used as a school textbook and so was widely available. Although its twelve books were named after signs of the zodiac, it is really a compendious moral treatise in verse which discusses, among other topics, marriage and celibacy and the duties of parenthood. See J.W. Binns, *Intellectual Culture in Elizabethan and Jacobean England: The Latin Writings of the Age* (Leeds, Francis Cairns, 1990), pp. 114–15.

25. 'Approbation', sigs. a3r–v.

26. 'Approbation', sig. a4r.

27. Accordingly, for scriptural notes on her text, I have used an edition of the Tomson/Junius Geneva Bible, printed by Robert Barker in London in 1610. Joscelin's biblical quotations were checked [using *The New Testament Octapla*, ed. L.A. Weigle (New York, Thomas Nelson, 1962)] against all the major Protestant English translations of scripture she could have known: Tyndale's, the Great Bible, the Bishop's Bible, the King James Bible, and the Geneva.

28. STC 22686.

29. Although the date on the title page is 1622, *Of Domesticall Duties* was entered into the Stationer's Register on 28 October 1620.

30. Kristen Poole has suggested that the two women may have been related. ' "The Fittest Closet for all Goodness": Authorial Strategies of Jacobean Mothers' Manuals', *Studies in English Literature 1500–1900*, 35.1 (1995), pp. 83–5. The funeral certificate of Thomas Brooke (Elizabeth's paternal grandfather) notes that three of Elizabeth's aunts married Leighs of Cheshire, *Cheshire and Lancashire Funeral Certificates*, Rec. Soc. Lancs. Ches., VI, 45–6. But whether Dorothy Leigh's husband was related to these high-status Leigh families in Cheshire is doubtful (see Dorothy Leigh, Introduction).

If Joscelin *was* led to Dorothy Leigh's mother's legacy through family connections, it is more likely to have been because Ralph Leigh was a distant poor relation of the Cheshire Leighs, or because the coincidence of name made the book interesting to her.

31. For Smith, the 'man and wife are partners, like two oars in a boat'. Still, the woman is the 'weaker vessel', and so in any disagreement must be entreated 'with gentlenesse and softnesse' rather than with blows. *Preparatiue to Mariage*, pp. 52–3. See also Margo Todd, 'The Spiritualized Household', in *Christian Humanism and the Puritan Social Order* (Cambridge University Press, 1987).

32. Compare Edward Dering's words to his wife Unton in 1630: 'God in heaven blesse thee, and oure hopefull burthen, for I cary in my heart ye paynes thou sufferest for me.' Quoted in Pollock, p. 52.

33. Mendelson and Crawford, p. 149.

34. 'Approbation', sigs. a4v–a5r.

35. R.C. Bald, *John Donne: A Life* (Oxford, Clarendon, 1970), pp. 528–9.

36. 'Approbation', sig. a4r.

37. A Visitation of Kent (Harl. Soc. 42.118) names Taurell's mother as Theodora, daughter of Edmund Cooke and widow of Clement Beere of Dartford.

38. 'Approbation', sigs. a5v–a6r. BL MS Add 5849, fol. 93r.

39. 'Approbation', sigs. A4v–a1r.

40. Edward Arber, *A Transcript of the Registers of the Company of Stationers of London; 1554–1640 A.D.*, IV (London, 1877), p. 72.

41. 'Approbation', sig. A4v.

42. Both Goad's editorial interference and Joscelin's self-corrections are more fully discussed in Sylvia Brown, 'The Approbation of Elizabeth Jocelin', *English Manuscript Studies 1100–1700*, 10 (2000).

43. Instead of Smith's morning prayer, the 1684 edition advises 'such Praiers as are publickly allowed, and chiefly those appointed by the Church'. *The Mothers Legacy to her Unborn Child* (Oxford: 'Printed at the Theater for the satisfaction of the *Person* of *Quality* herein concerned' . . . 1684), p. 47. See also pp. 78–80. Could the 'Person of Quality' have been Joscelin's daughter Theodora? In 1647, she married Samuel Fortrey, who later became a Gentleman of Charles II's Privy Chamber. Theodora would have been sixty-two in 1684.

44. For a detailed description of the manuscript, see Brown, Appendix, 'The Approbation of Elizabeth Jocelin'.

Elizabeth Joscelin's Manuscript Mother's Legacy

To my truly louinge and
most Dearly loued husband
Taurell Jocelin.[a]

Myne own deare loue I no   sooner conceyued a hope[b] that I   should bee made a mother by thee   but wth it entered the considera=   tion of a mothers duty and shortly after   followed the apprehension of   danger that might preuent me   for [sic] executinge that care, I so ex=   ceedingly desired. I mean in reli=   gious trayninge our childe, and   in truthe deathe appearinge in   this shape was doubly terrible   vnto mee first in respect of the   paynfullnes of that kinde of death   an[d] next the losse[c] my littell one   should haue in wantinge mee   but I thanke god theas fears wear   cured wth the remembrance that   all things worke together for the   best to those that loue god.[1] || [fol. 1v] And a certayn assurance that   hee will giue mee patience accor   dinge to my payn. yet still   I thought theare was som good   office I might doo for my childe   more then only to bring it forthe   (though it should pleas god to take   me) when I considered our   fraylty our apt inclination to   sin the diuells subtlety and the worlds deceytfullnes from[d] theas   how much I desired to admonish   it. but still it came into my   minde that deathe ~~would~~ [might] depriue   me of time If I should neglect   the present. I knew not what to doo   I thought of writinge but   then my own weaknes appea   red so manifestly that I was   ashamed and durst not vnder   take it. but when I could finde   no other means to express my   motherly zeale I encoraged my   selfe wth theas reasons first that I   wrote to a childe and though I   [fol. 2r] weare but a woman yet to a   childes iudgement: what I vnder   stood might serue for a foun   dation to better learning. agayn   I considered it was to my own   not to the world[e] and my loue   to my own might excuse my   errors: and lastly but cheefly   I comforted my selfe that my   intent was good and that I was   well assured god was the prosperer   of good purposes: thus resolued I   writ this ensuinge l^r [i.e. letter] to our little   one to whom I could not finde a   fitter hand to conuey it then thine   own: wch mayst wth authority   see the performance of this my   little legacy of wch my childe is   the[f] executor and

---

[a] Taurell Jocelin] Tourell Iocelin

[b] a hope] an hope

[c] the losse] of the losse

[d] from] against

[e] to my own not to the world] to my owne, and in priuate sort,

[f] is the] is

dear loue as thou   must be the ouerseer² for god sake   when ~~he or she~~ ⌈it⌉ shall
fayle in duty   to god or to the world do not let   thy fondenesᵃ winke at such folly
but   seuearly correct it: and that thy   troble may be littel when it coms   to years
I pray thee bee carefull ‖   [fol. 2v] when it is young first to pro   uide it a
religious nurse no matter   for her complexion³ as near as may   be chuse a house
wheare it may   not learn to swear or speak scurrilos   words:ᵇ I know I may be
thought   to scripulous⁴ in this: but I am sure   thou shalt finde it a hard matter
to   break a childe of that it learns   so younge: it will bee a great while   ear it
will be thought ould enough   to bee beaten for euill words and   by that time it
will be so perfectᶜ   that blows will not mend it. and   when some charitable body
reprooues   or corrects it for theas faults let   no body pitty it wᵗʰ the losse of   the
mother; For truly I should vse   it no better:ᵈ ~~then~~ ⌈next⌉ good sweet hart   keep it
not ~~like a~~⁵ from schoole   but let it learn betimes. if it bee a   son I doupt not but
thou willt de   dicate it to the L: [i.e. Lord] as his minister   if he will pleas of his
mercy to giue   him grace and capacity for that   great work: If it bee a daughter
‖   [fol. 3r] I hope my mother Brooke   if thou desirest her will take   it amonge hers
and let themᵉ   learn one lesson⁶ I desire her   bringinge vp may bee learninge   the
Bible as my sisters doo. good   huswifery, writing, and good workᶠ⁷   other
learninge a woman needs not   though I admire it in those whom   god hathe
blesst wᵗʰ discretion yet   I desire it not much in my own   hauinge seen that
somtimes women   haue greater portions of learninge   then wisdom wᶜʰ is of no
better   vse to them then A Maynsayle toᵍ   fly boat wᶜʰ runs it ~~vnd~~ vnder   water,
but wheare learning and   wisdom meet in a vertuous dispo   sed woman she is the
fittest closet   for all good∧⌈nes⌉ she is like a well ballacedʰ   ship that may bear all
her sayle⁸   she is; indeed I should but shame my   selfe if I should go about to
prays   her more; but my deare though   shee haue all this in her she will   hardly
make a poor mans wife   [fol. 3v] but I will leaueⁱ it to thy   will If thou desirest a
learned   daughter I pray god giue her   a wise and religious hart that she   may
vse it to his glory thy com   fort and her own Saluatyon but⁹   howsoeuer thou
disposest of her   educatyon I pray thee labor by all   means to teache her ~~truly~~

ᵃ   do not let thy fondenes] let not thy
indulgence

ᵇ   that thy troble . . . scurrilos words] and
that thy trouble may bee little when it comes to
yeeres, take the more care when it is young.
First, in prouiding it a nurse: O make choise,
not so much for her complexion, as for her
milde and honest disposition: Likewise if the
child be to remain long abroad after waining,
as neere as may be, chuse a house where it

may not learne to sweare, or speak scurrilous
words.

ᶜ   perfect] perfect in imperfections

ᵈ   the losse of the mother; For truly I should
vse it no better:] the losse of the mother.

ᵉ   let them] let them all

ᶠ   good work] good workes

ᵍ   to] to a

ʰ   ballaced] ballanced

ⁱ   but I will leaue] Yet I leaue

~~though~~   true humilitie though I as much[a]   desire it may bee ⌈as⌉ humble if it bee   a son as a daughter yet in a   daughter I more feare that vice   pride beeinge now rather accoun   ted a vertue in our sex worthy   prays then a vice fit for reproof   parents[b] read lectors[10] of it to theyr   children how necessary it is and   they haue principles that must   not ⌈be⌉ disputed agaynst as first   look how muche you esteem your   selfe others will esteem of you   agayn what you giue to others   you derogate from your selfe   and many more of theas kinde[c] || [fol. 4r] I haue heard men accounted   wise that haue mayntayned   this kinde of pride vnder   the name of generous[11] knowinge or   vnderstandinge themselues   but I am sure hee that truly   knows himselfe shall know so   much euill by himselfe that   he shall ⌈haue⌉ small reason to thinke   himselfe better then another man   Dearest I am so fearfull to   bringe thee a proud high minde[d]   childe that though I know thy   care will need no spur yet I   cannot but desire thee to double   thy watchfullnes ouer this vice   it is such a crafty diuelishe   insinuatinge sin[d] it will enter   little children in the likenes of   wit wth w[ch] theyr parents are   delighted and that is sweet norish   ment to it. I pray thee dear   hart delight not to haue a bould   childe modesty and humility   [fol. 4v] Are the sweetest ground   works for all vertue, let   not thy seruants giue it any   other title then the christen   name till it haue discretion   to vnderstand how to respect   others:[12] and I pray thee be not   profuse in the expence of clothes   for it[e] me thinks it is a vayn   delight in parents to bestow   that cost vppon one childe   w[ch] would serue too or three   if they haue them not of   theyr own[f] pauper vbiq̃ iacet[13]   Thus dear thou seest y̅ᵉ ⌈my⌉ beleeffe   if thou canst teache thy little   one humility it must needs   make thee a glad Father:

but I know thou wonderest   by this time, what the caus should   bee that wee too continually   vnclaspinge our harts one to   another I should reserue thi[s]   to write when thou think || [fol. 5r] thus,[g] dear remember how   greeuos it was to thee but   to hear me say I may dy   and thou willt confess this   would haue bin an vnplea   sing[h] discourse to thee and   thou knowst I ~~cou~~ neuer durst   displeas thee willingly so much   I loue thee: all I now desire   is that the vnexpectednes   of it make it not more greeuos   to thee but I know thou art   a christian and thearfore will   not doupt[i] thy patience: and   though I thus write to thee   as

---

[a] I as much] I much

[b] parents] Many Parents

[c] kinde] kinds

[d] a crafty diuelishe insinuatinge sin] a crafty insinuating deuill

[e] for it] vpon it

[f] if they . . . own] If they haue not children

enow of their owne to imploy so much cost vpon,

[g] one to another . . . think thus] one to the other, I should reserue this to writing. Whē thou thinkest thus,

[h] vnpleasing] vnpleasant

[i] doupt] doubt of

hartely desiringe to bee   religiously prepared to dy, yet   my deare I dispayr not
of   life nay I hope and dayly   pray for it if so god will   be pleased: nor shall I
think   this labor lost though I doo liue   for I will make it my own   [fol. 5v]
lookinge glasse whearin to   see when I am too seuear   when too remiss and in   my
childes fault thorough   this glass discern mine own   error,[a] and I hope god wil   so
giue me his grace that   I shall more skillfully act   then apprehend a mothers   duty:
my dear thoug   knowest me so well I shall   not need to tell thee I haue   written
honest thoughts in   a disordred fashion not   obseruinge method[14] for
thou   knowst how short I am of   learninge and naturall   endowments to take
such   a cours in writinge, or if   that stronge affection of thi[ne]   haue hid my
weakenes from\   thy sight I now professe   [fol. 6r] seriously my own ignoranc
and though I did not, this   following treatis would   betray[b] it, but I send it only
to the eys of a most louing   housband and a[c] childe ex   ceedingely beloued to
whom   I hope it will not be ∧ [alltogether] vn   profitable Thus humbly de
siringe god to giue thee all   comfort in this life and hap   pines in the life to
com I   leaue thee and thine to his   most gracious protectyon:

Thine inuiolable[15]
Eliza Joscelin[d]

[fol. 7r]
Hauinge longe often and   earnestly desired of god that   I might be a mother
to one   of his children, and the time   now drawinge on w[ch] I hope   he hathe
appoynted to giue   thee vnto me,[16] it drew me into   a consideratyon bothe
whearfore   I so earnestly desired thee and   (hauinge found that the true
cause; was to make thee happy)   how I might compas this   happines for thee,
I knew it   consisted not in honor wealthe   strengthe of body or frends   (though
all theas are great   blessings), thearfore it had   bin a poor and weake
desire[e]   to desire thee only for an heir   [fol. 7v] To my fortune no I ne   uer
aymed at so poore an   inheritance for thee as the   whole world:[17] neyther
would   I haue begged ~~thee~~ of god   so much payn as I know   I must endure to
haue only   possest thee wth earthly riches   of wch to day thou maiest   be a
great mã to morrow   A poore beggar: nor did a   hope[f] to dandle[18] thy
infancy   moue me to desire thee for   I know all the delight a pa   rent can take
in a childe   is Hony mingled wth gall[19]   but the true reason that   I haue so
often kneeled   to god for thee is that thou   mightest bee an inheritor of   [fol.
8r] The kingdom of heauen to   w[ch] end I humbly beseech   allmighty god thou

---

[a] error] errors   [d] Eliza Joscelin] Eliza: Iocelin
[b] betray] bewray   [e] a poor and weake desire] a weake request
[c] a] of a   [f] a hope] an hope

mayst bend   all thy actions and if it be   his blessed will giue thee so plen   tifull a mesure of his grace   that thou mayst serue him   as his minister, if he make   thee a man: it is true that   this age houlds it a most con   temptible office fit only for   poor mens children younger   brothers and such as haue no   other means to liue,[20] but for   gods sake be not discouraged w[th]   theas vayn speeches but fortefy   your selfe wth remembringe   of how great worthe the ~~saluation~~ [winning]   of one soule is in gods sight   [fol. 8v] And you shall quickly finde   how great a place it is to   be a priest vnto the liuing   god if it will pleas him to   moue your hart wth his ho   ly Spirit it will glow and   burn wth zeale to doo him   seruice, Oh L[ord] open thy lips   that thy mouthe may shew   forthe his prays.[21] if I had   ~~eloquence~~ [skill to write] I would write all   I apprehend of the happy   estate of true laboringe mi   nisters, but I may playnly   say that of all men they[a]   are the most truly happy   they are familiar wth god   they labor in his vineyard[23]

[6 blank folios]

[fol. 9r] wth out ceasing[b] and they are   so beloued of him that he giues   them abundance of knowledge   Oh be one of them let not   the scorn of euill men hinder   thee look how god hathe proui   ded for thee sufficient means   thou needest not hinder thy   study to look out for liuinge   as the Iseralites hindered theyr   work to look for straw,[24] if thou   beest not content wth this thou   willt not bee wth more. god   deliuer thee from couetousnes.   I desire thee that though thou   takest a spirituall callinge thou   willt not seek after the liuings   of the church nor promotions   [fol. 9v] Though I honor them as   I haue great cause.[25] but I   would haue thee so truly an   humble and zealous minister   that thy only end should be   to doo god seruice wth out   desire of any thing to thy   selfe saue the kingedom of   heauen. yet as I would not   haue thee seek theas things   so I would haue thee as   carefull not to neglect gods   blessings, but wth all thanke   fullnes to receyue what he   bestowes, and to be a carefull   steward[26] distributinge it to all[c]   that haue need. I could not   choose but manifest this desire   [fol. 10r] in writinge least it should pleas   god to depriue me of time to   speake and if thou beest a daughter   thou mayst pe[r]haps thinke I haue   lost my labor but read on and   thou shalt see my loue and care   of thee and thy saluation is as   great as if thou weart a son   and my fear greater: it may   peraduenture when thou comst to   som discretyon appear strange   to thee to receyue theas lines   from a mother that dyed   when thou weart born but   when thou seest men purchas   land and store vp tresure for   theyr ʌ[vnborn] babes wonder not at me   that I am carefull for thy   [fol. 10v]

---

[a] they] they by their calling   they labour in his Vineyard,

[b] they labor in his vineyard w[th]out ceasing]   [c] to all] to those

Saluatyon beeinge such an   eternall portyon.[27] and not   knowinge whether I
shall liue   to instruct thee when thou   art born let me not be bla   med
thoughe I write to thee   before.[28] whoo would not con   dem me if I should be
care   less of thy body while it is   w[th]in me:[29] sure a far greater   care belongs to
the[a] soule to   bothe theas cares I will en   deuor my selfe so longe as I   liue,
agayn I may[b] be won   derd at for writinge in this   kinde consideringe thear are   so
many excellent books whoos   least note is worthe all my   meditations: I
confess it   [fol. 11r] And thus excuse my selfe   first I write not to the   world
but to mine own   childe. whoo it may bee will   more profit by a few
weak   instructions cominge from a   dead mother (whoo cannot euery day   prays
or reprooue it as   it deserues) then far better   from much more learned   theas
things considered neyther   the true knowledge of mine own   weaknes nor the
fear this may   com to the worlds ey and bringe   scorn vppon my graue can
stay   my hand from expressinge how much   I couet thy saluation   thearfore
dear childe read hear   my loue and if god take   [fol. 11v] Me from thee bee
obedient   to theas instructions as thou oughtest   to be vnto me I   haue learnt
them out of gods   word I beseech him that they   may bee profitable to thee

1

The first charge I giue thee   I learned of Salomon Eccl.12.1[30]   Remember thy
creator in the   days of thy youth. it is an ex   ellent beginninge and a fit   lesson
for a childe looke w[th]   what the vessell is first seasoned it   retayns the taste[31] and
if thou be   ginnest to remember to serue   god when thou art young   before the
world the fleshe   and the diuell take hould on the[e]   god will loue thee and send
[fol. 12r] His holy Spirit to take posses   sion of thee whoo shall resist   those
enemis and not suffer   them to hurt thee. to moue thy   hart to remember thy
creator   betimes, meditate vppon the be   nefits thou continually receyuest: first
how he hathe created thee   when thou weart nothinge. redee   med thee by the
deathe of his   only son, when thou weart wors   then nothinge.[c] and how of
mear   grace he hathe giuen thee his   holy spirit, sanctifying thee to   an eternall
kingedom. thou canst   not possibly vnderstand how great   theas mercys are, but
strayght   thy soule must cry what shall   I doo for so gracious a god   [fol. 12v]
All the powrs of my soule and   body will I giue to his seruice   My first thoughts
will I dedi=   cate to him. like Abells sacrifice   I will present to him the
first   frutes of my youthe[32] in the   strengthe of my age I will[d]   fall down before

---

[a] the] thy

[b] I may] I may perhaps

[c] redeemed . . . nothinge] redeemed thee

being worse than nought,

[d] I will] will I

him and if   I liue to ould age that weaknes   will not let my knees bow nor   my hands be lifted vp yet   shall my hart meditate on his   goodnes night and day, and   my tong shall bee allways tel   linge of his marueylous works.[33]   when thou hast thus remem   bred the infinit mercys of god   it behooues the[e] to settle thy self   to a constant seruice of him   [fol. 13r] To order thy thoughts words   and actions to his glory   and to couenant[34] wth thy selfe   that thou wilt not breake thy   promises to god. that thou maiest   the more esily perform theas   dutis[35] Marke I pray thee theas   followinge rules for orderinge   thy ~~thoughts~~ [life] spend the day as I   instruct thee[a] and god will blesse   thee and all thy good endeuors

2

At thy first wakinge in the mor=   ninge be carefull of thy selfe   that thou harbor in thy brayn   no vayn or vnprofitable but   of all no vngodly fancy to   hinder thy morning sacrifice   but strayght frame thy selfe to   meditate on the mercis of god [fol. 13v] The maliciousnes of the diuell   and thine own weaknes, thine   own weaknes is apparant to   thee for euen but now thine   eys wear closed thou couldst   not see to defend thy selfe thy   strengthe was gon so that thou   weart not able to resist the   weakest creature a gnat or a   flea might glut themselues w[th]   thy bloud: The diuells malice   is as easily perceyued for   euen now he lyes lurkinge   ready to catche euery good   motion from thy hart suggestin[g]   things more delightfull to thy   fancy and perswadinge thee   to defer thy seruice of god   though but for a little while   but be warned and armed   [fol. 14r] Agaynst his tentations for bee assured if thou once yeeld to   neglect prayinge to god but one   halfe houre when that time coms   thou shallt finde thy selfe far   more vnapt thy hart more dull   to pray then before: wheare as   if thou disposest thy selfe to pray   though thou beest heauie and vn   cheerfull in it yet god whoo sear   ches the hart and sees thy desire   to pray though thou canst not   will enlighten thee and prepare   thy hart agaynst the next time   that thou shalt finde comfort.   thearefore take heed the diuell   deceyue you not for you see his   malice is not small that seeks   to cosen[36] you of all happines   present and to com for bee   [fol. 14v] Assured you can take noe   true Joy in earthly plesures   no longer then you seek after   heauen.[b] Hauinge thus discernd   The infinit malice of the diuell   and your own exceedinge   weaknes how do you thinke   you wear preserued from   his snares while you slept   or do you thinke he only besets   you when you are awake? no   be not deceyued he is not so   fayr an enemy his hate is   such to you that if hee could   hee would tear your body and   drag your soule too hell while   you sle[e]pe.[c] [37] Alas all this hee

---

[a] life spend the day as I instruct thee] life,   [c] sleepe] slept
[b] heauen] heauenly

might haue don your strength   was small to resist him now   [fol. 15r] you must needs confess whoo   it is that is only able to   preserue you that it is god   and that it is his mercy not   your desert that you are pre   serued, and gather to your selfe
a strong resolution wth all your   force to serue him all the day   and to resist all the tentatyons   of the diuell: Then beeinge tho=   roughly awake (for sure god likes   not sleepy^a prayr) begin to giue   ~~hi~~ God thanks and to desire the   continuance of his mercy towards   thee in theas words till thou canst   finde such as may better expresse   thine own soule   [fol. 15v]

| Oh Eternall God gracious   from the begininge and merci   full to the later endinge of the^38   world. I giue thee humble thanks   that accordinge to thine abun   dant goodnes thou hast gracious   ly defended me this night from   all dangers that might haue hap=   pened vnto me, I beseech thee   continue this thy fauorable good   nes toward me and so grant   mee thy grace that in all my
thoughts words and actions   I may seek thy glory and ~~for~~   euermore so liue in thy fear that   I may dy in thy fauor for thy   son my only sauiors sake amen

[fol. 16r]

3

Hauinge thus inuited god into your   soule take heed you offend not agaynst   so great and glorious a guest, thinke   if thou seest a superior entertayned   wth such obseruance of the m^r [i.e. master] such   diligence in the seruants such a ge   nerall care that all things may giue   a testimony of his wellcom, Oh think   sinfull soule what care oughtest thou   to haue when the liuing god vouch   safes to dwell in thee, Oh watch oh   be wary: do not my deare childe oh   do not willfully offend him for hard   ly are presumptuous sins forgiuen   but if out of weakenes thou offend
agaynst him run strayght before hee   can bee gon for he is mercifull and   will stay a while after thou hast sin   ned to expect thy repentance but if   thou doest not make hast then the   diuell whoo will not delay to seek thy   [fol. 16v] Destruction hee will accuse thee   mockinge thy impiety and god will   leaue thee^b more offended at thy neg   lect or rather contempt of his mercy   then at thy first offence thearfore   run quickly esteem no sin small   but what member soeuer caused the[e]   to offend him bringe it before him   and let it assist thee cheefly in thy   repentance if thine ey teache thee   wantonnes, couetousnes or the like   let them powr forthe tears to pur
chase thee a pardon if thy tonge   haue offended toward god [or] thy neygh   bor bringe it wth shame and sorrow   to confess in priuat what it was   not ashamed to glory of in publik^39   learn to be ashamed to comit sin   but beinge comitted hope

---

^a sleepy] sleeping   ^b thee] thee, being

not to hide   it from god by any other means   then[a] harty repentance So indeed thou   [fol. 17r] Mayst win his mercy to couer   thy transgression and in his sons   passion he will berry thine offences   so as he will hide them from himselfe   but then thou must delay no time   go quickly get thee alone go wear[b]   thy knees wring thy hands beat thy   brest know as little measure in thy   sorrow as thou didst in thy sin. the   lord will not dispise a contrite hart   and though he let thee kneele longe   he will haue mercy at the last   learn of Jaakob to cry wth a feruent   spirit I will not let thee go except   thou blesse mee[c] [40] our Sauior saythe y[e]   Kingdom of heauen sufferethe violence   and the violent take it by force[41]

4.

   Thus you see it must bee an eager   not a slothefull cours that must   bringe you to heauen: take heed   thearfore that you auoyd all the   [fol. 17v] Kindes of this sin whatsoeuer   you go about doo it wth cheer   fullnes be ashamed of idlenes as   thou art a man but tremble at it   as thou art a christian for be   sure the diuell neuer is so happy   in his tentations as when he   employs them on a slothefull man   whoo cannot endure to take so   much payns as to resist him[42]   Salomon promises no other pa=   trimony to A sluggard but   pouerty:[43] God hates a[d] slothefull   witnes the 5 foolishe virgins and   the vnprofitable seruant Math:25.   the one christe would not know   the other is branded wth too shame   full marks ~~Juste~~ ⌈euill⌉ and slothefull and   his talent taken from him[44] what   more wretched estate can thear bee   in the world: forst to bee hated   of god as an idle drone not   [fol. 18r] Fit for his seruice: then thorowgh   extream pouerty to be contemned   of all the world. Oh then at no   hand yeeld thy youth to slothe   but so soon as thou made[e] thy   prayr to god prepare to rise   and rising vse this prayer

In thy name oh blessed Sauior   I arise whoo wth the father and   the holy Spirit created me and   wth thine own most precious bloud   hast redeemed mee: I beseech thee   this day to gouern, keep, and blesse   me. Lead mee forthe, in euery good   way. thearin direct, and confirm   mee. and after this frayle and   miserable life. bringe me to that   blessed life. w[ch] hathe not[f] end, for   thy great merit, and mercy[g] sake: Amen

[fol. 18v]

[a] then] than by

[b] go wear] weare

[c] learn of Jaakob . . . blesse mee] Learne of *Iacob* to wrastle with God, and to cry with a feruent spirit, I will not let thee goe vnlesse thou

blesse me.

[d] a] the

[e] thou made] thou hast made

[f] not] no

[g] mercy] mercies

5

Thou art noe sooner broke out   of the arms of slothe but pride   steps in
diligently waytinge to   furnishe thee wth any vayn toy[45]   in thy attire and though I
beleeue   theare are diuers sorts of pride   more pestilent to the soule then   this of
apparell, yet this is enough   dangerous and I am sure betrays   a mans folly more
then any other   for, is it not^a a monstrous thinge   to see a man whome god hathe
created of an exc[e]llent form each   part answeringe the due propor   tion of
another should by a fan   tasticall habit make himself so   vgly that one cannot
find among^b   all gods creatures any thinge like   him. one man though not re=
sembling another in shape or   face yet for his rationall soule[46]   [fol. 19r] is like
another but theas   fashionists Haue I feare changed   theyr reasonable souls for
proud   souls wthout reason; could they els   to theas apish fashions ad apish   behauiour,^c
cringing, shrugginge,   startinge, and playinge the foole^d   euery way,[47] so that they
may truly   say when they are fashionable that   they are not like other men: and   I
beleeue wise men will not be sorry   for it, for whoo would be like them   I desire
thee for godsake shun this   vanyty whether thou be son or   daughter if thou bee^e
a daughter   I confesse thy taske is harder be   cause thou art weaker and
thy   temptations to this vice greater   for thou shalt see those whoo^f per=   haps
thou   wilt   thinke   lesse   able   exallted   far   aboue   thee   in   this
[fol. 19v] kinde and it may bee thou wilt   desire to be like them if not to   outgoe
them but beleeue and re   member that I tell thee the end   of all theas vanitys
is bitter as   gall,[48] oh the remembrance of mis   spent time; when thou shall
grow   in years and haue attaynd no   higher^g knowledge, then to dress
thy   selfe, when thou shalt see halfe   p^rhapps all thy time spent and   that of all thou
hast sowed thou   hast nothinge to reap but repen=   tance late repentance, how
wilt   thou greeue how wilt thou accuse   one folly for bringinge^h another   and
in thy memory cast ouer   the cause of each misfortuneⁱ hathe   befallen thee, till
passing from one   to another at last thou findest   thy corrupt will to be the first
cause[49] and then thou willt wth   [fol. 20r] Greef enough perceyue that
if   thou hadst serued god when thou   seruedst thy fond desires thou   hadst
now had peace of hart   god^j of mercy giue thee grace to   remember him
in the days of thy   youthe:[50] Mistake me not nor giue   your selfe leaue to

---

^a for, is it not] Is it not

^b among] amongst

^c could . . . behauiour] could they else
deforme and transforme themselues by these
new fangled fashions, and apish behauiour;

^d foole] fantastiques

^e if thou bee] If

^f whoo] whom

^g higher] other

^h bringinge] bringing in

ⁱ misfortune] misfortune which

^j god] The God

take too much   liberty wth sayinge my mother was   too strict: noe I am not, for I   giue you leaue to follow modest   fashions but not to be a beginner   of fashions nor would I haue you   follow it till it be generall so that   in not dooinge as others doo you   might appear more singular then   wise, but in one word this is all   I desire; that you will not set your   hart on such fooleris, and you shall   see that this modest cariage⁵¹ will   win you reputation and loue w^th   the wise and vertuous sort   [fol. 20v] And once agayn remember how   many hours mayst thou giue to god   wch if thou spendest in theas va   nitis thou shalt neuer bee able to   make account of if thou doest but   endeuor to doo well god will accept   the will for the deed but if thou   willfully spend the morninge of   thy time in theas vanitis god will   not be put of[f] wth such rekonings   but punishments will follow such   as I pray god thou mayst not   pull vppon thee:⁵²

yet alas this is but one sort   of pride and so far from bee   ing accounted a vice that if the   time mends not before you com to   vnderstandinge you will hear a   well drest woman (for that is y^e   stile of honor) more comended then   a wise or learned^a or religious   [fol. 21r] woman: and it may bee this may   moue you to follow theyr idlenes   but when you haue any such de   sire draw your selfe to consider   what maner of persons the comen   ded and comenders are and you   shall finde them all of one batche   such as beeinge vayn themselues   applaud it in others, but if you   will desire prays follow the ex   ample of those religious women   whoos vertuous fames time has^b   not powr to race out,⁵³ as deuout   Anna whoo serued the L: w^th   fastinge and prayr. luke 2 iust   Elizabet whoo serued god w^thout   reproof, religious Ester whoo taught   her mayds to fast and . pray Est.4.15.   and the chast Susanna whoos story   I hope the strictest will allow   for a worthy example⁵⁴

[fol. 21v]
I am so fearfull thou shouldst   fall into this sin that I could   spend my little time of life in   exhortinge thee from it, I know   it is the most dangerous subtle   sin that can steale the hart of   man it will allter shapes as oft   as the chamelyon dothe colors   it will fit it selfe to all dispo   sitions and wch is most strange   it will so disguise it selfe that   he must be cunninge whoo dis   cerns it from humility, nay it   may ly in thine own hart   and if thou beest not a diligent searcher of thy selfe thou shalt   not know it, but, if thou   watche well thou shallt take it   for it hathe one property that   cannot change, as the comon peo   ple beleeue the diuell cannot   allter the shape of one foot⁵⁵   [fol. 22r] It is true of pride that though   it bee transformed^c into [that] angell of   light humility, yet thou mayst know   it by selfe loue, if thou findest   that w^thin thee;

<hr />

^a learned] honest   ^c transformed] changed
^b has] hath

be sure pride   is not far of[f], for humility will   make the[e] seem vilde[a] in thyne   own eys, it will make thee see   thine own faults and confess   them, to be greater than other   mens, so that thou wilt respect   euery man aboue thy self.   but   the rules of selfe conceyt are iust   contrary, they stand on tiptoes   rekoninge theyr vertues like the   proud pharisee scorninge to bee   like other men,[56] shun it for gods[b]   sake for if thou entertayn it   it is such a shameles flatterer[c]   that it will make thee beleeue   thou are greater wiser learneder   [fol. 22v] Then all the company when   indeed thou willt prooue thy   selfe the greatest foole of them   wearyinge them all wth thy   vayn talke, ~~of this van~~   Salomon saythe x Pride goes   before distruction and a hy   minde before the fall {x prov 16 18} and our   blessed sauiour the true pattern   of humility exhorts vs to   learn of him that was lowly   and meek in hart, {Ma 11 29} and if wee   do so hee promises wee shall   finde rest vnto our souls   and he vses threatninge whear   perswasion will not serue[d]   whoosoeuer exalltethe himselfe   shall bee humbled, {L~~u~~ 14 11} read the holy   scriptures often and diligently and   thou shalt finde continuall threat   nings agaynst pride punishments   [fol. 23r] of pride and warnings from   pride, Thou shalt finde no sin   so heauyly punished as this it   made diuells of angells, a beast   of great Nabuchodonezer, doggs   meat of Jesabell,[57] and I will con   clude w[th] a good mans sayinge   if all the sins raygninge in the   world were burnt to ashes euen the ashes of pride would bee able   to produce[e] them all agayn[58]

I know in fewer words thear   might much more haue bin say[d]   agaynst this sin but ~~notw[th]stan~~   ~~dinge~~ I know not whoo will   say so much to thee when I   am gon, thearfore I desire   thou mayst bee taught theas   my instructions when thou   art young that this foule sin   [fol. 23v] May bee weeded out before it   take deep root in thy hart   I will return now to my   first purpose w[ch] is to set thee   down one day for a pattern   how I would haue thee spend   all the days of thy life

6

Thearfore auoydinge all ma   ner of pride make thy selfe   decently ready w[ch] beeinge don   retire to a place alone whear   humblinge thy selfe vppon thy   knees agayn renew thy prayrs   humbly confessinge and earnestly   desiringe forgiuenes for all thy   sins and vse D[r] Smiths mor   ninge prayr: then w[ch] I

---

[a] vilde] vile

[b] gods] thy soules

[c] flatterer] flattery

[d] and he vses . . . serue] Neither want there curses, threatning, where perswasions will not serue.

[e] produce] reduce

know   not a better nor did I euer finde   more comfort in any:[59] ~~th~~ in
adui   sing you to A set form of prayr   [fol. 24r] I do not prohibit
conceyued   prayr but humbly beg of   god to giue you grace to pray   often out
of your own meditaty=   ons accordinge to his will[60]   but when it shall pleas god
to   call you to the charge of a family   I will not direct but deliuer my   opinion,
that then a set form of   prayr is most necessary, my reaso[n]   is that your
seruants beeinge   vsed to it are allways ready   to go alonge wth you^a word
for   word as you pray and continu   ance makes them to vnderstan[d]   euery
word wch must needs   cause greater deuotion.^b

7

when you haue finished your   priuate prayr be sure that   you absent not your selfe
from   [fol. 24v] Publick prayr if it bee vsed   in the house whear you liue[61]   w^ch
ended go and vse any   lawfull recreatyon eyther for   thy profit or pleasure and from
all theas exercises reserue A time   to sit down to som good study   but vse that
most that may   make thee greatest; diuinity:[62] it   will make thee greater
richer   happyer then the greatest kinge   dom of the earthe though thou   couldst posses
it if any man   serue mee saythe christ him   will my father Honor,[63] if   Mardochey
wear [thought] so highly hono   red by Ahashuerous for a little   gay trappinge[64] what
shall bee don   to him whoom god will honor   thearfore if thou desirest honor   serue
the L: and thou art sure of   it, if riches be thy aym   [fol. 25r] St Paul assures thee that
godlynes   is great gayn[65] if thou couet ple   sure set Dauids delight before thine   eys:
I haue had more delight in   thy testimonys then in all maner   of riches Ps CXIX
and in the 92 Ps: he saythe thou L: hast made mee   glad by thy works in the
4 Psal: Thou hast giuen mee more Joy of   hart, &: and readinge the 91 Psal   thou shalt
see what maner of   blessings they are that god makes   his chilldren merry wth all[66]
and whe[n]   thou hast once fixt thy hart to thi[s]   study it will be so sweet that
the   more thou learnest the more thou   willt desire and the more thou   desirest the more
god will loue the[e]   thou willt study so well in priuat   and practis it in all thy
actions   publickly thou will weygh thy   thoughts so euen that thy words   [fol. 25v] shall
not bee light[67] and a few   lines I will vse to perswade   thee to be aduised in thy words

8

Though it is as much to say   Remember thy creator when thou   speakest as
if I could vse all y^e   exhortatyons and tell thee all y^e   perills y^t belongs to speech

---

yet so apt are wee to forget god in our foolishe taulk that somtimes wee by our discours would make gods of our selues thearfore it will not bee amiss to receyue a few instructions though weak from me for orderinge thy speech[68]

The morninge I haue dedica ted to meditatyon ~~good study~~ prayr good studys and honest recreatyon: The noon time is most vsed for discours it beeing all a man can doo while he eats [fol. 26r] And it is a time whearin a man ought to bee carefull of his speech hauing before him gods good blessings to refreshe his body and honest company to ~~refreshe~~ [recreate] his minde Thearfore[a] ought to be no way offensiue in his speech eyther to god or good men, but most especially take heed that neyther heedlesnes nor earnestnes in thy discours caus thee to take gods holy name in vayn[69] but allways speake of him wth reuerence and vnderstandinge next let not thy neyghbor suffer in thy speech but be rather silent then speak ill of any man though he deserue it and that thou mayst doo thus ob serue this rule whensoeuer thou hearest one ill spoken of before [fol. 26v] Thou second it examin thine own hart and it is odds but[70] thou mayst finde in thy selfe eyther ye same fault or a worse then hee is accused for; so thou shalt be forced eyther to mend thy selfe or not to ~~accuse~~ [condem] him: allso shun multiplicity of words and what thou speakest be sure to vnderstand fully for it is a gratinge to the ear to heare a man talke at random, if thou desirest to bet ter thy selfe; modestly aske a question of those whom thou seest haue[b] knowledge to resolue thee and bee lesse ashamed to confess thy ignorance then by houldinge a foolish argument, to betray it. and euer auoyd that scornfull fashyon of questioninge [fol. 27r] A man whoo thou knowest can not make thee a satisfyinge answear[71] neyther make a scorn of his igno rance for bee assured he knows somthinge that thou doest not know If god haue giuen thee a ready wit take heed thou abuse it not at no time mayntaine arguments agaynst the truth[c] for it is hard to do it wthout offendinge the god of truthe, and by it, thou maist harm thy weake brother,[72] but the greatest harm will bee thine own when thou comst to giue account for thy idle words; in thy mirthe shun suche jestinge as may make thee offensiue scoffinge becoms not a christian prise not thearfore the frothe[73] of an Idle wit before the faythe of a vertuous frend; and I pray thee as thou wouldst haue ~~my~~ blessings multiplyed vppon thee let noe [fol. 27v] Speech[74] passe from thee that may greeue chast ears how hatefull is obscean speech in rude people? but it makes one of gentile [i.e. gentle] birthe odious to all honest company Salomon says A wise man conceals knowledge but the hart of a foole publishethe foolishnes Pro 12 23 and he that keepethe his mouthe keepethe his life 13.3. and in the 14.5. the lips of the wise preserue them[75]

[a] Thearfore] and therfore

[b] haue] to haue

[c] the truth] the truth, especially in sacred or morall matter:

to conclude let thy tonge and   thy hart go together hate dissi   mulation and lyinge and god   will loue thee wch I humbly beg   of him :::} -

9

If thou [keep thy] thoughts holy and th[y]   words pure I shall not need to   feare but all thy actions will bee   honest yet[a] my fear thou shouldst   [fol. 28r] know the way and ~~yet~~[b] go aside   will not suffer my councell to   leaue thee alone till thou com to   thy iourneys end: first then bee   carefull when thou art alone that   thou doo nothinge that thou wouldest   not doo if men saw thee remembrin[g][c]   that gods ey is allways open, and   thyne own conscience will bee witnes   enough agaynst thee next be sure   that no action of thine may bee a   scandall to thy profession I mean   to the professyon of the true religion   this indeed is as much as to say to   thee eschue[76] euill: for thear is not the   least sin thou canst doo but the ene   mis of truth [will] be glad to say; loe   this is one of them that professes   god in his mouthe but see what   his life is; thearfore a great care   ought a christian to haue   [fol. 28v] especially those whome god has[d] set   as lights in his churche[77]

whatsoeuer thou art about to doo   examin it by gods commandement[s]   if it bee agreeable to them; go on   cheerfully and though the end an   swear not thy hopes neuer greeue   nor grudge but be glad that   gods will is performed and let th[y]   trust in him assuer thee that   all things work together for th[e]   best to them that loue god,[78] and though   it appear a crosse be assu   red it is a blessinge therefore[79]   make right vse of it, examin   thy selfe what sin thou hast co   mitted that may chalenge[80] that   punishment, repent[e] it and re   concile god vnto thee bearing   thy cross with patience, and dou[bt]   not, he that depriued thee of   thy hope to try thee: will   [fol. 29r] (If thou bear it well) ~~reward~~ [giue]   thee as great or a greater   blessinge then thou hopedst for   But if thou shallt finde that   thy attempts will not endure that   tryall break from them and tell   the diuell in playn tearms thou   hast a light to discern his snares   by and thearfore scornst to bee his   slaue; for beleeue me my childe   if thou shalt out of any worldly   respect doo a dishonest act. it may   bee thou mayst thriue in it a   while but the end is miserable   oh the burden[f] of a wounded   conscience whoo can beare: if   thou seest others thriue and grow   great in such courses; read the   73 Psalm thear thou

[a] yet] But

[b] ~~yet~~] yet

[c] remembrin] remember

[d] has] hath

[e] repent] repent of

[f] burden] burthen

shallt see   Dauid himselfe confesses his   [fol. 28v] Foot had wellnigh
slipt when   hee saw the prosperyty of the   wicked he describes all
theyr fe   licitys but at the last when he   went into the sanctuary he found
    what theyr end was how they   wear set in slippery places &.   and then hee
cryes whoom haue   I in heauen but thee, and I   haue desired non in the earthe
wth thee^81 Alas all theyr labor   is but to build a paper house   vppon the sand
wch though it   bee neuer so glorious to look   vppon a small tempest will
    shatter it: when if thou lay   the foundatyon of thy happines   vppon christe
the rock of thy   salluatyon and build it wth zelous   seruice of him accordinge to
truthe   then though the flouds beat   [fol. 30r] Agaynst it and huge tempests
    threaten it thou needest not fear   for thy walls will stand fast   and thy
foundatyon^a will secure thee^82   it wear enough to perswade   any man to be
honest if he   would consider the day of afflicti   on and store vp the comfort of
    a quiet conscience agaynst it came^83   for only that discerns the patien[t]   Job
from dispayringe kayn.   Kayn hideously cryes out his^b   punishment is greater
then hee   can beare: Job sighs forthe Loe: though hee slay me yet will I   trust
in him:^84 indeed till afflic   tion coms the worser sort of men   appear to be the
happiest but   then the chaf is soon known   from the wheat the good man
    knows his cross is good for him [fol. 30v]   bears it patiently and casts   his care
on christ. his hart   knows no repininge, nor his   tonge other complayninge
but   shall I receyue good from god   and not euill:^85 on the contra   ry when
affliction falls vp=   pon those whoo haue layd   thear foundatyon on the sand
    alas they haue noe comfort   they are eyther ashamed or   besotted^86 they
cannot finde god   nay they will not seek him   but instead of seeking councell
    from him they are not ashamed   (wth forsaken Saule) to implore   the diuell
what do they less that   seek after witches for lost goods   cure for themselues
theyr children or   cattell:^87 I hope there are but few   of theas but I know whear
god   is once forsaken, man is apt to   [fol. 31r] fall into the depth of sin it is
    grace^c mear grace that preserues gods   chilldren from theas dangerous falls
wch grace^c I beseech allmighty god make   vs all partakers of,^d and to conclude
    how I would haue thee square actions^e   whatsoeuer thou doest remember^f
thou art   in the presence of god (whoo will ex   pect an account from thee) so thou
    willt not dare to doo euill and thou   willt doo well chearfully becaus thou   art
sure it pleses the Lord whoo sees   thy willingnes and will not leaue thee
    vnrewarded: the vices most raygning   in theas^g I must particularly aduise   thee
[to] shun first swearinge for god sake   let your comunicatyon be yea yea and

---

^a foundatyon] foundations

^b his]this

^c wch grace] of which grace

^d partakers of,] partakers.

^e actions] thine actions,

^f remember] remember that

^g theas] these times

nay nay: for what is more saythe christ   comethe of euill,[88] keep not company
w[th]   a swearer lest custom make thee for   get how great the sin is and so by   little
and little thou mayst get thy   selfe a habit of it reprooue it in thy   frend if he
will brook reprooff, but it   is to no end to reprooue a scorner   [fol. 31v]
Rebuke not a scorner lest hee hate   thee but rebuke a wise man and hee   will
loue thee: Prou: 9.8.   allways keep a watche before thine   own lips and
remember that thou   needest not swear if thou doest not   accustom thy selfe to
ly for if thou   vsest to tell truthes thy word will   be as current as thy oathe[89] I
hope   thy callinge if god haue made thee   man[a] will be of authority to reproue
    this vice in others and not to de   light in it thy selfe if thou beest   a daughter
thou hast a callinge to   w[ch] thou must not dishonor thou   art a christian and
christ comands   thou shouldst not swear at all. Mat. 5. 3, 4[90]   beside thou art a
mayd and such ought   thy modesty to be that thou shouldst   scars speak but
when thou answerest   thou that art young speak if need   bee and yet scarsely
when thou art   twise Asked Eccle: 32 8[b 91]

[fol. 32r] The next vice too to[o] comon in   this age is Drunkennes w[ch] is the
    highway to hell a man may trauayl   in it from sin to sin till the diuell   show him
he can go no farther   as a trauayler from in to in till   hee com to his Jorneys end
oh thin[k]   how filthy is that sin that makes a   man a beast all his life and a diuel
    at his deathe Salomon asks to whom   is woe to whom is sorrow to who[m]   is
strife to whom is murmuringe   to whom are wounds w[th]out caus   and to whom
is rednes of the eys   and in the next verse answers   euen to them that tarry longe
at   the wine and to the end of the   chapter sets forthe the miseris   occasioned
by this vice Pro: 23[92]   that thou maist auoyd this sin be   carefull in the choyce of
thy frends   for it is they that [will] betray [thee] to   this sin neuer make choyce
of a   drunkard to thy companyon.   [fol. 32v] Much lesse thy frend for our
    kinged[om] hathe of late afforded more   examples of those whoo haue bin
slayn by theyr frends in a drun   ken quarrell then those that haue   fallen by
the enemies sword[93] and   how vnfit is he to be a frend   that when thou shallt
haue need   of his councell will haue his   head instead of wisdom fild   wth wine and
ad rather greef   then comfort to thy nesessitis   and agayn what secret thou shalt
    trust him wth thou maist be   sure shallbee vomited forthe and   all thy comfort
must bee he did   it vnwillingly when hee knew   not what he did thus thou seest

[a] man] a man
[b] if thou beest . . . twise Asked Eccle: 32 8] If
thou beest a Daughter, remember thou art a
Maid, and such ought thy modesty to bee, that
thou shouldst scarce speak, but when thou
answerest: thou art young, speake if need be,
and yet scarcely when thou art twice asked,
Eccles. 32. 8. Whatsoeuer thou be, thou hast a
calling, which thou must not dishonour: thou art
a Christian, and Christ commands thou shalt
not sweare at all, *Mat.* 5. 34.

to be a drunkard is to be a   man vnfit for gods seruice   or good mens
company I beseech   god giue thee grace to detest it

[fol. 33r] Next I must exhort thee   from a sin that I cannot   name thou must
search thine   own hart for it, it is thy   da⌈r⌉linge sin[94] that wch too enioy
   thou couldst resist all others at   least thou thinkest so; but do not   harbor
it search diligently for   it in thy own nature and   when thou hast found it
cast it   headlong from thee it is thy   souls subtle betrayer and all   thy other
sins depend vppon   it theare is not so much danger   in all the rest that thou
conten   dest wth as in this one that tho[u]   art lothe to call a sin thy othe[r]
   sins are like a rebellious multi   tude in a comonwealthe w^ch   wantinge a
head doo little harm   this is theyr head cut it of[f] and   thou shalt see ⌈all⌉
thy other sins   [fol. 33v] dispearsed as an army of   fearfull rebells when they
hear   theyr great leaders head has^a   kist the block[95] ~~Thus hauinge~~
~~spent   the~~

10

   when thou hast spent the   day in religious and honest   exercises in the
eueninge re   turn agayn to some good medi   tatyon or study wch conclude   w^th
prayr comendinge thy selfe   to god and so shalt thou ioy   fully go to thy supper
wch don   and the time of rest com as   thou begannest in the morninge   so shut
vp the day wth humble   thanksgiuinge for all the benefits   that day receaued
harty repentance   for all thy sins comitted naming   and bewaylinge them for
   [fol. 34r] Thou knowest not if thou re=   pentest not to night whether   thou
shallt liue^b to morrow   and though thou weart sure of   it yet the oftner thou
makest   euen thy accounts wth god thy   sleeps will bee the sounder and   thou
shalt awake wth a hart full   of ioy and ready to serue the   Lord: last comit thy
selfe and   all that is thine to god in zealous   praise^c vsinge Dr Smiths euening   prayr
as his morninge bothe   wch though ∧ ⌈they⌉ bee for a family   yet are they
easyly reduced too   a priuat mans prayr:[96] so goinge   to bed take thy rest
beginning   and ending in him that is both   first and last:[97] thus spend the
6   days thou hast to labour in, that   thou mayst bee redy to celebrate
the   Saboath to wch thear belongs another

remember[98]

[fol. 34v]

   ^a has] hath   ^c praise] Prayer,
   ^b liue] liue to repent

11

Remember that thou keep holy the   Sabathe day this duty so often and   earnestly comanded by god himselfe   so strictly obserued by the Jews (whoo   that day might kindell noe fire nor   vse any labor insomuch that the   L: whoo is the god [of] mercy him   selfe comanded the man that gathe   red sticks on that day to be stoned[99]):   and a long time after zealously kept   by the christians[a] yet in theas days   as if wee neyther had part in the   creation nor redemption of the world   wee[b] keep noe sabboath or ∧ [at] the most   but a shadow of a sabbathe whear   allmost[100] can wee finde one that   will loose a good bargayn rather   then make it on the Lords day   or that will bridle his own desires   to sanctify that day truly thear   are so few that it is hard to instance   one:[c] seeinge thearfore this danger in̶t̶   wch thou mayst easily bee intrapped by   [fol. 35r] The Diuells subtelty and followinge the   multitude I cannot but wth all my   powr exhort thee carefully to keep the   Sabathe to wch end I pray thee mark   well the 4th comandement[101]

Remember that thou keep holy the   Sabathe day: 6 days shallt thou labor   and doo all^d thou hast to doo: but y^e   seuenthe is the sabathe of the Lord thy   God in it thou shallt doo noe maner of   work thou nor thy son nor thy daughter   thy man seruant nor thy mayd seruant   nor thy cattell nor the stranger[e] that is   w^thin thy gates for in 6 days the Lord   made Heauen and earthe the sea and all   that is thearin and rested the 7th day   whearfore ye L blessed the 7th day   and Hallowed it:[102]

If thou willt be won to the due   obseruatyon of this day as an obedient   seruant; see god comands Remember   that thou keep holy the Sabbathe[f] if as   a louinge and dutyfull son see how   god perswades thee by reason[g] hee hathe   giuen thee 6 days to do thine own   [fol. 35v] works and hee requires but one   of thee what canst thou say for   thy [selfe] why thou shouldest not wholy   that day giue thy selfe to his seruice   lastly if thou willt learn how to   serue him as a good scholar hee   teaches thee an̶d̶ admirable way   bothe by rule and example first   by rule thou shalt do no maner of   worke in it, then by example. he   made the whole world in 6 days and   he rested ye seuenthe whearfore he   blessed it: &:[h] seeinge

---

[a] by god himselfe . . . by the christians] by GOD himselfe in the Old Testament, so confirmed to vs in the new, by the Resurrection of our Sauiour, in memory whereof it is called the Lords day, and perpetually celebrated by the Church,

[b] wee] too many

[c] that day . . . one:] that day?

[d] all] *all that*

[e] thy cattell nor the stranger] *thy cattle*

[f] Sabbathe] *Sabbath day*

[g] reason] equity, grounded vpon his owne bounty to thee:

[h] blessed it: &:] blessed it.

god thus comands   thee by his power perswades thee in   his mercy and teaches
thee bothe by   rule and his own most gracious   example: how canst thou bee so
deuoyd   of grace[a] as not to obey so iust a   master so mercifull a father so
graciou[s]   a teacher; if thou make not a consci=   ens of keepinge this day
howsoeuer   a dull security may possess thee to   flatter thy selfe, thou indeed
makest   conscience of nothinge for I am

perswaded[103]

[fol. 36r] if thou canst dispence wth thy selfe   to prophane this day; ~~thou will not~~
      eyther for thy profit or pleasure thou   wilt not stick vppon the like
occasion   to break all the rest of the comandement[s]   one after another,
thearfore for christs   sake be watchefull that the diuell deceyue   you not nor non
of his ministers[b]   draw thee away from this days duty   he is allways busy and
ready at hand   to draw thee[c] from god but this day   wthout doupt he doubles all
his forces   he will prouoke thine eys to sleep   he will send heauines and dullnes
to   thy hart and perhaps payn to thy   body if hee can so much preuayle any   slight
any trick to stay[d] from gods   house and from the congregatyon of his   people he
will   surely vse: nay hee will   somtime[e] do it wth religious pretenses   as to pray
at home read a sermon   study the scripture and to spend the   time in such
christian exercises as are   infinitly good at other times   [fol. 36v] but I once
heard a religious   preacher affirm (and I beleeued him)   that those whoo had
abilytie of body   to go to churche and yet out of   any euill disposition (for good
it cannot[f] bee) absented themselues though they   prayd they wear not heard, it
be   hooues the[e] by how much greater his   practises are agaynst thee that
day   so much the more to fortefy thy   selfe agaynst him at no hand let   him
stay thee from the churche   thear god hathe promised to be   present, and thear
he is. darest   thou then silly wretch absent thy   selfe from him? I know thou
darest   not. go then wth a hart prepared   to pray, by prayr, and goinge   meditate
on gods great mercys   in the creatyon of the world his   greater mercy in
redeeminge it   and mingle wth thy meditatyon   prayrs that may apply theas
great   blessings to thy selfe: so approche[g]   wth reuerent and feruent zeale   the
house of god an[d] throwinge   [fol. 37r] away all thoughts but such as   may
further the good worke thou   art about bend thy knees and hart   to god
desiringe of him his holy   spirit that thou maiest ioyn wth the   congregatyon in
zealous prayr and   earnest attentyon of[h] his word prea   ched and though[i] thou
hearest a mi   nister preache as thou thinkest weak   ly yet giue him thine

[a] grace] grace, nay of reason,	[f] cannot] can hardly
[b] ministers] instruments	[g] approche] approach and enter,
[c] thee] thee away	[h] of]to
[d] stay] stay thee	[i] though] though perhaps
[e] somtime] sometimes	

attention and   spend not the time in reading or   any other meditations,[a] and
thou   shalt finde that he will deliuer   somethinge profitable to thy soule   eyther
that thou hast not heard before   or not marked or forgotten[b] and it is   fit thou
shouldest bee often put in   mind of those things concern[c] thy sal   uatyon thus if
thou spend thy time   at church thou wilt be ready to giue   thy selfe to meditate
of the holy word   thou hast heard w^{th}out wch truly   hearinge profitethe little for
it is   wth the soule as wth the body though   meat be neuer so wholesom and
the   appetite neuer so great yet if any   [fol. 37v] ill disposition in the stomacke
hin   der digestion it turns not to nou   rishment but rather proues
more   dangerous so the word if after hea   ringe it be not digested by meditaty=   on
it is not nourishing to y^e soule[104] there   fore let the time thou hast to bee ab   sent
from churche be spent in pray=   singe god prayinge to god and apply   inge to
thy selfe what thou hast   heard if thou hast heard a sin re   prooued that thou art
guilty of take   it for a warninge do it no more   if thou hearest of a good action   w^{ch}
thou hast ouerslipt striue   to recouer time and resolue to   put it in act thus
by practising   what thou hearest thou shalt binde   it to thy memory: and[d]
make thy   selfe most happy: Learn of Isayah   the tru obseruatyon of the
Sabathe: If thou turn away thy foot from   the[105] Sabathe from dooinge thy
will on   my holy day and call the Sabathe a   delighte to consecrate it as
gloryous   [fol. 38r] To the Lord, and shallt honor him   not dooinge thy own
ways nor seekinge   thine own will nor speaking a vayn   word. Then shallt
thou delight in the   Lord and I will caus thee to mount vp   pon the high
places of the earthe and   feed the[e] wth the heritage of Jacob thy   father for
the mouthe of the L hathe   spoken it. Isaiah. 58. 13.[106] it is a wonder   to see
how often god hathe comanded this   one comandement and yet how
slack   wee are to keep it Exo: 31 from y^e   12 verse is all commandinge this
agayn   in the 34 21[107] and ~~infinite numbers of~~ [diuers]   places more learn
then to prepare   thy hart early for this day wch if thou   obseruest well god will
blesse the[e] and   thy Labors all the week: Thus far   I haue endeuored to
exhort thee to   thy duty towards god:

[12][108]

of wch the   honor due to thy Parents is such   a part as cannot bee seperated for
    god comands it Honor thy father   and thy mother it is ye first comandement   of
the second table as, Thou shall haue   [fol. 38v] Noe other gods but me is of y^e

---

[a] attention . . . meditations,] attention,   [c] concern] concerning

[b] forgotten] forgotten, or not well put in   [d] to thy memory: and] to thy memory, and by
practise.   making it thine owne,

first.[109] Idolatry beeinge ye greatest   sin agaynst god and disobedience to
Parents^a agaynst man wee are first   warned of them as if^b wee should   fall
into them it wear to late to   auoyd the other; for if wee once   becom^c Idolaters
it will be no hard   matter to bee a bower down to   an image, to abuse gods
holy name   and to prophane his sabbathes:^d so   if wee dare disobey good
parents   theft murder adulltery falsnes   couetousnes are easyly found out^e [110]   nay
I dare say if thou breakest   eyther of theas comandements thou   breakest all of
the first and second   table: for as thou canst not bee   idolatrous w^thout
breakinge all the   rest so canst not be a disobe   dient childe but thou are
~~first~~   a murderer^f a double one first   of nature in thy selfe wch if thy   wicked
purposes do not smother   [fol. 39r] will of her selfe breake forthe into   that
duty, for an example the story   of AEneas shows how much it was   obserued by
them that receyued not   the comandement from gods own   mouthe as did the
Jews yet hee   exposed himselfe to all dangers   rather then hee would forsake
his   father.[111] secondly thou art a mur   therer of thy Father whoo hauing   stored
vp all his ioy in thee hathe   by thy disobedience; his gray head   brought w^th
sorrow to ye graue[112]   wch god forbid, and what diffe   rence shall I say thear is
between   a disobedient childe and an adulterer   the one forsakes the wife of his
bosom   the other forsakes the holy spirit   the sweet guide of his soule^g
truly   this is a fearfull adulltery and sin   is a crafty strumpet she will allure   thee
and delude thee, agayn, in beeing   disobedient thou art a theef an impu   dent
one^h for thou doest not only   [fol. 39v] secretly steale but openly detayn   the
honour reuerence and obedient   duty wch all the world can wit   nes is ⌈thy⌉
fathers and how willt   thou auoyd beeinge a fals witnes   will not one sin draw on
another   willt not thou bee ready to ex   cuse thy selfe^i by throwinge calum   nious
aspertyons[113] on thy parents   giuinge thy tong leaue to ly   agaynst thy
conscience. and lastly   (oh Horrible how easy a step is   it to couet what thou
thinkest   thy parents life ~~parents life~~   too longe detayns from thee[114] thus   thou
seest in beeinge disobedient   thou breakest 6 comandements   from^j I beseech
allmighty god   deliuer^k thee and giue thee grace to   bee obedient to him and to
thy   parents I am sure thou hast a   father whoo will neuer comand   thee

---

^a Parents] parents, being the ringleader in
sinnes

  ^b as if] as if in case

  ^c becom] become in heart

  ^d sabbathes:] Sabbath:

  ^e good parents . . . found out] good Parents,
at that breach, theft, murther, adultery,
falsenesse, couetousnesse easily enter.

  ^f so . . . murderer] so thou canst not bee a

disobedient childe, but thou art a murderer,

  ^g the one . . . soule] the one forsakes her, by
whom he giueth being vnto others, the other
despiseth those from whom hee had his owne
being.

  ^h one] theefe,

  ^i selfe] vnnaturall obstinacy,

  ^j from] from which outrage,

  ^k deliuer] preserue

anything contrary to the || [fol. 40r] comandements of god thearfore   I haue
no need to speak to thee   how far a father ought to bee   obeyed but humbly
desire of god   to continew him in his good desire   wth long life to bringe thee
vp.^a   in the fear of the L: and to giue   thee a hart ready to embrace
all   religious learning

13

The next duty equall to this   thou must perform to all the world   in generall
doo to all men as thou   wouldst they should doo vnto thee.^115   this is the
comandement our sauiour   giues vs: loue one another by this wee   shall bee
known to bee his if wee loue   one another as hee hathe loued vs:^116   yet of all
that is comanded vs thear   is nothinge more contrary to our   wicked nature^b this
louinge our   neyghbor as our selfe^c wee can w^th   eas enuy him if he be riches or
scorn   him if hee be poor, but loue him?   nay ye diuell hathe more craft then so
|| [fol. 40v] it wear hard for him if men should   once begin to loue one another
thear   fore hee^d all art to stir dissentyon among   as many as hee can and to mixe
loue   wth dissimulatyon to auoyd this con   sider well that god is the author
of   peace and loue, and that strifes and   contentyons proceed of ye diuell, then
if   thou beest the childe of god doo the   works of god loue thy neyghbor as   he
hathe comanded least thou prouoke   our blessed sauiour (when he shall see   that
marke of the diuell: malice in thee)   to say as once to the vnbeleeuinge   Jews
you are of your father the diuell   and the lusts of your father will you   doo Joh:
8 44. Oh take heed thou offend   not god thus greeuously y^t hee shall   disclaym
thee as non of his because   thou doest not loue those that are his   this if well
weyghed weare enough   to make euery man charitable if it   wear only for fear
to hate whom   god loued and^e to beleeue or iudge   that god should hate whear
thou   doest ~~whe~~ wear such an impious || [fol. 41r] vncharitablenes as a good
christian   must needs tremble at god hathe   giuen thee no authoryty to
iudge   any man but he hathe comanded   thee to loue thine enemy, loue
your   enemis ~~to~~ blesse them that curs you doo   good to them that hate you and
pray for   them that hurt ʌ [&] persecute you that you may   bee the children
of your father wch is in   heauen Math. 5 44,^117 A man may finde   ways
enough^f to possess the diuell of his soule   but non wth lesse pleasure to himselfe
then   this; he may sell it as did Judas to satis   fy a couetous desire.^118 he may loose
it as does   many a lazy man his worldly estate be   cause he will not troble

---

^a to bringe thee vp.] that he may bring thee vp

^b nature] nature than

^c our selfe] our selues.

^d hee] he vseth

^e and] But

^f enough] enow

himselfe ~~he sinks~~   to look ouer an account of his fortune   he sinks ear he thinks of it so fares it   wth a negligent christian, 3dly he may   pawn it like a foolish vnthrift whoo   pawns that wch should keep him all his   life too purchase a gay toy wch shall   serue him a day or too so dothe he y^t   pawns that rich Jewell his soule ~~his soule~~   to ye couetous diuell for pleasure happely he || [fol. 41v] Means^a to redeem it but runs on   his selfe pleasing cours till the vse   hathe deuoured the principall[119] and   his vnmercifull creditor hales him   to a dūgeon whear he has time   foreuer to bewayle not only his   present misery but the loss of in   finit happines: Theas are strange   enough, that ⌈a man⌉ should sell eternyty   of ioy for welthe, or sleep away   the time whearin he might make   such a purchase, or pawn an   inestimable tresure for things not   worthe esteem. but yet they are all   better then hee that giues^b his soule   for nothinge as dothe the enuious   man. the couetous gets riches the   slothefull eas, the wanton pleasure   but this hater of his brother gets   nothing^c but torment frettinge   and vexatyon: he is not the   fatter for his meat nor dothe   he rest though hee sleep yet he   for whom he thus toyls his || [fol. 42r] Spirits happely eats sleeps and   laughs at his folly or peraduen   ture pittys him.^d the more easily   to auoyd this sin consider well   the ~~profit and~~ disprofits of it   ~~the dissuad~~ [?] read in the first: epist   of St John 3 chap 14 and 15 verses   and in the 4th ch the 8 and the   20 verses, read the 13 of the first   to the corinths thear St Paul shows   that all vertues are of no force   w^thout this loue.^e [120] as the want of   it brings infinit misery so the   possession infinit Joy first wee   perform christs comandement^f   whoo often requires this of vs as   if he should say I haue satisfyed   my father for all the comandemen⌈ts⌉   that you haue broke now your task   is easy I leaue you nothinge to doo   but to loue one another do this and   you doo all: you^g fulfill the law Ro   the 13, the 8 and 10 verses you^h abide   in the light the i Ep of St John 2: 10[121]   is it possible when theas are well   weyghed that any man should bee   [fol. 42v] so mad to bear an vncharitable   hart about him or so foole hardy   to harbor a spleen that shall hasard   his saluatyon can wee be so cru   ell to our selues as to deny christ   one comandement for all his loue   to vs he requires but this testi   mony of our loue to him w^ch   wee cannot chuse but perform   if wee doo loue him thearfore   take heed if thou feel any

---

^a ye couetous diuell . . . Means] the griping vsurer the deuill, for pleasure; haply he meanes one day

  ^b giues] giues away

  ^c nothing] nothing (no not in present)

  ^d yet he . . . pittys him.] yet he for whom, or against whom he thus toiles his spirit, haply eats, sleepes, & laughes at his enuiers folly, or

peraduenture pitties him.

  ^e St Paul . . . this loue.] Saint *Paul* shewes that without charitie euen spirituall graces are of no worth.

  ^f first . . . comandement] By Charitie we performe our Sauiour Christs commandement,

  ^g you] By it we

  ^h you] By it wee

malice   toward thy brother be sure thy   hart is not vpright toward god   thearfore
so root it from thy hart   that no string[a] [22] of it be left for   it will grow faster then
Jonahs   gourd:[123] Answear me not wth flesh   and bloud cannot doo this. I know   it
but if thou desire god to giue   thee his holy spirrit thou shallt be   strong to suffer
and ready to for   giue thou must not in any thing   be subiect to the fleshe for
the wi[s]   dom of the flesh is deathe but   [fol. 43r] allways make the spirrit
thy   guide for thear is life and peace[124]   the diuell would desire no
greater   aduantage then that thou wouldest   trust thy soule to the discretyon
of   thy corrupt fleshe he would soon   force[b] that to betray thee but   when thou
hast put thy selfe   vnder the spirrit submittinge thy   will to the will of god he
is   no more able to hurt thee

The next excuse I would take   from thee is a very foolish one   but so comon
that I fear you   may happen on it and that is   this if I should suffer wrongs
    patiently what will become of   my reputation what will the   world say:[125]
truly if you remember   Christ hathe suffered more for you   then it is possible
for you to suffer   yet he neuer reuiled any of his   enemis nor strake his
persecutors   but prayed for them and by his[c]   example teaches all that loue him
to   do the like he wills you to turn || [fol. 43v] The left cheek to him that smot   the
right to giue to him that   takes from you and to go w[th]   him that compells
you:[126] but theas   are strange rules for a generous[127]   spirit in theas times nay
sure if   I bee struck I must strike agay[n]   els I am a coward, indeed for   giuings[d]
if it wear to one tha[t]   would desire it at my hand[e] I   had rather giue a
fragment of   my right then go to law but   if he will not sue to me Ile   spend all
I am worthe eare I   yeeld,[128] or I would go out of m[y]   door to show a man his
way   but I would fayn see whoo   could compell mee[129] I marry   this is of the
right streyn but   now look wth a considerate e[ye]   vppon this custom of the
wor[ld]   and the former comandement of   christ and thou shallt finde the[f]
    iust oposit thearfore take hee[d]   [fol. 44r] and let it bee thy cheef
care   neuer to prise thy reputation   wth men equall to the salluation   of thyne
own soule but if thou de   [s]irest to keep thy credit vnblemishe[d]   serue god
wth an vpright hart   and doo nothinge to any man y[t]   thou wouldst not bee
content hee   should doo vnto thee open thy   hand to the poor according to   thy
ability meddle not wth oth[er]   mens occasions[130] but whear maies[t]   doo
good[g] and if it bee in thy   powr to hurt thine enemy let   it pass doo him good if

---

[a] thearfore . . . string] So root it out from thy
heart, that no sting

[b] force] inueigle

[c] and by his] And his

[d] indeed for giuings] Indeed as for giuing,

[e] hand] hands,

[f] the] them

[g] doo good] doe good, and hast a calling to it.

thou   canst and boast not of it he tha[t]   sees the[e] in priuate will openly
reward thee lastly let thy har[t]   be kept allways in aw of this   want of charyty
by continuall   remembringe that thou hast no   form of prayr to desire fogiuen
    nes for thy selfe if thou forgiue || [fol. 44v] not others all other petitions   god
grants vs freely[a] only this   is conditionall he forgiue vs   as wee forgiue others
our   sauior hathe taught vs no othe[r]   way to desire it and in the   18 of
Mathew he shows god   will no otherwise grant it[b] [131]

[a] thou hast . . . freely] thou hast of thy   couenantest to forgiue others. All the other
Sauiour no other forme of praier to desire   petitions we present vnto God absolutely:
forgiuenesse for thy selfe, than that wherin thou   [b] grant it] grant it. FINIS.

Notes

1. Romans 8:28.

2. *Ouerseer*: 'A person (formerly) appointed by a testator to supervise or assist the executor or executors of the will' (*OED*). The letter is Joscelin's will, whose instructions the child will execute or carry into effect, overseen by its father.

3. Patricia Crawford quotes one seventeenth-century woman advising her sister-in-law that she had found 'a brown ruddy complexioned nurse' the best: 'The Construction and Experience of Maternity in Seventeenth-Century England', in Fildes (ed.), *Women as Mothers in Pre-Industrial England*, p. 29. A child was thought not only to imbibe health or sickness, but a good or evil character from the milk of its wetnurse. Henry Smith writes, 'as the nurse is affected in her body or in her mind, commōly the child draweth the like infirmitie from her'. *A Preparatiue to Mariage*, p. 78.

4. *Scripulous*: scrupulous. Strict, or minutely concerned with what is right.

5. MS: the character struck out after *like* could be *a* or *v*.

6. Joscelin's father Sir Richard Brooke married Katherine Nevill as his second wife. They had five sons and three daughters – Mary, Anne, and Dorothy – the 'sisters' (step-sisters) with whom a daughter might live and be educated. It was common for children of the upper or middle ranks (even those who had not lost a mother) to be sent away to live and be educated in another household. In this case, that household would have been Sir Richard's seat, the old priory in Norton, Cheshire.

7. *Work*: in the singular, 'work' has the sense of needlework, a conventionally feminine occupation.

8. *Fly boat*: a small boat, especially a ship's boat, for which a mainsail (the principal sail of the ship) would be too large. *Ballace* is a possible form of 'ballast', the heavy material loaded into the hold to stabilize a ship when it is under sail and in motion (see *OED*, *ballast*). Joscelin may here be borrowing from Sir Thomas Overbury's popular didactic poem, *A Wife*. In enumerating the virtues of womankind, Overbury draws the line at learning, which 'doth not adde more *ballaste*, but more *saile*'. *A Wife Now the Widdow of Sir Thomas Ouerburye* (London, 1614). See p. 96.

9. MS: the shade of ink changes here, possibly indicating that Joscelin came back to writing this section after an interval.

10. *Lectors*: lectures, instructive or admonitory speeches.

11. *Generous*: appropriate to one of noble birth or spirit.

12. Joscelin seems to forbid the use of titles of respect (which might encourage vanity), and perhaps nicknaming. In *A Preparatiue to Mariage*, Henry Smith notes that the Jews gave their children names which would put them in mind of their religion: an 'admonition', Smith continues, 'to such as call their childrē at all aduentures, sometimes by the name of dogs euē as they proue after' (pp. 80–1).

13. *Pauper vbique iacet*: the poor lie (or languish) everywhere. Originally from Ovid's *Fasti* 1.218, and thence proverbial: see H. Walther, *Proverbia Sententiaeque Latinitatis Medii Aevi*, Teil 3 (Göttingen, Vandenhoeck & Ruprecht, 1965), #20949.

14. *Method*: 'arrangement of a discourse according to more or less formal rules' (*OED* sense 5). Joscelin may have been thinking specifically of Peter Ramus' strategy of ordering information from the general to the specific. The Ramist 'method' was popularly used in godly didactic tracts; for example, the writings of the Puritan minister William Perkins.

15. *Inuiolable*: not capable of being changed, broken, or degraded. 'Th'inviolable Saints / In Cubic Phalanx firm advanc't entire.' *Paradise Lost*, VI, ll. 398–9.

16. This may indicate that Joscelin started writing at an advanced stage of her pregnancy. She gave birth on 12 October 1622.

17. Joscelin was the only grandchild and heir of William Chaderton, who died in 1608 when she was twelve. Her only daughter Theodora also became an heiress. Joscelin may be thinking here of Matthew 16:26: 'For what shall it profite a man though he should winne the whole world, if hee lose his owne soule?'

18. *Dandle*: bounce gently up and down in the arms or on the knee.

19. 'No honey without gall' and 'Of honey and gall in love there is store' were proverbial sayings (Tilley H556, H557).

20. Under the system of primogeniture, the wealth and property of the upper ranks tended to pass undivided to the eldest son. Younger brothers of this class often had to find the means to maintain themselves: as ministers, for instance, but also as soldiers, administrators, and lawyers. For the perceived contemptibleness of the ministry, see Christopher Hill, *Economic Problems of the Church: From Archbishop Whitgift to the Long Parliament* (Oxford, Clarendon, 1956), pp. 207–8. Hill cites this passage from Joscelin.

21. A slight rephrasing of Psalm 51:15: 'Open thou my lips, O Lord, and my mouth shall shew forth thy praise.' The verse was also incorporated into *The Book of Common Prayer*'s liturgy for Morning and Evening Prayer, where the first clause was spoken by the minister, and the second by the congregation.

22. MS: the correction seems to have been made later, in darker ink and with a sharper pen.

23. In advising parents to choose a fit calling for their children, William Gouge writes: 'let parents be exhorted to traine vp such children as they finde fit, to the great and weighty calling of the ministerie: no calling wherein any may doe more good, and wherein (if they be able and faithfull Minsiters) they can receiue more comfort and contentment'. *Of Domesticall Duties* (London, 1622), pp. 534–5. *They labor in his vineyard*: from parables in Matthew 20 and 21 (see *OED*, vineyard, 1b).

24. When the Israelites in Egypt requested time off for worship, Pharaoh required them not only to make their usual tally of bricks, but also to gather the straw used in brickmaking (Exodus 5). See Tilley, B660.

25. Joscelin owed her wealth to her grandfather William Chaderton, who became Bishop of Chester in 1579 and Bishop of Lincoln in 1595. In 1575, the bishopric of Chester was nominally worth about

£420 per year, and that of Lincoln about £894. According to Hill, however, the real economic value of a bishopric was not its stipend, but 'the opportunity it gave for by-earnings'. *Economic Problems*, pp. 26–7.

26. *Steward*: a servant entrusted with the management of an estate or household.

27. MS: repeats *an*. Joscelin is here recasting a common New Testament opposition between worldly and spiritual riches. See, for instance, the parable of the rich man in Luke 12:16–21.

28. See Dorothy Leigh's very similar disclaimer, p. 23.

29. Under 'Duties of Parents', Gouge dedicates a section to '*a mothers care ouer her childe while it is in her wombe*'. *Of Domesticall Duties*, pp. 505–6.

30. The biblical book of 'Ecclesiastes, or the Preacher' was attributed to King Solomon, renowned for wisdom. The Geneva Bible headnote to Ecclesiastes summarizes: 'Salomon as a Preacher and one that desired to instruct all in the way of saluation, describeth the deceiuable vanities of this world.'

31. Under his heading '*Of instructing children so soone as they are capable*', Gouge writes, 'A vessell longest keepeth that sauour with which at first it is seasoned', giving the source of this sententious saying in the margin: 'Quo semel est imbuta recens seruabit odorem Testa diu. Hor.' *Of Domesticall Duties*, p. 543. The quotation is from Horace's *Epistles*, I.2, 'To Lollius', ll. 69–70, and is a favourite with writers on the godly education of children. See also Tilley L333.

32. Abel presented the first-born of his flock to God. His sacrifice was found acceptable, while his brother Cain's was not. Genesis 4:2–5.

33. A pastiche of the language of the Psalms. Compare, for instance, Psalm 63:4–6: 'Thus wil I magnifie thee all my life, and lift vp mine hands . . . my mouth shall praise thee with joyfull lips . . . when I thinke vpon thee in the night watches' and Psalm 9:1: 'I will praise the Lord with my whole heart: I will speake of all thy maruellous workes.'

34. *To couenant*: to enter into a solemn contract or agreement, as in the biblical covenants between God and his chosen people.

35. MS: leaves a space between *dutis* and *Marke*.

36. *Cozen*: cheat.

37. MS: *slept* is corrected to *sleepe*: the final *e* is superimposed on the *t*.

38. MS: *th[i]s* corrected to *the*.

39. This passage has some parallels with Matthew 5:29. 'Wherefore if thy right eie cause thee to offend, plucke it out, and cast it from thee: for better it is for thee that one of thy members perish, then that thy whole body should be cast into hell.' Joscelin's advice to allow the sinful member to assist in repentance is much milder.

40. Jacob wrestled with God (who appeared to him as 'a man'), and would not let him go until he blessed him. Genesis 32:24–30. *Jaakob* is the spelling of the Geneva Bible.

41. Matthew 11:12.

42. The association of the devil with idleness is proverbial. See, for example, Tilley B594, D281, I10, and Leigh, Chapter 40, p. 65.

43. The Book of Proverbs (also thought to be by Solomon) has this warning: 'How long wilt thou sleepe, O sluggard? . . . thy pouerty commeth as one that trauaileth by the way, and thy necessity like an armed man' (6:9, 11).

44. The five foolish virgins neglect to bring oil to light their lamps and so miss the Bridegroom (Christ) and are shut out from his marriage feast. Matthew 25:1–12. The slothful servant does

nothing with the one talent entrusted to him while his master is away. It is therefore given to the faithful servant who has multiplied his five talents by another five. Matthew 25:14–28.

45. *Toy*: a frivolous or worthless item or ornament.

46. MS: repeats *soule* at the start of fol. 19r.

47. Joscelin satirizes fashionable affectations using fairly topical vocabulary. *Fashionist* (one who studies and follows fashions) is first recorded from 1616. *Apish* (here with the double sense of 'foolishly affected and imitative') is a favourite word of poets such as Brathwait and Wither, who often collocate it with *toys*. *Cringing* (contorted, obsequious bowing) is satirized on one of Jonson's 1616 additions to *Cynthia's Revels* (V.iv.159). Finally, *shrugging* (raising the shoulders in a gesture of disdain) is satirized in the character of 'An affected Traueller', printed with Overbury's *A Wife* in 1614: he 'censures all things by countenances, and shrugs' (sig. E1v).

48. *Gall*: bile, proverbially bitter.

49. *Corrupt will*. The will is the mental faculty which enables one to choose good or evil. Calvinist theology emphasizes its corruption through Original Sin. Thus, Henry Smith's 'Morning Prayer', recommended by Joscelin (see note 59), states: 'the wil which was giuen vs to affect righteousness, is apt now to loue nothing but wickednes' (p. 252).

50. The injunction from Ecclesiastes 12:1 with which Joscelin opens her first numbered division. See note 30.

51. *Carriage*: manner of conducting oneself, behaviour.

52. MS: leaves a half-line blank and continues thereafter in a lighter shade of ink.

53. *Raze out*: obliterate, erase.

54. *Anna*: a widow who served God by fasting and praying in the temple at Jerusalem. When the child Jesus was brought to the temple, Anna prophesied that he would bring redemption (Luke 2:36–8). *Elizabeth*: the cousin of Mary and mother of John the Baptist. Both she and her husband 'were iust before God, and walked in all the commaundements and ordinances of the Lord, without reproofe' (Luke 1:6). *Esther*: the Jewish wife of King Ahasuerus. When her people were threatened with destruction, she fasted with her maidens and risked death by petitioning the King (Esther 4:16). *Susanna*: unjustly accused of adultery by two elders who lustfully spied on her as she bathed in her garden. The prophet Daniel cleared her name by exposing their contradictory testimony. Although the 'History of Susanna' was not considered one of the canonical books of scripture, it was included in the Geneva Bible under 'Apocrypha'. 'The strictest' might cavil either at the canonicity or the erotic scenario of the story.

Anna, Elizabeth, and Susanna are the female names recommended by Leigh for her sons' children. See Leigh, note 41.

55. It was popularly believed that the devil could be recognized, even under an assumed shape, by his one cloven hoof. See Tilley D252.

56. *They stand on tiptoes*: they raise themselves, or consider themselves higher than others. *Rekoninge*: counting, adding up. *Pharisee*: the Pharisees were pious Jews, characterized by their strict observance of Mosaic Law and, in the gospels, criticized by Jesus for their pretentions to superior sanctity. Cf. Luke 18:11: 'The Pharise stood and prayed thus with himselfe, O God, I thanke thee that I am not as other men'; and Leigh, note 73.

57. *Diuells*: the idea of rebel angels becoming devils is based on Isaiah 14:12–15, which recounts the pride of Lucifer in desiring to be 'aboue beside the starres of God'. For his punishment he was

'brought downe to the graue, to the sides of the pit'. *Nabuchodonezer*: Nebuchadnezzar, King of Babylon. He was divinely punished for his pride by being driven from human society: 'his heart was made like the beasts, and his dwelling was with the wilde asses: they feed him with grasse like oxen' (Daniel 5:20–1). *Jesabell*: Jezebel's 'wicked counsell' (as the Geneva note to 1 Kings 21:25 calls it) resulted in the murder of a man whose vineyard was coveted by her husband King Ahab. Her specific sin of pride, though, was her manner of greeting the new anointed King of Israel, Jehu: out of a window, having 'painted her face, and tired her head [put on a head-dress]'. The Geneva note comments on this (2 Kings 9:30): 'Being of an hautie and cruell nature, she would still reteine her princely state and dignitie.' She was cast out of the window and eaten by dogs, as prophesied by Elijah (2 Kings 9:36).

58. The good man whose saying this is was presumably either a minister or the author of a godly book. MS: leaves space at the end of the line, after which the writing resumes in a slightly larger hand and with a change in the shade of ink.

59. The Puritan minister Henry Smith's *Three prayers* were published separately as well as appended to *A Preparatiue to Mariage* in 1591, the year of his death. Smith's first prayer is 'for Morning'; the second, which Joscelin also recommends (see note 96) is 'for Euening'. The morning prayer is lengthy and Calvinist, beginning with a confession of complete human corruption. 'Our heart is a roote of corruption,' Smith writes, 'our eys are the eyes of vanity, our eares are the eares of follie, our mouthes are the mouthes of deceit, our hands are the hands of iniquitie' (p. 252). Even human prayer is inadequate: 'when we haue prayed, we had need to pray againe that thou wouldest forgiue our prayers' (p. 253). God's help is therefore beseeched at length, not least so 'that our time to come, may be a repentance of the time past, thinking alway of the ioyes of heauen, the paynes of hell, our owne death, and the death of thy sonne for vs' (p. 256). Smith ends with a household prayer: 'Blesse this familie with thy grace and peace, that the Rulers thereof may gouerne according to thy word, that the seruants may obey like the Seruants of God, and that we may all so loue one another, that we may all be loued of thee.' The whole is finished with the 'Our Father' (pp. 258–9). Joscelin's recommendation of Henry Smith's prayers was cut from the 1684 edition of her legacy. For this later excision, and discussion of which issue of the prayers Joscelin used, see 'Introduction'.

60. The most zealous Puritans tended to favour extemporaneous prayer – what Joscelin calls 'conceyued prayr' (see *OED*, *conceived* 2b) – as opposed to set (or pre-written) prayers, particularly those from *The Book of Common Prayer*. At the opening of her Chapter 33, Leigh declares herself opposed to the use of set prayers for personal devotions. For a different position on prayer, see Richardson, 'Introduction'.

61. *Publick prayr*: in this context, household worship, in which everyone living in the house (family, servants, guests) participates. Joscelin distinguishes this from *priuate prayr* undertaken in solitude – probably in one's closet or private room and just after one has risen or is about to retire to bed. Leigh begins her Chapter 18 by recommending prayer first thing in the morning, emphasizing that it should be in 'some priuate place'.

62. *Diuinity*: the study of all things pertaining to God, his nature, and relationship to humankind. Joscelin's citations from the Psalms below (see note 66) suggest that divinity involves the study both of God's 'testimonys' ('Gods word' according to the Geneva note to Psalm 119:14) and 'works' (Psalm 92:4) – that is, the material evidences of God's dealings with the world.

63. John 12:26.

64. King Ahasuerus honoured Mordecai, who had exposed an assassination plot, by clothing him in royal apparel. Esther 6:1–10.

65. 1 Timothy 6:6.

66. King David was thought to be the author of the biblical book of Psalms, which is indeed titled 'The Psalmes of Dauid' in the Geneva Bible. Psalm 119:14. (The verse in fact reads: 'I haue had as great delight in the way of thy testimonies, as in all riches.') Psalm 92:4. Psalm 4:7: 'Thou hast giuen me more joy of heart, then they haue had, when their wheate and their wine did abound.' In Psalm 91, the faithful are assured that they will be delivered from pestilence and a variety of other dangers: 'A thousand shall fall at thy side, and tenne thousand at thy right hand, but it shall not come neere thee.'

67. *Light*: without substance, trivial, unable to command respect.

68. MS: continues with a larger hand, a duller pen, and a different shade of ink.

69. To take God's name in vain is to break the Third Commandment (Exodus 20:7). Joscelin's point is that this may be done either out of frivolity or intense feeling, 'earnestnes' [see *OED*, *earnest* (as adjective), sense 1].

70. *It is odds but*: the odds are, it is probable that.

71. A familiar dramatic example of this practice is Prince Hal's quizzing of the tavern drawer Francis at the beginning of 2.4, *Henry IV, Part One*.

72. Joscelin is here pointing out the danger of the academic exercise (designed to develop rhetorical skill) of formulating arguments against an evident truth; for instance, demonstrating that the sun shines in the night sky. Her words recall the Apostle Paul's warning to abstain from practices which, although not prohibited, might nonetheless lead astray weaker Christians: 'It is good neither to eate flesh, nor to drinke wine, nor any thing whereby thy brother stumbleth, or is offended, or made weake' (Romans 14:21). See also 1 Corinthians 8:11.

73. *Frothe*: the bubbles or scum which form on the surface of a liquid; here, figuratively, unsubstantial or worthless words or behaviour.

74. MS: this line begins with a slight indentation.

75. The last citation from Proverbs is in fact from 14:3. MS: a small space left at the end of this line.

76. *Eschue*: eschew, avoid.

77. MS: leaves space at the end of the line. For Leigh, the *Preachers* are explicitly those whom God has set 'for a light' in the Church (see Leigh, p. 76).

78. Romans 8:28, as in the letter to Taurell (see note 1).

79. MS: leaves space at the end of the line.

80. *Chalenge*: invite, provoke.

81. This paraphrase of Psalm 73 is put together mainly from quotations (verses 2, 17–18, 25).

82. Here Joscelin amplifies Jesus' parable of the wise man building on rock, as opposed to the foolish man building on sand (Matthew 7:24–7). That the house on sand is 'a paper house' (that is, especially flimsy) is Joscelin's elaboration.

83. *Agaynst it came*: in anticipation of its coming (that is, in anticipation of or preparation for the 'day of affliction').

84. Cain's response (Genesis 4:13) to the curse of exile placed on him for killing his brother contrasts with the archetypally patient Job's acceptance (Job 13:15) of undeserved suffering.

85. The distinction between *chaff* and *wheat* is made by John the Baptist, speaking of the coming of Christ: the wheat (the godly) will be gathered in, while the chaff (the waste part of the harvest representing the wicked) will be burned (Matthew 3:12). The Geneva note on this verse reads: 'The triumphes of the wicked shall end in euerlasting torment.' The expanded use of *cross* for any affliction is ultimately biblical: 'And whosoeuer beareth not his crosse, and commeth after me, cannot be my disciple' (Luke 14:27). The last words in this passage are Job's. Covered with boils and urged by his wife to 'blaspheme God, and die', Job replies: 'shall we receiue good at the hand of God, and not receiue euill?' (Job 2:10).

86. *Besotted*: muddled, stupefied, intellectually or spiritually blinded.

87. When he was afraid for the outcome of a battle with the Philistines, Saul consulted a woman at Endor who had 'a familiar spirit', asking her to conjure the dead prophet Samuel to advise him (1 Samuel 28:7–14). Joscelin compares this to the practice of seeking remedies from 'witches' or wise women (or men), which William Perkins also condemns: 'For let a mans childe, friend, or cattell be taken with some sore sicknes . . . the first thing he doth, is to bethink himselfe and inquire after some Wise-man or wise-woman & thither he sends and goes for helpe. . . . And the partie thus cured, cannot say with Dauid: The *Lord is my helper*, but the deuill is my helper, for by him hee is cured.' *A Discourse of the Damned Art of Witchcraft* (1608).

88. Matthew 5:37.

89. *Thy word will be as current as thy oathe*: your mere promise will be generally accepted, with no necessity for oaths or swearing (calling upon God as witness, etc.).

90. Matthew 5:34: 'But I say vnto you, Sweare not at all.' The 1624 edition corrects the scriptural reference.

91. This reference to Ecclesiastes (reproduced also in the 1624 edition) is wrong. Could the correct reference be 5:2–8? Ecclesiastes 5:1 advises, 'let thy words be few', and subsequent verses discuss vows.

92. Proverbs 23:29–35. Among the miseries occasioned by drunkenness: 'Thine eyes shall looke vpon strange women, and thine heart shall speake lewd things.'

93. For cases of drunken homicide in Essex, see F.G. Emmison, *Elizabethan Life: Disorder* (Chelmsford, Essex County Council, 1970), pp. 150–1, 158–9.

94. Leigh also discusses the sin one's 'nature is most subiect vnto', likening it to a weed which will grow in one part of the earth but not in another. See Chap. 20, p. 37, also Chap. 33, p. 52.

95. *Kist the block*: euphemism for execution by beheading, which usually took place on a wooden block. Joscelin's metaphor recalls Leigh's advice for dealing with the prime sin: 'ouercome the captaine, and all the army will be discomfited' (see p. 53).

96. Like the morning prayer (see note 59), Smith's prayer for evening is long, Calvinist, and culminates in the 'Our Father'. Again the emphasis is on inescapable corruption. When at night, 'one day neerer to death' (p. 262), we examine our consciences, we find only unthankfulness for God's many benefits. Nonetheless God spares us, 'we sleepe, and to morrow we sin againe: this is the course of all our pilgrimage' (p. 263). The prayer thus asks again for God's grace, so that the petitioner – like the tree which brings forth leaves, then blossoms, then fruit – may bring forth good thoughts, good speeches, and a good life, 'to the honour of thy name, the good of thy children, and the saluation of our soules, remembering the time when we shall sleepe in the graue' (p. 265).

As previously (see note 61), the 'public' prayers of a family or household are distinguished from the solitary prayers of a man or woman retiring to bed.

97. Revelation 1:8: 'I am Alpha & Omega, the beginning and ye ending, saith the Lord.'

98. *Another remember*: Joscelin uses 'remember' as a substantive here; the subject of the Sabbath requires another injunction to remember. MS: 'remember' appears by itself at the bottom right-hand corner of fol. 34r. 'Remember' is also the first word of fol. 34v. By its placement at the bottom of fol. 34r, Joscelin seems to be treating 'remember' as a catchword, leading her reader's eye over the page to the beginning of the next section.

99. While the Israelites are in the wilderness, a man gathering sticks is condemned to death by stoning – God pronouncing judgement through Moses (Numbers 15:32–5).

100. *Allmost*: the obsolete use of *almost* to intensify a rhetorical question. (See *OED*, sense 4.)

101. MS: a line is left blank before the Fourth Commandment.

102. Exodus 20: 8–11. MS: space left at the end of the line.

103. MS: *perswaded* written by itself as the last line of fol. 35v.

104. Leigh uses the same common analogy between digestion and meditation on the Holy Word (see Chap. 7, p. 26). Leigh also emphasizes the necessity of putting it into practice (see Chap. 23, p. 41) – as Joscelin does in the next passage.

105. MS: *thy* corrected to *the*: the *e* is superimposed on the *y*. The 1624 edition reproduces *the*.

106. *If thou turn away thy foot . . . the L hathe spoken it.* Isaiah 58:13–14. Joscelin reproduces the wording of the Geneva Bible exactly. The Geneva note glosses 'turne away thy foote' with 'refraine thy selfe from thy wicked workes'.

107. MS: *34* corrected from *14* [?]; the 1624 edition reproduces *34*. For God's reiterated instructions to Moses that the children of Israel should keep the Sabbath, see Exodus 31:12–17 as well as 34:21.

108. MS: *12* inserted over the colon after *god*, and the line continues without a break until *honor*.

109. The Geneva headnote to Exodus 20 breaks the Ten Commandments into two 'tables' to correspond to the two stone tablets divinely given to Moses on Mount Sinai. These two tables or tablets of commandments were visually reproduced in churches.

110. Joscelin contends that breaking the first commandment of the first table (to worship no other god but the one God) will lead to the violation of the other three commandments of the first table: prohibitions against making graven images, taking God's name in vain, and violating the Sabbath (Exodus 20:3–11). Similarly, disobeying parents breaks the first commandment of the *second* table, and so leads to the sins prohibited by the remaining five commandments of the second table: murder, adultery, theft, bearing false witness, and coveting what belongs to one's neighbour (20:5–10).

111. Aeneas famously saved his aged father Anchises, carrying him on his shoulders from the burning city of Troy.

112. The words are those of Jacob anticipating the death of his son Benjamin. Genesis 42:38.

113. *Calumnious aspertyons*: insinuations or false accusations which would harm the good name of one's parents.

114. *To couet what thou thinkest thy parents life too longe detayns from thee*: to be impatient for one's inheritance, and so for the death of one's parents.

115. Matthew 7:12, and thence proverbial (Tilley D395).

116. John 13:34–5.

117. Matthew 5:44 and the first half of verse 45.

118. Judas betrayed Jesus to his enemies for thirty pieces of silver (Matthew 26:15).

119. *Till the vse hathe deuoured the principall*: until interest charges have exceeded the sum originally lent, or the value of the thing originally pawned, with a pun on the sense of 'principal' as the person chiefly concerned in the transaction (i.e. the 'foolish vnthrift').

120. 1 John 3:14–15: 'We know that wee are translated from death vnto life, because we loue the brethren: he that loueth not his brother, abideth in death. Whosoeuer hateth his brother, is a manslayer: and ye know that no manslayer hath eternall life abiding in him.' 1 John 4:8: 'Hee that loueth not, knoweth not God: for God is loue.' 1 John 4:20: 'If any man say, I loue God, and hate his brother, he is a lyar: for how can hee that loueth not his brother whom hee hath seene, loue God whom he has not seene?' The oft quoted thirteenth chapter of Paul's first letter to the Corinthians begins: 'Though I speake with the tongues of men and Angels, & haue not loue, I am as sounding brasse, or a tinkling cymball.'

121. Romans 13:8: 'Owe nothing to any man, but to loue one another: for he that loueth another, hath fulfilled the Law.' Romans 13:10: 'Loue doeth not euill to his neighbour: therefore is Loue the fulfilling of the Law.' 1 John 2:10: 'Hee that loueth his brother, abideth in that light' (i.e. the 'true light' of verse 8).

122. *String*: root. See *OED*, *string*, sense 2c, which cites John Bunyan: 'roots and strings of inbred errour'.

123. To shield the prophet Jonah from the sun, God caused a climbing plant (of the kind which bears a fleshy fruit called a gourd) to grow up over his shelter in just one night. Jonah 4:6–10.

124. Romans 8:6: 'For the wisedome of the flesh is death: but the wisedome of the Spirit is life and peace.'

125. For the code which forbade a gentleman to suffer wrongs patiently, see Lawrence Stone, *The Crisis of the Aristocracy 1558–1641* (Oxford, Clarendon, 1965), p. 246.

126. A paraphrase of Matthew 5:39–41.

127. *Generous*: noble (as in note 11).

128. *If it wear to one tha[t] would desire it at my hand . . .*: if asked nicely, I'll yield some of what is rightfully mine or due to me to avoid a lawsuit; but if not petitioned, I'll spend my last penny to frustrate my opponent in the law courts.

129. *I would go out of m[y] door . . .*: If I choose, I will inconvenience myself by stepping into the street to give directions; but I will not allow anyone to force me to do so.

130. *Occasions*: affairs, business.

131. The eighteenth chapter of Matthew contains the parable of the servant whose debt of ten thousand talents is forgiven by the King, but who will not himself forgive another servant's much smaller debt. On hearing this, the King throws the first servant in prison, to be tormented until he pays his ten thousand talents (verses 23–4). The parable (and chapter) ends with the words of Jesus: 'So likewise shall mine heauenly Father doe vnto you, except yee forgiue from your hearts, each one to his brother their trespasses.'

Part III

ELIZABETH RICHARDSON

INTRODUCTION TO ELIZABETH RICHARDSON

A Ladies Legacie to her Daughters (1645)

To express their maternal zeal, Leigh and Joscelin instruct and advise. Elizabeth Richardson's characteristic mode, however, is prayer. In one of the prayers in *A Ladies Legacie to her Daughters*, she disparagingly refers to her devotions as 'the poore fruit of my lips': a poor recompense to God for all his spiritual and temporal blessings. Richardson took care, nonetheless, to ensure that the fruit was plentiful. Throughout her long life, she wrote and rewrote prayers and meditations for the use of herself and her family. Besides the *Legacie* printed in 1645 (copies of which she annotated for her brother and grandson), two earlier manuscript books of prayers survive: one dated 1606 in the Folger Library, and the other, dated 1625 and presented in 1635 to a daughter, in the East Sussex Record Office.[1] Over a period of forty years, Richardson remained persistently interested in writing, revising, and distributing her prayers. Why did she write them, and why did she write so many?

Like Leigh and Joscelin, Richardson is not slow to justify her writing project. This 'poore book', she writes in her grandson Sir Edward Dering's copy of *A Ladies Legacie*, was intended 'for all my Children & Grand-children; for their instruction in their youth, & for their use, & remembrance of me afterwardes'.[2] Richardson's manuscript book of prayers presented to her eldest daughter Elizabeth contains similar sentiments. On the title page, Richardson writes, 'Sweet Besse, (as you loue me) keep this, though you lost ye first.' Like Joscelin, Richardson imagines her book posthumously replacing her lost self. This book too is for 'remembrance'. But it is also for use: she hopes it will be used 'dayly . . . to effect, & further your Saluation'.[3]

Richardson's prayer books were not mere family keepsakes but were meant to be *used* as devotional aids. It is certainly much easier to imagine the printed *Legacie* of 1645 consulted daily rather than read through at a sitting. The work itself explicitly invites this kind of practical, regular handling. It begins with a prefatory letter advising Richardson's daughters 'often to peruse, ponder, practice, and make use of this Booke according to my intention'. Richardson's intentions are made known partly by this sort of direct address to the primary recipients of the book, and partly by the structure of the *Legacie* itself. It is in fact divided into three books: the division serving the double purpose of ordering the reader's devotions and of memorializing three stages of Richardson's own life and devotional practice.

Book I is substantially the book of prayers she presented to her eldest daughter, 'Besse'. A note in that manuscript records the circumstances of its composition, 'at Chelsie, in September 1625. to spend away some of our malencholly time there; where yᵉ danger of death inclosed vs ⌈round⌉ about'.[4] A prefatory note to the 1645 *Legacie* specifies further that the danger came from the 'great sicknesse' in London, and that Richardson (at that time the widow of her first husband, Ashburnham) was staying with her children at the Duke of Buckingham's house in Chelsea. Additions and changes were made to the prayers composed under these melancholy circumstances before they appeared in the 1645 edition. Nonetheless, Book I of the *Legacie* reflects Richardson's earliest pattern of composition, a pattern which organizes both the 1606 Folger manuscript and the 1625 manuscript given to Besse. Meditations on passages of scriptures, supported by copious marginal citiations, are followed by prayers. In the Folger manuscript, for instance, a meditation on passages from Proverbs entitled 'The Profitt of wisdome, & holie knowledge, which is yᵉ science of Saintes' is followed by 'A praier for knowledge and understandinge before reading or studie'. Similarly, a meditation on biblical passages relating to faith is followed by 'A prayer for a true & fruitfull faith'.[5]

By the composition of Book II, written after the death of her second husband in 1634, Richardson has become notably less interested in meditating on scripture and now seems exclusively interested in prayers. Book I contains a number of prayers for specific occasions and settings: for example, at the first sight of morning light, before going to church, in bed before going to sleep. Book II takes these instructions for use a step further, by assigning specific prayers to each day of the week: two prayers, for instance, are given for Thursday morning and two for Thursday night. There is an attempt to differentiate each day's prayers by concentrating on different persons of the Trinity on different days. But the prayers are really so similar that the rationale for this cycle seems not to have been variety, but rather Richardson's desire to order her readers' use of her prayers into a regular daily and weekly pattern of devotion. Her annotations in a copy of the *Legacie* intended for her brother suggest that this ordering mattered to her. A weekly series of prayers for four o'clock in the afternoon was mistakenly printed in Book III rather than II, and Richardson notes, 'These should haue Joyned to yᵉ weekly exercise.'[6]

The prayers of Book III are, as a whole, the most personal, written out of crises of sorrow or sickness in her widowhood and old age. But even her 'sorrowfull widowes prayer', whose long title announces the circumstances of its composition shortly after the death of her second husband, invites wider adaptation and use: 'this may also serve any other upon the like occasion'.

Some prayers are to be read quietly and privately to oneself, on specific occasions and in specific places (like bed). Others may be adapted for 'public' use: that is, read aloud to household members during family prayers. The prayer to be read immediately after sitting down in one's pew in church suggests that

Richardson evisaged readers carrying about her book in their pockets; it was printed in octavo size, which would have made it easily portable.[7]

A present-day reader, used to reading novels from beginning to end, might keep in mind Richardson's 'intentions' for the practical, adaptable, not necessarily linear use of her prayers. It is positively in the spirit of the text to read the last prayers first, or to dip into the whole at random. If, on the one hand, Richardson is interested in ordering her readers' spiritual experience, she also deliberately leaves her prayers open to adaptation. This is perhaps why the majority of her prayers seem so impersonal: they are everywoman's, and everyman's. And although Richardson is very clear about originating and legitimating her writing in her 'private' maternal role – even manually changing the title of *A Ladies Legacie* to *A Mothers Legacie* in her presentation copies – she is equally clear that she sees an audience beyond the confines of the family. 'I shall be very glad and joyfull,' she writes at the beginning of the prayers of Book II, 'if my children, grand-children, kindred, friends, or any good Christian that shall peruse them, may make a good and right use of them to Gods glory.'

When we read Richardson's prayers, we don't get the glimpses of everyday life in a godly household that we do from Leigh or Joscelin. Her late prayers relating to widowhood and sickness, and her early prayer on the near-drowning of her eldest daughter in the Thames, are exceptions. We do, however, get a strong sense of what familial, social, and material uses she intended for her various writings. And despite the overt absence of autobiography from many of her prayers, we are nonetheless able to witness her return – almost obsessive in nature, and certainly personal in another sense – to the ritualized drama of sanctification through prayer. The point of her prayers was perhaps to transcend the everyday and the personal, both of which, in her case, were fraught with difficulties.

LIFE

While Leigh and Joscelin had solid connections with the gentry class, Elizabeth Richardson was related both by birth and marriage to high-ranking noble families with close connections to the monarchy. But although Richardson enjoyed the greatest social status of the three women, she also arguably suffered the greatest vicissitudes of fortune.

She was born Elizabeth Beaumont, eldest daughter of Sir Thomas Beaumont and Catherine Farnham of Stoughton, Leicestershire. Elizabeth would later declare, in the second book of her *Legacie*, that in writing prayers for her children and grandchildren she was following the 'example of my dear parents', who took 'much paines with us, more then is usuall, by their endeavours to bring us to know and feare God'. Elizabeth was the eldest of ten children. She memorialized her parents, siblings, and self by erecting a monument in St Mary's Church at Stoughton, depicting her parents kneeling in prayer either side of a table, each with their own open Bible on the table between them. The three sons kneel behind their father on the left; the seven daughters behind their mother on the right. Elizabeth is the first and tallest daughter kneeling behind her mother; this is the closest we can come to a visual self-representation, albeit conventionally stylized and mediated through the engraver. (See Illustration, p. x.)

The Beaumonts were a large gentry family in Leicestershire with literary and court connections. The well-known dramatist Francis Beaumont was a relation, as was the lesser-known Spenserian poet Joseph Beaumont. In February 1618, Elizabeth's first cousin, Sir Thomas Beaumont of Coleorton, hosted a masque; among the masquers were the third Earl of Essex, Lord Willoughby, and Sir Walter Devereux.[8] But Elizabeth's most famous and useful connection was the first Duke of Buckingham. The powerful favourite of James I and Charles I was Elizabeth's second cousin once removed: Elizabeth's grandfather, Nicholas Beaumont of Coleorton, was first cousin to Mary Beaumont, wife of Sir George Villiers, and mother of George, first Duke of Buckingham.[9] Elizabeth and her children benefited from the connection, for it was in fact Buckingham's wife Katherine who lent them a part of the Duke's Chelsea house to escape from the plague. Elizabeth commemorates her in the *Legacie* as her patroness: 'the good Dutches, my most honoured Lady'.

Being well connected, it is not surprising that Elizabeth married a hereditary landowner; although unfortunately for her and her children, he also turned out to be rather careless with his inheritance. In November 1590, when she can have been no more than fourteen years old,[10] Elizabeth married John Ashburnham, whose family had been landowners in Sussex since the twelfth century. John's father was a Roman Catholic, and had lost the family estate when he failed to pay recusancy fines. On his death in 1592, John recovered the estate – only to waste his patrimony by overgenerously taking on the debts of his friends. He was knighted upon King James's accession in 1603, but ended up in the Fleet, imprisoned for debt. He died there, ignominiously, in 1620.[11]

His widow was left bankrupt, with six children. A letter written to her four daughters in September 1625 recalls the difficulties of this period, which included the problem of raising 'portions of wealth' or dowries for the three daughters who were yet unmarried. Richardson states that her miseries were so great that, had it not been for her children, she would have 'forsaken the World before it despised me'. Later, in a presentation copy of the 1645 *Legacie*, she emends this passage to suggest that she had retirement in mind rather than suicide; yet the original wording strongly suggests, if not suicide, certainly a strong desire for death to take her from her troubles.[12] But she recalls too that she was helped through by a stoic determination to rise above 'vile and transitorie things' and seek 'such as are above, more certain and permanent'. This could serve as an epitome of the majority of Elizabeth's prayers; indeed, the discipline of prayer must have been a useful strategy for coping with the instability of her earthly fortunes in the early 1620s.

Fortune being mutable, however, Elizabeth Ashburnham's soon improved. The tomb of her eldest son John retells the story of his father's ruin (including the selling of all his estate, 'not leaving to his wyfe and six children the least subsistence'): not out of disrespect, the inscription hastens to reassure the viewer, but rather 'to give God the prayse, who so suddenly provided both for his wife and children as that within less than two years after the death of the said Sir John, there was not any of them, but was in condition rather to be useful to others than to want support themselves'.[13] Some time after 1625, Elizabeth added an expression of gratitude to the 'Letter to my foure Daughters', commending her 'honourable friends' who have been 'carefull and deare parents unto us'.[14] Elizabeth's high connections, almost certainly the Duke and Duchess of Buckingham, must have come to the rescue.

Elizabeth's next turn of fortune was her marriage to Sir Thomas Richardson on 14 December 1626, a year after she took refuge at Buckingham's Chelsea house. Perhaps the Duke and Duchess also helped to arrange what must certainly have been a financially advantageous match. Richardson was a wealthy man: there were rumours that he bought his way up the judicial hierarchy. In the month before he married Elizabeth, he became Chief Justice of Common Pleas, and in 1631, Lord Chief Justice of the King's Bench. He was also rumoured to have bought his wife a title, for in February 1628, Elizabeth was created Baroness Cramond in the peerage of Scotland. A female ennoblement would have been unusual at this time – it is said to have occasioned 'gibes and pasquinades for the amusement of Westminster Hall' – and it too may have been brought about by her cousin Buckingham, then at the height of his influence just a few months before his assassination in August.[15]

Her children, meanwhile, about whose futures she had been worrying, were making their own fortunes. Her eldest son John was on easy terms with the King (who called him 'Jack'), helped to this intimacy and to the position of Groom of the Royal Bedchamber in 1628 by the patronage of Buckingham. He also married advantageously – an heiress who sold her entire estate to help him buy back the Ashburnham lands.[16] Elizabeth Richardson herself contributed to the recovery of the old inheritance by lending money: a 1648 document notes her entitlement to a 'rent-charge of 50*l*. a year on the Sussex estate of her son, John Ashburnham, which she bought in 1639 for 1,000*l*.[17] By early in 1635, the family seemed so entirely settled that Elizabeth could give thanks to God in a prayer for 'my children, who were left destitute, now by thy provident provision and blessing, well setled for this life'.

It was during the renewed prosperity of her second marriage, and in the year that Sir Thomas became Lord Chief Justice of the King's Bench, that Elizabeth erected the plaque at St Mary's, Stoughton. As well as mentioning her husband's new position (her sister Frances' husband Sir Wolstan Dixie is mentioned, although not the fact that he was Lord Mayor of London), the inscription also commemorates her own recent ennoblement, noting that 'THIS MONYMENT WAS ERECTED AT THE CARE AND COST OF THE LADY ELIZABETH

RICHARDSON BARONIS CRAMOND . . . AÑO 1631.' This was not, however, the first monument which Elizabeth had commissioned. In the difficult years after her first husband's death, in 1622, Elizabeth set up a tablet in St Botolph's Aldersgate in memory of her mother, 'the religious and vertuous lady, Katharine Beaumont', who had died the year before. In 1627 too, at the request of her late uncle Francis, she had a tomb set into the pavement of Christ-church, Newgate Street, London to commemorate her grandparents Nicholas and Anne Beaumont. Like the Stoughton monument, neither of these monuments conceals its 'author'. On the contrary, each of Elizabeth's monuments asserts her identity, her connections to both the living and the dead, as well as her role as maker. The monument to her grandparents, although her uncle's idea, is also raised 'at the care and cost of Elizabeth lady Ashburnham, widow, late wife of sir John Ashburnham'; the memorial to her mother, which *is* her idea, declares itself 'set up out of the love and true affection of Elizabeth lady Ashbornham, widdow'. These works in stone are counterparts to the collections of prayers for her daughters: both media simultaneously memorialize members of her family and herself, and both set out examples of piety for the edification of future generations. The particular concern of her mother's legacies for the transmission of piety through the female line also finds its counterpart in Elizabeth's monuments: the St Botolph's tablet commemorates not only her mother, but also her daughter Mary, buried there in 1619. Commissioning material witnesses to familial and religious piety seems, like writing prayers, to have been a lifelong interest.[18]

Early in 1635, Elizabeth Richardson became a widow for a second time, and memorialized her husband in one of her most personal prayers: 'A sorrowfull widowes prayer and petition unto the gracious protector and defender of widowes, and father of the fatherlesse, which I composed shortly after the death of my dear husband.' The prayer certainly expresses a sense of great loss and a genuine fondness for her late husband, but it also recognizes that widowhood entails 'freedome from the bond of marriage', a freedom which she can now use to concentrate exclusively on her spiritual life. She compares herself with Mary – one of her favourite biblical exemplars – the disciple of Jesus who annoyed her sister Martha by preferring his words to the housework; and also with Anna, the elderly prophetess who spent all the years of her widowhood living in the Temple, dedicating herself to fasting and prayer. But Richardson does *not* see herself released from obedience into some kind of ungendered experience of spiritual freedom. It is notable that she thinks of Anna, and now herself, as a 'bondwoman': a female servant, really a female slave, to God. Her love and obedience to her husband are to be replaced by a far more rigorous (although self-imposed) regime under a divine spouse: 'Now deare God, make me to change and far exceed the fervent affection and carefull observance I have lived in towards my husband, into a holy feare, with devout and sincere love of thy Majesty and service, and due watchfulnesse over my selfe, that I displease not thee my God in any thing.'

In the next years, Richardson lived a nun-like existence as a dedicated spouse and servant of God. She retired herself 'in solitarinesse' to her late husband's house in Barking, Essex, and began to write the prayers of Book II of her *Legacie*, very possibly herself adhering to the daily and weekly discipline of prayer that they set out. In her retirement, Richardson was not only avoiding the distractions of the world – the kinds of businesses which preoccupied a Martha, not a Mary[19] – she was also avoiding the religious tensions which would eventually contribute to the outbreak of civil war in the next decade. The 1630s was a period of enforced conformity and Laudian 'innovations', which alienated or at least made difficulties for many, Dorothy Leigh's Puritan son William among them. One might read Richardson's emphasis on retirement and prayer as a deliberate disengagement from religious politics; one might also, however, see her prayerful retirement in Essex as a counterpart to the controversial community of Little Gidding in Huntingdonshire.[20] Although godly in the broad sense of 'pious', Richardson was not one of the self-consciously godly in the narrower sense of 'Puritan'. She shares Leigh's orthodox Calvinist conviction of original sin, for instance, but not her urgent sense of needing to keep separate from the unregenerate. And while Richardson aims for a stoic transcendence of the 'world', she feels no desire to preach against it, as Leigh and also Joscelin do.

She is certainly not worried about the standard of preaching, as Leigh vehemently is, and as Puritans continued to be in the 1630s. Richardson's references to preaching are rare and uncontentious: 'O God, indue thy servant the Preacher, with thy holy Spirit, to teach thy saving truth rightly and sincerely.' In her exclusive focus on prayer and the private drama of sanctification, she seems to be hardly concerned at all with public and communal religion.

On the other hand, a few of her prayers register a fear of apostasy.[21] One may well ask, from what orthodoxy did she fear to defect? There were certainly Roman Catholics in her family: her first husband's father, for instance, was a recusant, as was her patroness the Duchess of Buckingham. In her list of *Errata* added to the 1645 *Legacie*, Richardson directs that the petition, 'keep our soules and bodies in thy true faith', be changed to 'keep our soules and bodies in thy true Catholike faith'. Although 'Catholic' had developed the sense of 'Roman Catholic' by the mid-seventeenth century, Richardson almost certainly meant 'true' or 'universal' faith here. In 1645, what she could have meant in particular was the old established Church of England faith, which, by that year, had all but been dismantled.[22]

Richardson's orthodoxy was probably what we would now call 'Anglicanism' – tending perhaps to the Laudian side. One can certainly imagine a godly reader like Dorothy Leigh disapproving of her evident preference for set over conceived or extemporaneous prayer. From the godly perspective, indeed, some of Richardson's prayers have decidedly 'popish' features, in the same way that Laud's liturgical 'innovations' hearkened back to the unreformed times of popery: her seven petitions, for instance, for 'the seven spirituall and heavenly graces, wherewith to vanquish . . . the seven dangerous deadly sinnes'.[23] But while Richardson's attraction to the set rituals and rhythms of devotion have something in common with the Roman Catholic use of Books of Hours, Richardson is certainly not a Romanist.[24] Her prayers are personal and 'conceived', written by herself. But they are also 'set', made part of a regular discipline of devotion. Her devotional practice is neither popish nor Puritan, but takes something from both.

Richardson's detached retirement from the world did not shield her from further changes of fortune. Her 'Prayer to the God of mercy in time of affliction' in Book III of her *Legacie* refers to 'heavy troubles and visitations', and prays for mercy 'to this whole Kingdome, now in very great distraction, distresse and misery'. 'Now' is certainly some time between 1642 and 1645, and the 'visitations' the outbreak of civil war. Richardson's two sons John and William Ashburnham were both active for the Royalist cause. In 1643, John was discharged from the House of Commons (where he represented Hastings) for his loyal attendance on the King. Later he became paymaster of the King's army, while William was Major-General of the western forces. Tradition has it that Jack Ashburnham was with Charles at his execution on 31 January 1649, the King handing him his watch before going to the block. Certainly, the watch, the shirt and a pair of white silk drawers the King was wearing at the time, as well as the sheet which was thrown over his body, were afterward kept by the Ashburnham family and displayed as relics.[25]

Unsurprisingly, then, the family did not do well during the Commonwealth: once again their inherited lands were under threat. We know of Elizabeth Richardson's financial contributions to the recovery of her son's estate because she had to declare the annuity she derived from it to the Committee for Compounding when they were investigating John Ashburnham's assets. (The Committee seized the property of defeated Royalists and 'compounded' with them for a portion of their assets in lieu of prosecution.) Members of Richardson's family – not just her son John, but also her brother Henry Beaumont, and her son-in-law Sir Edward Dering – were punished severely, perhaps fatally, by the victors.[26]

Apart from her reference to the 'distraction, distresse and misery' of the kingdom, Richardson refrains – perhaps politicly – from direct comment on the civil war in her 1645 *Legacie*. One can presume she shared the royalist sympathies of her two sons. And although she does not write directly about the King, she does write about her God in the language of an awed and dutiful subject. Richardson has a definite penchant for meditating on the majesty of God, and of bowing (often the knee of her heart) before her own royal patriarch, 'with a child-like love, feare to offend thee, striving to please thee in all things'.

Furthermore, the fact that she chose to have her maternal prayers printed at last in 1645 – after forty years of writing and circulating them in manuscript – is itself significant. That year would not have been a hopeful one for those loyal to the monarchy or the old religion. The war turned decisively against the Royalists with the Battle of Naseby in July, but perhaps more important for Richardson was the fate of *The Book of Common Prayer*: in 1645 it was banned and replaced by the Presbyterian Directory for Public Worship. So, not only may Richardson have felt that prayers were especially needed in these discouraging times, she may also have been seeking, through her own prayers, to rehabilitate some of the old reassuring phrases and rhythms of common prayer. For she is as reliant on the old prayer book for the shape of her prayers and phrases as she is on scripture. Her prayers for morning and night, for instance, recall the prayer book's 'orders' for morning and evening prayer; the absolution pronounced by the minister during the former is clearly a favourite,[27] as is the 'General Confession' before Communion. With *The Book of Common Prayer* banned, it is no longer the minister but Richardson's legacy which transmits the words of absolution, by allowing her readers to pronounce it for themselves. Moreover, with the Directory for Public Worship in force, Richardson's petition to 'continue in thy right Church and true faith unto my end' takes on a new note of defiance from the circumstances in which it was printed.

Thus, prayers which seem otherwise impersonal and disengaged from religious or political controversy are, when reasserted in print in 1645, an act of intervention – even dissent. Even though Richardson clearly had her prayers reproduced so that they could then be circulated privately among members of her family, it is notable that she decided to use a printer (rather than a scribe) for this reproduction, and that she allowed her book to be offered for public sale (Thomason bought a copy on 24 November). The readership she envisaged for her prayers was both intimate and extended: as well as family members, 'any good Christian' could legitimately use, if not a Book of Common Prayer, at least one lady's or mother's book of prayers.

When Richardson sent her manuscript prayers to press in 1645, she was in her sixty-ninth year and conscious of herself as a very old woman. Prayers in the third book of the *Legacie* acknowledge her 'great age' and the illnesses attendant upon it. She was conscious that she could not live very much longer: an 'old age laden with infirmities and sicknesse is a sure messenger and forerunner of death'. Nonetheless, her prayers also record her recovery from an illness of many months' duration, and she was to live another six years after the publication of her prayers. She died in her seventy-fifth year, and was buried on 3 April 1651 in St Andrew's Church, Holborn, beside her first husband. Her eldest son's tomb memorialized her in her turn as a woman 'very eminent for her great temper and prudence'.[28]

THE TEXTS

If we are to go by the date of Elizabeth Richardson's printed legacy, then she writes the latest of our three mothers' legacies. But the 1606 date on her manuscript book of prayers in the Folger makes her one of the earliest practitioners of the genre – earlier than Dorothy Leigh by nearly a decade. Folger MS V.a.511 is dated 1606 from Ashburnham Place in Sussex and was clearly intended as a mother's legacy. (See Appendix 1 and Plate, p. 255.) It is primarily directed to her children, but she is already projecting an audience beyond them, for she gives it the title, 'Instructions for my children, or any other Christian, Directing to the performance of our duties, towardes God and Man; – drawne out of yᵉ holy scripture'. The work is evidently unfinished, but its projected contents include: (1) precepts for a civil and Christian life (2) a list of virtues and vices, with their rewards and punishments; (3) instructions for prayer, together with scripturally-based meditations and prayers and, finally (4) a treatise on life and death (which Margaret Hannay has shown to be based on the Countess of Pembroke's 1592 *Discourse of Life and Death*).[29]

Elizabeth Richardson does not seem to have reused any of the material of the Folger manuscript for the *Legacie* of 1645. She does, however, return to specific motifs and phrases which are already favourites in 1606, and in the endnotes to the text of the *Legacie* I indicate some of these echoes.

ASH 3501 in the East Sussex Record Office, on the other hand, is an early version of the first part of the prayers printed in 1645. It is dated 1626 and was given to Elizabeth Richardson's eldest daughter in 1635. With the exception of the second prayer, 'A Prayer to the Holy Ghost', prayers 1–15 of the printed *Legacie* all have counterparts in the earlier manuscript. The order has been changed somewhat, and longer prayers in the manuscript have been subdivided in the printed text (prayers 1 and 3 were originally one prayer, as were 8 and 9, and 10 and 11). The prayers are numbered erratically in the manuscript and are clearly under revision: Richardson must already have been thinking carefully about the ordering of the prayers, either for a subsequent fair manuscript copy, or even for print. As well, the wording of some of the earlier prefatory material and prayers was changed on its way to the 1645 *Legacie* – perhaps by Elizabeth Richardson herself, or a scribe, or both. (The East Sussex manuscript is itself a collaborative enterprise, written in three hands, with Richardson typically correcting or adding to the material written by the two other scribes.[30]) Some changes made for 1645 seem arbitrary, as the change from 'O Lord' to 'O God'. The number of doublets increases – 'he saueth us' becoming 'he saveth and delivereth us', for instance – perhaps in an attempt to lend the prayers the sonorous formality of legal discourse. Other changes, however, suggest changes in Richardson's devotional outlook appropriate to a woman growing older, and perhaps more ascetic, in troubled times. An earlier hope that she might 'continue in yᵉ true fayth' is given an emphatic amplification and becomes 'thy right Church and true faith'.[31] And in its 1645 version, 'A Prayer for the Lords day, before we goe to Church', seems more self-disciplinary and less fervent than its earlier counterpart. Richardson adds, for instance, a petition 'that I may heare [the preacher] with due attention, and resolve to follow and practice all good instructions'. On the other hand, age may also have brought increasing self-confidence: self-deprecating references to her legacy as 'a smale token' and a 'little labore' are removed in the printed version of her 'Letter to my foure Daughters'. In the text which follows, the critical apparatus at the foot of the page is primarily concerned with substantive differences between ASH 3501 and Book I of the *Legacie*. (Minor changes in spelling and punctuation are not noted.) All variants from the 1645 text, unless otherwise marked, should be assumed to come from ASH 3501.

The evidence of the two early manuscript mothers' legacies demonstrates, then, that Richardson was a constant reviser. Her impulse to add and emend, moreover, did not end with the publication of her prayers in 1645. *A Ladies Legacie to her Daughters* was printed in two issues: the second appends two poems or hymns, a meditation, and a list of *errata*.[32] Evidently, Richardson wished to add to the first issue, for the *errata* not only correct evident mistakes but continue the process of amplification, in one case suggesting a rather lengthy insertion.[33]

Furthermore, Richardson made emendations by hand for at least two personalized presentation copies of the 1645 *Legacie*. One was for her grandson, Sir Edward Dering, and is now in the Houghton Library, Harvard University; the other is in the Bodleian Library, Oxford, and was intended for her brother Henry Beaumont.[34] (Richardson's emendations to the Bodleian copy are reproduced in the critical apparatus and are marked as 'HB'.) Although her legacies, as well as the monument she commissioned in memory of her mother and daughter, suggest her interest in the female line, her presentation copies were notably both for male members of her family: both men, moreover, who had recently suffered personal loss because of the civil war, Sir Edward Dering losing his father shortly after he compounded, Henry Beaumont dying before he could himself compound and probably before his sister's book could be presented to him.[35]

As with the majority of Richardson's changes and additions, her emendations of the presentation copies tend to make cosmetic rather than material changes. The most substantive change to both presentation copies, however, is the title: from *A Ladies Legacie to her Daughters* to *A Mothers Legacie to her Sixe Daughters*. If the printing of her prayers did represent Richardson's response to the banning of *The Book of Common Prayer*, then stressing the private and particular nature of her text – it is a mother's address to her own daughters – may have been wise. And, despite her seniority, she may have been shy of characterizing her *Legacie* as a public venture before her male relatives. (She had, in her 'Letter to my foure Daughters', declined to address her prayers to her sons, 'lest being men, they misconstrue my well-meaning'.) Similarly cancelling the phrase 'to be sold' on the title page sends a usefully ambivalent message. The presentation copy is not only marked as a gift, but it is also symbolically removed from public circulation: the legacy becomes a 'private' printed text.

Richardson's ostensible reason for correcting printed copies for her grandson and brother was the printer's incompetence: 'indeed it is so falsely printed', she wrote to her grandson, 'as without it be corrected, you will meet with many absurdities'.[36] A number of the *Errata* do certainly duplicate corrections made in

Henry Beaumont's copy. On the other hand, it is notable that Richardson does not trouble to correct the many miscitations of scripture. She is less concerned with correctness than with personalizing her gift copies. Accordingly, each is handsomely bound with the recipient's initials on the cover. As with her early manuscript prayers, her presentation copies of the *Legacie* created a textual memorial for herself which was also to be used and appropriated by their ultimate owners.

Notes

1. Folger MS V.a.511. East Sussex Record Office, Asburnham Papers, MS ASH 3501. See 'The Texts' below. I am grateful to Victoria Burke for alerting me to the existence of these manuscripts, and also for allowing me to read, before publication, V.E. Burke and M.P. Hannay, 'Elizabeth Ashburnham's Manuscripts', *English Manuscript Studies 1100–1700*, 10 (2000).

2. The presentation copy to Edward Dering is in the Houghton Library, Harvard University; the epistle to Dering is reproduced in Charlotte F. Otten (ed.), *English Women's Voices 1540–1700* (Miami, Florida International University Press, 1992), pp. 301–3.

3. ASH 3501, fols. 1r, 4r. See Appendix 2 and p. 164 footnote f.

4. See p. 164, footnote f.

5. Folger MS V.a.511., fols. 4r–v, 67v.

6. See p. 219, footnote b.

7. Her two extant manuscript books of prayers are very small: the Folger MS about 16×20 cm, and the East Sussex MS about 7×14 cm. See Burke and Hannay, 'Elizabeth Ashburnham's Manuscripts', for exact measurements.

8. The masque was given in honour of Sir William Seymour and Lady Frances Seymour. See G.E. Bentley, *The Jacobean and Caroline Stage* V (Oxford, Clarendon, 1949), p. 1311. Sir William had previously been married to Lady Arabella Stuart, the rival claimant to King James's throne. After her death, he rehabilitated himself with James, was made a baronet, and in 1618, the year of the masque, would receive the courtesy title Lord Beauchamp (*DNB*).

9. *The Visitation of the County of Leicester in the Year 1619*. Harleian Society II (London, 1870) 60–1, 30.

10. Her son's tomb states that Elizabeth died in her seventy-fifth year in 1651 (see below). Her bridegroom was twenty.

11. Francis W. Steer, *The Ashburnham Archives* (Lewes, East Sussex County Council, 1958), p. v.

12. See 'A Letter to my foure Daughters', especially p. 163, footnote c.

13. Thomas Walker Horsfield, *The History, Antiquities and Topography of the County of Sussex* I (Dorking, Kohler & Coombes, 1974), p. 559.

14. See p. 163 footnote f. In seventeenth-century usage, *friends* include relatives and *parent* could have the sense of either protector or kinsman or kinswoman (see *OED* 'parent' sb. 1c, 2).

15. 'Cramond' in G.E. C[okayne], *The Complete Peerage*, 2nd edn. (rpt. Gloucester, Sutton, 1987), III, p. 490. GEC suggests (p. 488, note b) that Elizabeth might have been ennobled in lieu of her husband, since he was in public office in 1628 (although a Scottish, rather than an English, creation might have removed the difficulty). The title of Cramond was to pass from Elizabeth to Thomas Richardson's male heirs.

Interestingly, Buckingham's assassin John Felton came before Richardson in 1628. Richardson established an important precedent by refusing to allow him to be tortured on the rack to extract a confession. See Richardson, *DNB*.

16. See John Ashburnham, *DNB*, and Horsfield, I, p. 559.

17. *Calendar of the Proceedings of the Committee for Compounding 1643–1660*, Cases, 1647–June 1650 (London, Her Majesty's Stationery Office, 1891), Part III, p. 1863.

18. John Nichols, *The History and Antiquities of the County of Leicester*, II (part 2) (rpt. Ardsley, Wakefield: S.R. Publishers and Leicestershire County Council, 1971), pp. 858–9. Some time before 1647, Elizabeth had also given a gallery to the church of St Mary in Ashburnham. *The Victoria History of the Counties of England: A History of the County of Sussex*, IX (Oxford, 1937), p. 129.

The parallel between Richardson's mother's legacy and the monument to her mother and daughter is drawn in her entry in Maureen Bell *et al.* (eds) *A Biographical Dictionary of English Women Writers 1580–1720* (New York, Harvester Wheatsheaf, 1990).

19. Richardson does, however, seem to have undertaken works of charity after her second husband's death. See '*A prayer to God for charity*', p. 221 and '*A sorrowfull widowes prayer*', p. 229.

20. For the devotional possibilities for women at Little Gidding, and for opposition to it as an 'Arminian Nunnery', see Patricia Crawford, *Women and Religion in England 1500–1720* (London, Routledge, 1993), p. 46.

21. For example, she prays that she 'may continue in thy right Church and true faith unto my end'; and, in a later prayer, to be 'a true and faithfull member of thy right Church & Kingdom of grace here' (pp. 180, 236).

22. For Richardson, the universal or 'catholic' church *is* the Church of England. See, for example, her civil war prayer, where she prays for the 'distresse' of 'this whole Kingdome', and immediately after for 'all my fellow members in thy whole Church universall' (p.231). See also the exposition of the 'catholic faith' in the Office for Evening Prayer (the '*Quincunque vult*') in *BCP*.

23. See pp. 224–5. Richardson may be conscious of the possible charge of popishness, for in an earlier prayer she is careful to state that the seven petitions are all 'prescribed and allowed by sacred Scripture' (p. 180).

24. In both early and late prayers relating to Communion, Richardson makes very clear that she does not believe in transubstantiation. See her references to 'the outward signe of bread and wine' and again to the 'outward signes' (as opposed to the 'inward and inestimable graces bestowed upon our soules by the reall body broken') on pp. 177 and 233.

25. See John Ashburnham and William Ashburnham in *DNB*, and Horsfield, I, pp. 557, 559.

26. Henry Beaumont died in April 1646 before he could compound. On his suffering for his loyalty to the King, see Nichols, II (Part 2), p. 859. Sir Edward Dering compounded in February 1644 and died shortly afterwards. For the extreme poverty he suffered at the end of his life see *DNB*. See also *Calendar of the Proceedings of the Committee for Compounding 1643–1660*, Cases, 1647–June 1650, Part II, 831–2.

27. See *A Ladies Legacie* note 21.

28. GEC, *Peerage*, III, p. 490. Horsfield, I, p. 559.

29. For a full description and analysis of the Folger manuscript, including a transcription of the treatise on life and death, see Burke and Hannay, 'Elizabeth Ashburnham's Manuscripts'.

30. Again, for a full discussion of ASH 3501, see Burke and Hannay.

31. See Book I, 'A short Prayer for conclusion to any prayer'. ·

32. The first issue has been used as copytext, but the appended verses and meditation have been incorporated from the second issue. Where it has been possible to follow Richardson's directions for emending *errata*, I note emendations in the critical apparatus and mark them as '*Errata*'.

33. One of Richardson's directions under the *Errata* reads: 'also adde deare Lorde endue me with all other saving graces for thy glory and my salvation, as right humility, perfect patience, true faith, and unfeigned repentance for my sins, with grace to reform my life and former faults, that I may obtain thy gracious pardon'. I have not been able to locate where this addition should be made.

34. See note 2. The Bodleian presentation copy for Henry Beaumont is shelfmark Vet. A3 f.132.

35. The date of Henry Beaumont's death shortly after the publication of the *Legacie*, as well as the absence of a dedicatory epistle like the one to her grandson in the Harvard copy, suggest that the copy was never presented.

36. Otten (ed.), *English Women's Voices*, p. 301.

A
LADIES
LEGACIE
TO HER
DAVGHTERS.

In three BOOKS.

Composed of Prayers and
Meditations, fitted for severall
times, and upon severall
occasions.

As also severall Prayers for each day in
the Weeke.

By Madam *Elizabeth Richardson*, wife
to the late Sir *Thomas Richardson*
Knight, Lord Chiefe Justice
of the Kings Bench.

LONDON,

Printed by *Tho. Harper*, and are to be
sold[a] at his house in *Little Britaine*,
1645.

---

[a] to be sold] ~~to be sold~~ (HB)

A LADIES LEGACIE TO HER DAUGHTERS

1645

[sig. A3r]

The Contents of the Prayers contained in these three Books.

BOOK I.

[sig. A3v]

BOOK II.

BOOK III.

[p. 1]

A

LADIES LEGACIE

TO HER

DAVGHTERS.[a]

My dearly beloved Daughters (of which number, I account my two sons wives, my daughters in law, the Countesse of Marlborough, and Mrs. Francis Ashbournham, to be mine also)[1] assuring my selfe of your loves and kinde acceptance, I present this little Booke unto you all, which being mine, I hope you will carefully receive it, as comming from my love and affection

---

[a] A LADIES LEGACIE TO HER DAVGHTERS.] Written 1625. Printed 1645. The tytle is A Mothers ~~LADIES~~ LEGACIE TO HER six DAVGHTERS (HB; see also Plate, p. 161.)

Dedicatory epistle to Elizabeth Richardson's *A Ladies Legacie to her Daughters* (London, 1645). The annotated presentation copy for Richardson's brother, Henry Beaumont. Vet. A3 f.132, sig. A1r. (*By permission of the Bodleian Library, Oxford*)

towards you, and that you will please for my sake, the more to imploy it to your good; to which I will (while I live) daily adde my prayers and blessing for your present and future happinesse: and that this my poore labour may prove a happy furtherance to all your good endeavours towards vertue and piety: Therefore let me as a Mo- [p. 2] *ther intreat and prevaile with you to esteem so well of it, as often to peruse, ponder, practice, and make use of this Booke according to my intention, though of it selfe unworthy;*[2] *for you shall finde your greatest happinesse will be in the true feare, constant love, and faithfull service of Almighty God, which never faileth of comfort and reward, he being the only and most liberall giver of all good gifts and blessings, both spirituall and temporall; to whose infinite mercy and gracious guidance, I most humbly commend you all, and daily will doe the like in my prayers so long as I live. And further, most deare hearts, consider, That these Petitions are presented to a most bountifull and Al-sufficient Lord, that vouchsafeth in Christ to make us his adopted children, and to be our Gracious Father,*[3] *who gave his only Son for us, in whom he will deny us nothing: And greater benefits then here are asked, cannot bee received; therefore give me leave, since I have such great interest in you,*[4] *to perswade and obtaine of you all, often to beg these blessings of God, by these prayers faithfully offered up unto his Majesty: Whereby you shall glorifie his holy Name, make your selves eternally blessed, and bring much joy and comfort to*

Your most affectionate
Mother,
ELIZ. ASHBOURNHAM.[5]

[p. 3]

I had no purpose at all when I writ these books, for the use of my selfe, and my children, to make them publicke; but have beene lately over perswaded by some that much desired to have them.[a] *Therefore I have adventured to beare all censures, and desire their patience and pardon, whose exquisite*[6] *judgements may finde many blameworthy faults, justly to condemne my boldnesse; which I thus excuse, the matter is but devotions or prayers, which surely concernes and belongs to women, as well as to the best learned men; And therefore I hope herein, I neither wrong nor give offence to any, which I should be very loath to doe.*

This Booke was written at Chelsey *in the yeare* 1625.[b] *by E.A. at the Duke of* Buckinghams *house, a part whereof was lent me by the good Dutches, my most honoured Lady, when the great sicknesse was in* London.[7]

[p. 4]

A Letter to my foure Daughters, *Elizabeth, Frances, Anne,* and *Katherine Ashbournham,* of whom three were then unmarried, only *Anne* was married to Sir *Edward Deering* Knight and Baronet.[8]

---

[a] *to have them.*] *to have them. yt I would suffer* y[m] *to be printed* (HB)

[b] *at* Chelsey *in the yeare* 1625.] ffrom Chelsy in August. 1626. [NB, however, p. 164, footnote f]

My deare Children:

I have long and much grieved for your misfortunes, and want of preferments in the world:[9] but now I have learned in what estate soever I am, therewith to be content, and to account these vile and transitorie things to be but vaine and losse, so I may win Christ the fountaine of all blisse, wishing you with me, to condemne that which neglecteth you, and set your hearts and affections on better subjects, such as are above, more certain and permanent:[a] and feare not but what is needfull for this present life shall bee supplyed by him who best knows our wants:[b] and had it not been for your sakes (whose advancements love and nature bindeth me to seeke) I had prevented the spite of my enemies, and forsaken the World before it despised me:[c] But though I am so unhappy as to be left destitute, not able to raise you portions of wealth, yet shall I joy as much to adde unto the portion of Grace,[d] which I trust, and pray, that God will give to each of you, to whose mercy I daily commit you, nothing [p. 5] doubting but that he will receive you into the number of those fatherlesse he graciously taketh care of, if you omit not to serve and depend upon him faithfully,[e] for he never faileth them that trust in him. God is as free and ready to give us as we to aske, and contrary to the World, he grows not weary of importunate suters,[10] but often deferreth his blessings to make us the more earnest for them. Neither hath the Lord withdrawn his favour so from us as to leave us utterly desolate to despair, but hath graciously raised us comfort by honourable friends to be carefull and deare parents unto us, whom God preserve and shew mercy to them and theirs, as they have done to us.[f] And here I send you a motherly remembrance, and commend this my labour into your loving acceptance,[g] that in remembring your poor mother, you may be also put in minde to performe your humble duty and service to our[h] heavenly Father, who hath created us to his owne glory and service; and all we can performe, comes far short of what we owe unto him; yet is he well pleased, if we returne (for all his mercies, but obedience, and the sacrifice of praise and calling upon his holy Name. Now prayer being the winged messenger to carry our requests and wants[i] into the ears of the Lord (as David saith) he will praise the Lord seven times a day, and prevent the light to give thanks unto God;[11] and indeed, who can awake to enjoy the light and pleasure of the day, and not begin the same with intreaty of the Lords gracious direction in all things, and desire of his blessing upon us, and all that we have or doe? Or how can we possesse or hourely receive so many [p. 6] favours and benefits from God, and not offer unto him an evening sacrifice of thanksgiving? Or who dares adventure to passe the dreadfull night, the time of terror, and yeeld themselves to

---

[a] such as are above, more certain and permanent] such as are aboue, wch are more worthy, certaine & p[er]manent

[b] who best knows our wants] who best knoweth our wants yf we trust & depend vpon him

[c] the spite of my enemies, and forsaken the World before it despised me] the spight of fortune, & forsaken ye world before yt neglected me (ASH 3501); retyred my selfe from the World (HB)

[d] to adde unto the portion of Grace] to further the portion of Grace

[e] to serve and depend upon him faithfully] to serue him faithfully

[f] Neither hath . . . done to us.]

[g] And here . . . acceptance] And here I send you a smale token & Motherly remembrance, com̄ending this my little labore to yor louing acceptance

[h] our] yor

[i] our requests and wants] our wants

sleep, the image of death, before they are at peace with God, by begging pardon for their sins, and craving his protection and care[a] *over them in the night?*

I know you may have many better instructers then my self, yet can you have no true mother but me, who not only with great paine brought you into the world, but do now still travell in care for the new birth of your soules; to bring you to eternall life,[12] *which is my chiefest desire, and the height of my hopes: And howsoever this my endeavour may be contemptible to many, (because a womans) which makes me not to joyne my sons with you, lest being men, they misconstrue*[b] *my well-meaning; yet I presume that you my daughters will not refuse your Mothers teaching (which I wish may be your ornament, and a crown of glory*[c] *to you) who I hope will take in the best part*[d] *my carefull industrie, for your present and future happinesse, towards which I have not failed to give you the best breeding in my power, to bring you to vertue and piety, which I esteem the greatest treasure; and sure I am, it leads you to him that is the giver of all good things, both spirituall and temporall; to whose infinite mercy I most humbly commend you, who I trust will fulfill all your necessities, through the riches of his grace,*[e] *and make you perfect in all good workes to doe his will. And the God of peace sanctifie you throughout, that your whole spirits, soules and bodies, may bee* [p. 7] *kept blamelesse unto the comming of our Lord Jesus Christ,* {1 Thess. 5. 23.} *which shall bee the endlesse joy of your most loving Mother,*

Eliz. Ashbournham.[f]

A Preface, or inducement to Prayer.

The great God, and Lord of Heaven and Earth, whose wee are, and whom only we ought to serve, hath not left himselfe without witnesse: {Acts 17. 24. 27. 8. Cap. 23. 14. 17. Rom I. 19. 20.}[g] [13] For as much as that which may be knowne of God, is made manifest unto us, for the invisible things of him, that is his eternall power and Godhead, are seen by the creation of the world, being considered in his workes, to the intent wee[h] should bee without excuse. {His power Godhead. Rom. 5. 5. 8. 9.}[i] Also the infinite love of God is shed abroad in

[a] his protection and care] his p[ro]tection

[b] misconstrue] misconster

[c] crown of glory] crowne of honour

[d] who I hope will take in the best part] Therefore take in best p[ar]t

[e] {Col. 4.10. Heb. 13.21.}

[f] [ASH 3501 adds a postscript to Elizabeth Cornwallis, R's eldest daughter:] Composed at Chelsie, in September 1625. to spend away some of our malencholly time there; where ye danger of death inclosed vs [round] about, where[in]

(my sweet child) accept ye love, & care of a mother, who wisheth all Comfort, meeknes, & patience, may possess yor soule, to make you good in life, & happy in death. wch ye dayly vse of this, I hope will help to effect, & further your Saluation, to ye comfort of your affectionate mother. E.A.

[g] {Acts 17 ... Rom I. 19, 20.}] {Acts 17. 24. 27.}

[h] wee] all

[i] {His power Godhead.}] {Knowledge of God}

our hearts, {His love, Redemption.}ᵃ and set out towards us in the most gracious worke of our redemption, in that Christ died for us being sinners, and when we were enemies, God reconciled us unto himself by the death of his only begotten Son, {Jo. 3. 16. Jo. 4. 9. 10. 3. 16. Jo. 15. 23. 10. 15.}ᵇ whom God sent into the world that wee might live [p. 8] through him, and be saved by his life, {Christs love.}ᶜ greater love then this can none have, to lay downe his owne life for us.¹⁴

Now there are three speciall things amongst many that doe alwaies binde and urge us to the acknowledgement of God,ᵈ to the love of his Majesty, and the often calling upon his holy Name, *viz.* {His benefits. Of our sins. Our miseries and necessities.}ᵉ First, the multitude and greatnesse of his benefits towards us, for which we ought to give him continuall thanks. Secondly, the infinitenesse of our grievous sins, for which we must of necessity daily aske mercy, and pardon from him.ᶠ Thirdly, our owne manifold miseries and infirmities,ᵍ for which we are constrained to seek reliefe and remedy.

The first of those *David* considered, saying, What shall I render unto the Lord for all his benefits towards me? I will take the cup of salvation and call upon the name of the Lord. I will praise him with my whole heart all the daies of my life. {Psal. 116. 12, 13. 9. 1.} All his Psalmes are full of thanksgiving. To the second, Christ inviteth us saying, Come unto me all ye that are weary and heavy laden, and I will ease you. If any man sin, we have an advocate with the Father, *Jesus Christ the just*: He is the reconciliation for the sins of the whole [p. 9] world: {Matth. 11. 28. 1 Jo. 2. 1. 2. 1.}ʰ And if wee acknowledge our sinnes,ⁱ he is faithfull and just to forgive, and cleanse us from all unrighteousnesse. For the third, wee are incouraged by God himselfe, saying, Call upon me in the day of trouble, so will I deliver thee, and thou shalt glorifie me; for he will have mercy upon us, and heal all our infirmities; and when wee are in misery, he saveth and delivereth us.ʲ {Psal. 50. 15. Isay. Matth. 8. 17.}¹⁵

Now for the performance of our duty in thanksgiving, the blotting out of all our offences, and the release of our miseries, with the continuance of Gods grace and favourᵏ in all things, the chiefe and only way to find and obtain allˡ is rightly to seek,

---

ᵃ {His love, Redemption.}] {loue of god}

ᵇ {Jo. 3. 16. . . . 10. 15.}] {His benefitts John. 3.16 John 4. 9. 10. 13. 16 John. 15. 33. 10. 15.}

ᶜ through him . . . {Christs love.}] by him

ᵈ of God] of a God

ᵉ {His benefits . . . necessities}]

ᶠ pardon from him] pardon

ᵍ miseries and infirmities] miseries

ʰ {Matth. 11. 28. I Jo. 2. 1. 2. 1.}] {Mat: 11. 28. 14.}

ⁱ sinnes] sinn

ʲ he saveth and delivereth us] he saueth us

ᵏ favour] fauor towards vs

ˡ all] these

and truly to serve the Lord by prayer, who is the author and fountain of all goodnes, grace and mercy;[a] Every good gift comming from above, even from him that freely saith,[b] Aske, and yee shall receive; seek, and yee shall finde; knock, and it shall be opened unto you;[16] for hee that is Lord over all, is rich unto all that call upon him in truth; and the prayer of the faithfull,[c] avails much, if it be fervent; for faithfull and devout prayer is a[d] continuall intercourse and communion betwixt the Lord and us; and it is like *Jacobs* ladder,[17] by which our prayers make [p. 10] our wants ascend unto God, and his mercie descend downe upon us;[e] for with the heart man believeth unto righteousnesse, and with the mouth we confesse[f] unto salvation; but take heed in sending up thy desires, prefer the good of the soule,[g] before the pleasures or content of thy body; and set thy affections on things that are above: {Col. 3. 2.} First, seeke the Kingdome of God and his righteousnesse, and all other wants shall be supplied by his mercie, according to his will, and our necessities. {Mat. 6. 33.}

And when thou enterest into the house of God, take heed thou offer not unto him the sacrifice of fooles,[h] but before thou prayest, prepare thy self, thy heart and tongue, as *David* did, lest thou tempt God to displeasure: Be not rash with thy mouth, nor let thy heart be hasty to utter a thing before God:[18] {Col. 3. 2 Eccles. 4. 17. 18. 22.} But ere thou presume to present thy self, or service unto the Lord, {Psal. 108. 1.} meditate upon these three things: First, of the reverence we owe to the great Majesty of God, {Psal. 104.}[i] in whose presence we are, and to whom we must speake; this brings humility and lowlinesse of spirit, which makes us acceptable unto him. Secondly, of our knowledge and beliefe of the Lords sweet and gracious promises {Esay 65. 24.} which [p. 11] causeth boldnesse to come unto him, with sure confidence of being heard. Thirdly, of our[j] unworthinesse, {Job 15. 16} and what apprehension we have of our owne wants and miseries, and the great necessity of Gods helpe and mercy to relieve us.[k] This makes us to know and hate our selves,[l] and to love and honour God, in whom is all our help, hope, and happinesse; therefore with devout reverence, zeal, humility, and true faith, flye unto his mercy, and cease not to call often (as *David* did) seven times a day upon the holy Name of the Lord, Psal. 119. 164. by whom we shall bee saved, Rom. 10. 13.

---

[a] the author and fountain of all goodnes, grace and mercy;] y[e] Author & founder of all goodness:

   [b] even from him that freely saith,]

   [c] faithfull] righteouse

   [d] a] as a

   [e] our wants . . . upon us] o[r] wants assende vp vnto Heauen, & Gods mercies descend downe vnto vs {Gen: 2:8:12. Ro: 10:10:}

[f] we confesse] he confesseth

   [g] but take . . . soule] But take heed, in your requests, & desires, to prefer y[e] honor of God, & y[e] good of thy soule

   [h] {Eccle: 5:1:}

   [i] {Psal. 104.}] {Psal: 104:1:}

   [j] our] o[r] owne

   [k] to relieve us]

   [l] {Ro: 7:18:}

1. A preparation to Prayer.

O Everlasting fountaine of all goodnesse, and well-spring of grace, without whose speciall assistance, we are altogether unapt and unable to performe any duty or service that may be acceptable unto thee: Vouchsafe therefore (deare Lord) to helpe mine infirmities, who cannot of my selfe pray as I ought, but let thy holy Spirit direct and teach me truly to call upon thy divine Name, with a penitent and faithfull heart, an humble, contrite, and lowly spirit, a quiet, observant and recollected minde, freed from the vanities and cares of this vilde world,[a] or the love of [p. 12] this present life; so as I may dedicate my selfe wholly unto thee a living sacrifice, faithfully and devoutly to serve thee now, and all the daies of my life. O Lord,[b] make mee to lift up innocent hands, with a pure heart; and guide thou my lips with wisdome, and set a watch of grace before my mouth, that my tongue may not offend thee at any time, but duly praise thy glorious Name, now and for ever, Amen.[c]

2. A Prayer to the Holy Ghost.

O Gracious Lord Holy Ghost, I humbly beseech thee to fit and prepare my heart, and to direct and assist me in the right and true performance of this duty and service now of prayer towards my God: Thou understandest my disability of my selfe to any goodnesse: neither know I how to pray as I ought, except thy holy Spirit teach me: Therefore I earnestly and humbly pray thee to give mee thy grace and true spirit of prayer, that so I may now and at all times offer up my petitions and praises, in calling upon thy great and glorious Name, in a right faithfull and acceptable manner, to the glory of God, and the good and comfort of me thy poor servant, in soul and body, with the furtherance of my salvation, through Jesus Christ, my blessed and only Saviour, Amen.

[p. 13]

3. A Preface to any Prayer.

O my Lord, in all humility I come unto thee, the giver of all grace; thou knowest my unaptnesse to any goodnesse, thou hast given me an earnest desire to please thee, make perfect thine owne good worke,[d] and grant me a ready will and

---

[a] an humble . . . vilde world] an humble, & lowly spirritt, a quiet, & recollected minde, free from ye vanities, & cares of this ~~of this~~ worlde

[b] O Lord]

[c] that my tongue . . . Amen.] y^t my tonge may not offend thee, but dayly prayse thy gloriouse name. (O my / Lord), y^u hast giuen me an earnest desire [etc. see footnote d]

[d] O my Lord, in all humility . . . good worke] (O my / Lord), y^u hast giuen me an earnest desire to please thee, make p[er]fect thy owne worke

ability to performe my humble duty herein aright, that so I may sincerely and intirely love, fear and honour thee above all, and most carefully obey thy blessed will in all things: Good Father, let thy manifold mercies cover my infinite offences[a] from thy All-seeing eyes, and by thy grace cast all vaine thoughts, and sinfull hindrances out of my soule, that thy sacred Spirit may direct my spirit to pray with due reverence to thy Majesty, confidence in thy mercy, with sure trust[b] in thy promises, and feare of thy judgements. And that I may offer up all my supplications unto thee, with unfeigned zeale, true faith, humility and repentance: Sweet Lord, make me heartily thankfull unto thee for all thy blessings, and let all my petitions tend to thy glory; so as I may finde favour with thee, that thou wilt be graciously pleased to heare and accept of me and[c] my prayers, that they may enter into thy presence, and obtaine pardon of all my sins[d] past, with grace to frame my life in true obedience to all thy Commandements, the rest of my daies to come, that so my last end may [p. 14] be happy, and after death I may enjoy the felicity to live with thee, my Lord, for evermore, through the merits and passion of my only Saviour Jesus Christ, So be it.

4. A confession of sins, with a prayer for remission, taken partly out of the prayer of Manasses.[19]

Almighty Lord God of our fathers, who hast made heaven and earth, with all the ornaments thereof, who hast bound the sea by the word of thy commandement, whose terrible and glorious Name all men doe feare, and tremble before thy powerfull judgements; for the displeasure of thy great Majesty cannot be borne, and thy angry threatnings against sinners is importable,[20] and who can stand in thy presence when thou art offended? But yet (O Lord) thy mercifull promises to penitent sinners are unmeasureable, and unspeakable; for thou art the most gracious Lord, full of mercy and great compassion, and of long suffering, that desires not the death of a sinner, but that he should repent and live,[21] who of thy great goodnesse hast promised to give repentance and forgivenesse to them that sinne against thee, that they may be saved.

Now thou therefore (most dear Lord) who camest not to call the righteous, but sinners to repentance (of [p. 15] whom I am the chiefe[22]) thou of thy infinite mercy (I trust)[e] hast appointed repentance and remission unto me, whose sins are in number above the sands of the sea,[23] or the haires of my head; I have

---

[a] offences] sins
[b] with sure trust] & trust
[c] and] in

[d] sins] offences
[e] (I trust)]

committed much evill,[a] and have omitted to doe the good I ought, for I have
neglected all my duty and service towards thee, and am not worthy to be called
thy servant, nor to[b] behold the height of heaven, or to looke up unto[c] the place
where thine honour dwelleth, for the multitude of mine iniquities have bowed
me downe, and as a weighty burden are too heavy for me; I am depressed with
the load of my sinnes, and oppressed with the feare of due punishment for them;
for I have justly provoked thy wrath (O God) and multiplied my transgressions[d]
before thee: I have not done thy will, neither thy holy Commandements have I
obeyed.

Now therefore (O my Redeemer) to thee I humbly bow the knee of my heart,[24]
imploring thy mercy, and beseeching thee of grace: I will confesse my sins
against my selfe, and will not hide my unrighteousnesse from thee: I have
sinned (O Lord) I have grievously sinned, & I acknowledge my manifold
offences; for which I have nothing to answer, but (like the Publican[25]) Lord be
mercifull unto me a miserable sinner:[e] Wherefore I most humbly intreat thee to
forgive me, my sweet Saviour forgive me,[f] and destroy me not with mine
iniquities, be not angry with me for ever, neither condemne me in thy displea-
[p. 16] sure to the lower[g] part of the earth, and reserve not evill for me
hereafter: But (deare Father) make me of that blessed number, to whom thou
imputest not their faults, and whose sinnes by my Saviours righteousnesse are
covered;[h] for thou art the God of the just, and the God of them that will[i]
repent, and in poore me, thou wilt shew all thy goodnesse and pity;[j] for thou
wilt pardon and save me that am so vilde and unworthy, even of thine owne
great grace and mercy: Therefore I will turn my steps into thy waies, and will
seeke thy will, and obey thee with my whole heart: I will praise thee all the
daies of my life, and for ever: And let the heavens and the earth praise thy
eternall Majesty; for thine is all glory for ever, Amen.

---

[a] I have committed much evill] I haue (O
Lord) comitted much euill in thy sight

[b] be called thy servant, nor to] [be called thy
seruante or to] [an interlineation in ASH 3501]

[c] to looke up unto] to looke vppon [vnto]
[correction in R's hand]

[d] [exceedingly] [addition in R's hand]

[e] I have sinned . . . miserable sinner:] I haue
sinned, & I acknowledge my manyfolde offences,
for wᶜʰ I haue nothinge to answer, but lord be
mercifull to me a most miserable & wretched
sinner.

[f] to forgive me, my sweet Saviour forgive
me] to forgiue ∧ [me] (my ∧ [sines] sweet
Saui=/oʳ) forgiue me [interlineation in R's
hand]

[g] lower] lowest

[h] whose sinnes by my Saviours righteousnesse
are covered] whose sinnes ar couered

[i] will] will [do] (HB)

[j] the God of them . . . and pity] yᵉ god of yᵐ,
yᵗ repent, & in poore me, yᵘ wilt shew all thy
mercy, & goodness

5. A Prayer for the Lords day, before we goe to Church.

O Eternall God, most high Creator; preserver and disposer of all things: to thee is due all praise, honour, and worship, for thou art our gracious Lord, the only author of all our good, by whom we live, move, and have our being. O with what humble reverence, and devotion ought we to prepare our ears and hearts, to hear, receive and performe[a] any thing which concerneth thy [p. 17] most sacred Majesty; and even to take heed unto our feet when we enter into the house of God, that our waies may not offend thee: Neither ought we to presume to take thy holy Name into our mouths, except we endeavoured our selves to be reformed by thy lawes. Thou, O God, art Lord God of Sabbath, and hast inobled this day by the glorious resurrection of thy Son our Lord Jesus, and by the guidance of the Holy Ghost in thy blessed Apostles, and Catholicke Church,[26] hast ordained it for thy publicke service, honour and worship: so make me to serve thee therein with due feare and reverence. I most humbly beseech thee to sanctifie my heart and soule to the true performance of thy blessed will[b] in rightly observing the same; and leave me not unto my owne weaknesse and disability, who can of my selfe neither thinke well, nor doe any thing that is good,[c] for all my strength and righteousnesse is in Christ my Redeemer: Assist me therefore (sweet Saviour) with thy Spirit of grace to cease from sin, and all worldly workes, or earthly cogitations this day,[d] that may withdraw me from thy fear and[e] service: And give me an attentive eare to hearken diligently to thy divine word: Open my heart as thou didst the heart of *Lydia*,[27] that with true understanding, I may receive, and faithfully keep the same, with a conscionable care to practise what I shall learne thereby, devoutly calling upon thy most holy Name, and using due reve- [p. 18] rence in all my actions before thee: And good Lord, blesse thy servant whom thou hast appointed this day to instruct and direct us in thy word and will; open to him the doore of utterance, and give him the true understanding of thy holy word, that according to thy gracious pleasure all may be saved that come unto the knowledge of thy truth, and that he may be faithfull in thy service, rightly to dispose thy divine mysteries, and to teach in faith and verity: And grant that I may heare with due attention, and resolve to follow and practice all good

---

[a] to hear, receive and performe] to heare, & receaue

[b] Thou, O God . . . thy blessed will] thou O God, y[t] arte lord of y[e] Saboth, & hast ordained this day, for thine owne seruice: I most humbly beseech thee, to sanctifie my harte, & soule to y[e]

[c] who can of my selfe neither thinke well, nor doe any thing that is good] whoe, of my selfe, can nether will, nor doe any thinge, y[t] is good

[d] this day]

[e] fear and]

instructions, with true intention to thy glory, and the furtherance of my salvation, through Jesus Christ our Lord, Amen.[a]

6. An entrance to Prayer.

O God of mercy, thou wilt not the death of a sinner, but rather that he should turne from his wicked waies and live: Vouchsafe to knit (deare Lord) my soule unto thee, that I may truly fear thee, and unfeignedly love thee, dedicating my selfe unto thy service, and setting mine affections and desires in all true obedience, to seeke above all things thy glory, thy Kingdome, and thy righteousnesse; that so all thy graces may daily increase in me, and my humble and unperfect service in calling on thy holy name, may grow daily [p. 19] more faithfull and fervent, now and at all times to be acceptable unto thee, through the merits of thy deare Son, and my only Saviour, in whom thou art well-pleased, Amen.[b]

7. A short thanksgiving at the first sight of the morning light.[c]

O Lord, I blesse thee for my health, rest and preservation this last night, and all my time past: And now most humbly pray thee give mee grace so to spend this day, that some glory may redound unto thee by my service, some benefit and good unto them with whom I live, by my example, and some further assurance unto my selfe of thy favour, and my eternall salvation, through Jesus Christ my Redeemer, Amen.

8. A private[28] morning Prayer.

Eternall God, and my most loving Father, in all humility of soule, and unfeigned acknowledgement of my bounden[d] duty, I humbly present my sinfull

---

[a] open to him . . . Christ our Lord, Amen.] open to him yᵉ dore of vtterance, yᵗ he may be faythfull in thy seruice, rightly to dispose thy diuine Mysteries, & to teach in faith, & veritie; & giue him yᵉ true vnderstandinge, of thy holy worde, yᵗ all may be saued yᵗ com vnto yᵉ knowledge of thy trueth; for yᵘ willest not yᵉ death of a siñer, [etc. see footnote b]

[b] O God of mercy . . . well-pleased, Amen.] for yᵘ willest not yᵉ death of a siñer, but rather, yᵗ he should torne frõ his wicked wayes & live: Gaither & knitt (Deare Lorde) my strayninge soule, vnto thee if I may truly feare thee & vnfainedly loue thee,

dedicatinge my selfe vnto thy seruic[e] & settinge my affections, & desires, in all true obedience, to seeke aboue all things thy glory, thy kingdom, & thy righteousness, yᵗ all thy graces, may dayly increase in me, & my humble & imp[er]fect seruice, may at all times, be acceptable vnto thee. Through yᵉ merritts of thy deare sonn, & my onely Sauiour. in whom yᵘ arte euer well pleased. Amẽ

[c] This has some resemblances to a prayer in ASH 3501, 'When you a wake in the morning from sleep' (see Appendix 3).

[d] bounden] bounded

selfe here before thy Throne of grace and glory; beseeching thee to strike an awfull reverence into my heart, lest my presumption and [p. 20] want of due respect towards thy great Majesty, should turne my prayers into sinne. And seeing without faith it is impossible to please God,[a] indue me, good Lord, with true faith to believe, and apply unto my owne soule, all thy most gracious promises in Jesus Christ, whom thou hast appointed to be my righteousnesse,[b] redemption, and the reconciliation of my sins; his pretious bloud I know is allsufficient to satisfie thy just displeasure against me, and to make me, through him, to appeare pure, holy, and acceptable before thee: But of my selfe, alas, I confesse that I am poor, wretched, miserable, and wholly corrupt both in soule and body, the chiefe[c] of all sinners, guilty of the breach of all thy Commandements, such an one as in whom is no goodnesse, and to whom there is nothing due, but shame and utter confusion for ever! Lord give me a lively apprehension and sight of my wofull estate, that with true faith, contrition, and unfeigned repentance, I lay[d] hold on thy mercy and gracious pardon, in thy beloved Son my only Saviour, humbly beseeching thee (O dear Lord) to accept his blessed death, as an absolute discharge for all mine offences; so as my sins may never be imputed unto me, but that all my infirmities may be healed by his wounds; for I know thy mercy is above all thy works, and thou delightest not in the death of a poor sinner. Therfore I will wait for thy salvation, relie on thy gracious promises, and trust in thee for ever and ever, Amen.[e]

[p. 21]

9. A thanksgiving.

I will praise the Name of the Lord because he is good, and his mercy endureth for ever; for thou hast many waies extended thy great goodnesse[f] towards me, thine unworthy servant, which I acknowledge with all humble thankfulnesse; for who[g] am I, that thou shouldest be mindfull of me in mercy, to refresh me this night past with quiet rest, and to defend both my soule and body from all the perills thereof, preserving me by thy gracious providence all my life hitherto, from many evills and just[h] punishments that my sinnes have deserved, should have[i] fallen upon me: And thy mercies are renewed every morning:[j] O Lord, thy compassions faile not, but

[a] God] thee

[b] righteousnesse,]

[c] chiefe] vilest

[d] I lay] I ∧ [may] lay (HB)

[e] Therefore I will . . . Amen.] therefore, I will wayte for thy saluation, & trust in thy Mercy, for euer more. for y[u] hast many wayes

[etc. see note f]

[f] I will praise . . . great goodnesse] for y[u] hast many wayes extended thy great goodness

[g] who] what

[h] just]

[i] should have] or might haue

[j] vppon me

thou hast multiplied thy benefits towards me, both spirituall and temporall; which I beseech thee for Christ Jesus sake still to continue and increase, especially thy favour in bestowing all spirituall graces[29] on mee needfull to salvation. O let thy holy Spirit direct me in every word and good worke, and fill me with the fruit of righteousnesse, so as I may have a holy care this day and ever, to live as in thy sight, and to study to please and obey thee in all things, with reverence and feare, in a pure, holy,[a] and blamelesse conversation. O God, knit my soule unto thee, and create a new and upright[b] heart within me, and sanctifie me throughout, in soule, [p. 22] body and spirit, that I may give up my selfe a living sacrifice, holy and acceptable unto thee, and may be preserved from all sin and evill, this day and forever: crucifie my sinfull flesh with the lusts thereof, and withdraw mine affections from the love of this vile world, and fix my desires on things that are above, where my Saviour sitteth at thy right hand, who is my treasure, my hope and help,[c] with whom I trust to live for evermore, Amen. And further I beg all these blessings in the name, merits and mediation of Jesus Christ, concluding in that perfect prayer which he hath sanctified and left us saying, Our Father, &c.

10. A Prayer for the afternoone.

Most Gracious God, and my mercifull Father in Jesus Christ: how exceedingly are wee wretched creatures bound unto thy excellent Majesty for that unspeakable priviledge which thou vouchsafest unto mortall man, to have free liberty and accesse (through Christ)[d] unto thy gracious presence, there to unfold our woes, to powre out our soules, and lay open our griefes and desires before the immortall God, who is ready[e] to heare, and art both able and willing to relieve and helpe us? This imboldneth me (unworthy wretch[f]) to present my person and petitions unto [p. 23] thy grace,[g] and to call upon thy holy name through thy beloved Son: Lord let the words of my mouth, and the meditations of my heart, be alwaies right and acceptable in thy sight, my strength and my Redeemer;[30] for thou knowest my nature and substance, being but flesh and bloud, how corrupt and fraile it is, so that I am not of my selfe able to performe any holy duty as I ought, neither to will or do any thing that is good, without thou grant me the

---

[a] holy,]

[b] and upright]

[c] where my Saviour . . . Our Father, &c.] where my Sauiour sitteth at ye right hand, wth whome I trust to liue for euer more. & giue me grace, so to spend ∧ [my life] y^t sũm glory may redound vnto the, by my seruice, sũm benifitt, & good vnto them,

wth whome I liue, & sũm further assurance vnto my self of thy fauor, & my eternall saluatiõ through Jesus Christ my redeeme^r Amen. Amen.

[d] (through Christ)]

[e] ready] euer ready

[f] wretch] wretch y^t I am

[g] grace] heauenly Grace

assistance of thy holy Spirit,[a] to sanctifie my thoughts, to guide my tongue, and to helpe my infirmities: what am I but dust and ashes, a most vile and miserable sinner, conceived and borne in iniquity, and my transgressions are daily multiplied, adding sinne unto sinne till they be innumerable? how have I mispent this present day, the sinnes whereof, may justly provoke thy heavy displeasure against me, having throughout my whole life, committed all evill, and omitted all good, and have neglected the performance of my bounden duty[b] and service towards thee upon every slight occasion; and which is worst of all, custome of sinning, hath seared up[31] my conscience, and deprived me of the true sight and sense of my sins and wofull estate, and bred such a fearfull hardnesse in my heart, that I cannot duly repent as I ought, and as the greatnesse of my fault requires? Thou hast called often,[c] and sought to reclaime me, and hast waited to have mercy on me, but I have refused, [p. 24] and hated to be reformed, carelessely neglecting thy infinite patience, long sufferance, and goodnesse[d] towards me.

But now to thee, O God of mercy, I bring my heavy laden soule, casting my selfe downe at thy feet, beseeching thee, O Lord, to receive me to grace and favour, and reject me not as I have deserved, but convert thou me, and I shall be changed: make me turne unto thee in true contrition, that thou maiest returne unto me in gracious compassion, to forgive all mine iniquities, remit my ungratefulnesse, and remember my offences no more. O wash and cleanse my sinfull soule in the pure bloud of that innocent Lambe, that I may feele the vertue of his death, to slay all sin in me, and the power of his resurrection to raise me to newnesse of life, in true obedience to all thy Commandements; and with a child-like love, feare to offend thee, striving to please thee in all things, that so I may obtaine favour and mercy in thy sight, both for thy blessing in this life, and eternall salvation after death, through thy dear Son, and my only Saviour Jesus Christ, Amen.[e]

11. A Short Prayer for night.

O God, the fountaine of all goodnesse, I humbly and thankfully acknowledge, although I am altogether unworthy of the least of thy mani- [p. 25] fold mercies;

---

[a] any holy duty . . . holy Spirit] any holy dutie aright, nether to will nor doe, any thinge, y[t] is good, w[th]out y[u] grante me y[e] assistance of thy blessed spirit

[b] omitted all good, and have neglected the performance of my bounden duty] neglected all good, & haue omitted y[e] p[er]formance of my

bounded duty

[c] (O Lord)

[d] thy infinite patience, long sufferance, and goodnesse] thy infinite patience, & goodness

[e] that so I may obtaine . . . Amen.] For although I am alltogether vnworthy [etc. see prayer 11 below]

yet have I great experience of thy infinite goodnesse, bounty and favour, both towards my soule and body all my time past, this day, and alwaies, preserving me from all the evills which sin and nature[32] have made me subject unto, with a gracious supply daily ever since I was born,[a] of all things needfull for this present life: For all which I humbly bow the knee of my heart and soule unto thy glorious Majesty; but especially for all thy graces furthering my salvation by Jesus Christ,[b] I blesse and praise thy most holy name, yeelding all possible and hearty thanks for all thy benefits vouchsafed to mee, the continuance whereof I humbly beg at thy gracious[c] hands, commending and committing my soule and body into thy mercifull protection this night and ever, praying thee to preserve[d] me therein from all perills, sin or evill, for thou Lord only keepest mee in safety: now[e] stretch out thy wings of grace and mercy over me, that while sleep seizeth upon my body, let not security[33] oppresse my soule, but so sanctifie all outward refreshings unto me, as thereby I may bee the more fit and able to serve thee faithfully all my life to come, that[f] taking quiet rest, because thou Lord sustainest me, I may also when this life ceaseth, lay downe my head in thy peace, and be made partaker of thy glory, through thy mercies and Christs merits, with the assistance of the blessed Spirit.[g] To whom, O Father, Son, and Holy Ghost, be all praise, power, dominion, [p. 26] and glory now and for ever, Amen: Continuing my prayers further as Christ hath taught us, saying, Our Father, &c.

12. A short Prayer in bed before sleep.[h]

Deare Lord, receive me this night and alwaies, into thy gracious protection, to give mee now health, safety, and rest, if it be thy will: And dear God, when I shall enter into my long sleep of death, vouchsafe to sanctifie, and prepare my soule for eternall life, by the assistance of thy grace and holy Spirit, before thou call me away hence; and grant me a happy and blessed departure out of this world, that thou maiest receive me into thy favour and mercy, to be with mee in my death, that I may dye in the Lord, and rest in peace, and obtaine a blessed resurrection, that so I may be accepted to live with thee to praise thy great and holy name for ever, Amen.

---

[a] ever since I was born,]

[b] by Jesus Christ,]

[c] gracious]

[d] & defende

[e] now]

[f] that] y[t] now

[g] with the assistance of the blessed Spirit.]

[h] This has some resemblances to a prayer in ASH 3501, 'At night: being in Bedd' (see Appendix 3).

13. A Prayer before the receiving the Sacrament of the Lords Supper.

O most sweet Saviour Jesus Christ, and my deare Lord, who art the authour and finisher of my faith, redemption, and salvation, the life [p. 27] and food of my soule: I most miserable sinner, presuming[a] nothing at all on mine owne merits or worthinesse,[b] but trusting wholly in thy infinite mercy[c] and goodnesse, doe feare and tremble to appeare before thy Majesty, or to come unto the table of this[d] heavenly banquet: But thou Lord Jesus[e] who graciously callest me, and all heavy laden sinners, accept in mercy the will for the deed, in that I am unworthy and ill prepared to presume into thy presence; and vouchsafe me the assistance of thy divine Spirit, I humbly beseech thee, in this holy action, that my duty and service therein may bee acceptable in thy sight: And powre down thy heavenly blessing upon[f] this thy holy Ordinance of thy Word and Sacraments,[g] that they may be effectuall to revive,[h] strengthen, and supply in me all sanctifying and saving graces needfull to the due and right performance of this sacred duty in an acceptable manner, whereby to enlighten[i] my understanding with thy grace to the right knowledge of thee and thy truth; and work in me a lively true faith, wherewith I may lay hold and apply unto my sicke soule all the sweet and comfortable promises and benefits purchased by the bitter death of my sweet Saviour: Indue me also with most[j] unfeigned and hearty sorrow and repentance for all my[k] great and grievous sins and offences committed against thee; for all which I most humbly beg thy gracious[l] pardon: and grant me such perfect love and[m] charity, that I [p. 28] may sincerely, with all due reverence and devotion, love thee, my God, with all my heart, soul and strength, and may love my neighbour as my selfe,[34] yea my very enemies for Christs sake, that so I may rightly receive this blessed Sacrament, being prepared by thy grace as I ought to bee:[n] And let, O Lord, thy pretious bloud shed for me, cleanse and wash away all my sins, and the breaking of thy pretious body, heale all the wounds of my

[a] presuming] trustinge

[b] ∧[w^h is none at all] [interlineation in R's hand]

[c] but trusting wholly in thy infinite mercy] but wholy ~~trustinge~~ [relying] on thy mercy [correction in R's hand]

[d] thy

[e] Jesus]

[f] upon]on

[g] Sacraments] sacrament

[h] revive] renew

[i] in an acceptable manner, whereby to enlighten] in acceptable manner, humbly prayinge thee, deare Lord) to enlighten

[j] most]

[k] my]

[l] gracious]

[m] love and]

[n] being prepared by thy grace as I ought to bee] as I ought to doe

corrupt soule, that by the gracious operation of the Holy Ghost, I may be inwardly and inseparably joyned to thee my head Christ; that thou maiest supply all my weaknesse and defects in soule or body, out of thy infinite fulnesse of grace and mercy; that being cloathed with thy righteousnesse, I may be accepted by thee, and through thee;[a] and so be accounted worthy to be partaker of all thy merits, that with the outward signe of bread and wine, I may blessedly[b] receive the true signified Christ, with all his benefits, and may have grace to hunger and thirst after the[c] spirituall food of Christs body and bloud,[35] to nourish my soule unto eternall life, and to make me become a new creature in holinesse of living, with all true and humble thankfulnesse, to thy glory and my everlasting salvation: beseeching thee to accept my poor endeavours for perfect performance, and reach forth thy helping hand from heaven to save me, thy unworthy servant, pardoning my sins, and covering my imperfections, with the pure in- [p. 29] nocencie of that immaculate Lambe, Jesus my Saviour.[d] And so I humbly commend my selfe unto thy mercy, who art able to doe abundantly, above all that I can aske or thinke; to thee be all honour, power, and praise for evermore, Amen.

A short meditation, direction, or preparation before you presume to enter into the presence and sight of God, to approach unto the heavenly banquet, humbly desiring this, or the like by prayer. As thou drawest near unto the holy table, pray earnestly in thy heart unto Christ:

{Knowledge of God and ourselves.} That he will draw near by grace unto thy soul, to strengthen thee with knowledge, true faith, unfeigned repentance, and perfect charity, that thou maiest rightly, reverently, and faithfully receive this holy Sacrament to Gods glory, and thine owne comfort, and salvation. {Ps. 14. 23. 1 Jo. 1. 8.}[36] Now when thou commest to communicate[e] and receive this blessed Sacrament of the Lords Supper: First, banish all vaine and earthly thoughts, {Col. 3. 2. Rom. 12. 1.2. & 1. 15.} and recollect thy heart to the serious me- [p. 30] ditations, of that which is the life of the Sacrament,[f] even the death of thy Saviour; {1 Tim. 2. 4} and humbly and devoutly present thy selfe and service to

---

[a] and through thee]

[b] blessedly] happily

[c] the] this [corrected from 'the' in R's hand]

[d] Jesus my Saviour] Christ Jesus

[e] That he will draw near . . . to communicate]
When y[u] comest to cõmunicate

[f] Sacrament] sacraments

the Redeemer of thy soule, and Lord of the feast, the only saviour of mankinde, Jesus Christ our righteous Lord.[a] {Humility. 1 Pet. 5. 6. 1 Jo. 2. 2. & 4. 14.}

Then apply thy minde to these contemplations: First, remember with great reverence the infinite Majesty of God, his mercy, goodnesse,[b] and justice, in whose presence we are. Secondly, consider thine owne vilenesse, misery, and unworthinesse, being wholly corrupt both in soul and body. {True repentance. 1 Jo. 9. Prov. 28. 13.} Thirdly, confesse all thy sins plainly, for in hiding our sins this work will not prosper, but with most hearty[c] and unfeigned sorrow, in all humility cast thy self at Jesus feet, earnestly begging for pardon, with hatred to all sin, and purpose of amendment: For who so confesseth and forsaketh their sins shall finde mercy. {True faith 1 Pet. 1. 18.19 21. 2.14. 1.3. 21.}[37] Fourthly, trie and acknowledge thy faith, and stedfast beliefe in Christ Jesus (the blessed Son of God the Creator) to be the only Saviour and Redeemer of the world, who dyed for thy sins, and rose againe for thy justification, and is ascended up to heaven[d] for thy salvation, where sitting at Gods [p. 31] right hand, he maketh intercession for thee, {1 Pet. 3. 22 Heb. 12. 24. 1 Jo. 2. 1.} and powreth downe all graces and blessings upon thee,[e] who giveth himself with all his merits, unto thee in this Sacrament, covering all thy offences with his perfect obedience: {1 Tim. 21 5. Jam. 1. 17.}[38] So making thee righteous, and leaving thee a pledge and seale of thy future and eternall happinesse, this his holy institution, which the divine word hath sanctified to that end and purpose. {Sanctification. 1. Jo. 17. 19.[39] Heb. 13. 12.} Now call to minde the exceeding[f] love of God and Christ towards thee, {Gods love to us.}[g] the one in sending his only deare Sonne, to become man and suffer death: The fifth,[h] in giving his most pretious body and bloud, to bee crucified and shed upon the crosse, to satisfie the just wrath of God due for thy sins; of which this bread broken, & wine powred out (that we see) is a remembrance which we ought often to celebrate, and set our hearts and soules duly and truly, {Our love to God. 1 Ja. 4. 9.10.[40]} to love and honour this gracious God and Lord, who hath loved us first, and done such great things as to give himself for us.[i] 6. Ponder well in thine heart all the divine mysteries of this holy Sacrament;[j] to which heavenly banquet, Jesus thy Saviour now inviteth thee, taking away thine hatefull[k] iniquities, and [p. 32] cloathing thee with his

[a] the only saviour of mankinde, Jesus Christ our righteous Lord] ye Sauiour of ye world

[b] goodnesse]

[c] confesse . . . hearty] confess plainely all thy sinnes, wth most hartie

[d] to heaven] into glory

[e] thee] us

[f] exceeding] infinite

[g] both ye father & ye son [addition in R's hand]

[h] The fifth] ye other

[i] as to give himself for us] for us

[j] {Diuine meditatiõ ye benefit of ye sacrament. Justification.}

[k] hatefull]

innocencie; so to make thee acceptable in the sight of God the Father, and by the gracious operation of the Holy Ghost, joyning thee unto himselfe, as thy head, and all of us in true love one to another, {Jo. 15. 12. Charity to our neighbours. 1 Jo. 4. 21.} as members of one body, to walke in newnesse of life the rest of our dayes. {Amendment. 1 Jo. 33. 10.[41] 1 Pet. 4. 2.} 7. And lastly, forget not to be ever truly thankfull for these inestimable benefits of God the Father, of the blessed Trinity;[a] and of Jesus Christ our Lord towards us, who hath laid downe his own life to redeem us, such vile and miserable sinners, all which the Holy Ghost applieth unto us. {Thankfulnesse. 1 Jo. 5. 7 Eph. 5 20. 1 Thess. 5. 18.} Infinite[b] mercies, we are never able sufficiently to acknowledge and admire. Prepare not thy belly, but thy soule; believe, and thou hast eaten; this saith St. *Augustine.*[c] [42]

14. A thanksgiving after the holy communion of the Lords Supper.

Oh! blessed and praised for ever, be the Name of the Lord my God, who hath done great and many things for me; and holy is thy gracious and[d] glo- [p. 33] rious name, and let thy mercy and thy truth (O Lord) never forsake me, but vouchsafe to continue thy goodnesse and loving kindnesse towards me for ever, and say[e] unto my soule thou art my God, my helpe and my salvation for evermore. And now especially (O Lord) as I am infinitely bound, I render unto thy divine Majesty all humble and possible praise and thanks[f] for this present and particular favour shewed unto me thy unworthy servant, in feeding my soule to eternall life, with the most pretious food of thine owne sacred body and bloud, blotting out all my sinnes, and sanctifying mee by thy holy Spirit, imputing to me thy righteousnesse, and admitting mee (so unworthy) to be a happy partaker of this blessed Sacrament: The benefit whereof is unspeakable, and the mercy therein unexpressable;[g] only I admire thy goodnesse towards mankind, and magnifie thy great mercy, beseeching thee (my God) as thou hast vouchsafed to accept mee at this holy Table; so (good Lord) let mee not[h] depart without a blessing, but be pleased to receive me into thy gracious care and[i] favour, that I may live and die therein; and give mee

---

[a] of the blessed Trinity] wth ye blessed spirrit

[b] Infinite] these Infinite (HB)

[c] to redeem us . . . St. *Augustine.*] to redeeme vs such vile & miserable sinners wch mercy we are neuer able, sufficiently to acknowledge & admire. Amen

[d] gracious and]

[e] alwaies

[f] thanks] thanks [corrected from 'thankfulnes' in R's hand]

[g] unexpressable] beyond my expression

[h] returne unthankfull, nor [interlineation in R's hand]

[i] care and]

grace[a] to spend the rest of my time in a carefull reformation of all evills past, a diligent performance of thy most holy will in all things, and true obedience to all thy Commandements, with a faithfull and right application of all thy mercies and merits;[b] so that I may feele thy bitter passion[c] (O Lord) sweet unto my soule, and [p. 34] by the assistance of thy Spirit, bring forth the fruits of amendment of life, and most hearty thankfulnesse all my daies;[d] that at the end of this life, I may obtaine a blessed roome in the Kingdome of glory, there to praise thy holy name for evermore, Amen.

15. A Short Prayer for conclusion to any prayer.[e]

O God the Father, blesse and governe my soule and body, in all things to thy service: O Lord the Sonne my Saviour Jesus, protect me, and direct me at all times to doe thy will: O holy Ghost, blessed Spirit, preserve mee from falling into any sinne or evill: but instruct, sanctifie and lead me into the waies of truth and righteousnesse, that I may live in thy feare, and dye in thy favour, and may continue in thy right Church and true faith unto my end: So that in the houre of my death, and in the dreadfull day of judgement, I may finde grace in thy sight that thou maiest pardon and passe by my sins, and receive me to mercy through Jesus Christ, that I may live with thee my God for evermore, Amen.

[p. 35]

16. A Prayer for the Lords day in the afternoone when you are from Church;[43] being seven humble petitions from a poor sinner to our Saviour Jesus Christ, the Lord and fountain of mercy, prescribed and allowed by sacred Scripture.

Most great and gracious Lord, and my only Saviour Jesus Christ, whom the Angels doe admire, all the Saints doe magnifie, and at thy name (O Jesus) doth every knee bow in heaven and earth: I most humbly beseech thee, to have mercy on me that presume to speake unto thee, who am but dust and ashes; {1. Remission of sins, and amendment of life. Luke 18. 13.[44] Rom. 6. 6.} yet Lord I

---

[a] (deare Sauiour)

[b] vnto my ~~oure~~ selfe [interlineation in R's hand]

[c] passion] death

[d] thankfulnesse all my daies] thankfullness all my dayes to comme

[e] 'The conclusion' in ASH 3501 is an early version of this prayer (See Appendix 3.)

beg of thee to forgive all my grievous and manifold offences, and cast all my sins out of thy sight, and not only to pardon all my past misdeeds, but also by thy mighty power and spirit, to slay all sin in me for the time to come.

{2. To rise from sin, Rev. 20. in this life} And of thy gracious favour vouchsafe while I live in this world to make mee a blessed partaker in the first resurrection to arise here, from remaining or lying dead in sin, and so the second death shall [p. 36] have no power to hurt me,[45] but by thy grace and assistance, I may become a new creature in all holinesse of life before thee, that I may daily bee raised from sin by thy holy Spirit to a new life of grace in Christ.

{3. In death Rev. 14. 13 21. 3.4. Luke 22. 32.36.}[46] But when the appointed time of my death doth approach, sweet Jesus leave me not, but keep and deliver mee from that great houre of temptation, when Sathan will sift[47] mee, and seeke my destruction, then deare Lord, pray for me that my faith may never faile, neither let my soules enemies prevaile over mee, but make thy poore servant one of those blessed that shall die in thee, O Lord, whose tears God will wipe from their eyes, and they shall rest from their labours, and their workes follow them.

{4 The first judgemẽt. Mat. 25. 34.41.}[48] Now, good Iesus, grant also in the last day and houre of death, when I shall come to my first account before the Throne of God, and the dreadfull Majesty of the Father; O my Saviour, appeare with mee, that by thy gracious mediation I may finde favour in his sight, and through thee obtaine to bee received into the society of thy Saints[49] and servants; and also by thy infinite mercy and bitter passion, that I may in and through thee have my sins [p. 37] covered and pardoned, and may be accounted worthy to escape thy just and great wrath, which my iniquities have deserved, and say alwaies unto my soule thou art my God, and my salvation for ever. And so I miserable sinner, through thy merits, sufferings, and unspeakable mercy, may be made able to stand before thee the blessed Son of God and man, at my appearance in thy glorious and awfull presence when thou commest to judge the world, and hast full power to save or to condemne us, then looke Saviour on me as one of thine.

{5. At the last judgement, 6. Is after death. Rev. 8. 20. 15.}[50] And sweet Saviour, I further beseech thee by thine owne former and free election and meer grace towards me, vouchsafe in the dreadfull time of thy great visitation, that my poore name may be found written in heaven in the booke of life, so as sin nor Sathan may not bee able to blot mee out; but that thou, gracious Iesus, wilt be pleased to acknowledge me (thy most unworthy servant) to be thine, before God and all his holy Angells.

{The 7th. For eternall life, John 17. 22. 24. Ps. 16. 11. Conclusion.} Now lastly, Lord by thy great goodnesse and mercy, that[a] I may be received into thy grace and favour, and so accepted as to injoy that most happy place and heavenly inheritance of everlasting glory, [p. 38] which thou our Jesus hast dearly purchased for us: that where he my blessed Saviour is, I may live with him, who loved me so much as to die for me, and through him being admitted into the glorious presence of God, which is the fulnesse of joy, at whose right hand are pleasures for evermore: I shall there eternally serve, praise and magnifie his most holy name, who liveth for ever and ever, Amen.

17. A Prayer to the Trinity for direction and acceptance from God, of all our prayers.

Most glorious God, and our heavenly Father in Christ, I most humbly pray thee for his sake to heare and accept mee, and my supplications that I offer up unto thy Majesty in the name of thy beloved Son: And I beseech thee sweet Iesus, in thy love and mercie, which made thee become our Redeemer; vouchsafe also to be my gracious advocate, and to direct and receive my petitions, and present them to the Father, for by and through thee only, I must obtaine acceptance. Now further I beg of thee, Lord Holy Ghost, who best can teach us to pray as we ought, to take compassion on my frailties and infirmities, to heale and helpe them, and be pleased to sanctifie and assist my heart and soule to performe this duty [p. 39] and service at all times, rightly, faithfully, and constantly; to Gods glory, and mine owne comfort and furtherance of my eternall salvation in Christ my Saviour, Amen.

18. Another Prayer for the afternoon for many severall blessings.

Oh most dear Lord, who knowest my manifold infirmities, and innumerable miseries: In mercy let thy gracious care and holy hand bee over me now and ever, to guide me into thy right paths, that I may walke in the wayes of thy Commandements, and keepe them with my whole heart unto my end. And vouchsafe, good God, to clense and change the thoughts of my corrupt heart from vaine and idle imaginations, to good and godly meditations, which may produce in me by thy assistance, holy actions agreeable to thy most blessed will; and by thy spirit let my affections be reformed, and my love withdrawne from the vanities of this vile world, and may bee fixed on heavenly things above, that there may be my heart and only joy, where my Lord Christ sits in glory at the right

---

[a] that] graunt that (HB)

hand of his Father; and so I may with blessed *Mary* chuse the better part,[51] to forsake all the world, and my selfe also, to follow and heare Iesus; and first and chiefly so to seek as [p. 40] to obtaine that which is most needfull, even thy glory, O God, thy Kingdome, and the righteousnesse thereof, and leave all other things to be bestowed on me as shall seem best unto thee.

And Lord grant that my understanding may be inlightned to discerne, imbrace, and practice the holy workes of thy blessed Spirit, and that my memory may be strengthned to retaine and make right use of all the good instruction that I heare or read according to thy will, and make my heart the storehouse of all thy divine precepts,[52] that by thy grace I may bring forth good fruit in my life; and make mee able rightly and reverently, to read and heare thy holy word, and heavenly will daily as I ought to doe, and by thy grace to frame my life thereafter; and direct thou me thy poor servant in all I goe about to doe that which is best, and most to thy glory, that howsoever all the powers and faculties of my soule, or the members or senses of my body may be decayed or lost by age, griefe, or sicknesse, for the occasions of this life, yet so[a] Lord all that is needfull for thy constant service, I beseech thee, continue to my last breath. And also be pleased to grant, that my death be neither sudden, nor unexpected, nor my pains violent, whereby to be made unable earnestly and faithfully to pray and call upon thy holy name; but if it be thy will, give mee knowledge of my death when thy time is come to call mee out of this world, and assist me fervently to crie unto thee [p. 41] for grace and mercie, in the needfull time of dread and danger; then (deare Lord) fit and prepare me for thy selfe, and give me a blessed departure hence to dye in thee, my Lord, and so I shall remaine safe and ever happy; and sweet Iesus; make me pray unto thee with my last breath, and yeeld up my spirit to God that gave it with praises in my mouth unto my gracious God, the Father, Son, and Holy Ghost.

Now vouchsafe, good Lord, while I live to indue me thy most unworthy servant with thy grace and holy Spirit, whereby devout love, and feare of thy Majesty, with true faith, stedfast hope, perfect charity, and unfained repentance, with all other saving graces, may be daily renued and increased in mee, towards thee, to thy glory, and the furtherance of my salvation through Christ: O sweet Saviour, who hast performed and suffered great and many things for mee; deare Jesus, continue thy infinite favour, and finish thy worke of mercy towards me the least of thy servants, still to call and draw me daily unto thee, and make me faithfull, constantly, and wholly thine in all humble obedience and true humility to serve thee in uprightnesse of life, and a holy conversation[53] towards all so long as I live, and wilt[b] assure my

---

[a] so] ~~so~~ (HB)   [b] wilt] Lord (*Errata*)

soule, that thou art my mercifull God, and after death make[a] me a happy partaker of thy everlasting Kingdome of glory. So be it. Amen.

[p. 42]

19. A Prayer of three petitions, to the blessed Trinity, the Father, Son and Holy Ghost, for the spirit of prayer, for repentance and remission of sins, and grace to amend and lead a new life.

O my Lord Holy Ghost, our sanctifier and comforter, and preserver, the giver of all heavenly gifts and graces, and the directer and assister of us to all goodnesse: I most humbly pray thee to indue me thy poore sinfull servant, with thy true spirit of grace and prayer, to helpe and teach me how to pray as I ought, and to drive away, and banish from me in the performance of this my duty, all evill temptations, and wicked hindrances that seek to pervert and withdraw my heart and soule from the true service of my God; and suffer not the world, the divell, nor any his agents to have power over me, or part in mee, to prevaile against me, and to cause God to turn his eare and face of mercy, from hearing and receiving my prayers and supplications: but Lord, by thy grace make my petitions now and alwaies right, faithfull, and acceptable to Almighty God, through Iesus Christ my blessed Saviour.

But O my God heavenly Father, the originall of all goodnesse, and mercy, who graciously commandest us to call upon thee in the time of trouble, that thou delivering us, we may glorifie thee; [p. 43] what greater misery and danger, then a heavy load of sins that will not easily be cast off, and a wounded spirit who can beare it? for I confesse I have most grievously sinned against thee, and my iniquities are multiplied before thee, as the starres which cannot be numbred. O Lord, whose compassion never faileth those that seek and trust in thee, as thy mercy exceedeth all thy great workes, so let that through thy deare Son move thee to release mee of this intolerable burthen; which else will throw mee out of thy presence and favour, wherein is the fulnesse of joy; and presse me down to hell into everlasting torments amongst the enemies of God and man. Now mercifull God, who hast pity on thy poore creatures, and delightest not in the death of a sinner; Lord turne me from all my evill waies, that I may be converted unto thee, to feare, love, and obey thee unto my end: And vouchsafe to pardon all my transgressions past, and remove my sins from me as farre as the East is from the West, and bury them in oblivion, that they

---

[a] make] ⌈wilt⌉ make (HB)

may not be able to separate my God from mee, as far as heaven from hell: but Gracious Lord, be pleased to give me, thy unworthy servant, the blessed gift of true sorrow and repentance to salvation, to fit me for thy mercy, and prepare me with grace by the amendment of all my misdeeds, for thy loving acceptance of me in thy favour againe, and say to my lost soule, I am thy God, and thy salvation for ever; and so [p. 44] thou working in me, both the will and the deed, the praise, honour and glory be only thine, for evermore.

Now swe[e]t Jesus, the fountaine of mercy, and Saviour of all that trust and believe in thee, who graciously callest all heavy laden and penitent sinners to come to thee, that thou maiest ease them; have mercy on me, and heale my sinfull soul with thy most pretious bloud; and thy righteousnesse I know is alsufficient to cover a world of sinnes, if thou please to impute it unto mee. O shrowd mee under thy innocent wing, that the great wrath I have deserved may never fall upon mee: but vouchsafe, dear Lord, to receive mee sinfull creature into thy favour, as thou didst *Mary*,[54] to become wholly thine, and be thy faithfull disciple so long as I live; and stretch forth thy hand of mercy, as thou didst to *Peter* from sinking in the sea;[55] so Lord save me thy unworthy servant, from perishing in my sins; and by thy assistance, according to thy blessed advice, that I may make my peace here, where I have transgressed, before I goe where the utmost farthing must bee paid. O Lord, by thy grace make me a new creature, daily to worke out my salvation, with sorrow for my time lost, feare to offend again, and trembling at the heavy judgements due unto me, and striving to make my calling and election sure, by a holy life and godly conversation both towards God and man all the rest of my dayes. And make mee [p. 45] cast utterly off all love of this deceitfull world, which is but lost, and my owne vaine desires that hang so fast on, and only apply my heart and soule to seek after thee and thy Kingdome, with the righteousnesse thereof, and then I shall obtain the end of my faith and hope; even thy glory, and my owne salvation, through thee only dear Jesus, my blessed Lord and alone Saviour. To whom with God the Father, and the Holy Ghost, three Persons, one eternall God and glorious Trinity, be rendred as is due, all praise, honour and glory, for ever and ever, Amen.

20. The conclusion to this booke. A short Prayer so to performe our duties here towards God, that we may obtaine heaven hereafter.

Oh most mercifull Lord God, thou knowest my unaptnesse to any good: I humbly pray thee to give me thy poor unworthy servant grace so truly to feare thee, as not to offend thee; so constantly to beleeve in thee, and confidently to relye upon all thy gracious promises, in all my troubles and necessities; and so entirely and sincerely to love and honour thee above all things, that nothing in this world may withdraw my minde from thee, nor any vaine hopes, or earthly desires make mee neglect my service to thee; but that I [p. 46] may daily study and strive, rightly and carefully to obey thee my Lord at all times, diligently to seek thee, and know thy will, and faithfully to serve and please thee as I ought to doe as long as I live. For thou, O God the Father, lovedst us first, and sent thy deare Son out of thy bosome to redeeme us, and our sweet Saviour Jesus in his love gave himselfe, and laid downe his owne life to save us from eternall death; greater love cannot bee found then for one to dye for a friend,[56] but thou Lord diedst for thine enemies; much more having now reconciled us to the father, and to thy selfe: I trust being united to thee also by the Holy Ghost, by sanctification and true faith wrought in me by that blessed Spirit, I shall obtaine mercy through the merits and sufferings of my deare Jesus, to live with thee in heaven hereafter, to glorifie the great Name of God, the eternall Father, Son and Holy Ghost, to whom bee all praise and honour for ever; and let heaven and earth, Saints and Angells, and all creatures, give glory to him for evermore, Amen.

Here is one Prayer more which I joyne to these, because it concerned one of my daughters, to whom this Booke belonged, though it was lately penned upon a very strange accident.[57]

[p. 47]

21.   *A thanksgiving to Almighty God, for his most mercifull preservation of my noble kinswoman the Lady* Eliz. Feelding, *and of my owne daughter, the Lady* Eliz. Cornwalleis, *from drowning under the Bridge, and was long under water: and one worthy Gentlewoman in the company could not bee recovered. This may serve upon any such fearfull accident.*

Most Mighty God, Creator of heaven and earth, and the only disposer of all things therein, thou art the defender and protecter of all thy children and servants, and the gracious preserver of all those that depend upon thee: thy power ruleth both by sea and land, and thy all-guiding providence directeth all things in the world, according to thy own high will and good pleasure, and for the good of all them that trust in thee. Whereof thou hast given many, and mee the unworthiest of thy servants, an especiall testimony of thy infinite mercy towards my deare daughter and kinswoman, in that great and miraculous deliverance lately of them, in the dreadfull danger of sudden death by drowning in the Thames; for thou didst mercifully provide and take care to save their lives, when they were past sense to take care of themselves, or to call upon thee for helpe: yet beyond all hope, thou didst bring them back from the gates of death, praised [p. 48] for ever be thy most glorious Name; and let neither us, nor any of our generation forget this thy great mercy. Now Lord, make us duly to acknowledge all thy benefits, and let us not passe them out of our mindes without true thankfulnesse for all thy favours continually vouchsafed unto us undeserved: for all which we poor creatures have nothing to returne to thee, but devout love, faithfull service, and carefull obedience, with the humble sacrifice of praise and thanksgiving; which by thy assistance, I will performe towards thee with a gratefull heart, so long as I live, and for ever, Amen.

22. A Petition of the Author for herselfe.

O Lord, as *Paul* said, he would readily performe the duty in his charge that lay upon him, lest while he preached to save others, himself should become a cast-away:[58] so dearest Lord, I having taken pains to compose many Prayers for the use of others (under my care) to further them in the constant performance of this duty of prayer; which being rightly used, will draw many blessings from thee: Almighty God, I most humbly beseech thee, to heare and receive their supplications, that call upon thee by these Prayers. So, Gracious Lord, suffer not me to neglect my [p. 49] duty and daily service herein, towards thy Majesty, but make me carefully, rightly and reverently to offer up due praises and prayers, daily unto thee in a faithfull and acceptable manner all the daies of my life. And give me thy poor servant the assistance of thy grace and holy Spirit, to reform all my waies before thee; to suppresse and overcome the corruption of my heart, the vanity of my mind, and to forsake and abandon the love of this vile world, with all the deceitfull vanities thereof, and to cast off those great & superfluous cares and desires after the things of this mutable life, which passe away like a shadow or dream. Wise *Solomon* that had the plenty, and triall of all things under the Sun, tells us what it will prove, only vanity of vanities, and vexation of spirit.[59] Wherefore let me learne with *Paul*, in what estate soever I am, therewith to be content,[60] and to submit with humble patience to thy pleasure in all things thou sendest, who knowest what is best and fittest for me; and keep me from repining and despairing in thy chastisements; for thou canst heale as well as wound, when thou pleasest. Therefore I will dedicate my heart and soule, and all my endeavours unto thy faithfull service, striving to make my calling and election sure, by looking after thee my God, thy Kingdome, and thy righteousnesse, which is the only thing needfull: This grace grant unto mee, O God, for Jesus Christs sake, Amen.

The end of the first Book.

[p. 51]

BOOK II.ᵃ

This Book I began to write at my house at Barking *in* Essex, *where I retired my selfe in solitarinesse, after the death of my worthy and dear husband, Sir* Thomas Richardson, *Knight, Lord chiefe Justice of the Kings Bench: who dyed at Candlemas,* 1634.⁶¹

Where shortly after I finished these Prayers following for my owne private use; being the fittest imployment for my time, who was then in so much heavinesse.

I call this Book a weekly exercise of Prayer, either for a private person, or in their owne family: To which there are added some other necessary Prayers, very usefull for those particular occasions, whereto they are directed: which I shall be very glad and joyfull, if my children, grand-children, kindred, friends, or any good Christian that shall peruse them, may make a good and right use of them to Gods glory: And I doe most heartily and humbly pray, that God will vouchsafe to heare in heaven, and to receive, accept, and grant their just requests, to his owne honour, their comfort, and [p. 52] *my great happinesse, who am a wel-wisher, and true lover of their soules in the Lord.*

Eliz. Richardson.

These Prayers I composed for the instructions of my children, & grand-children, after the example of my dear parents, Sir Thomas Beaumont, *and his Lady, of* Stoughton *in the County of* Leicester,⁶² *who I thinke were as carefull and industrious to breed up their children (which were living)ᵇ in the instruction and information of the Lord, to serve and obey God, as any parents could possibly be, which made them take much paines with us, more then is usuall, by their endeavours to bring us to know and feare God, and to keep his Commandements: Which* Solomon *saith, is the whole duty of man.⁶³ But when parents have done the best, and all we can, it is Gods grace and blessing that must perfect the worke: which I humbly pray him to adde to accomplish my desire, to their eternall happinesse.*

[p. 53]

An Exhortation concerning Prayer.ᶜ

Before thou goest to pray: consider seriously of these three things, which are very necessary to fit and prepare thee the better for that holy and blessed exercise: First, ponder with thy selfe, into whose presence wee come, and to whom we presume to speak, being before the great Majesty of God Almighty. Secondly, in what manner we pray, and to what end our prayers tend, which must chiefly respect the glory of

---

ᵃ written 1625 Printed 1645 | Called A weekly exercise of prayer. (HB) [NB: the dates of writing and printing are added either side of the running title 'to her Daughters.']

ᵇ which were living] ~~which were living~~ (HB)

ᶜ Prayers for each day of yᵉ weeke./ (HB) [Added above the printed title.]

God and his service; and then our owne desires and necessities, both for soule and body. Thirdly, weigh well what good or hurt, what benefit or danger may ensue, by the performing of this duty carefully or negligently.[a]

1. A short Petition to precede any other Prayers.

O Lord Holy Ghost, who knowest my corrupt heart, and the frailty of my soule, which can performe no good but by thy grace. Vouchsafe, my Lord, to sanctifie, assist and teach me the unworthiest of thy servants, by thy holy Spirit, so to pray now and alwayes, that my supplications may be faithfull and acceptable to my God, to his glory, and the comfort and good of my selfe, both in soul and body for ever, Amen.

[p. 54]

2. A Prayer to God the Holy Ghost, for the true spirit of grace in prayer.

O God Holy Ghost, the giver of all good gifts and graces, give mee thy true Spirit Lord, who art the comforter and sanctifier of thine Elect: thou knowest my great and manifold infirmities, and frailties; all which, I humbly pray thee in thy love and mercie to heale and helpe. And Lord give me power, strength, and grace, by thy assistance, to resist and overcome all wicked assaults and temptations of the divell, that seeke to draw me from God and goodnesse, and lead mee to all evill: but vouchsafe Lord, I beseech thee, still to be present with me in this holy exercise, and indue thy poore servant with thy blessed Spirit and gift of prayer to call upon thy glorious Name faithfully and sincerely, whereby my unworthy petitions (though full of imperfections) may be received and accepted by thee. And Lord, banish all wandring thoughts, and wicked hindrances from my soule, in the performance of this my bounden duty and service, that I owe unto thee, my God, Father, Son, and Holy Ghost: And be pleased Lord, to assist mee now and ever with thy grace to worship thee at all times, in spirit and truth, as thou requirest: and not to present a dead, dull and corrupt offering unto my Lord, of the lips without the heart, or by joyning in my [p. 55] thoughts God and the world, or mammon together, which thou hatest,[64] and so make my prayers abominable to thy Majesty; for thou hast made the heart, who ought and must be served and honoured with it.

Therefore I humbly pray thee, to inable me by thy assistance, to offer unto thee, my God, a holy and living sacrifice, of my selfe, my prayers, and praises daily, in

---

[a] Before y[u] prayest p[r]pare thy selfe, and tempt not God./ (HB)

a right and acceptable manner, not looking so much to the benefit and recompence of reward that shall bee received thereby from thy mercifull hands to my owne good, but chiefly for the honour and glory of thy great Name, whose I am, and whom I am bound to serve, and from whom I have already received so many great blessings and benefits both spirituall and temporall: for which I render most humble and hearty thanks unto thy Majesty.

Now lastly, deare Lord Holy Ghost, I earnestly beg of thee, daily to unite mee unto thy glorious head, and only Saviour Jesus Christ, that so I may performe with true faith, good devotion, humility, and sincerity, this, and all other holy duties and services, according to thy blessed will and word, to thy glory and my great comfort; now and for ever: So be it.

[p. 56]

3. A short preface before any other Prayers, for the Lords day.

Almighty Lord God, in whose glorious presence I am, presuming to take thy sacred name into my sinfull mouth: before thee, Lord, I most humbly prostrate my selfe; thou seest the heart, and knowest our wants before we aske, yet hast thou commanded us to ask in thy Sons name,[65] promising for his sake, to grant us all needfull blessings both for soule and body. O Lord, thou understandest my great weaknesse and disability, who can doe no good, but by thy assistance: I now most humbly pray thee, to keep all evill interruptions from my heart and soule, and so to indue mee with thy true Spirit of grace and prayer, in performing this duty and service to thy glorious Majesty; that so all my supplications may now and at all times be right, faithfull, acceptable, and pleasing unto thee; and by thy great mercy also, prevailing for my good, and furtherance of my salvation, through my only Lord and Saviour Jesus Christ. Amen.

4. A Prayer for the Lords day at first awaking.

O Most glorious Lord God, the high and gracious Creator of heaven and earth, with all [p. 57] things therein; Thou didst finish that mighty work in six dayes, and rested the seventh, commanding thy Church and people of the Jewes to keep holy the seventh day, to thy due service and praise. But our Lord Jesus having finished the redemption of mankinde by his crosse and passion, and bitter sufferings didst bury that Sabbath in his grave upon that day, and by thy Spirit didst guide thy Apostles and Christian Church to sanctifie and keep holy this first day of the weeke,[66] in perpetuall memory of his glorious resurrection and eternall rest from that labour, and suffering for our redemption, to thy due service and praise; blessed be thy holy name therefore.

And now, dear Lord, for[a] all my former neglects of my duty herein; for Jesus his sake, pardon my sinfull breaches of this, and all other thy holy Commandements heretofore: and vouchsafe, O God, alwaies to knit my straying heart, to the true feare of thy great name, to keep me from offending thee, and fill my soul with the infinite love of thy divine Majesty, that I may daily strive to lead the rest of my life in all obedience to thy holy will. And Lord, vouchsafe to inspire me thy most unworthy servant, I humbly pray thee, with thy blessed Spirit, that I may withdraw my minde this blessed day, from all worldly cogitations, thinking my owne thoughts, speaking my owne words, doing my daily works, or going my owne waies; but assist me with thy grace, that I may apply my heart and soule wholly to medi- [p. 58] tate of thy wonderfull works, and manifold mercies, with thankfulnesse, and to attend thy service either publique or private,[67] with care and faithfulnesse, and to obey all thy Commandements henceforth with diligence, and constantly serving thee all my life to come, that so I may praise and glorifie thee, and thou maiest pardon my sins, and save my poore soule, through thy great and unmerited mercie in Jesus Christ, my Lord and only Redeemer, Amen.

5. A Prayer for the Lords day in the morning before going to Church.

My soule praise thou the Lord, and all that is within me praise his holy name,[68] who is most worthy of all honour and glory.

Almighty God, our heavenly Father in Jesus Christ thy beloved Son, who of thy infinite goodnesse by thy great power and divine word, didst in six dayes create heaven and earth, the sea and the whole world, with all things therein, and resting the seventh day, didst blesse and hallow it, commanding all thy people in purity after thine owne image, to keep the same holy to thy due honour and praise; having also given us six dayes for our owne occasions:[69] and after this great and [p. 59] unexpressible worke, thou didst also in thy appointed time accomplish by thy beloved Son Jesus, that happy redemption of mankinde, who were lost by sin, and fallen from thee; which unspeakable mercie and benefit was as upon this first day of the week consummated by the miraculous blessed resurrection of our Saviour; which wee Christians now keep in commemoration of these thy infinite benefits; that according to thine appointment thy servants may rest this holy Lords day, from all worldly affaires to thy honour and glory: blessed and praised now and for ever, bee thy glorious Name, for these thy marvellous workes.

---

[a] for] for ʌ⌈giue⌉ (HB)

Therefore I most humbly beseech thee, O Lord, of thy great mercie, by thy Spirit of grace, to sanctifie mee thy most unworthy servant, both in soule and body, that I may at all times, but especially this Lords day, and upon all other daies consecrated by thy Church to the memory of any of thy blessings, benefits and deliverances, wholly devote my selfe, to thy true feare, holy devotion, and faithfull service, in performance of thy blessed will and commandement: And so thy worthy name may be glorified, my salvation furthered, and thy favour and blessing rest alwaies upon me and mine. And likewise I most humbly pray thee, O God, for thy Son Jesus sake, to forgive all my sins done in my whole life past, in breaking this and all other thy divine Laws, that through the death and bitter passion of my deare [p. 60] and innocent Saviour, which hee suffered to redeem us, thou wilt vouchsafe to be reconciled unto me, thy guilty and sinfull creature; that as this is a day of rest to thy due praise, so by thy mercy it may bee a happy day of joy and peace to my poore soule and conscience, through my only Lord and blessed Saviour Jesus Christ, Amen, Amen.

6. A Prayer to be said at the Church, as soone as we are come into our seat.

O Lord our God, who art here present amongst us, thou seest and understandest all things, and knowest my heart; prepare, sanctifie, and assist my heart and soule, with thy grace, so to behave my selfe, both outwardly and inwardly, as in the presence of thy glorious Majesty, in this thy blessed house of prayer and hearing thy word, with such due reverence, feare, humility, true faith and devotion, as may be best pleasing and acceptable unto thee, and most profitable and available for the good of mine owne soule. O God, indue thy servant the Preacher, with thy holy Spirit, to teach thy saving truth rightly and sincerely, that it may be powerfull to our edification,[70] and effectuall to the beating downe, and banishing of all sins from our soules, and the en- [p. 61] crease of faith and grace in us that heare him; to thy glory, and the furthering of our salvations, through Jesus Christ our Lord, Amen.

7. Another shorter Prayer to the same purpose.

Good Lord, that knowest my infirmities, prevent and remove all sin and evill hindrances and impediments of drousinesse, and wandring thoughts from me fraile sinfull creature, and open my ears and heart like *Lidices*[71] to attend and marke diligently what is taught out of thy most sacred word. Inlighten, Lord, my understanding, to conceive rightly what I heare, and keep my mind wholly intentive upon thy faithfull service; in hearing thy holy word with true devotion before thee; and make my memory retentive of all the good instructions that I learne, and give me grace carefully and conscionably to practice them throughout my whole life, to the honour of thy great name, the performance of thy most holy will, the amendment of all my faults; and finally, the salvation of mee thy poore servant, through my Saviour Jesus Christs merits and mercies, Amen.

[p. 62]

8. A Prayer after the Sermon is ended, before we go out of the Church.

Most Gracious Lord God, I humbly beseech thee, to pardon all my sinfull neglects, defects, and want of due preparation, or any infirmities that have overtaken mee in the performance of my duty towards thee, in this thy house, and blessed exercise of Prayer, and hearing of thy divine Word. And let me not depart out of this holy place without thy blessing, whereby my knowledge, faith, holinesse, and comfort in thee may be daily increased in me: And Lord, adde thy grace to what I have now heard, that by thy gracious assistance, it may bring forth plentifull fruit in me, to the reformation of my life and conversation, in avoiding all evill, and doing all good, which may be serviceable and acceptable to thy Majesty, and best pleasing in thy sight, through Jesus Christ, my only Saviour. Amen.

A Prayer for the Lords day at night, of three Petitions.

First, thankfulnesse for benefits already received, with prayer for the continuance of all Gods mercies. Secondly, for repentance, true faith, remission of sins, and amendment of life. Lastly, so to live and dye unto God here, that after death, we may live with him in heaven for ever.

[p. 63]

9. The Prayer.

My soule praise thou the Lord, and forget not all his benefits, which forgiveth all thine iniquities, and healeth all thine infirmities, which redeemeth thy life from death, and crowneth thee in mercy and compassion, who provided a ransome for thee, before thou hadst being to understand thine owne wretched estate. Oh, my Lord God! how good and gracious hast thou ever been in all thy mercies both spirituall and temporall towards me, the least and unworthiest of thy servants, before I was borne, and ever since, from time to time?

Now Lord,[a] I humbly pray thee, in the same love and favour, from which I have hitherto received so many and great benefits, vouchsafe thou alwaies to continue thy blessings unto me, especially in daily renewing all spirituall graces in my soule, for the true performance of all holy duties and service, in a right and acceptable manner towards thy Majesty: and Lord, make my humble thankfulnesse unto thee, appeare in my true obedience of thee in all things, that I may duly praise and glorifie thy name for ever.

Now deare God,[b] let not thy mercy in prolonging my daies, encrease the number of my sinnes, and so to heap up wrath[72] unto my selfe against the day of wrath, by drawing upon me due punishments for my offences; but mercifull God, adde thou grace [p. 64] unto my daies; and for Jesus sake, forgive all my sinnes past that I have done before thee in my whole life time, especially in my many breaches of this holy and blessed Lords day, which we keep in remembrance of our Saviours resurrection; with all my neglects and defects in the performance of my duties towards thee this present day, and heretofore, according to thy Commandements.

And grant,[c] O God, through thy mercies, and my Saviours merits, that my iniquities may never bee imputed unto mee; but Lord, let thy goodnesse, patience, and long sufferings, lead me to daily and unfaigned repentance; and give me true faith in all thy gracious promises, and by the assistance of thy holy Spirit, to bring forth amendment of all my former faults, with true obedience unto thy blessed will and holinesse of living all my life to come: That so I may obtaine grace and favour in thy sight, to prevent and keep mee hereafter from all sin and evil, or offending thee, my God, in thought, word and deed; and direct thou my waies right before thee, in all godlinesse and uprightnesse of heart, that I may be enabled through my Lord Jesus Christ, to doe every good worke, and by thy grace to live here according to all thy Commandements; and when thou pleasest to call for mee out of this wicked world unto thy selfe, Lord assist me with thy spirit and grace to make a blessed end, and to die in thee, my Lord, and so I shall finde mercie through the merits of my Saviour [p. 65] Jesus, after death to be accepted and received into the Kingdome of heaven, and through Christ my Saviour, may bee admitted into thy glorious presence, O God, where is the fulnesse of joy, and at thy right hand there are pleasures for evermore, of which Lord make me a happy partaker, when this life is ended. Amen, Amen.

[a] {i.} (HB)
[b] {2.} (HB)

[c] {3.} (HB)

10. A Prayer for Munday to God the Father, at first awaking.

I will praise thee[a] with my whole heart, for thou hast dealt lovingly with mee. Blessed and praised now and ever, be thy most glorious Name, O my God, heavenly Father, for all thy great and manifold mercies and blessings, both spirituall and temporall in soule and body, vouchsafed unto mee thy most unworthy and sinfull servant, before I was borne, and hitherto, this last night, and all my life past; for thy favours have ever been right, good and gracious towards mee, having done great and many things for mee, praysed be thy most holy Name, who hast been my only stay, succour, helpe and comfort in this world; and thy infinite mercy in Christ, is all my hope and confidence, for the life to come. Now Gracious Lord, who hast been my good God and guide from my youth, have pity upon my infirmities: and for [p. 66] Jesus sake, forgive all my sinnes that I have committed before thee in my whole life past, and let thy mercy and truth, never leave me nor forsake me, neither in life, in death, nor in the last judgement, but be pleased by thy Spirit, to say alwaies unto my soule, especially at my death, thou art my God and my salvation, for in thee will I trust so long as I live, and for ever. So be it.

A short supplication before the weekly Prayers.[b]

11. A morning Prayer for Munday to God the Father.

Heare me when I call upon thee, O God of my righteousnesse, have mercy upon mee, and hearken unto my prayer. Most Gracious Lord God, and my heavenly Father, in Christ Jesus my Saviour; thou knowest my great and grievous infirmities, that I can of my selfe neither will nor performe any good, nor think a good thought, but by thy grace; therefore I most humbly pray thee to indue mee thy poore unworthy servant with thy holy Spirit, whereby these and all other my prayers and petitions, that I presume to offer unto thy Majesty, may by thy assistance be made in a right manner, and in an acceptable time, when thou wilt please to be found of me, and graciously to heare and receive me and my supplica-[p. 67] tions. And now vouchsafe, dear God, to sanctifie, prepare and assist my heart and soule, with thy true Spirit of grace and prayer, to drive away all vaine and wandring thoughts, sluggish dulnesse, and all evill temptations out of my minde; and knit my heart and soule to the true feare of thy great Name, and to the devout love of thy divine Majesty; and teach mee with all due reverence, and such true humility and devotion, as is fit to appear in thy sacred presence, that I may

---

[a] ∧ ⌈o Lo.ᵈ⌉ (HB)   [b] This left out (HB)

rightly, faithfully, and humbly, now and at all times, call upon thy holy Name as I ought to doe, and daily pray unto thee, O my blessed Lord God, who hast awaked mee in health and safety to this daies light, which I most thankfully acknowledge, with all other thy blessings and benefits, both spirituall and temporall, bestowed on me thy sinfull servant, from time to time; beseeching thee of thy infinite mercy alwaies to continue them unto me. And as thy gracious providence hath brought me to begin this new day, so Lord, by thy power defend me therein from falling into any sin or evill, to offend thee; but give me grace at this present to performe, and ever continue to lead a new, a holy, and an upright life in thy sight, all the rest of my daies to come, to frame my heart, and reforme my waies, in all true obedience hereafter to thy most holy will and Commandements.

And further, I humbly praise thy glorious Name, for thy gracious preservation of me and mine, and all o- [p. 68] ther thy benefits vouchsafed me the last night, and all my life past unto this instant houre, having hitherto given me health, maintenance and safety; which, I pray thee, whilst I live, still to vouchsafe me, and make me truly thankfull to thee for all thy mercies; and let thy benefits never slip out of my minde, but that I may daily and duly acknowledge them to the true praise of thy most holy Name. And grant me grace to spend the rest of my time to come more carefully and faithfully then I have formerly done, to seeke, serve, feare, love, obey, and please thee my Lord, in all things as I ought to doe, so that it may bee more then meat and drinke unto me, to doe the will of thee my heavenly Father. And I most humbly beseech thee, O God, the fountaine of mercy, to forgive and pardon all my sinnes and offences past that I have committed against thee, either in soule or body throughout my whole life; Lord blot them out of thy remembrance, with the most pretious bloud of thy deare Son, my only Saviour Jesus Christ; and grant through thy mercies, and his merits, and sufferings, that my iniquities may never be imputed unto me.

But vouchsafe, O God, now and ever, to keepe me thy poore servant, as the apple of thine own eie from all sin and shame, and hide mee under the shadow of thy wings from falling into any evill or danger this day;[73] especially, O Lord, preserve mee alwaies from the great wickednesse of committing any presumptu- [p. 69] ous sin before thee, and from the fearfull sinne against the Holy Ghost (which is unpardonable)[74] and from the dangerous sins of neglect towards thee, hardnesse of heart, senselesse security, or falling into wicked despaire, whereby I may prevent my soule of thy mercy in Christ for my salvation.[75] But, good God, direct thou my thoughts, desires, words, and deeds, to be ever agreeable to thy most holy will, and obedient to all thy Commandements, that I may henceforth live before thee with an upright heart, daily studying and striving to serve and please thee in all things, so long as I live, that after death, I may praise and magnifie thy Name in heaven among thy Saints and servants, for ever and ever. These great mercies, O gracious God, with all other thou knowest needfull for me, either for this life or the life to come, I further beg of thee, in the name, merits and mediation of thy deare Son, and my sweet Jesus, concluding in that perfect forme of prayer, which hee hath taught us, saying, Our Father, &c.

12. A Prayer to God the Father for Munday night.

O Lord my God, how excellent is thy name in all the world, who hast done great workes, and brought mighty things to passe.[76]

Almighty Lord, and my heavenly Father in Christ, most high and mighty God, Creator, [p. 70] possessor, preserver, and disposer of heaven and earth, and all that is therein, the fountaine of grace and mercy, and Father of light, from whom commeth all good and perfect gifts: I most humbly pray thee of thy great goodnesse to give mee thy poore sinfull servant, thy grace and holy Spirit, to direct my heart and all my waies aright in thy sight, and to guide me in the paths of truth and righteousnesse; and Lord, lead mee into that streight way, and through that narrow gate, which bringeth unto life eternall;[77] that so of thy infinite mercie through Christ, I may enter in (though most unworthy) with them that obtaine grace to finde it, and there to live with thee, my God, in joy and blisse for evermore. And further, I yeeld and render unto thee, my Lord, all humble and possible praise, honour, and thankes, for all thy great and manifold mercies and benefits, spirituall and temporall, vouchsafed unto me thy most unworthy servant in soule and body from time to time; and also for thy gracious preservation of me and mine, and all other thy blessings bestowed upon me this day past, and all my life hitherto. Now, good God, for Christs sake, I humbly pray thee, to forgive and pardon all my sinnes and trespasses that I have committed before thee, inwardly or outwardly in soul or body, by thought, desire, word or deed, this present day, or any time of my life heretofore. Mercifull Father, wash away all my sinnes out of thy sight, [p. 71] with the most pretious bloud of that All-sufficient sacrifice, the innocent Lamb of God, Jesus, who was slaine for our transgressions: hide all my sins in his wounds, and bury them in his grave, so as they may never bee able to rise in judgement against me, either to accuse or to condemne mee. But Lord, make me of that blessed number, whose sinnes thou wilt cover, and whose iniquities thou wilt pardon. And vouchsafe also to forgive my omission of all those good deeds I ought to have done, and my sinfull neglect in the true performance of all duty and service that I owe unto thee; especially my wicked negligence in calling upon thy holy Name, and daily praising thee for all thy mercies: and likewise I beg pardon for my often omitting, or slightly performing this duty of praying unto thee as I ought, now and at all times; which Lord give me grace more carefully, faithfully and devoutly to perform towards thee, by the assistance of thy holy Spirit ever hereafter, that so of thine infinite mercy thou maist bring mee to that eternall Kingdome which thou hast prepared, O God the Father, before the world began, for all that truly love and beleeve in thee, to thy great praise and honour, and my salvation in Christ, through thy mercy, O blessed Lord God, to whom be glory now and ever. Amen.

[p. 72]

13. The conclusion for Munday, to be said last, or in bed.

O my God, I most humbly commend and commit my selfe both body and soule, my children and grand-children, my kindred, friends and family, and all that doth belong unto me, here or else where, with all my fellow members in thy whole Church,[a] into thy most gracious protection and preservation, this night and alwaies. Good God, I beseech thee, vouchsafe to blesse, sanctifie and keep our soules and bodies in thy true faith, feare and favour, with safety, this night, and to our lives end. Amen.

14. A Prayer at first awaking, for Tuesday, to our Saviour Jesus Christ.

My soule shall magnifie thee, O Lord, and my spirit rejoyceth in God my Saviour, who hath done and suffered great and many things for me,[78] blessed be thy most holy Name for thy infinite benefits and blessings, both spirituall and temporall bestowed upon mee thy unworthy sinfull servant from time to time. And chiefly (Gracious Lord) for thy accomplishment of my redemption before I had any being: who didst vouchsafe to [p. 73] come into the world amongst evill men, and to be borne of a Virgin, to take the shape and nature of man upon thee, and in our flesh didst work and performe all righteousnesse to bee imputed unto us; and also submitted thy selfe to suffer the most bitter and ignominious death of the Crosse, to free us from that eternall death, which our sinnes have deserved; and also rose againe from the grave the third day, to overcome sin, death, the grave, hell and Sathan, with all other things for us. And so thou, sweet Jesus, art become our reconciliation, redemption, righteousnesse, and justification, with hope also through thee of salvation and glorification hereafter. Of all which thy inestimable benefits, I humbly pray thee, O Lord my Saviour, of thy infinite mercy both in this world, and after this life is ended, to make me thy poor unworthy servant a happy partaker amongst thy Saints and servants, that I

---

[a] Church] Catholike Church (*Errata*)

may live hereafter with thee and them, to praise and glorifie thy Name, my deare
Jesus, for ever. Amen.

15.   A Prayer for Tuesday morning, to God the Son, our Redeemer.

I know that my Redeemer liveth, and shall stand the last day upon the earth,[79]
to judge the world in righteousnesse, and all the people with equity. [p. 74] O
sweet Iesus Christ, who art my Lord and perfect Saviour, the beloved Son of
God, the blessed Redeemer of the world, the only searcher of mans heart, before
whom all things are manifest, all desires knowne, and from thee no secrets can be
hid: Lord cleanse and reforme the thoughts of my wicked corrupt heart, by the
inspiration of thy most holy Spirit,[80] to purge my heart, soul and conscience from
all sin, evill, and dead works,[81] rightly and faithfully, to feare and serve thee, the
true and living Lord, that I may unfainedly love thee, and constantly praise and
magnifie thy holy and blessed Name all the daies of my life, and for ever. Now,
Gracious Iesus, grant that the words of my mouth, and the thoughts, and
meditations of my heart, in these and all other prayers and petitions that I make
unto thy Majesty, may bee alwaies guided by thy blessed Spirit, and that all my
waies and actions, be directed according to thy holy word, and so by thy merciful
assistance, all things I goe about, shall be ever right and acceptable in thy sight,
O Lord God of truth, that art my strength and my Redeemer.

And deare Saviour, who knowest the infinite corruption of my wretched nature,
and my unaptnesse to all goodnesse, vouchsafe to draw and knit my heart and
soule, to thy true feare and faithfull service, and suffer no worldly respects, regard
of persons, nor any pleasures, to withdraw my minde, or hinder my soule from
the true performance of my daily [p. 75] duties and service towards thee, my
God, with due observance of thy great Majestie, faithfully, devoutly and
constantly serving thee, and calling on thy holy name, now and at all times, and
daily worshipping thee in spirit and truth, as thy selfe hast commanded. And be
thou pleased, dear Lord, by thy grace, to guide and direct my heart, soule, and
body, with all my desires, waies, and workes, according to thy owne good will and
pleasure; for I humbly commend and commit my selfe, my children and grand-
children, with all belonging to mee, and all things that any way concerneth me,
to thy most gracious protection, direction, and disposing, now and ever.

And I humbly pray thee, O my sweet Iesus, so to prevent[82] me with thy holy Spirit,
that I bee led into no temptation this day by the divell or his evill agents, the vaine
world, or my owne corrupt flesh, neither suffer any sinfull thoughts to possesse my
soule; but assist me, I beseech thee, to set a watch over my heart and waies, and
before my mouth, and set a seale of grace and wisdome over my soul, and upon my

lips, that I offend not with my tongue, or in my actions, either against thee my God, my neighbour or my owne soule; but Lord, make my heart cleane and upright before thee, and keep me from falling into my former sins againe, but indue me with grace so to number my daies, that I may apply my heart to wisdome and goodnesse, and daily endeavour and strive to [p. 76] lead a new and godly life in thy sight; and make me firme, stedfast, and constant in thy right Church, saving truth, and true faith unto my lives end, to live and die therein; but if I hold any errors contrary to thy will and word (O Lord) speedily convert my soule unto thee, and shew me the paths of life, and teach me thy truth, and suffer me not to slide from it, but so long as I live here, constantly to set my whole heart, soule, and delight, to seek, to serve, to love, and to fear thee, my Lord, in all true obedience, humility, repentance, and purity, with stedfast faith in thee, and true holinesse of living, as is required of thy children and servants, through the assistance of thy blessed Spirit, and the blessing of thy heavenly Father, who liveth and reigneth with thee, three Persons, and one true eternall God, blessed for ever. Amen. Concluding my humble petition, with that perfect prayer, which Christ our advocate hath sanctified, and taught us saying, Our Father, &c.

16. A Prayer for Tuesday at night to our blessed Saviour, for my selfe and children.

O sweet Iesus Christ, that art both God and man, my blessed Saviour, Redeemer, and Mediator, who understandest all things, and seest what we want before we aske, and knowest best [p. 77] what is in miserable mortall man, that is made of earth,[83] how corrupt my nature and substance is, how many and great my frailties and infirmities are, and how subject I am to fall into all manner of evill both in soule and body, if thy grace uphold me not: therefore I most humbly beseech thee, O Lord, to receive me and mine now and ever, into thy provident and gracious care, to protect and direct us in all our waies to doe thy blessed will, and to live in all[a] thy holy feare, to save and guide us waking from all sinne and shame, and to keep and defend us sleeping from all perills and dangers either of soule or body, that so by thy mercie we may rest in peace and safety this night, and also awake in thy grace and favour, and doe all things to thy honour and glory, and may live and dye thy true and faithfull servants; and after death vouchsafe, dear Lord, by thy merits and sufferings to give us eternall life with thee in heaven, which thou hast dearly purchased for us.

Now sweet Jesus, vouchsafe to indue and assist mee with thy grace and holy Spirit, that I may be able rightly, faithfully, and confidently (as I ought to doe) to

---

[a] all] all (HB)

cry and pray unto thee, my God, for grace and mercie, that I may finde favour in thy sight, and that my trust in thee may never cease, that so I may obtaine true contrition for all my offences, and pardon for my sins past, with all saving graces for my salvation both in life and death, and assured hope of everlasting life when [p. 78] this is ended, through thy pretious death and bitter passion, sweet Iesus my Saviour. Now, good Lord, indue me with grace, to fit and prepare my soule as I ought, before my day of death approacheth, that I be not taken unprovided; but assist me with thy blessed Spirit to worke in my heart a true and lively faith, to lay fast hold upon all thy mercies, merits, and gracious promises, and rightly to apply them to my owne soule. And further give mee, I humbly pray thee, unfaigned repentance and remission of all my sinnes, with other needfull graces for the performing of all holy duties to thy Majestie, that so I may be inabled rightly and faithfully to serve and please thee while I live here; and also make me carefully to fit and prepare my soule for thy mercifull acceptance, before thou call me to thy selfe out of this vale of misery; and give mee grace daily to die unto this world, and forsake it while I am in it, that I may live more and more in true holinesse and righteousnesse before thee; and so I shall obtaine blessednesse here to be directed by thee in all in things, and to have thy protection over me to die happily in thee, and live eternally with thee, who art my only Saviour and Redeemer, Iesus Christ the righteous, to whom be all glory for ever and ever. So be it.

[p. 79]

17. The conclusion for Tuesday, to be said at night or in bed, to the Son, for my selfe and children.

My sweet Iesus, by thy grace and holy Name, keep mee thy poore servant, and all mine from all sinne and shame, and by thy bitter death and passion, save us from thy great wrath, and endlesse damnation, and by thy powerfull resurrection, raise us daily from sin to grace and newnesse of life, and by thy glorious ascension, draw me thy unworthy servant continually to heaven after thee by a holy life and godly conversation; and of thy great mercie, after death, reserve[a] me to be where thou art, and make me partaker of thy everlasting salvation; and in all my troubles, sorrows and distresse, doe thou my griefes redresse, and be my blessed consolation; and vouchsafe to receive me this night and alwaies into thy mercifull preservation: for now I will lay me downe in peace, and also rest and sleep, because thou Lord, dost only mee sustaine, and wilt in safety keep: for on

---

[a] reserve] ~~reserve~~ [ceaue] (HB); preserve (*Errata*)

thee alone I wholly doe depend, who art all my hope, helpe, comfort, and confidence, sweet Iesus my Saviour. Amen.

[p. 80]

18. A Prayer for Wednesday to the glorious Trinity at first awaking.

Great is our God, and worthy to be praised,[84] I will speake of all thy marvellous workes, for thou hast done great things, and holy is thy Name.

To thee O God, heavenly Father, our gracious Creator of all things; with God the Son, that blessed Redeemer of mankinde, and God the Holy Ghost the sanctifier of thine elect; unto thee, O Lord, three Persons, one true and everliving God, be given and rendred as is due by mee, and all other thy children and servants, all humble and possible praise and thanks, now and ever. For I thy most unworthy servant, doe humbly and thankfully acknowledge, that I finde thy blessings and benefits both spirituall and temporall, sleeping and waking, daily and howrely, to be renued towards me, for which I blesse and magnifie thy holy Name, especially for those spirituall graces[85] thou hast vouchsafed unto my soule from time to time, before I had any being, for my election by the whole Trinity, and my creation by God the Father,[a] which thou didst fully performe in thine owne innocent person: but chiefly in that infinite love token[86] unto mankinde, of God the Father in ordaining and sending thy deare Son out of thy bosome into the world; and thou, O Christ, [p. 81] in comming amongst wicked men, to put thy selfe into their cruell hands for our redemption, and so become our righteousnesse, justification, and salvation, which thou hast dearly purchased for us with thy own bloud. And since I was borne, O blessed Spirit, for my continuall preservation, and daily supply of all needfull blessings for my soule and body, especially for my vocation,[87] and calling to the right knowledge of God and his saving truth, with some measure of true faith, sanctification, and regeneration from sinne to grace, all wrought in mee by the holy operation of thee Lord Holy Ghost; by whom also we are united unto our Lord and head Christ Jesus, from whom Lord let me never be separated. Now vouchsafe O God, still to continue all thy mercies towards me; and chiefly in giving me daily a supply and increase of all heavenly gifts, and spirituall graces, whereby I may be able rightly, faithfully, and constantly, to feare and love, to seek, serve, and please thee my God, in all things as I ought to doe; that so I may obtaine thy grace and favour (by thy assistance) to live a holy life here according to

[a] wᵗ my redemption wrought by thee, sweet   thee my Saviour (*Errata*)
Jesus my sauiour, (HB); and my redemption by

thy will, that thou of thy infinite mercie, Almighty God, and glorious Trinity, maiest make me partaker of thy heavenly Kingdome of glory hereafter. Amen.

[p. 82]

19. A Prayer to the Trinity for Wednesday morning.

O God the Father of heaven, the gracious Creator of all things, the righteous judge, that searcheth the heart, and trieth the children of men, and beholdeth all our waies, and knowest my substance is but dust, flesh and bloud, and my nature as it is corrupted by sin, is of it selfe, earthly, sensuall and divelish, and can merit nothing from thee, O Lord, but condemnation. Deare God, the originall of all goodnesse, I most humbly beseech thee to have mercy upon mee miserable sinner, and enter not into judgement with thy poore servant, for no flesh living is righteous before thee; neither reward me after my wickednesse, for I am a wretched and most sinfull creature, and have done exceeding much evill in thy sight; but I humbly pray thee, O God, for thy dear Son and my Saviours sake, to withdraw thy great wrath and heavy displeasure from mee, which my sinnes have justly deserved; and if it be thy will Lord release my present afflictions, which now and long have lain upon me: and vouchsafe also to prevent and remove those weighty judgements, that hang over my head for my iniquities, that by thy unspeakable mercies I may escape them; yet if thou please further to visit mee with fatherly chastisements for the amendment of my [p. 83] faults; Lord give me wisdome and patience to beare all things as I ought to doe, without offence towards thee, and by thy grace to make the best and rightest use of all thou sendest, so as in the end they may turne to thy glory and the furtherance of my salvation in Christ my Lord.

O God the Son, Redeemer of mankinde, who didst vouchsafe to bee borne of a woman, to become man for our redemption, and camest into the world to seek and save all those that were lost by sin, that they might live by faith in thee; which Lord grant unto me, sweet Jesus my Saviour, and have mercie upon me a wicked sinner, to forgive and pardon all my sinnes and offences that I have done before thee all my life past in thought, word and deed; and impute not my iniquities unto me, neither destroy mee with my transgressions, nor let thy heavy displeasure reserve evill for me hereafter: but deare Lord, of thy great goodnesse grant me thy poore servant true faith, and unfeigned repentance, with thy gracious remission of all my trespasses, and wash my sinnes out of thy sight with thine owne most pretious and innocent bloud, which thou didst so freely shed for our redemption; naile all my offences upon thy crosse, and bury them in thy grave, so as they may never be able to come in judgement against mee, either to accuse or shame me in this world, or to condemne and confound mee in the world to come, for thy mercies sake, sweet Jesus my Savi- [p. 84] our: But I most humbly beseech thee, O Lord, to sanctifie and cleanse my heart and soule from all sinne and evill, by thy holy Spirit, that I may be upright in thy sight, to reforme all my waies before thee, and let thy grace and holy Spirit[a] lead mee into the paths of truth and righteousnesse all my life, that after death thou maiest of thy infinite mercy bring me to that everlasting inheritance of happinesse which thou hast so dearly purchased for us with thine owne bloud, in whom is all my trust, who art my only Saviour, Mediator and Advocate for ever.

O God the Holy Ghost, our comforter, preserve and sanctifie thou my heart and soule, that I may unfeignedly love thee, truly feare thy holy Name, and faithfully serve, please and obey thee, as I ought to doe now and all the daies of my life: And vouchsafe, O blessed Spirit, to instruct and inlighten my soule and understanding, with the true knowledge, devout love, and stedfast beliefe of thy sacred truth, and keepe me therein for ever. O Holy Ghost, vouchsafe to make thy seat and dwelling in my soule, and let thy holy Spirit take full possession of my heart, and abide alwaies with mee to fill me with all saving graces, whereby I may bee preserved from falling into any sinne or evill, and bee inabled to doe all good that may be best pleasing unto thee, and to performe all duty and service (by thy assistance) in an acceptable manner unto my gracious and Almighty God, the Father, the Son, and [p. 85] the Holy Ghost, three Persons, and one ever glorious Trinity, to whom be rendred all praise, honour, power, and thanks, as is right due, for ever and ever. Amen.

20. An evening Prayer to God the Holy Ghost for Wednesday.

O God the Holy Ghost, blessed Spirit, by whom we are sanctified and sealed unto the day of redemption, and by whose holy operation, we are joyned unto our blessed Lord and head Christ Jesus; from whom let nothing in heaven or earth ever separate me: And mercifull Lord I humbly pray thee, cast me not in thy displeasure out of thy care and favour for my sinnes, and withdraw not thy grace and holy Spirit from me, neither forsake me, nor leave me to my selfe, who am wholly subject to all wickednesse. But I most humbly beseech thee, to creat[e] in me a new, a clean, an upright, a faithfull and perfect heart in thy sight, to walke in all true holinesse before thee, as thou requirest, all my daies to come; and good Lord, daily renue thy grace, and a right holy spirit within mee, to sanctifie and cleanse my soule from sinne, to preserve mee from falling into evill, and to guide me into the waies of truth and righteousnesse. Now dear Lord, marke me thy [p. 86] poore servant for thine owne, and prevent mee with thy grace that I never grieve, despight, or neglect thee my

---

[a] and holy Spirit] ~~and holy Spirit~~ (HB)

God in any thing, neither to resist or quench the good motions of thy holy Spirit in my heart at any time; but I most humbly pray and desire to bee led and directed in all things by thee, who best knowest my frailties and infirmities, that I can (of my selfe) neither will nor performe any good at all, much lesse call upon thy holy Name as I ought, all my best works and endeavours, being full of imperfection and corruption; but I humbly beseech thee, good Lord, to accept in me the will for the deed, the affection for the action; and vouchsafe to heale and helpe my great disability to any goodnesse, and teach, and assist me rightly, faithfully and constantly, to pray unto thee my God, now and at all times according to thy holy will, and daily to call upon thy great Name in truth and sincerity.

And be pleased, O Lord Holy Ghost, to prepare, assist and lift up my heart and soule towards thee, and bend downe thine eare of mercy to heare me, and vouchsafe thou blessed Lord, to make request by thy grace in mee, with such inward and faithfull devotion, humility, sighs and groans as cannot be expressed, that so my supplications may bee acceptable to God my heavenly Father, through the merits and sufferings, of my dear Saviour Jesus, and the holy working of thee O God the Holy Ghost, my com- [p. 87] forter, who art the sanctifier and preserver both of my soule and body; I humbly pray thee to inflame my heart and spirit with fervent zeale and unfeigned devotion to the true and constant performance of all duties and services that I owe unto thee my God. And vouchsafe Lord, by thy holy Spirit to infuse into my soule everlasting and devout love towards thy Majesty, with Christian charity towards all my brethren, thy children and servants: And Lord, put thou a right and stedfast hope into my heart that my trust in thee may never faile, till I have attained to the eternall felicity, which God the Father hath prepared, and our blessed Saviour hath purchased, and thou blessed Spirit by thy holy assistance wilt[a] bring us unto, to glorifie the Name of my God in heaven hereafter for ever. Amen.

21. The conclusion for Wednesday at night, to the blessed Trinity.

Mercifull God, heavenly Father, blessed Son, and Holy Ghost, who hast appointed the night for all mortall creatures to take rest, without which our weake natures cannot subsist: I am now in health by thy gracious providence, by thy favour, and laid downe in my bed, which representeth the grave, and by thy mercie hope al- [p. 88] so to take quiet rest and sleepe, that is the image of death, from which I know not whether ever I shall awake againe to this worlds light, for my life dependeth on

---

[a] wilt] wilt p[r]ᵉpare and (HB)

thy good pleasure; therefore I most humbly pray thee of thy infinite mercy, O God, to forgive all my sins past that I have committed against thee, this present day or heretofore, through the merits and sufferings of my Redeemer Jesus; and vouchsafe heavenly Father to bee reconciled unto mee, thy most guilty sinfull servant, in and through thy dear and innocent Son, who is my righteous Saviour: And grant while I live here, that in Christ I may hereafter live to thee, and thy faithfull service; and when I sleepe, Lord let me safely rest by thy blessed preservation, and by the assistance of thy holy Spirit, that I may continue in thy true faith, feare and favour with a good conscience unto my last breath; that so if thou call me away this night, or any other time in my sleep, thou wilt in Christ pardon my sinnes, and after death receive my soule to thy grace and mercy, to remaine with thee for ever, and may praise thee, my God, everlastingly. Amen, Amen.

[p. 89]

22. A Prayer for Thursday morning at first awaking to God the Father.

My God, I heartily praise thee for my present health, rest and preservation this night and formerly, and safe approach by thy providence to this light. I humbly beseech thee, vouchsafe this day and alwaies, to bee my present helpe in all dangers, and my mercifull God to pardon all my sinnes and wickednesse, that I have done heretofore, and to prevent and to[a] protect mee by thy grace and favour from falling into any sin or evill to offend thee hereafter; and direct me by thy holy Spirit in all things I goe about, to doe that which is acceptable in thy sight (through Christ) and to the best for my owne soule. Deare Lord, give me thy sinfull servant thy grace, whereby I may be able rightly and faithfully to seeke, serve, and please thee my God, as I ought to doe, this day and at all times throughout my whole life: These great blessings I beg of thee, O God the Father, by thy gracious assistance, in, and through, and for the sake of thine owne deare Sonne, and my only Saviour, Jesus Christ the righteous. So bee it.

[p. 90]

23. A Prayer for Thursday morning to God the Father.

Most mighty God, and my mercifull Father, the giver of all good gifts: grant mee thy grace and the light of thy countenance, to guide mee this day and ever, to walke

---

[a] to] ~~to~~ (HB)

in thy paths of truth and righteousnesse all my life, and to runne in the way of thy Commandements unto my end; for thy beloved Sonne hath taught us before all things to seek that which is most needfull, even the Kingdome of God, and the right[e]ousnesse thereof, and then our heavenly Father will supply all things else which he knoweth to be necessary for us:[88] Good Lord, make me (with *Mary*) to choose the better part,[89] to seek, heare, and follow our Saviour Jesus, and let that never bee taken from mee thy poore servant. To which end, I humbly pray thee, O God, to weane and withdraw my heart and soule, from the cares, love or liking of this vilde world, and all the vanities thereof, all which like a dream and shadow fade away: And Lord, drive all wicked thoughts out of my minde, and banish covetous desires (the root of all evill) from my heart, and make me ever consider what it would advantage me, if I could win the whole world, and should lose my owne soule.[90] Therefore I beseech thee, O Lord, by thy holy Spirit, to settle my heart and soul, my desires, [p. 91] affections, and delight, only upon thee my God, thy glory, thy Kingdome, thy righteousnesse; and make me to account all earthly things but drosse and dirt so that I may win Christ, and attaine to the excellent knowledge of Jesus my Saviour, who is the Lord of life; him chiefly, O God, let me finde and obtaine to be mine, with whom I shall have all other good things, by thy infinite mercie I beseech thee,[a] that so I may be able rightly and faithfully to serve and please thee as I ought, while I live heare, that after death thou of thy unspeakable goodnesse, maiest make mee partaker of thy heavenly Kingdome of glory.

And now, deare God, vouchsafe unto me thy most unworthy servant the grace of daily and unfeigned sorrow and repentance for all my sins, with a sound sense and feeling of them in a contrite spirit, with care to reforme all my former faults in the rest of my life, and make me strictly to examine my owne heart, soule, knowledge, and conscience, of all the evills I have done before thee, and severely to judge, hate and condemne my selfe for them, that so I may escape thy great wrath, and may not bee judged and condemned by thee in thy heavy displeasure, which I am not able to beare; for who can stand in the sight of thy great Majesty when thou art angry? therefore I most humbly pray thee, good God, in the multitude of thy mercies, to forgive and grant me thy grace and pardon of all my sins and offences past that I am guilty of, [p. 92] for thy beloved Sonnes sake, that so my iniquities may never be imputed unto me; but Lord give me true faith to lay fast hold upon thy mercies, and all thy gracious promises, and the merits and sufferings of Christ, with grace rightly to apply them to my owne salvation, through Jesus my Saviour; that so I may be quit[91] through him, and freed of my account with thee before I die; and grant that I may daily die unto the world, and hate all the vaine pressures thereof, and may live more and more unto thee in all righteousnesse and true holinesse of living before

---

[a] I beseech thee] ~~I beseech thee~~ (HB)

thee as becommeth thy Saints: that so when thy appointed time is come for me to enter into my long sleep of death, that thou wilt be pleased by thy holy Spirit to fit and prepare me, and to give me a happy and blessed departure out of this life, to die in the Lord that I may rest in peace and safety, and be raised up by my Saviour to grace and glory, that thou pardoning all my sinnes, and receiving me to mercie, thou maiest wipe all teares from mine eies, and remove all sorrow from my soule, and for Jesus sake to admit me into thy glorious presence, and there to enjoy eternall felicitie, and be a happy member of thy blessed Church triumphant to praise thee there for evermore. Amen. And the blessing of God Almighty, the eternall Father, the beloved Son, and the Holy Ghost, be ever with mee, to sanctifie, blesse and preserve my soule and body in thy feare and favour, and true faith, stedfast [p. 93] hope, and perfect charity unto my lifes end. Amen.

24. A Prayer to God the Father for Thursday night.

Have mercy upon me, O Lord, and hearken unto my prayer, for I know thou Lord wilt blesse the righteous, and with thy favour wilt compasse him as with a shield.[92] Lord thou lovest not wickednesse, neither shall evill dwell with thee, thou shalt destroy them that speake lies, for thou abhorrest all them that worke iniquity: yet thou desirest not the death of a sinner but that he should returne and live; therefore deare Lord, deliver my soule and save me in thy manifold mercies, for I have grievously sinned before thee, and my iniquities are gone over my head into thy presence, and are too heavy for mee to beare. But I most humbly beseech thee, for thy beloved Son Jesus sake, to give me unfaigned sorrow and repentance for all my sinnes past, which are great and many, and grant me thy gracious pardon and remission for all my offences committed this day or heretofore against thee; and Lord, indue me with true faith to lay hold of all thy mercies, and my Saviours merits and sufferings, with grace to amend,[a] reforme my life, according to thy most holy word and Commandements, all the rest of my [p. 94] daies to come: to which end Lord give me a soft, a penitent, upright and contrite heart, with a tender conscience, and a true and sound sense and feeling of all my sinnes, infirmities, and spirituall wants, with grace earnestly and faithfully to cry and pray unto thee for mercie and reliefe in all my necessities, and chiefly for all spirituall graces to my soule. And as I trust thou wilt awake mee from the dulnesse of this nights sleep in safety to the morning light; so dear Lord, by thy holy Spirit daily quicken my soule from the deadnesse of sinne, to newnesse of life, and raise me up in mercie hereafter, from the darknesse of death, unto light and life eternall, to live with thee my God for evermore. Now gracious Lord, receive mee with all that doth belong unto me into thy mercifull protection now and alwaies, to keep and deliver us from

---

[a] ∧ [&] (HB)

all sinne and evill, giving us this night quiet sleep, health and rest if it be thy will; and grant whether I sleep or wake, live or dye, I may be wholly thine, and doe all to thy honour and glory; that so both in life and death, Christ may be to me an advantage, through thy infinite mercie, O my blessed Lord God.

Now I humbly pray thee, so to inlighten the darknesse of my soul and understanding with thy grace, that I may see clearly the right way to heavenly happinesse, and by thy assistance follow hard after it untill I have attained to it; and also for thy holy Names sake defend mee from all perills and dangers of this [p. 95] night either to my soule or body, to me or any of mine, for the love of thy only Son, my deare Saviour Jesus Christ: for whose sake, grant me also the guard of thy holy and good Angells now and ever, that they may pitch their tents about mee to preserve mee from all my enemies bodily and ghostly;[93] and commit mee Lord to the custody of thy blessed Spirit to keep me from falling into any sinne or evill, and to guide my waies into the paths of truth and righteousnesse, that I may live in thy holy feare, and dye in thy faith and favour; and good God, grant that in the howre of my death, and in the day of judgement, thy dear Son and my sweet Jesus, may bee my mercifull judge and Saviour, to pardon and passe by all my sinnes, and cover them with his righteousnesse, that after death I may bee received and accepted into thy grace and favour, to live and remaine in joy and blisse eternally with thee my God, Father, Son, and Holy Ghost. Now, O God, who canst doe abundantly, more then I can aske or thinke, to thee be all praise, honour and glory, for ever and ever. Amen.

25. The conclusion for Thursday night in bed.

O Lord my God, I thanke thee for all thy mercies vouchsafed unto mee this present day [p. 96] and formerly: and now be pleased, O Lord, by thy holy Spirit to sanctifie me thy poor unworthy servant, in soule, body and spirit throughout, to thy right faithfull and constant service all my daies; and assist me with thy grace that I may daily confesse, lament, hate, leave and amend all my former misdeeds, and may become faithfully and unfainedly thine in all true obedience and sincere and perfect love toward thy Majesty, both living and dying, and for ever; that through thy mercy and Christs merits, I may be found blamelesse at the appearance of my Lord Jesus, by whom I trust to obtaine to live in heaven with thee, and to bee presented by my Saviour unto thy gracious acceptance in that great day of the Lord, to remain with thee my God for ever. Amen.

26. A Prayer for Friday at first awaking to God the Son.

Deare Saviour Jesus, have mercy upon mee a miserable sinner: Thou immaculate Lambe of God, that knewest no sinne, but diedst for our transgressions, and shed thine owne most pretious bloud to cleanse us from sinne:

I most humbly praise and magnifie thy holy Name for all thy mercies who hast done and suffered great and many things for mee, but especially I blesse thee for [p. 97] those spirituall blessings thou hast bestowed upon me before I was borne, and hitherto. Now sweet Jesus, who knowest my fraility, I doe most humbly pray thee never to leave me to my self, nor to my soules enemies, neither while I live, at my death, nor in the great and dreadfull day of judgement, when all things shall bee made manifest before thee, and it will be wholly in thy power to save or to condemne; then Lord Jesus looke in mercie on me as one of thine, whom thou lovest to the end, to pardon and cover all my sinnes, and receive me into thy grace and favour, for by thee only commeth my salvation, and in thee, O Lord, is my whole trust: Therefore vouchsafe Lord, to continue thy goodnesse, thy favour, and thy loving kindnesse towards me this day and for ever, in forgiving all my iniquities, that I have committed in my whole life past; and also my sinfull omission of those duties and good workes, which thou hast commanded, and I have wickedly neglected. But I most humbly beseech thee, my Saviour, to indue mee thy most unworthy servant with thy grace and holy Spirit, to direct my heart, and all my waies aright before thee, and preserve me at all times in the sincere and perfect love of thy divine Majesty, and in thy feare and favour, with unfaigned repentance and amendment of life, that I may obtaine thy gracious pardon for all my offences, and Lord, give me true faith, stedfast hope, and perfect charity unto my lifes [p. 98] end. These great mercies I aske at thy gracious hands, deare Jesus Christ, who art my only Saviour, Redeemer, Mediator, and Advocate: to whom be all praise and glory for ever. Amen.

27. A morning Prayer for Friday, to God the Sonne.

Sweet Saviour, none can come to the Father but by thee; and whosoever commeth unto thee thou castest not away, but wilt raise him up at the last day unto eternall life.[94]

Now deare Jesus, thou blessed Son, and innocent Lambe of God, that takest away the sinnes of the sinnes[a] of the world, who graciously callest unto thee all heavy laden and penitent sinners that thou maiest ease and refresh them; have pity on me, and vouchsafe to sanctifie and cleanse my soule and body, from all sinne and evill by thy holy Spirit, and make mee pure and upright in thy sight, and be pleased to protect and direct my heart and soule, and all my waies before thee, and to indue me with thy blessed Spirit, to preserve mee from falling into any sin or offence towards thee; but assist me with thy grace in all things I goe about to doe, that I may doe that which may be most acceptable and best pleasing in thy sight. Now Lord, I confesse that I was concei- [p. 99] ved and

---

[a] of the sinnes] ~~of the sinnes~~ (HB) (*Errata*)

borne in sinne, and I am a miserable and wretched sinner above all others, and unto whom should I come, but to thee the Saviour of mankinde, who camest into the world to save sinners by thy grace, of whom I am chiefe?

O fountaine of mercy, who didst vouchsafe to bee borne of the blessed and pure Virgin Mary, (to become man) and tookest our wretched nature upon thee, therein to suffer death, to reassume[a] us from eternall death, sinne, the grave, hell and Sathan, and didst willingly lay down thine owne life for us, which no man could take from thee, that wee might live by faith through thee; and also thou hadst power to take it up againe, and didst rise from the grave the third day for our justification, and to vanish[95] all our spirituall enemies: and lastly, thou our Lord didst gloriously ascend into heaven, there to take possession, and make intercession for us unto thy heavenly Father, with whom thou dost reigne in heaven for ever, whither thou dost graciously and daily draw to thee all those that truly beleeve in thee, there to live hereafter with thee; of which number, deare Lord, in the fulnesse of thy mercies make me one. Now I further humbly pray thee, sweet Jesus, the Saviour of all that trust in thee, that thou wilt have mercy on mee, to forgive and pardon all my sinnes and offences past, and present, both originall and actuall,[96] of omission and commission, of infirmity or presumption, whatsoever I stand guilty of be- [p. 100] fore thee, and even those secret sinnes, that none but thy All-seeing eyes, and my owne conscience can testifie against mee, which is more then a thousand witnesses: I humbly pray thee to cast them all behinde thy backe into the pit of oblivion, never to come in remembrance with thee; and wash all my faults out of thy sight with that blessed streame of thine owne most pretious bloud, which thou didst so plentifully shed for us in thy most bitter passion. O blessed Lord, let not all these thy mercies and benefits which thou hast done and purchased for mankind, be fruitlesse or in vaine towards mee, thy poore unworthy servant, whose confidence is only in thee, that thou wilt make mee a happy partaker of all thy great benefits and favours: And sweet Iesus, grant through thy mercies, merits and infinit[e] sufferings, that my transgressions may never bee laid to my charge; for there is no other name under heaven[b] but thine only, blessed Iesus our righteous Lord, by which we can be saved. To thee bee rendred as is due all honour, praise, thanks, and glory, forever and ever: Concluding my petition with that perfect Prayer, which thy selfe hast taught us, saying, *Our Father which art in heaven, &c.*

[p. 101]

---

[a] reassume] ransome (*Errata*)
[b] under heaven] on earth nor under heaven (*Errata*)

28. A Prayer for Friday night, to God the Sonne, our blessed Saviour.

I will love thee dearly, O Lord my strength, for thou art my helper, my refuge, and the lifter up of my head, and I will praise thy name so long as I have breath. O Lord Christ, by whom was fulfilled the Law and the Prophets, and in thee all the promises of God are Yea and Amen,[97] to the glory of God the Father, and the comfort of all thy servants; thou art that pure and innocent Lambe of God, that was killed and is alive, to thee was given all power, honour and glory, who liveth and raigneth for ever in heaven and earth, of whose Kingdome there is no end; to thee Lord bee all possible praise and thanks for ever. This is my only Lord and blessed Saviour Jesus Christ the righteous, who died for our sinnes, and rose againe for our justification, and art our Advocate in heaven; so that whatsoever we shall ask the Father in thy name, according to thy will, if we beleeve, we shall obtaine it for thy sake, who art the beloved Son of God, in whom only hee is well pleased. My deare God, have mercy upon me a most grievous sinner to pardon all my offences past, in soule or body, of ignorance or wilfulnesse, of frailty, neglect, contempt or wicked stubbornesse; bury them all, sweet Jesus, in thy grave, and cleanse them from before thine eyes, [p. 102] with thy most pretious bloud, which thou didst of thine owne accord and infinite love shed for us, to free us from eternall death which by our sinnes are[a] due; therefore gracious Lord, grant through thy merits, and manifold sufferings, that my iniquities may never be able to appeare before thee against me, either to accuse or condemne me, neither in this life, at my death, nor in the great and last judgement: but in that dreadfull day, Lord by all thy mercies I beseech thee, shew thy self my loving Saviour, to passe by & cover all my misdeeds with thy righteousnesse, that so I may escape thy just wrath which my transgressions have deserved.

Now, deare Iesus, while I live here, make me thy unworthy servant wholly thine, to be thy faithfull and constant disciple, and so to love thee as to keep thy Commandements which are not grievous, but in obeying them there is great reward; and let me so follow thee here, as to bee lowly and meek, to forsake my selfe and the world, and to take up all my crosses with patience, and strive to goe after thy steps, thou I be farre unable to drinke of that heavy and bitter cup of Gods wrath of which thou so deeply tastedst, who art the propitiation for our sinnes to deliver us from that fearfull condemnation due unto us: my offences Lord, I confesse did adde unto that weighty burden of Gods heavy displeasure, and our grievous sinnes which thou didst beare upon the crosse for all true

---

[a] are] ~~are~~ ∧ is (HB)

beleevers, who shall passe [p. 103] from death, to life eternall, which thy sufferings, O Christ, hath purchased for us; whereby I, the unworthiest of thy servants doe also hope to follow thee hereafter, from the grave to heaven at the resurrection of the just, that according to thy will declared before thy death, all that are thine shall bee with thee, even where thou art to enjoy all blisse and happinesse; in thine owne love by thy unmerited mercies, we shall bee made partakers with thee of thy heavenly Kingdome of glory, there to serve and praise thy glorious Name, who art most worthy, world without end. Amen.

29. The conclusion for Friday night.

Lord Iesus, vouchsafe to receive me this night into thy gracious protection both in life and death: And deare Lord, I humbly pray thee to inlighten me with thy grace rightly and faithfully to serve and obey thee in all true devotion, and with due submission to thy holy will in all things so long as I live; and now Lord, I am in health laid downe in my bed by thy loving permission, hoping to take quiet rest and sleep, which I beseech thee to give me, and also I trust by thy mercie to awake in thy grace and favour to the morning light againe, because thou gracious Lord, [p. 104] dost only me sustaine, and wilt in safety thy poore servant keep; who doe most humbly commend and commit my selfe, my soule and body, my children and grand-children, and all I have to thee, from whom I have received all the good I doe enjoy, for thou hast shewed great mercies unto me; for which I blesse and praise thy holy Name, beseeching thee to give me grace, never to forget thy benefits, but to continue Lord thy true and faithfull servant unto my death, and for ever. Amen.

30. A Prayer to the blessed Trinity, at first waking for Saturday morning.

I will praise the Lord because he is good, for his mercy endureth for ever; by whom we live, move, and have our being,[98] our maintenance, safety and preservation. Now glorious Trinity, Father, Son, and Holy Ghost, I humbly pray thee, vouchsafe unto mee thy most unworthy servant, such grace and favour[a] to knit my heart and soule fast to thee, so that my sinnes, nor my soules enemies, the wicked world, my owne corrupt flesh, nor the malice of the Divell, may not be able to pluck mee out of thy mercifull and powerfull hands; but Lord assist me with thine owne blessed Spirit, that I may daily continue and increase [p. 105] in all sincere and perfect love and obedience towards thy Majesty; and in thy feare and favour, and all other saving graces, to have a good conscience before thee, with true faith, stedfast hope, and perfect charity unto my lifes end. Amen.

[a] ∧ ⌈as⌉ (HB)

31. A Prayer unto the Trinity for Saturday morning.

O Lord our God, how excellent is thy Name in all the world, for thou hast laid the foundation of the earth, and the heavens are the workes of thy hands, and thou didst create, and dost governe, dispose and rule the whole world, with all things therein, according to thy good pleasure.

O most divine and adored Trinity, Father Son and Holy Ghost, three persons, but one true, eternall and everliving God, to whom be all praise, honour and glory as is right and due for ever. Thou only by thy word and power didst make all things for thine owne glory, especially mankinde after thine image in purity and holinesse to thine own service; for by thy providence and mercy commeth all good gifts and blessings unto us, and also deliverances only from thee, of those evills and dangers which sinne hath made us subject unto in falling from thee, and our first integrity, by the subtillty and malice of Sathan and [p. 106] our owne frailty, yet of thine owne free grace thou didst elect a number by thee selected of thy chosen servants to inherit an eternall Kingdome, with and through thy beloved Son, whom thou didst ordain and send into the world at thine appointed time to be the redemption of all that beleeve in thee.

O God the Son our blessed Lord Jesus Christ, it is written of thee that thou shouldest doe the will of God the Father, who ordained thee to be our Redeemer, and wert made of God unto us, wisdome, righteousnesse, sanctification and salvation, with glorification hereafter. Now deare Jesus, who hast paid our ransome, even the all-sufficient and acceptable sacrifice of thine own pretious bloud to wash away our sins, who was lifted upon the crosse between heaven and earth to make an attonement betwixt God and man, his heavy wrath and our grievous offences, and so thou art become our Priest, to offer up thy innocent selfe to cleanse us from our sinnes, who art our Prophet to instruct and teach us and direct our waies aright, to shew us the path of life, and make the way plaine before our faces, and by thy example, to beare our crosse patiently, and follow thee that art the way, the truth and the life, to lead us to eternall salvation; also thou art our King to protect, defend, and reigne over us in mercy, truth and righteousnesse, till thine enemies be made thy footstoole,[99] and all that hate thee be destroyed before thee, for God hath [p. 107] put all things in subjection under his feet, then shalt thou judge the whole world in righteousnesse and equity, and wilt bring thy servants, to that eternall inheritance, which thou hast by thy merits and sufferings so dearly purchased for us, who wert borne unto us to be the joy and comfort of all people, and the glory and salvation of all that truly beleeve and trust in thee our Saviour.

O God Holy Ghost, the giver, worker and sealer of all graces unto us; by thee we are called to the knowledge of God and his saving truth, sanctified to the performance of his will and Commandements certified by the holy Spirit of our salvation in Christ Jesus, and by thee applied unto us to bee regenerated and borne againe by thy holy operation from sin to grace, to thy glory and our endlesse felicity. And thy Spirit also witnesseth to our spirits that we are the children of God and heires with Christ of the Kingdome of heaven to the eternall comfort of all thy servants, being by thee also united to our blessed[a] Christ, and sealed to the day of redemption,[100] and continually assisting us to all goodnesse.

Now great and glorious Lord God, Father, Son, and Holy Ghost, thou hast plentifully powred downe thy manifold mercies and favours upon us, and multiplied exceedingly thy blessings and benefits spirituall and temporall towards us before we had being in the world, since we were borne, and after death thou hast laid up an eternall weight of glory for all [p. 108] those to possesse that truly beleeve in thee, which give me grace to doe, for none hath or ever can deserve them. Oh the abundant mercy, bounty, and goodnesse of our gracious God towards mortall mankinde! who can declare the height and depth of Gods unspeakable love, or be sufficiently thankfull to him for such unexpressible benefits; but with *David*, we may say (Lord) What is man that thou art mindefull of him?[101] Or what shall we render to thee for all thy mercies, having in us no good at all, but what we receive from thy selfe? therefore Lord, adde this further grace unto thy former favours, by the assistance of thine owne Spirit, to make us thy unworthy servants, able, rightly, faithfully, and constantly to feare, love, honour, serve, obey and praise thy most glorious Name while we live, and for ever and ever. Amen.

32. A Prayer to God the Holy Ghost, for Saturday night.

O God Holy Ghost, the giver of all graces and my gracious sanctifier, comforter and preserver, thou knowest my infirmities, my inclination to all evill, and backwardnesse to any goodnesse: vouchsafe Lord, to sanctifie mee thy poore sinfull servant, in soule, body and spirit [p. 109] throughout, to thy true feare, intire love, and right faithfull and constant service, all my time to come: And be pleased Lord, by thy grace to enlighten my dull soule and understanding, with the sound knowledge, sincere love, and stedfast beleefe of thy saving truth, and keepe me ever constant therein. And vouchsafe, deare Lord, to inrich me thy poore unworthy servant, with the infinite treasure of that heavenly wisdome from above, which waiteth about thy Throne, that may teach me thy holy will, and what is good and acceptable unto thee; and inable me with grace to doe it, that so I may

---

[a] head (HB)

discerne between good and evill, and make me shunne and hate that which is evill, and follow and cleave unto that which is good; and to withdraw my love from this vaine world, and fix my affections upon thee my God, and on heavenly things that are above, that my chiefe treasure may be settled there in heaven, and my heart also; and so I shall first seek to obtaine that which is most needfull, even thy glory, thy favour, and thy blessed Kingdome, and then Lord, I know thou wilt supply all the defects of grace in my soule, and heale all the infirmities of my body; but chiefly vouchsafe daily to continue and increase all spirituall graces in my soule by thy mercy and mighty power, O my blessed Lord God; to which end, O gracious Spirit, give mee an upright and penitent heart, an humble and lowly spirit, a quiet recollected[102] minde freed [p. 110] from the vanities and cares of this present world, and the love of this vile life; but Lord teach mee with *Mary* first and above all things to seek after thee my God,[103] thy Kingdome, and the righteousnesse thereof, so that I may have grace wholly to devote and dedicate my selfe, my time and best endeavours unto thy true and faithfull service, and daily study and strive to doe thy holy will in all things, and seek thy glory here, that so I may be partaker of thy heavenly Kingdome hereafter.

And deare Lord Holy Ghost, inspire me with thy grace daily to heare and read thy holy and blessed word as I ought to do, and that I may so imploy my time therein as to frame my life hereafter to thy glory and my soules good. And grant mee graciously, O God, to chuse, to speake, and to walke in the waies of truth and righteousnesse, and to set thy heavy judgements against sin continually before my face to deter[a] and make mee daily to remember my owne last end, and by thy assistance to prepare for it, and to consider the end in all my actions before I doe them, that I may never doe amisse; and let me still remember thy all-seeing eyes are ever upon our waies that I may not displease or offend thee in any thing: But Lord, indue me with thy holy Spirit to direct my heart and all my waies aright before thee, that so thou maiest witnesse to my spirit that I am the childe of God, and ever continue unto mee that unspeakable comfort to give me the joyfull hope [p. 111] of my salvation, through my Lord Jesus Christ, unto my end: and in my end especially establish me with thy free spirit to worke in my soul all saving graces that may make me acceptable in thy sight, through my Lord Jesus Christ, for whose sake I beseech thee further to extend thy goodnes towards me, to forgive all my sinnes and offences that I have done before thee in my whole life past, and preserve me in soul and body from all sin and evill, either committing or falling on mee; but deare Lord, vouchsafe daily to supply and bestow upon me all the benefits and blessings necessary for this present life; but chiefly be pleased to sanctifie my soule and body unto thy faithfull service, and indue me with all saving graces for my

---

[a] me from as euill (HB)

salvation both in life and death, that so I may bee able rightly and constantly to serve and please thee whilst I live here, that also by thy gracious assistance I may obtaine a place hereafter to live with thee eternally, O Holy Ghost, and my blessed Lord God, to whom be all thanks and praise for ever. Amen.

33. The conclusion for Saturday night in bed to the weeks Prayers for mornings and nights.

I most humbly beseech thee, my Lord God, mercifully to lo[o]ke upon me and my manifold infir- [p. 112] mities, and for Jesus my Saviours sake, vouchsafe to forgive and pardon all my sinnes and grievous offences that I have committed in thy sight all the daies of my life past; and in thy great mercy turne from me all those evils that my transgressions have justly deserved; and Lord, grant me thy preventing grace and fatherly providence to bee still with mee to preserve me at all times from falling into any sinne or evill, either to offend thee my God, or to hurt my owne soule. And vouchsafe, Lord, so to direct and dispose the heart and waies of me (thy most unworthy servant) towards the right performance of all duties and services that I owe unto thee my God, and the happy obtaining (by my Lord Iesus) of everlasting salvation to my owne selfe; that amongst all the changes, chances and adversities of this miserable, mutable, and mortall life, I may ever be defended by thy ready helpe and favour from falling into sin, shame, harme or danger, either in soule or body, and may be directed and assisted by thy grace and providence to walke in the waies of righteousnesse and true holinesse before thee, that thou my Lord Holy Ghost, maiest guide me in all things I goe about, to doe that which may be most serviceable, acceptable, and best pleasing in the sight of my Lord God, to whom be all praise, honour, power and eternall glory, for ever and ever. Amen.

The end of the second Book.

[p. 113]

BOOK III.

Short Prayers which may belong to any the three Books, when time serves, not for longer devotions.

1. A short Preface before other prayers or petitions.

O Lord Holy Ghost, who best knowest my manifold infirmities, have mercy and pity upon me; and vouchsafe to prevent, or to banish and drive away all evill hindrances and temptations that may withdraw my heart from God in the offering up of my prayers and humble petitions unto thy Majesty; and be pleased Lord, to sanctifie, teach and assist me herein with thy holy Spirit and grace, that I may rightly and faithfully performe this duty and service before thee, to thy glory and my good, and comfort of my soule through Christ Jesus. Amen.

2. A short thanksgiving at first sight of the morning light.

My blessed Lord God, I most humbly praise thee for thy gracious preservation of mee with quiet rest and health this night past, and brin- [p. 114] ging me in safety to this light; Lord blesse and sanctifie me this day and ever unto thy faithfull service, and keep me alwaies in thy true faith, feare, favour and ready obedience; and make me constantly and unfaignedly thine all my life time, but in my death especially, that when it pleaseth thee to call for me out of this miserable world, thou maiest bring me to eternall salvation by thine own merits and meer mercy, sweet Jesus, I most humbly beseech thee. So be it.

3. A Prayer for helpe in present temptation, in the time of prayer to our Lord Jesus, who overcame and subdued the old tempter, the subtile Serpent our everlasting enemy,[104] from whom God defend us.

Oh my God, heavenly Father, who hast made and seest all hearts, and knowest my great affection and fervent desire rightly to serve thee, and my weaknesse and frailty in performance thereof, have pity on my infirmities, and assist me with thy grace. And sweet Jesus my Saviour, who didst suffer thy selfe to bee tempted by the Divell, that thou mightest overcome the tempter, and succour all those that are tempted; to thee Lord, I call and pray, for helpe and defence against this malicious adversary. O God the Holy Ghost, indue me with thy blessed Spirit and power so to resist him that he may flye from me, and banish thou Lord, all wicked hindrances and tem- [p. 115] ptations away from thy poore servant in performing all my duties towards thee. Now deare God, have mercy upon me most miserable sinner, and in thy infinite mercy drive away this subtill enemy of my poore soule, with his pernitious agents, the vaine world, and the corruptions of our owne nature, let them not prevaile over me at any time, for these are very ready to assault, tempt and draw my minde from thee in all my devotions and services that I endeavour to offer unto thy Majesty; and to make my prayers vaine and void, and drive me to fall into wicked neglect towards my God, whereby to prevent, destroy, and divert all my comforts and hopes in thee O Lord, which is the whole life of my soule. But Gracious God Almighty, whose power and strength is above all, vouchsafe to overcome and banish all[a] from mee, never to returne againe; and let thy blessed Spirit rest constantly in me to withstand all disturbances in the performance of my duty before thee; and deare Lord, make new, cleane, and upright my heart, and frame it to thy holy will, that so by thy gracious assistance, I may faithfully serve and honour thee, please and praise thee my God, now and at all times, in this life and for ever, to thy glory, and my eternall comfort. Amen.

[p. 116]

The afternoone prayers at foure a clock for each day in the week.[b]

Munday.   *1. A thanksgiving to the blessed Trinity, Father, Son, and Holy Ghost.*

O my good and gracious God, great and many are thy mercies and blessings I have received from thee both spirituall and temporall, from time to time; and now what shall I render unto thee, having no good to returne, but the poore fruit of my lips, which is nothing unto thee but the performance of our duties to praise thy great Name, and to acknowledge all thy benefits? therefore now I will give thanks to God the Father, our gracious Creator, who so loved us when we were his enemies, and had lost our selves by sinne, that he ordained, and after sent his only begotten and beloved Son into the world, that whosoever, beleeveth in him should not perish but have everlasting life; Christ being the propitiation for our sinnes, that we may live by faith through him. And also I yeeld all possible praise unto my blessed Saviour, who became man, and in his infinite love willingly laid downe his life for us, and washed away our sinnes with his owne pretious bloud, and made us by his merits and sufferings, Kings and Priests unto God, and adopted children to his Father, and heires with himselfe of an eternall Kingdome, by whose resurrection we [p. 117] have a lively hope of an inheritance that cannot be shaken, and withereth not, reserved in heaven for us. Now to thee Lord Holy Ghost, the preserver, sanctifier, and comforter of mankinde, by whom we are sealed unto the day of redemption, and by whose holy working wee are united unto Jesus our blessed head, and are certified by thy Spirit, witnessing to our spirits that wee are the children of God to our great comfort; and further by thy assistance and grace, our weake prayers are rightly and effectually offered up unto the Lord our God.

---

[a] euill temptations (HB) (*Errata*)

[b] These should haue Joyned to y[e] weekly exercise. (HB)

Now to thee, Almighty God, three Persons and glorious Trinity, but one true and everliving God, from whose mercifull hands we daily receive all the good we doe injoy in this present world, with further and full assurance of far greater happinesse by thy infinite mercies in the life to come,[a] be all praise and glory. Amen.

Tuesday.   *2. A Prayer to the Trinity for grace and true faith.*

O sweet Jesus Christ, Son of God, who art the divine word, without whom nothing was made, and being made had been utterly lost, hadst thou not been our powerfull and mercifull Redeemer; thou art the way, the truth, and the life, and thou who hast said, that no man can come unto the Father but by thee, who camest into the world, and didst willingly lay down thine owne [p. 118] life only to save sinners by thy grace, of whom I am chiefe; have mercy upon me miserable sinner, who can of my selfe neither will nor performe any good worke towards God as I ought to doe: but vouchsafe Lord, to indue mee with grace to serve and obey thee, to learne thy will and to doe it, and through faith to lay hold of thy mercies, that so thou my Saviour maiest in thy righteousnesse present me to thy heavenly Father, that hee may looke upon me poor sinfull creature, through thee his deare Son, and for thy sake to receive and accept me into his gracious favour, to pardon all my sinnes, and save my soule, through thy perfect righteousnesse, and manifold sufferings all performed for me.

Now thou Lord hast further said that none can come unto thee except the Father draw him, therefore I most humbly pray thee, O God the Father, by that infinite love towards mankind, which caused thee to send downe thy beloved Son out of thine owne bosome into this wicked world, that whosoever beleeveth in him should not perish, but have everlasting life: I earnestly pray thee, O God the Father, to draw me to thy Son Jesus, that I may lay fast hold by faith on him to be my Saviour, and to be his faithfull and constant servant, and to be made through him, and by thy mercie a happy member of him our blessed head, & then I shall be sure never to fall into condemnation, but by stedfast faith in him obtaine eternall salvation: And deare Lord Holy Ghost, [p. 119] the giver of grace, by whom we are joyned to our Lord and head Christ, and sanctified to a new and holy life: Lord cleanse and frame my heart and soule by the holy working and assistance of thy Spirit and grace, unto the right, faithfull and constant service of my Lord God my Saviour Jesus, with thee O Holy Ghost, so long as I live: Lord daily increase my faith and all saving graces in me for my salvation, and may by thee be directed and lead into the waies of righteousnesse, untill thou hast brought me unto endlesse happinesse through Jesus Christ. Amen.

[a] to thy great maiesty (HB)

Wednesday.   *3. A prayer to God for charity.*

O mercifull Lord God, the giver of all graces, I humbly beseech thee to frame my heart, will and affections, in all ready obedience to thy most holy will and Commandements in all things, especially in the workes of mercy, and charity, they being a sweet smelling sacrifice wherewith thou art well pleased, and wherein we may imitate thee, and shall thereby gaine the honour to be made like unto thy selfe, and be knowne to bee one of thy disciples if we love our brethren as our selves.[105] O God, as thou hast blessed mee of thy meer goodnesse with an estate above some others, to give me the grace of compassion and charity, and inlarge my heart towards thy service, to shew mercy unto them that want, as thou hast been [p. 120] mercifull unto me, that I may willingly distribute, communicate to those that are in need, and be liberall of my earthly vanishing wealth to relieve thy childrens necessities, for thy sake, that are dear unto thee, who wert free of thy very bloud, and sparedst not thine owne life to ransome them and me from utter destruction: and so the loynes and bellies of the poore shall praise thee and blesse me in their comforts; and thou maiest vouchsafe to receive and accept at my poore hands that small mite[106] of thankfulnesse and obedience towards thee my God, from whose most gracious hand I have received many bountifull blessings and benefits throughout my whole life, which let mee never forget, gratefully to acknowledge while I have breath, and to praise thy holy Name for all thy mercies now and for evermore. Amen deare God. Amen.

Thursday.   *4. A Prayer to the Trinity for spirituall graces.*

Most gracious Lord God, who didst create man of the dust of the earth, and knowest we are by nature the children of wrath, and wholy inclined to evill; for thou best understandest how unapt and unable I sinfull creature am to doe any good before thee, much lesse to call upon thy great and glorious Name as I ought to doe, yet thou in mercy hast appointed prayer to bee the chiefe [p. 121] meanes betwixt thy great Majesty, and the unworthinesse of us thy poore sinfull servants, wherby to declare our wants, griefes, and desires unto thee, who art our only hope and helpe: Therefore deare Lord, indue me thy unworthy servant with thy true spirit of grace and prayer, to teach mee how to pray as I ought, that thereby I may have power and strength to withstand all evill temptations that seek to draw me from thy service, and by thy assistance that I may be able to resist the Divell that hee may flye from me in the performance of all duties towards thee; and give mee grace with faith and fervency, humility and true devotion, to cry and pray daily and constantly unto thee for relief and distresse^a in all my troubles and wants, and faithfully to call and relye upon thee for all thy blessings and benefits both spirituall and temporall, to be bestowed on my soule and body as thou shalt thinke fittest; that so I may render all thanks and magnifie thy Name, as I am right bound to doe, for all thy mercies and favours vouchsafed unto me the most unworthiest of all thy servants from time to time.

And I humbly pray thee, O Lord, to give me the blessed gift of true faith, without which it is impossible for me to please thee my God, but thereby I may lay hold, and rightly apply unto my owne soule all the infinite benefits purchased by the bitter death and passion, and precious bloud-shedding of my Lord and Saviour Jesus Christ, that I may bring [p. 122] forth the fruits of righteousnesse and true holinesse before thee as becommeth that[107] Saints and servants; whereby I may glorifie thee, and have assurance to my owne conscience that I am thine by constantly obeying thy will: And also Lord grant me hearty and unfaigned repentance and true sorrow for all my sinnes originall and actuall, in omitting the good I ought to do, and committing the evill I should not doe against thee, that so I may obtaine pardon of all my trespasses, through the merits of Jesus Christ the righteous; and let thy blessed Spirit produce in me amendment of my life all my time to come, and assist mee with thy grace to shun and hate all approaches of evil, and Lord shew me the way of life, and turne my steps into the right paths that I may walke in true obedience to all thy holy Commandements. Now deare God of thy mercy, give me the true feare of thy holy Name, with assurance of thy gracious favour towards me, and continuall joy and comfort in the Holy Ghost, that I may strive alwaies to keep faith and a good conscience before thee towards all; and indue me with grace, will, understanding and ability, to do good workes to thy glory, and bring comfort and profit to my soule in praying, reading, and hearing of thy most holy word at all times, and most devout love towards thy Majesty, with affection to all my brethren, thy children, servants and all the daies of my life to come, by thy gracious assistance dear God, Amen.

[p. 123]

Friday.   ## 5. A Prayer for defence against our soules enemies, in all temptations.

Good Lord God, who knowest the power and great malice of our spirituall enemies, from whõ none can defend or deliver us, but only thou, O Lord, whose power and strength is over and above all; and if thou please to receive me into thy

---

^a distresse] ~~dis~~ ∧ [re] dresse (HB) (*Errata*)

gracious protection, who can hurt or plucke mee out of thy mercifull hands? Therefore I most humbly beseech thee, O God, to defend me both in soule and body, in life and death, from all the temptations of my owne wretched nature within me, the wicked inticements of this vaine world round about me, with the malicious snares, and evill temptations of the Divell that are ever at my backe ready to intrap me, and draw my soul from thee my God and all goodnesse, and to lead mee captive into all wickednesse, sinne and evill, to seperate me from thee, all which like roaring Lions seeke to devoure and destroy me everlastingly.[108] But I most humbly pray unto thee, O Lord, who understandest my frailties, to preserve and deliver me from all their assaults, that they may never be able to prevaile over me to draw mee to sin against thee my God, in any thing; neither suffer them to prevent, hinder, disturbe or carry away my minde, or possesse my vaine heart with wandring thoughts in the performance of any holy [p. 124] duty or service towards thy Majesty; nor give them power to bring those harmes, dangers or mischiefes upon me either in soule or body which they desire to doe. But let thy blessed Spirit so fully possesse me, and ever direct and assist mee in all my waies, to doe all things in a right, faithfull and acceptable manner before thee, that so at all times thy Spirit may witnesse unto my spirit,[109] that I am thy childe and servant; and of thy infinite mercy good Lord, vouchsafe thou alwaies to say unto my soule, especially at my death, that thou art my God, my helpe and my salvation for ever: and by thy grace make my heart and soule to answer and performe unto thee againe, that I am, and will bee thy true, faithfull and obedient servant unto my last breath for ever. Amen.

Saturday.   6. A Prayer for the true spirit of prayer, or a meditation. With a short prayer to Jesus our Saviour.

Deare Lord Holy Ghost, the helper of our infirmities, the preserver and sanctifier of mankinde, I most humbly begge of thee to indue mee thy unworthy sinfull servant, with thy true Spirit of grace and prayer, that I may rightly performe that duty towards thee of calling upon thy holy Name, and all other thy service this day and at all times, with true and right devotion, that so my petitions being humbly presented to thy great [p. 125] Majesty lowly and meekly on the knees of my heart & body; they may by thy mercifull assistance be lifted up and ascend by the wings of faith and devotion unto the highest heavens, and there with confidence through my Saviour Jesus, enter into the glorious eares and presence of Almighty God, where all mercy, grace and goodnesse aboundeth. And then my supplications by thy favour, may be heard and accepted by thee my God, to prevaile and draw downe from thy mercifull hand all graces and blessings needfull, upon me thy poore creature both in soule and body; and so my unworthy sacrifice of due praise and thanks that I offer unto thee may be received and accepted by thee, the Lord of all mercies, who doth often take in good part even the will for the deed, from thy fraile unworthy servants, and then my poore prayers shall bring much joy and comfort to me, and give glory to thee, my Lord. To whom (as of right belongs) be all honour and praise, for evermore. Amen.

A short Prayer to our blessed Saviour Jesus, to be joyned to the former prayers.

Oh my deare Lord Jesus, who didst in thy infinite mercy give thy innocent selfe to death for me a poore miserable sinner; Lord by thy grace make me to dedicate and offer up my selfe a living sacrifice holy and acceptable unto thee, in [p. 126] daily striving rightly and faithfully to serve and obey thee, that I may be wholly thine; and as thou hast bought me with an unvaluable[110] treasure, even thine owne most pretious bloud, so sweet Jesus by thy holy Spirit unite me unseparably unto thee, my blessed head; and by thy asistance, that I may become a new creature, to hate and forsake all sinnes, the vaine world, and my wicked selfe, and to be a true, carefull and constant servant unto thee, to feare, love, honour, and glorifie thy great and heavenly Name, who art the comfort and salvation of all that beleeve and trust in thee, which Lord, let me unfaignedly doe, so long as I live.

7.[a]   *A Prayer to God, the Lord of all grace and mercie, containing seven humble petitions from a penitent sinner: 1. For true faith. 2. For the Holy Ghost. 3. For wisdome. 4. For the feare of God. 5. For the love of God, and charity to our neighbours. 6. For repentance and true contrition of heart. 7. And for the grace and right spirit of prayer.*

O most bountifull Lord God, which giveth to all men liberally, and reproacheth none, if we aske in faith and waver not: and our blessed Saviour maketh us a large promise, saying, Aske and yee shall receive, seeke and you shall finde, knock and it shall bee opened unto you: And whatsoever you shall aske in my Name I will doe [p. 127] it, if you beleeve when you pray that you shall have it; for your heavenly Father if you aske in my name, will give the Holy Ghost to them that desire him, and wisdome to such as aske it of God, and no good thing shall be wanting or with-held from them which feare the Lord, and walke

---

[a] for ye Lo.^ds day. (HB) (*Errata*)

uprightly in his sight; so that we may well say with *David*, What is man that thou Lord art mindefull of him, and dost visit him with thy mercie, and crownest him with glory and honour?[111] Most mercifull Lord, these thy gracious promises and great goodnesse towards mortall man imboldneth mee, though a miserable sinner, and most unworthy of thy favours, now to offer up my supplications, and become an humble suter to thy Majesty, to begge these great blessings at thy hands, who have justly deserved grievous punishments from thee for my offences. But of thine owne meer mercie, deare God, who desirest not the death of a sinner, but our repentance, conversion, and salvation; and for thy best beloved Sons sake, in whom thou wilt deny us nothing, vouchsafe to incline thine ear to receive the humble petitions of me thy poore servant, who presumeth to crave of thee, the Father of mercie, and the originall of all goodnesse, from whom only commeth all good and perfect gifts, the seven spirituall and heavenly graces, wherewith to vanquish and banish us from[a] the seven dangerous deadly sinnes,[112] which like Serpents slay and destroy so many soules, the least sinne [p. 128] we commit, being sufficient to condemne us for ever.

And now first,[b] Good God, I humbly pray thee to bestow upon mee the blessed and most needfull gift of true faith, without which it is impossible to please thee, whereby I may stedfastly believe and trust in thy goodnesse, and lay fast hold of all thy mercies and gracious promises, especially upon the merits and sufferings of thy dear Son, and my Saviour Jesus for my redemption, and by thy grace rightly to apply them all to my salvation. And grant I may with thy assistance, bring forth such fruits of true holinesse and righteousnesse, as may be most to thy glory and the peace and comfort of mine owne conscience.

And since I have begun to speake to thee,[c] O Lord, who am but dust and ashes, vouchsafe for Jesus sake, further to give me the most excellent gift of the Holy Ghost, to unite me inseparably to my blessed head and Saviour Christ, and inspire my soule with all saving graces, which may change all the evill in me to goodnesse, darknesse to light, vices to vertues, and so wholy to cleanse and sanctifie my soule, body, and spirit, throughout, that I may be made perfect to every good worke, and renewed and inabled to all obedience, godlinesse and holinesse of life before thee:

and I also most humbly beseech thee[d] (O gracious God) to inrich me thy poore unworthy servant, with the unvaluable treasure of that heavenly wisdome from above, which abideth about thy Throne, to direct [p. 129] and reforme my heart,

---

[a] us from] ~~us~~ from ∧ [me] (HB)

[b] {i.} (HB)

[c] {2.} (HB)

[d] {3.} (HB)

and all my wayes aright in thy sight, and to teach me thy holy will, and what is good and acceptable unto thee, and inable me with grace to doe it; and likewise Lord indue me with the true understanding of thy holy Lawes, that I may keepe them with my whole heart unto my end.

Now,[a] O my Lord, we are taught by *Solomon*, That the beginning of wisdome is the feare of the Lord,[113] and the knowledge of divine things, true understanding; therefore I doe most humbly intreat thee to knit my rebellious heart to the holy feare of thy glorious Name, who only art to be feared, with the due consideration of thy righteous and terrible judgements, who canst cast both body and soul into hel; let this detaine me from falling into any evill or offence towards thee, and thereby also draw my sinfull soule unto thy faithfull service, with true contrition for all my past transgressions against thee.

But especially,[b] good God, be pleased to indue my poore soule with the infinite gift and blessing of thy sincere and perfect love of thy divine and heavenly Majesty who art the true and only good. And, O God, grant that I may love and honour thee above and beyond all other things, with all my heart, all my soule, all my strength, and with all my minde, setting my affections not on things that are below, but upon heavenly treasures that are above, which are permanent and fade not, where my sweet Saviour who dyed for mee on [p. 130] earth, now liveth and reigneth with thee in heaven for ever, and maketh intercession for mee there, that by thy assistance I may continually study and strive, carefully and willingly to performe all duties towards thee in obeying thy Commandements with an upright and perfect heart before thee: and in all true charity being ready to doe good to others as thou commandest, and to love my neighbour as my selfe, even my enemies for thy sake.

Most mercifull Lord, who knowest our fraile and wretched natures,[c] and desirest the conversion, & not the confusion of poor miserable sinners; thou sweet Jesus, camest to call, not the righteous, but sinners to repentance, such as I am, and to save that which was lost; Oh let not my poore soule be lost which cost thee thy deare pretious bloud to save; but Lord, make mee by true faith lay hold of my redemption by thee, and all other thy workes of mercy; and though I have grievously offended in thy sight, yet I beseech thee, with-hold not thy favour from me thy poor sinfull servant, but give me the grace of unfeigned sorrow and repentance, with a true contrite spirit, and a broken heart for all my sinnes committed before thee, from the greatest to the least, wherein I have displeased thee, by thought, desire, word or deed; hating, judging and condemning my selfe,

[a] {4.} (HB)   [c] {6.} (HB)
[b] {5.} (HB)

for so offending thee my Lord God; and most earnestly and humbly crave thy
assistance, that I may now happily returne to thee with a [p. 131] penitent and
grieved heart, from whom I have so unhappily gone astray by a vaine corrupt
mind and sinfull soule, whereby I hope in thy great mercy to escape thy just wrath
and condemnation due to my grievous offences; and may also obtaine thy
gracious pardon for all my passed misdeeds, with the assistance of thy holy Spirit,
which I most humbly crave, to amend my former faults, and to reforme my wayes
the rest of my life in all things according to thy blessed will. Now lastly, O gracious
Lord our righteousnesse, my sure hope and heavenly Father, the fountaine of all
goodnesse, in whom is all mercy and compassion, from thee only we receive all
good gifts and graces; for thou hearest the prayers, and to thee shall all flesh come,
who understandest our wants before we aske, and knowest our wretched natures
and disabilities to all goodnesse, so that thy grace only must worke both the will
and the deed of all that is good in us, and then of thine owne mercie accept the
same through the merits and mediation of our Saviour Jesus; so doubling thy
favours towards us miserable mortall creatures, whose hearts are vile and false
unto our selves and to thee also, and our thoughts are only evill continually:
Therefore sweet Jesus the mirrour of mercie, vouchsafe to heare and helpe me, to
call and draw me to thy selfe, and knit fast my heart and soule unto thy true feare,
devout love, and faithfull service for ever; that so by thy selfe, [p. 132] I may be
inabled to run willingly and joyfully after thee, rightly and readily to performe all
duties towards thee, and keep all thy Commandements constantly.

Oh gracious Lord Holy Ghost,[a] our blessed preserver, comforter and sanctifier,
soften thou my hardened heart by thy grace, and inlighten my dull and sinfull
soule, with all the powers thereof, my understanding, memory, will and affection,
with all saving graces; especially as the chiefe means to gaine the rest, vouchsafe
to inspire me with thy true spirit of grace and prayer rightly, humbly, fervently
and faithfully to call daily on thy sacred Name, and to worship thee in spirit and
truth, even as thou requirest to be served, that so by thy favour I may obtaine
grace, power and strength, to banish all wandring thoughts, and to vanquish and
resist all wicked hindrances cast in by the divell or his agents, the world, and
mine owne corruptions, which distract and disturbe my serious and devout
attendance of both soule and body in rightly performing this duty of prayer unto
my Lord God, whereby I may be duly thankfull for all thy benefits and mercies,
already bestowed on me and mine, and also to begge and obtaine the gracious
countenance[b] of all thy blessings spirituall and temporall, in whatsoever thou
seest necessary for this present life, and that which is to come; but more especially
in giving me all saving graces, which may fit, prepare and further me here for thy

---

[a] {7.} (HB)   [b] countenance] ~~countenance~~ continuance (HB)

hea- [p. 133] venly Kingdome hereafter. To which my Saviour and Redeemer bring me by all thy merits and sufferings, and in the fulnesse of thy mercies, I humbly beseech thee, dear Jesus. Amen, Amen.   —

1.   A sorrowfull widowes prayer and petition unto the gracious protector and defender of widowes, and father of the fatherlesse, which I composed shortly after the death of my dear husband:[114] *And this may also serve any other upon the like occasion.*

Almighty God, and most gracious Lord, who art full of pity and goodnesse, vouchsafe to heare, assist, and accept the humble devotion and supplication of me thy poore unworthy servant, in Jesus Christ thy deare Son. Most mighty God, whose mercies are above all thy great works, and whose power and divine providence directeth and disposeth all things to the best, for those that doe love and depend upon thee. Thou hast ever been pleased to shew mercie unto me thy poore handmaid, the most sinfull of all thy servants, and hast taken care of mee even from my mothers wombe, and vouchsafed me many benefits and blessings, and delivering mee out of very great crosses and troubles, still holding me up by thy gracious hand from sinking in the midst of a sea of sorrowes; and like a most loving Father in my divers change of fortunes, hast at all times provided for me and mine beyond our deserts, or the [p. 134] worlds expectation, having in thy mercifull goodnesse made me see with comfort all my children, who were left destitute, now by thy provident provision and blessing, well setled for this life: All which by thy infinite favours, Lord make me ever thankfully to acknowledge, and grant that I and all mine, may serve, obey, praise, and glorifie thy great and blessed Name for ever, and ever. And as thou Lord, hast stretched forth thy hand of bounty to supply all my worldly wants; so dear God, vouchsafe more especially to extend thy gracious care over my soule, to prevent and keep me from sin, and indue me with all spirituall graces, so that my whole life and waies may ever be serviceable and acceptable to thy heavenly Majesty.

And now, O Lord, since it hath been thy will and pleasure, to take away, and call to thy selfe my deare husband out of this transitory life before me, and to bereave me of him who was my chiefe comfort in this world: I humbly beseech thee, vouchsafe to take me into thy care, and give me grace to choose with *Mary*, that better part which may never be taken from mee, chiefly to serve and follow thee, that so I may turne this freedome from the bond of mariage only the more to thy service, and may become thy bondwoman to serve and praise thee day and night like *Hanna*,[115] so long as I live. And Lord, assist me with thy grace to obey thee in all things according to thy holy will, daily endeavouring to [p. 135] work out my salvation with feare and trembling, and continually striving by a godly life and holy conversation, to make my calling and election sure, which is one of the chiefest things needfull. Now deare God, make me to change and far exceed the fervent affection and carefull observance I have lived in towards my husband, into a holy feare, with devout and sincere love of thy Majesty and service, and due watchfulnesse over my selfe, that I displease not thee my God in any thing. And good God, by thy holy Spirit, withdraw my heart from the covetous seeking, desiring and longing after the vanities, riches, delights, preferments, or vaine pleasures of this wicked deceitfull world, but instead of my former care and troubles in worldly businesses, to please my husband, and for the good of my children, let me now bend my minde, and wholly set my heart and soule, to seeke after thee my good God, thy glory, thy Kingdome, and the righteousnesse thereof, that so I may walke before thee all the rest of my daies, with an upright, faithfull, and perfect heart in thy sight. Lastly, indue mee with true thankfulnesse to thy gracious Majesty for all thy manifold mercies vouchsafed unto me, Lord give me grace to use those benefits thou bestowest on me conscionably as may be best pleasing unto thee, and to imploy all I have to thy glory, the relievement of thy truest servants, and my owne comfort, especially the good of my [p. 136] soule in performing my duty towards thee, in striving to doe all the good I can, while I have time, for I desire so to use and receive thy blessings here, as I may be also received into the place of eternall blessednesse hereafter, through Jesus Christ my Lord.

Finally, I most humbly beg that thou wilt vouchsafe to be a loving and gracious Father in thy care and comfort to me, and all mine, and let thy mercie, blessing and favour, rest alwaies upon me, my children and grand-children kindred and friends, with all that thou hast given thy poore servant, who doth in all humility commend and commit my selfe, my waies and workes, wholy to thy most blessed protection, and direction, to dispose according to thy good pleasure; that so I may doe all things to thy glory here, and by thy mercy be a happy partaker of thy eternall Kingdome of glory hereafter, through Jesus Christ my Lord, Amen.

2. A Prayer to the God of mercy in time of affliction.

O most gracious Lord God, the originall of all goodnesse, and fountaine of mercie, thou hast commanded thy poore servants to call upon thee in the day of trouble, that thou maiest deliver us, and we may glorifie thee; great are the troubles of thy children, but thou deliverest them out of all; thine eyes, O Lord, are upon thy ser- [p. 137] vants, and thine eares are open to their cry, for thou art near unto all that call upon thee in truth, and wilt save such as bee afflicted in spirit: the sorrows of my heart are increased, Lord draw me out of my troubles; the poore crieth, and the Lord heareth, he prepareth their hearts, and bendeth his eares to them, and delivereth them out of all their feare and care; for the hope[a] afflicted shall not perish before thee for ever. The Lord also will be a refuge in due time, even in affliction, and they that know thy Name will trust in thee, for thou wilt not faile them that seek thee: have mercy upon me, O Lord, consider my troubles which I suffer of them that hate me without cause, thou hast been my defense, and hast lifted me up from the gates of death: O Lord my God, in thee I put my trust, save me from them that persecute mee, and deliver me in thy good time. But, dear God, I most humbly confesse that my sinnes are so many and grievous, as they have deserved farre greater punishment then I am able to beare, and I can hope for no helpe or release but from thine owne goodnesse, who art my only hope and sure refuge; for thou hast mercy on whom thou wilt have mercy, and takest compassion on whom thou pleasest; but I acknowledge that my sufferings are not answerable to my sinnes, for thou hast corrected me with favour, not in rigor; therefore if thou shouldest kill me, yet will I trust in thee,[116] for thy mercy exceedeth all thy workes, and un- [p. 138] der the shadow of thy wings will I rest in confidence, till all my afflictions be overpassed.

Yet Lord, if it seem good unto thee to continue these heavy troubles and visitations, that now lye sore on me, I humbly pray thee to sanctifie all my afflictions unto me thy poore servant, which I hope are but fatherly chastisements for the amendment of my faults, and not the fearfull judgements and ensignes[117] of thy wrathfull displeasure; from which Lord, for thy Sonnes sake, preserve me thy poore sinfull creature, and lay no more upon me then thou wilt make me able to undergoe as I ought to doe, saying with *Ely*, It is the Lord, let him do what he pleaseth: and make me to consider like *Job*, that naked I came into the world, and naked I shall returne, the Lord gave, and the Lord hath taken, praised be his name for ever;[118] but thou Lord art my strength and my stay in all distractions. I further humbly beseech thee, to give me grace and patience in all things, and at all times, to keep my selfe from any offence towards thee, by repining at thy just and favourable corrections for my transgressions; but grant that I may as Christ hath taught us, meekly and humbly, submit my selfe to thy most righteous and blessed will, that so I may (by thy assistance) make the best and right use of whatsoever thou sendest, that all may be to the best for thy honour, and turne to my good when thou art pleased to give a happy issue to this temptation, and in thy good time to ease and de- [p. 139] liver me out of these great adversities to thy glory. But I know that the afflictions of this present world, are not worthy of the glory that shall bee revealed to us hereafter; yet I humbly desire if it so please thee, that I may live the rest of my daies in peace and quiet, constantly to attend thy service, and seek after my owne salvation.

---

[a] ∧ of yᵉ (HB) (*Errata*)

Lord be mercifull to this whole Kingdome, now in very great distraction, distresse and misery,[119] and also to all my fellow members in thy whole Church universall, wheresoever any of us are afflicted, inwardly or outwardly in body or minde, grant us either speedy delivery, or else grace to performe thy good pleasure, and with patience to wait thy leasure, untill thou please to have mercy on us to our release and comfort, and to thy owne praise and glory, who never failest those that depend upon thee. Now I most humbly acknowledge with all possible praise and thanks, which I am bound ever to render unto thee, that thou hast formerly delivered me out of many sorrowes, cares, troubles and vexations, both in body and minde, and also I blesse and magnifie thy holy Name for all thy great and manifold blessings which thou hast bestowed upon me, thy most unworthy servant; and I pray thee Lord, of thy infinite goodnesse, not to let my sinnes and wickednesse hinder thy mercies towards me, but pardon and cast all my offences out of thy sight, through Jesus Christ my Saviour; and vouchsafe alwaies to con- [p. 140] tinue thy grace and favour to mee, and especially in daily renewing all spirituall graces in me, that so, when, or how soone soever thou hast appointed an end unto my daies here, I may then obtaine the end of my faith and hope, even thy glory and my owne salvation, through thy beloved Son and my only Saviour Jesus: for whose sake, Lord heare me, and grant these my humble requests, with all things else which thou best knowest necessary either for my soule or body, for this life, or for the life to come, in which, deare God, make mee in thy manifold mercies partaker of eternall happinesse, for evermore. Amen.

3. A Prayer for due preparation before the holy Communion of the Lords Supper.

O most gracious God, and our heavenly and mercifull Father in Jesus Christ, who hatest nothing thou hast made, and desirest not the death of sinners, but that we should return to thee and live; thou absolvest all those that truly repent and beleeve thy holy Gospell, and didst send thine only and beloved Son Jesus into the world, to seek those that were lost, and to save sinners by thy grace, of whom I am chiefe. O sweet Jesus, thou callest to thee, those that are heavy laden and truly penitent, and weary of their burthensome sinnes, that thou maiest mercifully ease and refresh them; thou camest to call sinners to repen- [p. 141] tance, and restore us that were lost by sinne, and to lay downe thine owne life to redeeme mankinde from eternall death, and hast left us a gracious remembrance thereof in thy most holy Supper of that unspeakable worke of our redemption, which we are exceedingly bound often to celebrate, in acknowledgement of thy unexpressible mercy and favour towards us.

But oh my Lord! I tremble and feare, knowing that I am a wretched and wicked sinner, and my offences have made me abominable in thy sight, being wholy corrupt both in soule and body, from the crowne of my head, to the soal of the foot, the worst deserving of all thy servants, and if thou shouldest strictly marke what I have done amisse, or enter into judgement with me, how should I dare to come into thy presence having nothing to answer for my selfe, but (to cry with the Publican) I have grievously offended, Lord be mercifull to mee a sinner? (and as another saith of himselfe, how should I presume to appeare in the presence of God, can the Lord be mercifull to so miserable a sinner as I am?)[120] But Lord, I have learned, and do beleeve that there is mercy with thee, and plentifull redemption; therefore we are infinitly bound to love and feare thee; but I doe humbly confesse that I am altogether unworthy of my selfe to approach unto thy blessed table, but thou Lord that givest both the will and the deed in all good workes, so Lord I pray thee to worke in me a due [p. 142] preparation for thy acceptance, and then inable me to performe my duty herein in a right and faithfull manner, for there at thy heavenly banquet, thou Lord, Father, Son and Holy Ghost, art present in thy great Majesty beholding our unperfect devotions, wants in preparation, and manifold infirmities; but thou Lord by thy powerfull grace cleansest us from sin, and changest us into new creatures, and in thy highest bounty giving thy selfe really unto us to be received spiritually by faith, and by the working of the Holy Ghost; thou art the heavenly food of our soules unto eternall life, powring such great and wonderfull treasure into poore earthen vessels, as we are, and so making us partakers of all the benefits of thy unspeakable merits, and bitter passions and sufferings.

Oh Lord, who invitest me thither, continue thy mercy to perfect the good worke thou hast begun for my salvation, and heale thou my corrupt soule, converting my straying and deceitfull heart, and knit it unto thee my God, and by thy grace prepare and fit me, rightly, reverently, faithfully and worthily, to receive that high and divine mystery, in all humility, contrition, true faith and charity, with such devotion as I ought to doe. Now deare Lord, give me grace rightly to understand, and duly to consider and ponder of thy greatnesse to feare thee, of thy goodnesse to love thee, of thy power and manifold mercies towards me, ever to beleeve and trust [p. 143] in thee: And also to looke into my owne rebellious disobedience, and shamefull ingratitude towards thee, and my most miserable estate, who am in danger of everlasting damnation by my innumerable transgressions committed against thee; Lord touch my hardened heart with the oyle of thy grace, that it may be softened to receive a sound and sensible feeling and sight of all my grievous sinnes past, both in committing the evill I was forbidden, and omitting the good I am commanded, with a true sense of thy just wrath against me for the same, which may worke in mee by thy assistance, such unfaigned sorrow and penitencie, even to breake my stony heart with hatred of my self and all sinne for so offending thee, with such true contrition and repentance unto salvation, as I may obtaine thy mercifull pardon sweet Jesus, that by thy wounds I may bee healed, and all my offences hidden, never to bee imputed unto me hereafter; and by thy grace heartily purposing, constantly to endeavour the amendment of all my misdeeds for the time to come, and by thy helpe to lead a holy and a sanctified life so long as I live. Now I humbly beseech thee, oh dear Lord, to indue me also with the blessed gift of true faith, which is the only hand to lay hold of thee, and all thy mercies whereby thou maiest dwell in me, and I in thee for ever; I beleeve, Lord helpe my unbeleefe, and strengthen and increase in me a right hope, [p. 144] and lively faith, stedfastly to beleeve, and rightly to apply to my owne soule all thy gracious promises, benefits, merits and sufferings for me to my salvation.

O my God Holy Ghost, vouchsafe to inspire my heart with true and perfect charity towards all my brethren and neighbours, yea even to my very enemies for thy sake, that I may forgive them, as thou dost pardon me. And thou Lord, preserver of mankinde, by thy gracious operation in this blessed Sacrament, joyne me an unworthy member unseparably unto thy[a] blessed head Christ Jesus, especially at this time, grant that through thy holy working and assistance, I may bee a happy partaker not only of the outward signes, but also of the inward and inestimable graces bestowed upon our soules by the reall body broken, and pretious bloud shed of our deare Saviour Jesus, which was crucified for us, to be the pretious food of our soules, all which Lord rightly apply unto my soule, with all other benefits thereby signified and assured unto us, and through his righteousnesse and merits, that I may be reconciled and accepted by God our heavenly Father, to my eternall comfort and happinesse; that so I may devoutly and everlastingly love and honour, magnifie, and admire the infinite mercy, love and favour of God, the Father, our deare Saviour Jesus, and of the Holy Ghost, to whom be all praise and glory for ever. Now Almighty God, grant me thy poore servant grace to live in true faith, [p. 145] ready obedience, and continuall thankfullnesse all the rest of my daies here, that I may live hereafter in heaven with thee, in joy and blisse for evermore. Amen.

4. An humble thanksgiving after the receiving of the Sacrament of the Lords Supper.

I yeeld unto thee my mercifull Lord God, Father, Son and Holy Ghost, all humble and possible praise and thanks, for all thy great benefits and loving favours vouchsafed unto me, thy poor sinfull creature both spirituall and temporall all my life hitherto; and deare Lord, the fountaine of all mercie, thou hast been exceeding good and gracious towards mee, which I humbly acknowledge, especially in vouchsafing so great and manifold blessings to me thy most unworthy servant in this thy present favour, which thou hast been pleased to

---

[a] thy] my (*Errata*)

make me partaker of amongst thy children. Now, deare Lord, make me ever truly thankfull with all my heart and soule unto thee for all thy mercies bestowed on mee, who with shame and sorrow doe confesse, I have deserved no good, but all evill at thy hands by my manifold offences committed against thee; therefore in all humility I doe beseech thee, to cast all my sinnes and wickednesse out of thy sight, and let them be no hindrance to thy grace and mercy towards me; but Lord still continue and increase thy [p. 146] fatherly care and loving kindnesse both to my soule and body to prevent and preserve me from falling into any sin or evill; and vouchsafe to bestow all spirituall graces on mee, that may inable me to live a more holy and acceptable life before thee ever hereafter; and seale thou my pardon for all my sinnes past, for Christ Jesus sake, who dyed for me, and with his owne unvaluable bloud paid my ransome, and fully satisfied thy great and just wrath against me.

But gracious God, how unspeakable is thy goodnesse and infinite favour towards mankinde, that instead of powring down punishments upon us for our great offences against thee, thou didst thy selfe in thy tender love ordaine the meanes for our redemption, justification and eternall salvation, through Christ thine owne deare Son: praised be thy glorious Name for ever, and chiefly at this time I magnifie thee sweet Jesus (the mirrour of mercy) who before thou hadst finished the great worke of our redemption, didst also institute the blessed Sacrament of thy holy Supper that inestimable benefit, to all thy servants which rightly receive the same, it being a pledge of thy love, a remembrance of thy mercy, a renuing of grace in us, a testimony of thy favours, a confirmation of our faith, a uniting of us (by thy Holy Ghost) to our blessed Lord and head Christ Jesus, and all our fellow members in perfect charity one towards another, with assurance thereby of the pardon of all our sinnes, and [p. 147] eternall salvation to our soules: the great benefit thereof is beyond my expression, of which this day thou hast graciously vouchsafed to make mee (though unworthy of my selfe) yet by thy favour a happy partaker. Now deare Lord, enlarge thy goodnesse further toward me thy poor servant, to give me daily the spirituall gifts of sound repentance, encrease of true faith to beleeve all thy gracious promises, with grace rightly to apply them to my owne soule, and all the infinite benefits which thou my deare Saviour hast purchased for me, that so this Sacrament may worke those good effects in me which thou hast therein offered unto us, and that I may by thy assistance, bring forth the fruits of righteousnesse, obedience, and true holinesse of life, all the rest of my daies, and to make such thankfull and constant acknowledgement and right use of all thy mercies, as I may glorifie thy blessed Name; reforme my waies, and frame my heart in all things to be faithfully and constantly thine, and then I know that thou wilt ever be my gracious God, to thy honour and my endlesse felicity, through my Lord Jesus Christ the righteous. Amen.

1. A meditation concerning death.

O Lord God Holy Ghost, our sanctifier, preserver and comforter, who best knowes my corrupt nature, that cannot of my selfe performe [p. 148] any true service towards God, being inclined to all evill, and unapt to any goodnesse, I humbly beseech thee, that understandest my manifold infirmities, be pleased to indue me with all saving graces in the performance of all holy duties towards God. And I humbly pray thee sweet Jesus to call and draw me daily unto thee; and vouchsafe Lord by thy holy Spirit to possesse my heart and soule, to make mee wholly and constantly thine, truly to feare and love thee, to serve and obey thee in all things, that so thou in thy infinite mercy maiest never leave me, but be my gracious Lord, and mercifull God for ever. And I humbly pray thee Lord Holy Ghost, to sanctifie and assist me thy poore sinfull servant, with all spirituall graces for my salvation in Christ, both living and dying, that I may strive to become what I ought to be, and to doe thy holy will in all things while I live.

Now O good God, Father, Son, and Holy Ghost, thou knowest that many and evill have been my daies in this world, and by thy providence I have attained to a great age, but have not performed the ends for which I came into the world, who being made only to serve God in holinesse and righteousnesse all the daies of our lives to his glory, and our salvation, which is the chief thing needfull; but alas, for the most part it is the least regarded or thought upon, where I confesse (with sorrow) that I have been too much neglectfull, having sometimes been drawne by the [p. 149] cares and troubles of this life, which necessity brought upon me, to set my heart ever carefully upon earthly things, and likewise, too often have I been carried away with the vanity of my owne heart in following after the preferments, or delighting in the pleasures of this vile world, all which perish in the using, by which delusions and deceits, that old subtill serpent Sathan (that first wrought our ruine) he now steals away our time and hearts, only to make us lose our souls also. But deare Lord, though I have too long gone astray, yet while I am going towards my God, Lord let it be thy worke of grace and mercie to make me see and understand when I am out of the right way before I goe too far to fall into irrecoverable danger, from which I cannot returne. Oh shew me the paths of life and lead mee into the true way to heaven that I may first turne to thee in true faith with a contrite spirit, and a broken heart for my lost time past which I have mispent, that so I may obtaine pardon for all my sinnes formerly committed before thee, and then I know thou wilt receive me as one of thine, and in mercie bring me to thy salvation.

Now Lord, although our times are only knowne to thee, yet I cannot have long to live, for the life of man is but short, and old age laden with infirmities and sicknesse is a sure messenger and forerunner of death, and then draweth near the first appearance when [p. 150] my breath ceaseth, of my poore soule before the tribunall seat, of thy great Majesty, O God, and before all thy holy Angels there to bee called to give an account of all my life and time mispent: Alas, how can I answer one thing of a thousand; now what should I doe, if I had not there in heaven an All-sufficient Saviour, who is also my blessed advocate to mediate for me, in whom is all my trust, comfort and confidence; therefore gracious Lord Jesus helpe me now while I am here, and assist me to make my peace (as thou dost advise) while I am in the way before the grim and cruell Sergeants[121] of sicknesse and death lay hold upon me to prevent me of the freedome, and ability of my senses, and spirit, being aided with thy power, strength and grace by unfaigned repentance, and true faith to obtaine through Christ my release, and pardon of those grievous debts and trespasses that I stand guilty of before God, which I am no waies able to satisfie, but only by thee my Saviour Jesus, or else I shall be throwne into that dreadfull dungeon, from whence there is no escaping: Therefore now I doe most humbly beg and pray thee, that I may finde such favour in thy sight, knowing my owne disabilities, that thou Lord wouldest knit[a] and prepare my heart and soule, for thine owne mercifull acceptance, before thou call and ceise[122] upon me by death, to take me out of this life, and make me continually mindfull of my last end while I live in health, and [p. 151] of that strict reckoning which then I must make unto thee, the great God of heaven and earth, who seeth and knoweth all things of all my life past, even to my very words.

And let me still remember that thou Lord searchest the hearts and triest the reines,[123] and beholdest all our waies, and will bring each worke to judgement, with every secret thing, whether it be good or evill: Therefore I most humbly beseech thee, while I am in this world, give me the grace of daily and unfaigned repentance for all my sinnes past, with care to amend all my former faults in the rest of my life, and narrowly to examine my own heart, soule and conscience of all the evills I have done before thee, hating and severely judging and condemning my selfe for them, that so I may escape thy great wrath, and not be judged and condemned by thee, O Lord, in thy heavy displeasure, which I am not able to beare; for who can stand in the sight of thy great Majesty when thou art angry? Therefore gracious God, let me here obtain thy mercifull pardon for all my offences past, with grace to reforme my former misdeeds, and by thy blessed assistance become a new creature all my daies, that so I may gaine a blessed end through my Saviour to dye in him, and make my peace with God here, before I goe hence and be no more: To which purpose I humbly pray thee while I live, to make me a true and faithfull member of thy right Church & Kingdom of grace here [p. 152] to professe and practice true Religion, and all holinesse of life to my last end; but chiefly, Lord, give me a blessed

---

[a] knit] fit (*Errata*)

part in the first resurrection, that I may not lye dead in trespasses and sinnes, but may by thy holy Spirit be daily raised from the grave of sinne, and enabled to live the life of grace, that so the second death may have no power to hurt me; and at the last when it shall please thee to appoint a stop to my daies, and to set a period unto my time, grant that my death be neither suddaine, nor unexpected, neither my paines violent, whereby I should be unable, faithfully, earnestly and constantly to cry unto thee my God, and call upon thy holy Name, for reliefe and comfort in that great and dreadfull day and time of death and danger, when my soules enemies will seek my utter destruction; then Lord, depart not from me, but pray that my faith in thee faile not, and strengthen my weaknesse by thy power, and supply my soule with all saving graces, and defend me from the malice and subtill temptation of my spirituall adversaries, that they may never be able to prevaile against me in any thing.

But I humbly pray thee sweet Saviour, to grant that in the day of thy great visitation, my poore name through thy unspeakable goodnesse, may be then found written in thy blessed booke of life, so that my sinnes, nor my soules enemies, may not be able to blot it out; but that by thy infinite mercy and favour, sweet Jesus, unto me, I may then be ac- [p. 153] counted in thee worthy to escape thy just wrath, and by thy power and clemency, who didst vouchsafe to be borne of a woman, and shalt bee judge of the whole world, grant through thy mercies, merits, and manifold sufferings, that I poore sinfull creature, may be made able to stand before thee the blessed Son of God and man in that great and dreadfull day of judgement, when all our secret wickednesses shall be made manifest, and thou Lord, to whom all judgement is given by the Father, art to give our finall sentence: Oh then dear Jesus, in whom only I trust, receive me into thy gracious favour as one of thine, that my sinnes may be covered with thy righteousnesse, that so I may be preserved from thy wrath, and that wofull doom, Go ye cursed into hell fire, appointed for the Divell and his Angells; but Lord, in the fulnesse of thy mercy, make me one of that happy chosen number, to whom that joyfull call shall belong, Come ye blessed of my Father, inherit, and enter into that Kingdome, which he hath prepared for you before the beginning of the world;[124] and also thou our Saviour hast purchased for us; then Lord in thy infinite love grant me a part in that everlasting happinesse, to live with thee, and glorifie thee there, for ever and ever. Amen.

[p. 154]

2. A Prayer to live blessedly, and dye happily.

Oh gracious Lord God, who didst create all things by thy omnipotent power, and lastly made mankinde! thou best knowest the frailties and corruption of our wretched nature which we inherit from our first parents, whose substance was but earth, and we are of our selves inclined onely to earthly and evill things, and such is the condition of mortall man, that all that are borne must dye, and returne to dust from whence they came, but the spirit returnes to thee, O God, that gave it, to receive either joy or blisse with thee for ever, or else eternall banishment from thee, who art the only good; therefore I doe most humbly beseech thee, deare Lord, to looke mercifully upon me, to helpe my manifold infirmities, and daily to prevent and keep me from falling into any sinne or evill to offend thee. But especially in the time of my death, dear Lord, be mercifull unto me a most miserable sinner, to forgive all my sinnes and offences past, that I have committed against thee my God, my brethren, or my owne soule; and grant through the merits, and many sufferings of thy beloved Son, and my only Saviour Jesus, that they may never bee imputed unto me thy poor servant, but vouchsafe good God, in thy manifold mercies to indue mee thy most unworthy suppliant, with all saving graces leading [p. 155] to my salvation both in life and death; for we daily see by example how suddainly death may surprise us when we least expect it; therefore while this life is in being, and I am going on in the way of all flesh, which can be of no long continuance; Lord teach and assist mee to make my peace for my offences with thee my God while I am here, who else wilt take an account of me in a dreadfull place, and art able if thy wrath be not pacified, to cast me into hell fire, from which there is no redemption; therefore have mercy on me, sweet Jesus, that I may by thy helpe, grace and assistance, rightly fit and prepare my self for thy acceptance before sicknesse lay hold on me; for when death seiseth it will carry mee immediately before the judgement seat of thy great Majesty: Oh there let me finde thee, deare Jesus, to be my gracious Saviour and Advocate, and so I shall obtaine mercy and favour, and by thy sufferings, my offences pardoned, and Gods severe justice satisfied. And thus in thee and through thee only, my blessed Redeemer Iesus Christ, I shall be received to grace and mercy, and made partaker of eternall life, and remaine with Almighty God, in whose presence is the fulnesse of joy, and at his right hand there are pleasures for evermore, which Lord make me partaker of, there to glorifie the Name of Almighty God, Father, Son, and Holy Ghost, for ever. Amen.

[p. 156]

3. A Prayer to be prepared for a happy death, and to gaine a joyfull resurrection.

Most glorious Lord God, who didst make all things, thou well understandest that we poor creatures (how highly soever we are conceited of our selves) are but dust and ashes, and must returne to earth from whence we came; our lives and times are in thy hand and power, and what thou hast appointed we cannot change, and all things to our selves are most uncertaine; for when thou with just rebuke dost chastise man for iniquity, thou makest his strength and beauty to consume away like a flower

of the field that withereth and falleth:[125] for when thou callest, man cannot retaine
the spirit, nor adde one houre to his time, but it returnes to thee that gave it, and
hee goeth downe to the grave, from which he shall not returne againe till this world
is at an end: Therefore, deare Lord, I now most humbly beseech thee, for thy
beloved sonnes sake, who hath satisfied thy just wrath by his infinite and innocent
sufferings, and redeemed me from sin and Sathan by his death, Lord forgive and
pardon me all my sinnes and offences past, either in soule or body, that I have
committed against thee ever since I came into this miserable world, which I confesse
are innumerable, more then the haires of my head, or the sand upon the Sea shoare,
but vouch- [p. 157] safe, O mercifull God, to be reconciled unto mee a wicked
sinner, in thy deare and righteous Son Christ Iesus my only Saviour, who hath paid
my ransome with his owne pretious bloud, wherewith, oh God of mercie, blot my
debt to thee by sinne, out of thy sight; and also he did fulfill all righteousnesse for
me, who is now my blessed Mediator in heaven, to impute all this unto mee:

Therefore, deare Lord Holy Ghost, by thy gracious and holy Spirit, joyne and
unite me unto my Lord and head Christ, never to be separated from him while I
live here, and when I goe from hence carry me to be where he is, and give mee
grace and faith in and through him, to make my peace while I am in the way and
passage of this life, and while I have breath to call upon thee, before I am laid
into the darke dungeon of the earth, when the wormes shall eat my corrupt flesh;
yet I trust and doe believe through him, that hath overcome death, the grave, and
hell for me, that at the blessed resurrection of thy children and servants, that my
corruption shall put on incorruption,[126] and I shall see my blessed Lord and
Saviour with these my eyes, who did redeeme me, and shall be my mercifull
judge to save me; therefore I have sure confidence in his favour, and under the
wings of his mercie shall I rest in safety. Now I humbly pray thee, O God the
Holy Ghost, to sanctifie, fit, prepare, and assist my heart and soule with thy
Spirit, to fill me with all saving [p. 158] graces for my salvation; while I live, to
enable me to call, pray and strive to please thee here in all things; but especially
Lord at my death stand by me and pray for me that my faith faile not: fit and
prepare me for thy gracious acceptance, before thou call and seise upon me to
take me out of this present life; and make me alwaies mindefull both in health
and sicknesse of my owne last end, and then of my appearance before thee, to
make answer before the great God of Heaven & Earth (from whom nothing can
bee hid) of all my life and deeds past, even to my very words; for thou art only
and above all to be feared, who canst both save and kill, and cast both soule and
body into utter perdition in hell: Therefore Lord, vouchsafe to assist me with thy
grace to worke in me all things which may make me acceptable unto thee before
the day of my departure, that when it doth approach it may not bee fearfull and
terrible, but happy and comfortable unto me in Christ Jesus my Lord, that
through him, my last day may be my best, and most welcome to my soule; that I

may then call and pray, and say with confidence, Come Lord Jesus, come quickly,[127] for into thy hands I most humbly commend my spirit, for thou hast redeemed me, O Lord God of truth; and vouchsafe thou even to my last breath, alwaies to say unto my soule, thou art my God, and my salvation for ever. Amen.

[p. 159]

4. A Prayer in sicknesse, with expectation of death.[128]

Oh heavenly Father, who hast been my gracious God before I had being, and my mercifull guide from my youth, be pleased especially now at the houre and point of my death which I shall shortly expect, to be mercifull, O God, unto me a miserable sinner, to pardon for Jesus sake all my sinnes and iniquities that I have committed formerly; and vouchsafe to heale and save my wretched soule that hath infinitly offended thee, and strengthen my weaknesse with thy power, and supply all graces wanting in me by thy mercie, and defend me from all my spirituall adversaries, who will endeavour my destruction if they can, but let them not prevaile against me; and Lord Jesus, be not farre from me, neither forsake me in a time when so much trouble and danger is about me; but in the multitude of thy mercy, Lord pray for mee that my faith faile not, and stretch forth thy hand to save me, as thou didst to *Peter*,[129] lest I perish. Now, O God, give me such sound and unfaigned repentance, as may obtaine from thee remission of all my sinnes, with true faith to lay hold of all thy gracious promises, and a right and a stedfast hope in all thy mercies; but chiefly indue me with devout and perfect love toward thy Majesty, which may make me faithfully and [p. 160] constantly thine to serve and obey thy holy will in all things, with Christian charity towards all my brethren: but Lord, if it be thy will give mee knowledge of my death when it is neare, that I may faithfully pray unto thee, and call on thy most blessed Name with my last breath, and may joyfully and willingly yeeld up and commend my spirit backe to thee my Lord, who gave it unto me: And deare Lord, prevent and remove all evill hindrances in my way to heavenly happinesse, that through Christ Jesus my Saviour, I may bee received amongst thy children and servants, and admitted into the presence of thy Majesty, O heavenly Father, there to enjoy eternall felicity with thee in heaven when this life is ended by death.

But if thou shouldest please at this time to continue and prolong my daies upon earth; Lord, so long as I live, teach me by thy grace so to number my daies that I may apply my heart to wisdome and godlinesse and holinesse of life, seeking to redeem my lost time past which I have mispent, by daily repentance and amendment of life, striving to make my calling and election sure, by a holy and good conversation the rest of my time to come, that by thy mercy, and merits of my Saviour Jesus I may be freed of my trespasses, and heavy account with thee before I dye, and may escape thy just and great wrath which is due for my manifold transgressions.

Now Lord Jesus, I willingly submit my selfe to thy good pleasure to [p. 161] dispose of me as thou seest best: but I most humbly beg of thee, when my last and appointed hour is come, that I shall enter into my long sleep of death, and goe to lye downe in the dust; deare Lord, give me a happy departure out of this life, that I may dye in thee, O Lord, to rest in peace and safety, and may be raised up by thee at the last day to grace and glory, that thou receiving mee into thy mercy and favour, I may live and remain with thee in eternall happinesse to glorifie thy blessed Name, and sing hallelujah amongst thy Saints for ever and ever. Amen.

5. A Prayer unto the Lord of mercy in the time of sicknesse to be fitted for death, and assisted in that dreadfull houre against all temptations, to gaine a blessed passage out of this world at Gods appointed time.

O great and mercifull God, who reignest and disposest of all things in heaven, and in the whole world as it pleaseth thee, and understandest all the passage here below on earth, be it never so secret, and by thy mercie and power dost work all things to the best for those that love and depend upon thee; for thou art full of goodnesse, patience and long-suffering towards us poore weak and fraile creatures, and thy abounding mercy, doth exceed all other thy great workes in pardoning sinners; but beyond all other thy favours to- [p. 162; misnumbered 161] wards us, thy infinite love to mankinde did most appeare in sending thine owne dear Son into the world to save sinners by thy grace, that all that beleeve in him might be saved; without which thy mercie, what hope, comfort, or helpe were there left unto us miserable sinfull creatures; for the just man falleth seven times a day, but the wicked much more, and if the righteous scarcely be saved, where shall the ungodly and sinner appear, such as I am?

Therefore I come and cry and pray unto thee, who only canst relieve me, in all humility, contrition and confession of my manifold transgressions, and in the blessed Name of thy dear beloved Son, my only Saviour, I do beg and beseech thee, O Father, full of compassion, not to enter into judgement with me, nor to remember what I have done amisse; but to consider what thy Christ hath done and suffered for mee, and looking on mee through him, have mercy and pity upon me a most grievous sinner; I know too well, how justly thou maiest condemne me; but Lord, to save a poore sinner by thy grace is farre greater honour and glory unto thee: And gracious God, who of thine owne meer mercy didst give us thy most deare Son to be our reconciliation and redemption whē we were thine enemies, much more being reconciled, and having performed all things for us, thou canst deny us no good thing that wee aske in his beloved Name: Therefore, O God, for Christ innocent sake, vouchsafe to be recon- [p. 163; misnumbered 162] ciled unto me, thy most unworthy sinfull servant, and cast all my offences into his grave, where my Saviour paid the last part of my ransome; and by his power rising againe the third day from death, he conquered and overcame all my soules enemies, sin, death, hell and Sathan; and deare Lord, with his pretious bloudshed upon the crosse, wash my soule cleane before it appeare in thy presence, and take away all my iniquities out of thy sight, never to come in remembrance before thee, so that Christ may be unto me both in life and death an advantage.

And now most deare God, my life and time here is only in thy hand and pleasure, and thou hast cast me upon the bed of sicknesse, from which I know not whether I shall recover, or rise any more while I live in this world; therefore I most humbly pray thee, sweet Jesus, never to leave or forsake me, but stand thou alwaies in mercy by me, and let thy right hand uphold and sustaine me to preserve me from all my spirituall enemies that wait to destroy my soule: But thou my Lord, art sufficient for me, O Lord, vouchsafe me thy grace to direct my heart and words towards thee, and by thy ready helpe to assist me in all things, and at all times, that in thy mercie at the last thou maiest finish all thy favour in mee, which is the accomplishment of my faith and hope in thee: And Lord grant that I may willingly and readily come unto thee when thou callest; and vouchsafe, O blessed Spirit Holy Ghost, to [p. 164] fit and prepare me by unfeigned repentance to obtaine remission of all my sinnes that I have done before thee, with true faith to lay hold of all the mercies of my God in Christ, and with stedfast hope to rest on all thy gracious promises, O Lord, who never failest those that trust in thee.

Now Lord, give me strength and patience to wait thy good leasure and pleasure, untill thou have pity and compassion on me, either to recover and restore my health here (if it be thy will) that I may live and glorifie thee longer in this life, or else that thou wilt please to receive and prepare me for thy selfe, and give me all saving graces for thine own mercifull acceptance, when thou pleasest to call and take me to thee out of this wretched world, that so my faith and sure trust in thee may never faile unto my last breath. Now lastly, Lord grant, that as the outward man (the body) decayeth and groweth weaker, so the inward part (the soule) may by thy gracious assistance grow together in faith and confidence towards thee, with full assurance of thy Spirit within me of thy favour to me for my eternall salvation: Then come Lord Iesus when thou pleasest, for into thy hands I humbly commend my spirit, that when this life shall leave me, thy grace and mercy may receive mee into that endlesse happinesse in heaven, which my Lord and only Saviour hath purchased for me, that I may praise God everlastingly. Amen.

[p. 165]

6. My Prayer of thanksgiving after my long and great fit of sicknesse, which begun on Twelfth day at night and held me till Whitsontide:[130] This may serve upon any other occasion.[a]

Most gracious Lord God, I blesse and praise thy great and holy Name, for all thy blessings and benefits both spirituall and temporall vouchsafed to my soule and body; but especially I magnifie thy glorious Majesty for all those spirituall graces thou hast bestowed upon my soule before I was borne and hitherto, which I beseech thee of thy mercie daily to continue and increase towards me: Now deare Lord, make me thy unworthy servant ever truly thankfull to thee for all thy goodnesse extended towards me, and grant me grace to make such right use of all thy mercies as may be most to thy glory, and my salvation in Christ. But now, O Lord, that art my God, I must at this time render thee humble thanks in particular, and not forget to acknowledge thy benefits, and to praise thy holy Name for all thy mercies shewed unto me; for in my late and long sicknes, thou hast heard my groanes, and taken pity on me, and released me from all my paine and griefs, for thou dost visit my transgressions with favour (not in wrath) and hast alwaies been my stay and comfort from my youth, and thou art my deliverance and ready helpe in all my adversities, thou [p. 166] didst bring me downe for my sinnes almost to the grave, and hast in mercy lifted me up again from the gates of death, and restored me to health, who healest all my infirmities, pardonest all my iniquities, and givest me present supply in all my necessities, blessed be thy glorious Name for ever.

Now O God, as thou art pleased to prolong my dayes on earth, so especially I humbly pray thee daily to increase all saving graces in mee for thy true and faithfull service, and vouchsafe alwaies to continue all thy goodnesse and mercies towards me, that I may truly feare, perfectly love, and carefully obey thee in all things; and by the assistance of thy holy Spirit, make me to become, and ever to continue to bee more and more thy unfeigned servant: And now I am aged, and fit to leave the world when thou pleasest, yet while I am in it, Lord make me continually to grow from grace to grace unto the knowledge of the Lord Jesus Christ, with faith in him rightly to please and praise thee so long as I live. And gracious Lord vouchsafe never to withdraw thy grace and favour from me, untill thou hast finished thy greatest worke of mercy, and the height of my hopes, and happinesse, which is the salvation of my poor soule, through thine owne deare Sonne, and my only Saviour Jesus Christ; and when it shall please thee to call me away to thy selfe out of this vaine world, be pleased to give me a happy and blessed departure to dye in my

---

[a] in the like visitation (*Errata*)

Lord Jesus, and in thy true [p. 167] faith and favour, that thou having pardoned all my sins, and passing by my unworthinesse, in Christ, thou maiest after death receive and accept mee poore sinner into thy grace and favour through thy dearly beloved Sonne, in whom only thou art pleased, who is my righteousnesse, Lord, and my Redeemer; and so when I have left this life, I shall rest in peace and safety, sleep in Christ, and bee raised by him hereafter to great glory amongst his servants, and may obtaine favour to be accepted into the society of holy Angels and blessed Saints, and admitted into the glorious presence of Almighty God, there to praise and magnifie his Name, for ever and ever. Amen.

7. My conclusion. A Prayer to my blessed Lord and Saviour Jesus Christ.

Oh my deare Lord Jesus, I most humbly begge for thy love and mercies sake to pardon all my sinnes past, that thou maiest looke downe in pity and compassion on me, to heare the prayer of thy unworthy sinfull servant, who doth earnestly intreat thee, to vouchsafe me thy gracious and continuall helpe, protection and direction, in all my weake endeavours, wants and troubles, that so all my desires wayes and actions, being begun, continued, and ended in thee, I may bee able rightly and faithfully to serve and please thee at all times, really to love and honour thee above [p. 168] all things, truly and carefully to feare and obey thee according to thine owne will; confidently to relye upon thee, and willingly to submit to thy pleasure in all my crosses and calamities; and constantly to praise and magnifie thy most worthy and holy Name, for thy great and manifold blessings and benefits bestowed upon me of thy meer grace and mercy: O my blessed Lord and Saviour Jesus Christ, who art the author and finisher of my good, and finally of my eternall salvation, to thee be all praise, honour and glory, for ever and ever. Amen.

8. Another short Prayer.

O Lord my God, have pity upon me that am a most miserable sinner, and full of frailty, unapt and unable to doe any good, I earnestly desire rightly to serve thee, but without thy grace and help I cannot doe it, a fit subject for thy great mercy. Dear Iesus, pardon all my sinnes past, and give me grace henceforth to become a new creature in thee, daily to attend thy service constantly, and to performe all holy duties which I owe unto thee faithfully; and to shun and resist all sinfull neglects towards thee carefully; that so while I live, I may duly feare and obey thee rightly and truly to love and praise thee, here and for ever. Amen.

FINIS

[sig. M1r]

My owne Prayer in Meeter, or to be sung
as a Hymne.[a] [131]

1   IN mercy Lord heare my requests,
           for which to thee I call,
      My griefes are great, my soul's opprest,
           thou canst me helpe in all.

2   A gift of God I doe require,
           which Lord me not deny;
      Give me thy spirit of grace and prayer,
           with this still me supply.

3   In thee Lord I confide alone,
           turne not away thy face;
      My hearts desire to thee is knowne,
           I sue to have thy grace.

4   My vaine heart cleanse and knit to thee,
           and for thy service frame me;
      Thy constant Spirit in me let stay,
           my raigning sinnes to slay.

5   From neglectfull[b] wandring thoughts keep me,
           in my devotions free,
      They draw away from God my soule,
           and all my service spoile.

6   No earthly things let me imbrace,
           or on this world cast my mind,[c]
      Thy Kingdome, favour and thy grace,
           make me still seek and finde.

[sig. M1v]

7   For of my selfe no strength I have,
           to doe thy blessed will,
      Thy helpe O holy Ghost I crave,
           my duties to fulfill.

8   O God I will not let thee rest,
           unlesse thou heare my prayer,

---

[a] Sigs. M1r–M2v occur only in the second issue of the 1645 *Legacie*.

[b] neglectfull] ~~neglectfull~~ ∧ [wicked] (HB)

[c] this world cast] th~~is world cast~~ [em sett] (HB)

Till me thy servant thou hast blest,
    in granting my desire.
9   To pardon my offences great,
    and from all sinne deliver,
Lord make me thine in soule and heart,
    thy faithfull servant ever.
10   From all the sins that I have done,
    Lord quit me by thy mercies true,[a]
And free me from those judgements great,
    which for my sinnes are due.
11   O Christ thy mercy and grace now beg I,
    which Lord unto me grant,
That I in thee may live and dye,
    in heaven to be a Saint.
12   Amen, so be it[b] Lord say thou with me,
    that I these gifts may obtaine;
Then shall thy servant ever praise thee,
    whose goodnesse is my endlesse[c] gaine.
13   All glory, thanks and praise be to thee,
    that sitst on heavens Throne,
Who shewest mercy unto me,
    when I to thee make moane.

[sig. M2r]

Other short Verses to the like purpose.

1   Lord lead me in thy truth, and thy right way,
Be thou my God I thee most humbly pray.
2   Teach me thy will, and all thy Lawes divine,
Which to fulfill Lord make me wholly thine.
3   To serve, love, feare, obey, and praise thee ever.
who from my sinnes and hell wilt me deliver.

[a] mercies true,] ~~mercies true,~~ [grace,] (HB)   [c] endlesse] ~~endlesse~~ (HB)
[b] so be it] ~~so be it~~ [now] (HB)

A Rule which I have gathered out of the Scriptures to my owne use for the governing and ordering both of soule and body at all times, especially in the service of God, to make us acceptable to his majesty, and to bring all blessednesse and happinesse to our selves.

First, especially endeavour to make thy heart cleane, upright and faithfull, without doubting, which is the chiefe receptacle of most good, or all evill. Secondly, have an innocent and gratefull minde, thankfully to acknowledge all Gods mercies and benefits, and requite all humane courtesies as farre as thou canst. Thirdly, let thy prayers to the Almighty proceed from lippes unfeigned, free from falshood or guile. Fourthly, lifting up pure hands with a penitent, fervent, and devout soule toward God. Seventhly, set a watch [sig. M2v] before thy mouth, to prevent thy tong from wicked cursing, slandering, lying, dissembling and swearing. Eighthly and lastly, be sure to keep a good and cleare conscience in all things, both before God and towards all the world; this will be thy ready and true witnesse, a continuall feast, and a continuall consolation to thy selfe in this life, and an assurance of eternall happines hereafter.

But *Salomon* the wisest amongst the sonnes of men gives one short rule, for our duties towards God, were we but able to performe it; saying, Let us heare the end of all, feare God and keep his Commandements, for this is the whole duty of man,[132] for God will bring each work to judgement, what ever secret thing, whether it be good or evill.

FINIS.

Notes

1. Frances (née Holland) married Richardson's eldest son, John Ashburnham, and helped to restore the estate his father had wasted. Jane, widow of James Ley, Earl of Marlborough, married the second Ashburnham brother, William. Richardson's own daughters are named in the 1625 'Letter to my foure Daughters'.

2. The characterization of her work as 'unworthy' recalls Richardson's epistle, 'Of the intent and effect of this booke', in Folger MS V.a.511 (see Appendix 1). The exhortation to 'peruse, ponder, practice' echoes the dedication to ASH 3501 (see Appendix 2).

3. The heavenly Father's divine capacity to provide contrasts sharply with the shortcomings of the Ashburnham's earthly father. See Richardson, 'Introduction'.

4. *Interest in you*: concern for you; investment or stake in you.

5. The use of Elizabeth's first married name here suggests that the letter was originally composed before her marriage to Thomas Richardson in 1626.

6. *Exquisite*: over-nice.

7. The Duchess was the former Katherine Manners and was married to Elizabeth Richardson's second cousin once removed, George Villiers, the Duke of Buckingham. The house in Chelsea must

have been the one once owned by Thomas More and known in the eighteenth century as Beaufort House. Lionel Cranfield, Earl of Middlesex, purchased it around 1619, but it was forfeited by him and granted to Buckingham in 1627 according to the *London County Council Survey of London IV: The Parish of Chelsea (part II)*, eds. Sir Laurence Gomme and Philip Norman (London, London County Council, 1913), p. 23. Could Buckingham and his wife already have been inhabiting it as early as 1625?

8. Richardson is recalling the marital states of her daughters in 1625. Sir Edward Dering was a Member of Parliament and possibly owed his baronetcy to his mother-in-law's connection to Buckingham. He married Anne in January 1625, and she died in 1628 (see *DNB*). Later, Elizabeth was to marry Sir Frederick Cornwallis, Frances Frederick Turville, and Katherine John Sherlock.

9. In this letter, Richardson is alluding to the death of her children's father, but also to his improvidence which has left her, and them, 'destitute'. Until the family fortunes rose again, the daughters may have experienced serious social difficulties. 'Portions of wealth' or dowries were required to make a good marriage; being presented at court was similarly important and expensive.

10. *Importunate suters*: Richardson takes her image of 'importunate suters' from the custom of presenting requests or 'suits' to the King or to powerful courtiers. Richardson suggests that God, unlike earthly patrons, never tires of requests for help.

11. Psalm 199, verses 164 and 147.

12. Galatians 4:19, used also by Leigh (p. 23).

13. Acts 17:24 and Romans 1:19–20 clearly speak of 'witnesses' of God in the world. Romans 1:20, for instance (which Richardson copies nearly *verbatim* from the Geneva Bible), reads: 'For the inuisible things of him, that is, his eternal power & Godhead, are seene by the creation of the world, being considered in his works, to the intent that they should be without excuse.' I have not been able to make sense of the other references in this marginal note. *Cap.* is *caput*, or chapter.

14. A conflation of John 10:15, cited in the marginal note above, and John 15:13: 'Greater loue then this hath no man, when any man bestoweth his life for his friends.'

15. The unspecified reference to Isaiah could merely be mnemonic, or Richardson's reminder to herself to seek out the applicable verse later, for Matthew 8:17 reads: 'That it might be fulfilled, which was spoken by Esaias the Prophet, saying He tooke our infirmities, and bare our siknesses.' (The Geneva Bible gives a cross-reference to Isaiah 53:4.)

16. Matthew 7:7.

17. *Jacobs ladder*: Jacob dreams of a ladder between heaven and earth, on which he sees the angels of God ascending and descending (Genesis 28:12).

Some of this section is anticipated in Folger MS V.a.511 (fol. 65v): 'aske and ye shall receaue, seeke and you shall finde, knock and it shalbe oppened vnto you. Cease not then to call vpon ye name of ye lorde by wch we shalbe saued; but pray with vnderstanding, in truth, & feruentnes of spirit; for ye prayer of ye righteous auayleth much, if it be feruent.' Also on fol. 66r: 'True prayer, is ye exercise of faith, the nourisher of hope, the fier to kindle charity; and it is like Jacobs ladder, y^t reacheth from earth vnto heauen.'

18. Ecclesiastes 5:2, rather than the evidently muddled marginal citations.

19. 'The prayer of Manasseh, King of the Iewes' is an apocryphal prayer printed in the Geneva Bible between 2 Chronicles and Ezra. Richardson follows it closely, directly borrowing some parts and rephrasing others.

20. Very close to Folger MS V.a.511, fol. 68v, where Richardson is already relying heavily on the prayer of Manasses: 'Most mighty god great and terible wch hast made heauen and earth w^t all y^eir ornament and boũde ye sea by the worde of thy cõmaundement wch hast shut up ye deep and sealed it by thy glorious name whome all do feare and all flesh doth tremble before thy powre by because ye maiesty of thy glory canot be borne and thine angry threatning against siñers is importable.' *Importable*: unbearable; used in the Geneva Bible's 'prayer of Manasseh'.

21. Richardson here (and many times more throughout her *Legacie*) echoes the 'Absolution' given by the minister in the Order for Morning Prayer, *BCP*.

22. Richardson appropriates the words of Paul in 1 Timothy 1:15 – evidently one of her favourite formulae.

23. From 'The prayer of Manasseh': 'for I haue sinned aboue the number of the sand of the sea'.

24. This odd metaphor is also taken from 'The prayer of Manasseh': 'Now therefore I bow the knee of mine heart, beseeching thee of grace.' It occurs too in Folger MS V.a.511 (fol. 71v): 'I sinfull woman, am bolde to approach into thy presence most humbly bowing ye knee of my hart before thy throne of grace.'

25. *Publican*: the archetypal sinner of the New Testament. See note 44.

26. *Catholicke Church*: not the Roman Catholic but the universal Christian Church.

27. *Lydia*: 'whose heart the Lord opened, that shee attended vnto the things, which Paul spake' (Acts 16:14). The Geneva note connects this explicitly to preaching – 'The Lord onely openeth the heart to heare the word which is preached' – although Richardson is probably thinking of scripture readings, as she writes of preaching separately, below.

28. The sense of 'private prayer' noted in Joscelin (see note 61) applies, suggesting that Richardson meant other prayers for 'public' family use.

29. *Spirituall graces*: the gifts from God which make salvation possible. In later prayers, Richardson accounts her creation, election, and the incarnation of Christ spiritual graces. She also devises her own idiosyncratic scheme of seven spiritual graces to counterbalance the seven deadly sins: faith, the Holy Ghost, wisdom, the fear of God, the love of God and neighbour, repentance, and the right spirit of prayer.

30. Psalm 19:14.

31. *Seared up*: made insensitive, as flesh is made insensitive by being burnt (after 1 Timothy 4:2: 'consciences burned with an hote yron').

32. *Nature*: see Leigh, note 159.

33. *Security*: spiritual complacency.

34. Matthew 22:37–9.

35. 'The spirituall food of Christs body and bloud' recalls the *BCP*'s prayer after Communion. Richardson is careful to distinguish between the outward signs and 'the true signified Christ'. Arguably the punctuation of ASH 3501 makes the distinction even clearer: there it is 'ye true signified (Christ)' (fol. 16r).

36. The reference to Psalm 14:23 is certainly wrong (although this seems to be the reference in ASH 3501 as well). Psalm 14's emphasis on human corruption does, however, relate to 1 John 1:8: 'If we say that we haue no sinne, we deceiue our selues, and trueth is not in vs.'

37. 1 Peter 2:14 seems inapplicable, although that is also the reference given in ASH 3501.

38. The references to 1 Timothy 21:5 and James 1:17 are repeated twice in the margin; the first is evidently wrong, probably a misprint for 2:5: 'For there is one God, and one Mediatour betweene God and man, which is the man Christ Iesus.'

39. Probably a misprint for 1 John 1:7, 9.

40. Probably 1 John 4:9, 10.

41. Probably 1 John 3:10.

42. *Believe, and thou hast eaten*: I have not been able to trace this.

43. *When you are from Church*: when you are not in church; after the morning service, or between the morning and afternoon services.

44. The publican of Luke 18:13 is also favoured by Leigh and Joscelin as the typological figure of repentance: 'But the Publican standing a farre off would not lift vp so much as his eyes to heauen, but smote his brest, saying O God, bee mercifull vnto me a sinner.'

45. Richardson is modifying the millennial predictions of Revelation 20:6: 'Blessed and holy is he, that hath part in the first resurrection: for on such the second death hath no power: but they shall be the Priestes of God and of Christ, and shall reigne with him a thousand yeere.' For Richardson, the first resurrection is definitely a spiritual one: a revivification from the death of sin, which takes place in this life.

46. Two of the scriptural citations here may be pertinent for Richardson's decision to write books of prayers. Revelation 14:13: 'Then I heard a voice from heauen, saying vnto mee, Write, The dead which die in the Lord are fully blessed. Euen so saith the Spirite: for they rest from their labours, and their works follow them.' Luke 22:32: 'But I haue prayed for thee, that thy faith faile not: therefore when thou art conuerted, strengthen thy brethren.' Luke 22:36 seems inapplicable.

47. *Sift*: test, make trial of. After Luke 22:31 (in King James Version): 'Satan hath desired to have you, that he may sift you as wheat.' See also *OED*, 'sift', v. 2a.

48. The citations refer to the judgement of the Son of Man on his throne, separating the dead into the righteous and the unrighteous, like a shepherd separates sheep from goats. Richardson distinguishes this 'first judgement' at death from the last universal judgement 'after death', at the end of time.

49. *Saints*: see definition at Leigh, note 40.

50. Probably a citation of the eighth chapter of Revelation as well as 20:15: 'And whosoeuer was not found written in the booke of life, was cast into the lake of fire.'

51. Mary, sister of Martha (see Leigh, note 169). Luke 10:42: 'Mary hath chosen the good part, which shall not be taken away from her.'

52. Compare Folger MS V.a.511. (fol. 5r): 'Good father open yᵉ eyes of my soule, and enlighten my vnderstandinge, yᵗ I maie perceaue thy trueth and walke therein, enlarge my hart yᵗ I maie praise and magnifie ✙ thy holy name, strengthen my memorie yᵗ it maie be a storehouse of all goodnes.'

53. *Conversation*: behaviour.

54. See note 51.

55. In Matthew 14, Peter tries to imitate Jesus walking on the water. When he starts to sink for lack of faith, Jesus stretches out his hand to save him (verse 31).

56. See note 14.

57. The headnote to the prayer gives the essential details of the accident, which presumably happened at London Bridge between whose piers the river could flow dangerously fast. ASH 3501, a version of Book I of the *Legacie*, was presented to Elizabeth Cornwallis in 1635 (see Introduction and Appendix 2).

58. 1 Corinthians 9:27: 'But I beat downe my body, & bring it into subiection, lest by any meanes after that I haue preached to other, I my selfe should be reproued.' By analogy at least, Richardson is here thinking of her prayers as preaching.

59. Ecclesiastes 1:14.

60. Philippians 4:11.

61. *Candlemas*: 2 February, the Feast of the Purification of the Virgin Mary (or the Presentation of Christ in the Temple). Richardson counts Lady Day (25 March) as the first day of the year; thus Richardson actually died early in 1635.

62. For the monument Richardson erected to commemorate her parents, see 'Introduction' and Illustration, p. x.

63. Ecclesiastes 12:13.

64. 'You cannot serve God and mammon.' This is proverbial (see Tilley G253), originally from Matthew 6:24. In the Geneva Bible, the verse, 'Ye cannot serue God and riches', has a note referring to 'mammon': 'The word is a Syrian word, and signifieth all things that belong to money.'

65. John 14:13.

66. The Jewish sabbath was on the seventh day (Saturday), commemorating the day God rested after six days of creation (Exodus 20:11). The Christain sabbath became the first day, in memory of the day on which Christ rose from the dead (see Matthew 28:1).

67. *Thy service either publique or private*: Richardson may mean attendance either at the parish church or a private chapel; she could also be suggesting that the alternatives are church service or private devotions. If the latter, she contrasts with Joscelin's hard line on church attendance (p. 125).

68. Psalm 103:1, corresponding exactly to the Geneva version.

69. *Occasions*: affairs, business.

70. *Edification*: instruction, specifically religious instruction which will build up the recepients in faith. See *OED*, 'edification', 2.

71. Probably a printer's error for 'Lydias' (see note 27).

72. The phrase 'heap up wrath' is from Job 36:13 (King James Version): 'But the hypocrites in heart heap up wrath: they cry not when he bindeth them.' (In the Geneva, it is 'increase the wrath'.)

73. Psalm 17:8: 'Keepe me as the apple of the eye: hide me vnder the shadow of thy wings.'

74. Matthew 12:31: 'Euery sinne and blasphemie shall be forgiuen vnto men: but the blasphemie against the holy Ghost shall not be forgiuen vnto men.'

75. Compare Folger MS V.a.511 (fol. 69r): 'O good lorde deliuer me from yᵉ bondage of sin and sathan, and let me not lie drowned in deadly & senceles security; wherby I am euen shut out from thy fauour.'

76. Psalm 8:1.

77. Matthew 7:14: 'the gate is strait, and the way narrow that leadeth vnto life, and fewe there bee that finde it'.

78. Richardson is quoting loosely from the first verses of Mary's Magnificat (Mary's song of praise inspired by the Incarnation) in preparation for writing about it herself below. See Luke 1:46–7, 49.

79. Job 19:25.

80. This closely recalls the collect which begins the *BCP*'s service for the administration of the Lord's Supper.

81. Hebrews 9:14: 'How much more shall the blood of Christ, which through the eternall Spirit offered himselfe without fault to God, purge your conscience from dead workes, to serue the living God?' The Geneva commentary writes of *dead works*: 'sinnes which proceede from death, and bring foorth nothing but death'.

82. *Prevent*: to go before; to anticipate human need with spiritual help (see *OED*, 'prevent', 4).

83. See Leigh, note 99.

84. Psalm 48:1.

85. See note 29.

86. *Love token*: something given to express affection, a keepsake.

87. *Vocation*: God's calling of a soul to salvation. Compare Joscelin's thoughts about her daughter's calling (p. 122).

88. Matthew 6:33.

89. See note 51.

90. 1 Timothy 6:10: 'the desire of mony is the roote of all euill'. Matthew 16:26.

91. *Quit*: paid up, owing nothing; also set free, delivered.

92. Psalm 5:12. *Compasse*: encircle, protect.

93. Richardson may vaguely have in mind the Israelites pitching their tents in the wilderness wherever the guiding cloud or fire (both signs of God's presence) lead them. See Numbers 9:17.

94. John 6:44: 'No man can come to mee, except the Father which hath sent me, draw him, and I will raise him vp at the last day.'

95. *Vanish*: to cause to disappear.

96. Original sin is the inherent sinfulness which belongs to all the human race, while actual sin pertains to the acts of individuals which realise or actuate this fallen condition.

97. 2 Corinthians 1:20. The Geneva note explains that this means 'all the promises of saluation are sure and ratified in Christ'.

98. Psalm 107:1 and Acts 17:28.

99. In Hebrews 10:13 Christ sits at God's right hand, 'And from hencefoorth tarieth till his enemies be made his footstoole.'

100. Ephesians 4:30: 'And grieue not the holy Spirit of God, by whom ye are sealed vnto ye day of redemption.' *Sealed*: guaranteed; set apart (see *OED*, 'seal' v. 2b).

101. Psalm 8:4.

102. *Recollected*: absorbed in contemplation.

103. See note 51.

104. Matthew 4:1–11 recounts Jesus's forty-day sojourn in the wilderness, where he successfully resisted Satan's temptations.

105. John 13:35.

106. *Mite*: Richardson may have in mind the story of the widow's mite, told in Mark 12:41–4. The poor widow's 'two mites' are judged by Jesus to be more than the riches cast by the wealthy into the treasury, for the widow gave 'all that she had'.

107. Probably a printer's error for 'thy'.

108. 1 Peter 5:8: 'Be sober, and watch: for your aduersary the deuill as a roaring lion walketh about, seeking whom he may deuoure.'

109. *Spirit* capitalized refers to the Holy Spirit; *spirit* means soul.

110. *Unvaluable*: invaluable, priceless.

111. The first part of this prayer depends on some of Richardson's favourite biblical texts: Matthew 7:7, John 14:13, Psalm 8:4–5.

112. For Richardson's idiosyncratic idea of the spiritual graces, see note 29. Here she may have in mind medieval schemes such as the seven gifts of the Holy Spirit (which partly overlap with her spiritual graces), or the three theological plus the four moral virtues; that is, groups of seven which balanced the seven deadly sins of anger, avarice, envy, gluttony, lust, pride and sloth.

113. Proverbs 9:10.

114. That is, shortly after 2 February 1635.

115. Hanna or Anna was a widow and prophetess of a great age who recognized the child Jesus as the Messiah: 'shee was a widow about fourescore and foure yeres, and went not out of the Temple, but serued God with fastings and prayers night and day'. See Luke 2:36–8.

116. Job 13:15: 'Loe though he slay me, yet will I trust in him.'

117. *Ensignes*: emblems, signs; the banners of an army.

118. Eli's words are a response to hearing that he and his house will be punished because of his sons' wickedness (1 Samuel 3:18); Job is responding to the destruction of his wealth and children (Job 1:21).

119. This suggests that the prayer was written sometime after the outbreak of civil war in 1642.

120. For the *Publican*, see note 44. The other sinner may be Manasses or Manasseh (see note 19), who says in his apocryphal prayer: 'I am not worthy to behold and see the height of the heauens for the multitude of mine vnrighteousnesse.'

121. *Sergeants*: officers whose job is to arrest offenders and to bring persons to appear before a court.

122. *Call*: to summon, as for attendance at court. *Ceise*: to seize, arrest. To 'call and ceise' is what the sergeant does (see previous note).

123. Psalm 7:9: 'the righteous God trieth the hearts and reines'. *Reines*: the kidneys; in biblical use, the seat of the feelings or affections (see *OED*, 'reins' 3).

124. See note 48.

125. Isaiah 40:6–7: 'All flesh is grasse, and all the grace thereof is as the floure of the field. The grasse withereth, the floure fadeth.'

126. 1 Corinthians 15:53: 'For this corruptible must put on incorruption: and this mortall must put on immortality.'

127. This was a common seventeenth-century deathbed utterance, taken from the penultimate verse of Revelation (22:20): 'He which testifieth these things, saith, Surely I come quickly. Amen. Euen so, come Lord Iesus.'

128. This prayer and the next two relate to a serious illness lasting several months. See headnote to Prayer 6.

129. See note 55.

130. Twelfth Night is 6 January; Whitsunday is the seventh Sunday after Easter, and Whitsuntide the days immediately following this Sunday.

131. The first prayer alternates tetrameter and trimeter lines in a four-line stanza: the dominant metrical pattern, in fact, of the immensely popular versification of the Psalms by Thomas Sternhold and John Hopkins. Sternhold and Hopkins also provided tunes to which their Psalms – and presumably Richardson's prayer – could be sung. (Copies of *The Booke of Psalmes, Collected into English meeter, by Thomas Sternhold, John Hopkins, and others*, were sometimes bound together with Bibles. A 1610 edition printed in London for the Company of Stationers was, for instance, bound together with the 1610 Geneva Bible I consulted.)

132. See note 63.

APPENDIX 1

Excerpts from Folger MS V.a.511

[fol. 1v]

psal: 78.5.	God established a testimony in Jacob, & ordeined a Law in
6.7.	Israell, wch he comãunded y^t y^ei should teach y^ir children, that y^e
	posteritie might know it, & ye children wch should be borne, might
	declare it to their children; y^t they may set their hope on God
	& not forget his workes, but keepe his comaũndements.
deut:6.6.7.	And these my wordes wch I comaund thee this day; ye shall
ii.18.19.	lay up in yor harts, & in yor soules, & ye shall teach & rehearse
4.9.	y^m continually to yor children; y^t they may obserue & do all
32.46.	ye wordes of this law; I know saith ye Lord, y^t Abraham will
gene:18.	comaund his sonnes, & his houshold after him, y^t y^ei keepe y^e
19.	way of ye Lord, to do righteousnes & iudgement, y^t ye Lord
	may bring upon Abraham, y^t he hath p[ro]mised him
ephe:6.4.	Therefore parents ought to ∧⌈be carefull to⌉¹ bring up their children, in
pro:22.6.	instruction & information of ye Lorde; for what a childe
	is taught in youth, he will not departe from in his age.

E. A.

[fol. 2r]

Of the intent and effect of this booke.²

A Booke of Precepts, Instructions, and Prayers, wch I haue   written, and for the
most part collected,~~all~~ out of ye holie scriptures,   for the direction of my
children; that as god hath made me a meanes   for ye life of their bodies, so I
may discharge ye care y^t is comitted to   me (wch I most respect ∧ ⌈for⌉ ye good of
their soules, y^t they may both liue,   and die, in ye feare & fauour of God, and
may inioye after death,   a blessed inheritance amongst ye saintes of god in his
kingdome of   glorie; whose saluation wilbe an vnspeakable comforte to me, and
    euerlasting felicity to y^mselues: <u>And</u> therefore I humbly beseech   the lord of

---

¹ Added in a different pen.   ² See Plate opposite.

Of the intent and effect of this booke.

A Booke of Precepts, Instructions, and Prayers, wch I haue
written, and for the most part collected, out of ye holie scriptures,
for the direction of my children; that as god hath made me a meanes
for ye life of their bodies, so I may discharge ye care y^t is comitted to
me (wch most respect,) for ye good of their soules, y^t they may both liue,
and die, in ye feare & fauour of God, and may inioye after death,
a blessed inheritance amongst ye sainctes of god in his kingdome of
glorie; whose saluation wilbe an vnspeakable comforte to me, and
euerlasting felicity to y^mselues: And therfore I humbly beseech
the lord of mercie, to giue y^m all his grace, y^t they may of this small
helpe, & all other good & better meanes offered y^m make such true
& profitable vse, as may aduaunce Gods glorie, giue good example to others, & bring eternall happines to their owne soules.
Now if any other shall by chaunce come to veiw these my poore
endeauours (wch I know are full of defects, & vnworthy as I purpose to make it publike) but to my best frends, who would phaps af-
force me a partiall censure, or at least a louing acceptance of the
booke for my sake, let me intreat ye wise & learned (if such happen to
see it) to fauour me wth this excuse, y^t from my sexe is expected no p-
found knowledge of science, or true arte of learning to add grace to my
labor w^ I intend further then ye instructing of mine
owne children, who while they are yong, are ignorant of ye little I am
able to teach y^m, & when they come to better discretion & iudgment,
I hope they will still respect it out of affection, because it was thar
mothers paines out of carefull loue & desire of y^r weldoing, but cheefly they are bound to respect whatsoeuer ye worde of god,
out of wch if it is gathered, for their good. And if any of small knowledge, doe thinke it worthy their paines of reading, & shall finde
therein any help to encrease their knowledge, or amend y^r practise
in vertue & godlines, I shall esteeme y^r profit & benefit, a great hapines
to my selfe, especially if thereby ye true worship & seruice of god, may be
any way furthered.   written at Ashbortham in Sussex anno domini
                             g. Elizabeth Ashbornham   1606.

Prefatory epistle to Elizabeth Richardson's earliest manuscript mother's legacy book.
V.a.511, fol. 2r. (*By permission of the Folger Shakespeare Library, Washington, DC*)

mercie, to giue y^m all his grace, y^t they may of this small   helpe, & all other good & better meanes offered y^m, make such true   & p[ro]fitable vse, as may aduaunce Gods glorie, giue good exam=   ple to others, & bring eternall happines to their owne soules.   Now if any other, shall by chaunce come to veiw these my ~~poore~~ ⌈motherlie⌉   ~~labors,~~ ⌈endeauors⌉ (wch I know are ⌈simple &⌉ full of defects ⌈†⌉ & ⌈‡⌉ so vnworthy as I ~~neuer~~ pur=   pose to   make it puplike ⌈keepe yt fram ~~all euen~~ from y^e light ∧ ⌈even⌉ of⌉ ~~not to~~ my best frends, who would p[er]haps af=   forde me a partiall censure, or at least a louing acceptance of the   booke for my sake ∧ ⌈but I ‡ †⌉ let me intreat y^e wise & learned if such happen to   see it to fauour me wth this excuse, y^t from my sexe is expected no p[ro]=   found knowledge of science, or true arte of learning to add grace to my   ~~endeauours~~ ‡ ⌈labor wch I thinke ‡⌉ neyther doe I intend ∧ ⌈nor presume⌉ further then y^e instructing of mine   owne children, ∧ ⌈to lead a godly & vertuous life⌉ who while they are yo⌈u⌉ng, are ignorant of y^t little I am   able to teach y^m, & when they come to better ~~discretion~~ ⌈vnderstanding⌉ & iudgment, yet   I hope they will still ~~regarde~~ ⌈respect⌉ it out of affection, because it was their   mothers paines ⌈p[ro]ceeding frõ⌉ ~~out of~~ carefull loue & desire of y^{ir} weldoing, but cheif=   ly ∧ ⌈I charge y^m to follow what y^{ei} finde in it agreeable to⌉ ~~they are bound to respect y^e vnreprouable author,~~ y^e worde of god,   out of wch it is ∧ ⌈~~for y^e most p[ar]te~~ almost all⌉ gathered, for their good. And if any of small know=   ledge, doe thinke it worthy their paines of reading, & shall finde   therein any help to encrease their knowledge, or amend y^{ir} practise   in vertue & godlines, I shall esteeme y^{ir} p[ro]fit & benefit, a great hapines   to my selfe, especially if thereby y^e true worship & seruice of god, may be   any way furthered.

written at Ashbornham in Sussex anno. domin
p[er] Elizabeth Ashbornham 1606.

APPENDIX 2

Title Page of ASH 3501, East Sussex Record Office

A Rememberance for my
foure Daughters. /
Elizabeth. Frances. Anne. & Katherine.
This to my most deere, and entirely
beloued Daughter, as she well deserueth.
Elizabeth Ashbornham.
From yor affectionate Mother. E. A:
with my blessing, & prayers, for your
present, & future happines.

Which for my sake, accept, esteeme,
and ymploye, though in it selfe vnworthy.
Peruse, Ponder, & Practise./

Sweet Besse, (as you loue me) keep this,
though you lost y^e first. Eliza: Cramond
1635./

APPENDIX 3

Prayers from ASH 3501, fols. 19r–v

[fol. 19r]

3. When you a wake
in the morn=
ning from
sleep.

O swet Lord that hast awaked me   in health, & saftie, to this present   light, I humbly prayse   thy holy name   for thy gratiouse p[ro]tection of me, this   night past, & all my life hetherto; &   grãte yᵗ I may spende this day, &   all my dayes to come, in thy true   feare, & faythfull seruice; to thy   glory, yᵉ ayde, & releafe, of thy chil   dren, & seruants, & yᵉ furtherance   of my owne saluation, through my   blessed Sauiour Christ Jesus.

ii. The conclusion./

O god yᵉ Father, bles, saue, & gouer   me, in all thinges; O lord yᵉ Sonn, directe, g∧[u]ide, & p[ro]tecte me at all   times; O Holy Gost blesed spirrit, instructe, sanctifie, & preserue   me, in yᵉ waye of truth & righte

[fol. 19v]

ousnes yᵗ I may liue in thy feare, & dye   in thy fauor, & continue in yᵉ true   fayth, vnto my liues end; so agin yᵉ howrᵉ   of death, & in yᵉ dredfull day of iudgẽt,   I may finde grace in thy sight, yᵗ yᵘ   pardoning my sinns, mayest receaue me   to mercy, & I may liue wᵗʰ thee for   euermore. Amen. So be it. //

12. At night: being in Bedd.

O Lord giue me thy seruant quiet rest this night,   And grant] (O God) when I shall en-   ter into my longe sleepe of death, yᵗ   yᵘ Lord wilt sanctifie, & prepare my soule, by yᵉ asistance of thy   blessed spirrit, for thine owne gra   tious acceptance, before yᵘ call fore   me by death; & be pleased, to giue me ⌈so happy⌉ a   departure out of this life, yᵗ I may   rest in peace, & saftie; yᵘ wipeing   away all teares from mine Eyes, &   through thy Mercy, raysing me   vp to grace, & glory; I may liue   wᵗʰ thee, & praise thy holy name   for euer, & euer. Amen. Amen.

[The two following folios are torn out.]

FURTHER READING

Beilin, Elaine, *Redeeming Eve: Women Writers of the English Renaissance*. Princeton, Princeton University Press, 1987.

Brown, Sylvia, 'The Approbation of Elizabeth Jocelin', in *English Manuscript Studies 1100–1700*: 10 (2000).

——. '"Over Her Dead Body": Feminism, Poststructuralism, and the Mother's Legacy', in Viviana Comensoli and Paul Stevens (eds), *Discontinuities: New Essays on Renaissance Literature and Criticism*, Toronto, University of Toronto Press, 1998.

Burke, Victoria E., and Margaret P. Hannay, 'Elizabeth Ashburnham's Manuscripts', in *English Manuscript Studies 1100–1700*: 10 (2000).

Crawford, Patricia, *Women and Religion in England 1500–1720*, London, Routledge, 1993.

Cressy, David, and Lori Anne Ferrell, *Religion and Society in Early Modern England: A Sourcebook*, London, Routledge, 1996.

Ezell, Margaret, *Writing Women's Literary History*, Baltimore, Johns Hopkins Press, 1993.

Feroli, Teresa, '"Infelix Simulacrum": The Rewriting of Loss in Elizabeth Jocelin's *The Mothers Legacie*', *English Literary History* 61 (spring 1994), 89–102.

Fildes, Valerie (ed.), *Women as Mothers in Pre-Industrial England*, London, Routledge, 1990.

Hannay, Margaret (ed.), *Silent But for the Word: Tudor Women as Patrons, Translators, and Writers of Religious Works*, Kent, Ohio, Kent State University Press, 1985.

Haselkorn, Anne M. and Betty Travitsky (eds), *The Renaissance Englishwoman in Print: Counterbalancing the Canon*, Amherst, University of Massachusetts Press, 1990.

Hobby, Elaine, *Virtue of Necessity: English Women's Writing 1649–88*, London, Virago, 1988.

Houlbrooke, Ralph, *The English Family 1450–1700*, London, Longman, 1984.

Mendelson, Sara, and Patricia Crawford, *Women in Early Modern England 1550–1720*, Oxford, Clarendon Press, 1998.

Otten, Charlotte F. (ed.), *English Women's Voices 1540–1700*, Miami, Florida International University Press, 1992.

Poole, Kristen, '"The Fittest Closet for All Goodness": Authorial Strategies of Jacobean Mothers' Manuals', *Studies in English Literature 1500–1900*, 35.1 (winter 1995), 69–88.

Rose, Mary Beth, 'Where are the Mothers in Shakespeare? Options for Gender Representation in the English Renaissance', *Shakespeare Quarterly*, 42 (1991), 291–314.

Schleiner, Louise, *Tudor and Stuart Women Writers*, Bloomington, Indiana University Press, 1994.

Schofield, Roger, 'Did the Mothers Really Die?', in Lloyd Bonfield, Richard M. Smith, and Keith Wrightson (eds), *The World We Have Gained: Histories of Population and Social Structure*, Oxford, Basil Blackwell, 1986, pp. 231–60.

Sizemore, Christine W., 'Early Seventeenth-Century Advice Books: The Female Viewpoint', *South Atlantic Bulletin* 41 (1976), 41–8.

Todd, Margo, 'The Spiritualized Household', in *Christian Humanism and the Puritan Social Order*, Cambridge, Cambridge University Press, 1987.

Travitsky, Betty, 'The New Mother of the English Renaissance: Her Writings on Motherhood', in Cathy N. Davidson and E. M. Broner (eds), *The Lost Tradition: Mothers and Daughters in Literature*, New York, Frederich Ungar, 1980.

Wall, Wendy, 'Dancing in a Net: The Problems of Female Authorship', in *The Imprint of Gender: Authorship and Publication in the English Renaissance*, Ithaca, Cornell University Press, 1993.

Wayne, Valerie, 'Advice for Mothers by Women and Patriarchs', in Helen Wilcox (ed.), *Women and Literature in Britain 1500–1700*, Cambridge, Cambridge University Press, 1996.